1~14	Introductory Information
15~25	Attractions & Shopping Museums & Historical Societies
26~29	Sports
30~37	Trips
38~64	Lodging & Restaurants
65~96	Arts Guide
97~136	New Haven History
137~196	Communities & Neighborhoods
197~215	Historic & Contemporary Architecture
216~231	Area Prep Schools & Colleges
232~264	Yale
265~277	Medical Services
278~281	Charitable Organizations National Organization HQs
282~284	Business & Industry
285~303	People

DEDICATION

In honor of my grandfathers, Raphael Harrison & Abraham Starin

In the 1880s, when they were both in their early teens, my grandfathers left Russia, to escape being drafted into Czar Alexander II's army, which for young Jewish boys was often a one way trip to Siberia. Following signs that offered jobs in Connecticut, they walked along the railroad tracks from New York City to New Haven.

Ralph Harrison was a farmer who started out as a fruit and vegetable peddler, and later owned a series of small grocery stores in the Orange Street area. I knew him very well as he lived to be 93 years old, and walked to my Whitney Avenue office from his home in Westville almost every day for the last 10 years of his life to visit and chat with me.

Abraham Starin was a fine tailor, who opened his own successful store on Chapel Street before 1900. He made millions in downtown New Haven real estate, only to lose most of his fortune in the Great Depression. He was especially proud of the beautiful home he built on Livingston Street, across from East Rock Park.

Published by the Real Estate Educational Foundation, Inc., New Haven, CT
Distributed by The H^2 Company, 315 Whitney Avenue, New Haven, CT 06511 • 1(800) 243-4545

Library of Congress Catalog Card Number: 95-79505

Harrison, Henry S. with David F. Highnote
Harrison's Illustrated Guide: Greater New Haven
1. New Haven, Connecticut, City of
2. Cities of the Northeast.
   l. David F. Highnote ll. Title.

ISBN 0-927054-39-6
1st Printing, June 1995

Copyright ©1995 by Henry S. Harrison, New Haven, CT

All rights reserved. No part of this book may be reproduced
in any way or by any means including electronic transmission
without permission in writing from the author.
Printed in the United States of America

Artist Tony Falcone created the oil paintings which were used for the covers of this book. His murals and canvases enhance public spaces, corporate collections and private homes in the U.S. and abroad. A professional artist for 21 years, Tony is on the ARTSPACE board, a member of the Arts Council and City Spirit Artists, Chairman of the Public Art Committee of the Chamber of Commerce, and Director of the *Legacy Project,* a mentoring program for middle school students to create murals in honor of the 1995 Special Olympics. The scenes on the front and back covers of this book work together, although they are separate scenes. *New Haven* represents the flavor and spirit of this great city with its library, court house, offices, churches and people enjoying the Green. *Yale* is pictured from an imagined aerial perspective offering a compelling and unusual view.

Harrison's Illustrated Guide
GREATER New Haven

A Great Place to Live, Work, Study & Visit

GREATER NEW HAVEN CITY LIGHTS New England Sights

To: President Lawrence J. DeNardis and the University of New Haven

Best wishes!

Henry S. Harrison
7-15-95

Henry S. Harrison

with David F. Highnote

Ruth Lambert, Editor

AUTHOR'S NOTES

Foreword

I was "conceived in prosperity and born in the Depression" in 1930 at what was then Grace (now Yale-New Haven) Hospital.

Most of my childhood was spent in the East Rock neighborhood, just a few blocks from my current home on Saint Ronan Street, and around the corner from my office at 315 Whitney Avenue (an old Tudor mansion my father converted to medical offices before World War II) where I have worked for 40 years. After the War, my parents moved the family to Woodbridge, and I lived in Hamden for a few years during my first marriage.

Back in the 1960s, Bruce Lehman and I won an award from Mayor Richard Lee for remodeling the first building in the Wooster Square Redevelopment Project to be financed with an FHA mortgage. I lived there on Court Street for 17 years. Living in the Wooster Square Historic District stimulated my interest in architectural styles, and I began collecting pictures of its many different buildings. I also started my New Haven antique map and historic picture collection at about the same time.

My architectural styles picture collection became the foundation for my first book *HOUSES: The Illustrated Guide to Construction, Design & Systems*, which I wrote when I was 40 years old. Of the sixty different architectural styles I identified for the book, almost half were buildings I found in greater New Haven.

I was astonished (and delighted) to discover that I could produce a successful book. I still remember almost flunking English at Hopkins and the Wharton School. I wonder what my old English teachers, especially Miss Carver at Hopkins, would think to learn that *HOUSES* is still in print, and has sold over 300,000 copies since it was published in 1973 by the National Association of Realtors. *HOUSES* gave me the confidence to write more than 20 books over the past 25 years. My success as an author put me on the lecture circuit, and I have taught in 49 of the 50 states. (I've never been to North Dakota.)

Our family owns a mail order business, which means we could locate anywhere. Each time I return from a trip, we discuss where I have been and whether it would be a good place for us to live.

In the past two years, I have been to Russia (my "ancestral home") three times, invited by the World Bank to help jump-start the Russian appraisal profession by writing Russia's first real estate appraisal text.

Ruth, Kate, H Alex and I visited Moscow together in 1994. We all agreed that Russia is a great place to have come from, but not a place to live today.

We feel the same way about the many other foreign countries we have visited. (One of my appraisal textbooks has been translated into Japanese, but we haven't checked out Japan yet.)

My wife, Ruth Lambert, and I have spent our 19 years of marriage in New Haven. My children, Julie, Eve, Kate and H Alex were born in New Haven and for now continue to live in the area. My granddaughter Nina spent her infancy at our New Haven office daycare facility.

The two questions I was asked most frequently as I gathered information for this book is why I continue to live in New Haven, and why I decided to write a book about it. The answer to the first question is simply that I have never found another place where I would prefer to live.

The answer to the second is that I wrote this book to tell other people how I feel about New Haven. When I began collecting material for this book, my working title was "Greater New Haven: America's Best Kept Secret." I'm tired of hearing and reading only bad things about cities. I wanted to share my version of New Haven. I believe that even with its current problems, as the new subtitle says, greater New Haven is "A Great Place to Live, Work, Study & Visit."

My family has a long history of giving. My mother, Helen Starin Harrison, devoted the majority of her time to charity work (as she called it). She was the founder of the 60 Plus Club, now a national program of the National Council of Jewish Women. Watching her, I learned how much one person can do to make a difference.

As Robert Leeney, Editor Emeritus of the *New Haven Register* pointed out in a recent speech, New Haven historically has had its ups and downs — but it has also always had citizens prepared to put forth sincere efforts to successfully turn it around. 1995 is such a turn-around year. The Special Olympics World Games will mean a lot to our city and the region. Everywhere we look, we see people who are giving their time and money to make improvements.

Ruth and I wanted to help too. We felt that with the writing, editing and production skills we have developed in our business, it would be appropriate for us to create a book which would tell visitors and residents all about greater New Haven. In honor of my 65th birthday, we decided to donate our royalties and profits from the book to the *Real Estate Educational Foundation*, which I founded.

We sincerely hope you will enjoy reading this book and find it interesting and useful, and that it will enrich your experience of New Haven and its surrounding communities. If so, we will have succeeded.

HSH

AUTHOR'S NOTES
Acknowledgements

When I began working on this book in 1985, I hired Sarah Shapiro to take pictures and Nancy Polk to collect information about Yale and the community facilities. In 1989, I put the book aside to manage my trade magazine *Real Estate Valuation*, and continue to write my expanding set of real estate related texts.

About a year ago, I caught Special Olympics fever and realized there would never be a better time to produce a book about New Haven. In January 1995, I hired David Highnote, a Yale senior, to help with production. He has contributed so much to the writing, research and compilation of this book, that his role has evolved from part-time assistant to Project Czar. He also receives credit as a co-author.

I began, as always, "pasting up" my text and photos onto lay-out boards, using old-fashioned rubber cement. David and my wife Ruth Lambert, who volunteered to be the editor, convinced me to utilize computer technology for this project. I agreed, though somewhat skeptically, and we were off and running. This decision allowed us to scan hundreds of photos, mementos, and maps which would otherwise have been too expensive to include. We also retained complete control of type, which we set in-house on our desktop computers. We were able to size and place type and pictures at will, and make corrections right up to press time.

Despite my best intentions, much of this material was difficult to research and pull together. For the last 5 weeks of production David, Ruth and I worked an *average* of 18 hours a day to finish it in time for my 65th birthday party. Without their complete dedication to the task, this book would still be just a dream.

I have many people to thank for their unselfish help in this project. First are those who actually assembled major sections of the book, the Contributing Editors who helped make this book what it is. Jacqueline Koral, Editor of *Real Estate Valuation* Magazine and a close family friend, provided the Education, Yale and Medical sections with formatting help from Maura Gianakos. Dorie Baker put together the Arts information. Journalist Paul Bass wrote the commentary on living in New Haven. Julie Harrison wrote up all the material on Long Island Sound, the New Haven Police Department, Parks and Education. Robert Frew updated the Upper State Street facts, and Gerald Kagan assembled the Contemporary Architecture Tour.

Thanks also to Melanie Ginter, who arranged for me to use the New Haven Preservation Trust's Historic Building Walking Tour, Peter Halsey who "poked at" the sports material and Marnie Halsey for the Hopkins data. An historian, who wishes to remain anonymous, helped with the New Haven history. Peter Hall also reviewed the history sections and made contributions. Greg and Helen Mulherin, Roberta O'Hare, Leonard D'Agostino and Gregory Scott helped on the Community section. Elinor Gregory and Suzette Benitez of the Convention and Visitors Bureau, and Kathleen Cei at *The Advocate*, provided material and excellent photos of the community and its many attractions, as did my cousin Alan Sagal, who works for AAA.

Carol Cheney and Matthew Nemerson collaborated on the slogan "A Great Place to Live, Work, Study & Visit." Matt, with Judith Pitcher at the Greater New Haven Chamber of Commerce, provided listings on people, restaurants, business and industry. Upper Chapel Street information came from Evelyn Schatz and Joel Schiavone, and his assistants Cathy Garrity and Liz Carpenter.

Fred Maretz was my emissary to Mayor John DeStefano who assigned Pat Smith and Catherine Sullivan-DeCarlo to help. Pat provided maps and neighborhood information and arranged for Bonnie Winchester and Judy Mongillo to collect the Board of Education and Police Department material. Bryan McGrath helped me define neighborhood boundaries. Yale's Public Relations Director Gary Fryer assigned Laurie Trotta to the project. She collected the deans' pictures and biographies, arranged for the Yale map, and loaned me her personal archive on Harkness Tower.

The Knights of Columbus data and photos were supplied by Harvey Bacque and Timothy Hickey. Material about New Haven people was supplied, reviewed or verified by all of the following people: Elizabeth Curren, Gail Thompson, Steve and Judy August, Bitsie Clark, Matthew Nemerson, Jackie and Kurt Koral, Laurie Trotta, Tom Ficklin, Howard Schultz, and Carol Cheney. The decisions about who and what to include were made solely by me, with help from my wife Ruth Lambert, who gathered the information and organized the "More People" section.

Being able to reach the right person at critical moments in data gathering was made easier by Penny Taylor at the Arts Council, who was unfailingly helpful and resourceful.

Harold Sosnow was the book and cover designer. He also drew the pen-and-ink section and tab icons, and meticulously hand-lettered the cover title. The cover illustrations are oil paintings by Tony Falcone, created especially for this book.

Many pictures we used are from the New Haven Colony Historical Society. We have tried to correctly credit all of them. We are fortunate to have a resource like the Historical Society to preserve a record of our heritage.

The book was printed by father-son team Harry and Daniel Davidson of Pyne-Davidson Company in Hartford. It was printed flat-by-flat rather than all together, in order to meet the deadline. Proofreading was done under intense time pressure by Jean Liskow and Jackie Koral. My cousin and partner, Roger Harrison, helped by "running the show" while we were totally absorbed in writing and editing.

Finally, my special thanks to the officers and directors of the New Haven Real Estate Educational Foundation for publishing this book. They are listed on the inside front cover. Thanks also to Roberta O'Hare and Sue Ciaburri who act as the Foundation's volunteer staff.

Mayor DeStefano says in his letter "a book about New Haven is long over due." I agree – and thank you all for your help in making my personal dream such a satisfying reality. It's a great birthday gift!

Henry S. Harrison
New Haven   June, 1995

GREATER NEW HAVEN

City Lights...New England Sights

Mission Statement
The purpose of the Greater New Haven Convention & Visitors Bureau is to promote the fifteen-town region of greater New Haven as a destination or stop-over point for individual and group tourism. This is accomplished by engaging in visitor promotions and soliciting/servicing conventions and other related group business. The goal is to ultimately generate overnight stays and business for area attractions, thereby enhancing the economic fabric of the region.

For a free visitor's guide/calendar of events or hotel reservations, call: 1-800-332-STAY. For a recorded 24-hour events update, call the SNET Access hotline: (203)498-5050, code 1315.

Convention & Visitors Bureau

Board of Directors 1994-1995
Vincent Romei, Chairman
Gregory Mulherin, Vice Chairman
Richard Legg, Treasurer
Dorothy Larson, Secretary
Harvey Bacque
Edward Bottomley
Christopher Carter
Henry Criscuolo
Charles J. Dowd, Jr.
Jan Finch
Gwenn Fischer
Gloria Ireland
Mark Izzo
Reneson Loisel
William Meddick
Matthew Nemerson
Frank Pifko
Lalia Rach, Ed. D.
Daisy Rodriguez
Robert L. Seneca
Michael Schaffer
Joan C. Simpson
Lynda Smith

VINCENT ROMEI
Chairman

ELINOR GREGORY
Executive Director

Staff
Elinor B. Gregory, Executive Director
Suzette A. Benitez, Director of Sales
Alison B. Cummings, Director of Marketing & Communications
Betsy Plank, Convention & Tourism Services Coordinator
Carrie Beecher, Director of Events and Special Promotions
Patricia Watkins, Receptionist
Virginia Kozlowski, Bookkeeper

*Ansonia Bethany Derby East Haven Hamden Milford New Haven North Branford
North Haven Orange Prospect Shelton Trumbull West Haven Woodbridge*

One Long Wharf Drive Suite 7 New Haven CT 06511   203 777 8550   FAX 203 495 6949

BARBARA JOHNSON
Chairman of the Board

The Chamber

1794 – 1994
200 Years of Leadership

THE GREATER NEW HAVEN
CHAMBER OF COMMERCE

Branford
Bethany
Cheshire
East Haven
Guilford
Milford
Hamden
Madison
New Haven
North Haven
North Branford
Orange
Wallingford
West Haven
Woodbridge

The Chamber

Dear Reader,

As you look through *Harrison's Illustrated Guide to Greater New Haven*, we hope you'll agree that this region is indeed a great place to live, work, study, and visit. Waiting for you is a cornucopia of cultural riches from art to theater to music, diverse towns and neighborhoods, and a community of educational institutions – including Yale University, considered to be the best in the country.

The Greater New Haven region offers bustling business and retail districts, sprawling industrial parks filled with high-tech and high-growth companies, vital urban and suburban developments and one of America's premiere health, medical, and science communities.

We encourage you to experience the many flavors of area restaurants, and to appreciate the beauty of our extraordinary mixture of historic and contemporary architecture. From the quaint tree-lined streets in the Westville neighborhood to the turn-of-the-century architecture of Yale, from the beaches of Madison and Milford to Sleeping Giant Park in Hamden, to the fields and meadows of Wallingford and Bethany, the aesthetic landscape of the region is as breathtaking as it is varied.

Whether it's walking the ivy paths of Yale University or the white sandy shores of our region's beaches, you'll enjoy the riches this community has to offer.

Barbara Johnson
Chairman of the Board
The Greater New Haven
Chamber of Commerce

Matthew Nemerson
President
The Greater New Haven
Chamber of Commerce

195 Church Street
New Haven, CT 06510
(203) 787-6735
Fax (203) 782-4329

MATTHEW NEMERSON
President

Convention & Visitors Bureau
Chamber of Commerce

Special Olympics World Games Connecticut 1995

Special Olympics Pages 12-13

Yale Art Gallery Page 20

New Haven Ravens Page 26

Dinosaur State Park Page 32

Restaurants Pages 40-64

Neighborhood Music School Page 81

The Amistad Page 112

Introductory Information

Tabs	1
Copyright	2
Title Page	3
Dedication & Foreword	4
Acknowledgments	5
Visitors & Convention Bureau	6
Chamber of Commerce	7
Table of Contents	8
Calendar of Annual Events	10
Special Olympics World Games	12
Transportation	14

Attractions & Shopping Museums/Historical Societies

Attractions	15
Long Island Sound	19
Museums	20
Historical Societies	22
Shopping	24

Sports

New Haven Ravens	26
Volvo & SNET Tennis	27
Public Golf Courses in CT	28
Miscellaneous Sports	29

Day Trips

In-State Day Trips	30
Out-of-State Trips	36

Lodgings & Restaurants

Hotels & Motels	38
Restaurants & Night Clubs	40

Arts Guide

Arts Council	65
Theatre	67
Music	78
Arts Institutions	82
Galleries	84
Public Outdoor Art	86
Dance	88
Arts Programs	90
Museums & More Galleries	91
Arts Commission, Councils & Organizations	92

New Haven History

History & Firsts	97
Tour of Hillhouse Avenue	133

Communities

Introduction & Map	137
Ansonia	138
Bethany	139
Branford	140
Cheshire	141
Derby	142
East Haven	143
Guilford	144
Hamden	145
Madison	146
Milford	147
North Branford	148
North Haven	149
Orange	150
Prospect	151
Shelton	152
Trumbull	153
Wallingford	154
West Haven	155
Woodbridge	156

New Haven

Mayor's Welcome	157
Schools	158
Parks	160
Police	162
Wards & Voting	164
Service Directory	165
"New Haven Wannabes"	166

New Haven Neighborhoods

Neighborhoods Introduction	168
Downtown Introduction	169
Downtown Ninth Square	170
Downtown Church St./Coliseum	171
Downtown College & Chapel	172
Downtown Whitney Audubon/Lower State	173
Downtown Church St. South	174
Long Wharf	175
New Haven Property Sales	176
Dwight/Edgewood/West River	178
East Rock	179
Dixwell	180
Newhallville	181
East Shore	182
Hill	183
Fair Haven	184
Fair Haven Heights	185
Upper State Street	186
West Hills	188
Beaver Hills	189
City Point	190
Prospect Hill	191
Westville	192
Wooster Square	194
Problems	196

Guilford Page 144

Milford Page 147

New Haven Mayor's Welcome Page 157

Audubon Arts District Page 173

Downtown New Haven Page 168-174

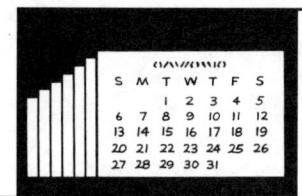

Harrison's Illustrated Guide • Greater New Haven
Table of Contents

Walking Tours
Pages 197-215

Hopkins
Page 218

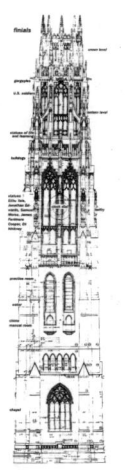

Harkness Tower
Page 258

Historic & Contemporary New Haven Architecture

Showplace of
    Modern Architecture 197
Walking Tour of
    Historic Buildings 209

Area Prep Schools and Colleges

Choate Rosemary Hall 216
Cheshire Academy 217
Hopkins 218
Hamden Hall 219
Country School/Foote 220
Lauralton Hall/Milford Academy ... 221
St. Thomas/Wightwood 222
Gateway 223
Southern State College 224
Albertus Magnus College 226
Quinnipiac College 228
Univ. of New Haven 230

Yale University

History 232
Yale College 238
Graduate & Professional Schools 240
Campus Map 248
Libraries 250
Athletics 252
Senior "Secret" Societies 254
Harkness Tower 258
Religion 259
Dwight Hall at Yale 260
Science Hill 261
Art & Performance Spaces 262
Yale Co-Op 264

Medical Services

Yale-New Haven Hospital 266
Hospital of St. Raphael 268
VA Medical Center/Gaylord 270
Masonic Home /Milford Hospital .. 271
Hill Health Center &
    Fair Haven Health Clinic 272
Clifford Beers/Gesell 273
Nursing Homes 274
Hospice/VNA 275
CMCH 276
Yale Psychitratric Hospital 277

Charitable Organizations National Headquarters

Community Initiatives 278
Community Foundation 279
Jewish Community Center 279
YMCA / Dixwell Q House 279
Knights of Columbus &
    Daughters of Isabella 280

Business & Industry

Business & Industry Statistics 282
Science Park 283
Media 284

People

Judges 285
New Haven Aldermanic Board 286
State Representatives & Senators .. 288
More People Who
    Make New Haven Great 289

Gaylord Hospital
Page 270

Community Foundation
Page 279

St. Mary's Church
Page 280

Science Park
Page 283

People
Pages 285-303

Summary of Tours

40 In-State Trips
10 Out-of-State Trips
Pages 30-37

Walking Tour of
Historic Hillhouse Avenue
Pages 133-136

Showplace of
Modern Architecture
Pages 197-208

Walking Tour of
Historically Significant Buildings
Pages 209-215

January

Icebreakers Ice Sculpting Competition
WPLR Radio, New Haven Green. 287-9070

February

Elm City Dog Show
New Haven Coliseum, So. Orange St. 772-4200

Orange Sleigh Rally
603 Orange Center Road, Orange. 799-6495

March

Saint Patrick's Day Parade
Along Church and Chapel Streets in downtown New Haven. Colorful marching units from New England & Ireland. 389-0160

Women in the Arts
A month-long celebration of women as inspirational forces in visual and performance arts. Exhibits, special tours, performances. City Spirit Artists: 773-1777

The annual Summertime Street Festival coincides with the Volvo International Tennis Tournament each August. Three blocks of Chapel Street are closed each evening for a week to host a celebration of local food and entertainment.

April

Spring Antique Show
New Haven Coliseum, So.Orange St. 772-4200

Goldenbells Festival
Hamden's three-week festival of concerts, nature walks, and athletic competitions. 248-3077

May

Springtime Crafts Festival
Arts Council of Greater New Haven's annual extravaganza on Audubon St., New Haven. Buy pottery, jewelry, baskets, greeting cards, etc. Call for schedule and events. 772-2788

May Day
Celebrate at the Eli Whitney 1816 Barn, 916 Whitney Ave, Hamden. Sponsored by the Greater New Haven Acoustic Music Society. 624-4200

WELI Kite Fly and Spring Festival
Radio Towers Park, 495 Benham St., Hamden. Kite fly contest, food, music, and much more! 281-9600

Freddy Fixer Parade
Shelton Ave. & Ivy Street, New Haven. 865-6941

Meet the Artists and Artisans
Over 200 exhibitors will display their crafts on the Green, Broad St. in Milford. 874-5672

Woodbridge Antique Show
Sponsored by the Amity and Woodbridge Historical Society's at The Center, Meeting House Lane, Woodbridge. Over 50 dealers. Plant sale, quilt raffle, and food. 387-2823

June

Picnic in the Park
The New Haven Symphony Orchestra, Edgerton Park, Edgehill Rd, Hamden. 776-1444

Fair Haven Festival
Quinnipiac River Park, New Haven. 467-7425

Arts and Crafts Show on the Green
West Haven Council of the Arts' annual show. Cambell Avenue, West Haven. Traditional and contemporary New England Artists. 937-3669 or 933-7777

Strawberry Festivals
St. Francis Church, 397 Ferry St., New Haven. 777-5356
Woodmont United Church of Christ, 1000 New Haven Ave., Milford. 878-3885

St. Andrew's Feast
St. Andrew's Club, 515 Chapel Street, New Haven. Traditional Italian celebration with live entertainment and good food. 865-9846

Connecticut Irish Festival
North Haven Fair Grounds, Washington Avenue. Music, dancing, & great food at the biggest Irish Festival of the year. 874-7950

SEASONAL EVENTS

Music

Greater New Haven Acoustic Music Society
University of New Haven, 300 Orange Avenue, West Haven. 624-4200

New Haven Symphony Orchestra
Woolsey Hall Series and Great Performances Series both held at Woolsey Hall at Yale, corner of College and Grove Streets. (October–June) 776-1444, (800) 292-NHSO

Orchestra New England
Concerts at Battell Chapel at Yale, College and Elm Streets, New Haven. (October–June) 934-8863

Outdoor Summer Concerts on the Green
Evening concerts on area town greens. 777-8550

Toad's Place
300 York Street, New Haven. 624-TOAD

Yale School of Music
Sprague Hall at Yale. Corner of College and Wall Streets, New Haven. (September–May) 432-4157

Sporting Events

Milford Jai-Alai
The world's fastest ball game at 311 Old Gate Lane, Milford. (May–December) 877-4242

New Haven Ravens AA Professional Baseball
An affiliate of the Colorado Rockies. Home games played at Yale Field, Derby Avenue, New Haven. For information, call 782-1666 or (800) RAVENS-1

Yale Athletics
Seasonal college sports. For information, call 432-YALE.

Theatre

Amarante's Dinner Theatre
62 Cove Street, New Haven. 467-2531

Artspace
70 Audubon Street, New Haven. 772-2377

The Alliance Theatre
Resident company, University of New Haven, Dodds Hall, 300 Orange Ave., West Haven. 789-1198, 932-9055

Long Wharf Theatre
222 Sargent Dr., New Haven. (October–June) 787-4282

Lyman Center for the Performing Arts
Southern Connecticut State University, 501 Crescent Street, New Haven. (January–July, September–December) 397-4435

New England Actors' Theatre, Inc.
Audubon and Orange Streets, New Haven. (October–May) 458-7671

Nutmeg Players
920-8 Quinnipiac Avenue, New Haven. 466-8000

Orange Players
A spring drama or comedy, a summer musical and a fall children's show. Orange. 891-2188

Stony Creek Puppet House Theatre
128 Thimble Island Roads, Branford. 488-5752

Shoebox Theatre Company
8 Svea Avenue, Branford. 483-7188

Shubert Performing Arts Center
247 College Street, New Haven. (September–May) 562-5666 or (800) 228-6622

Yale Repertory Theatre
Corner of Chapel and York Streets in New Haven. (October–May) 432-1234

Yale University Theatre
222 York Street, New Haven. (October–May) 432-1234

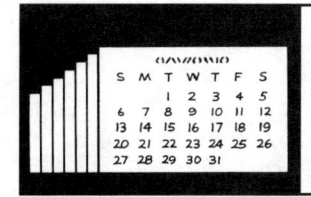

GREATER NEW HAVEN
Calendar of Annual Events

July

Great American Sand Castle Sculpture Competition
Open to families, clubs & friends. Silver Sands State Beach. Milford Fine Arts Council: 878-6647.

New England Art and Craft Festival
On the Green in Milford. Over 100 art & craft displays, demonstrations, food court, & entertainment. 878-6647.

Family Day Celebration
West Haven's scavenger hunt, sand sculpture contest, fishing derby. A day of events along the waterfront off Captain Thomas Boulevard, West Haven. 937-3651.

Bethany Carriage Rally
At the old airport site, 719 Amity Road, Bethany. This is a driving horse show of obstacle races, light harness and draft horses. 393-2100.

August

Hamden Italian Festival
Hamden High School, 2040 Dixwell Ave. Rides, entertainment food & cultural exhibits. 281-3897.

Savin Rock Festival and Catfish Classic Regatta
Three days of great food and entertainment on West Haven's Boardwalk! 937-3710.

Summertime Street Festival
Great food, spirited atmosphere and fantastic entertainment every night during the Volvo Tennis Tournament! The celebration takes place on Chapel Street between College and Park Streets. 777-8550.

Volvo International Tennis Tournament
World-class tennis at the Connecticut Tennis Center, Derby Ave., New Haven. 772-3838 or (800) 54-VOLVO.

Milford Oyster Festival
A canoe race to Charles Island, entertainment, games, crafts, and food. A great day on Broad Street in downtown Milford. 878-0681.

September

WPLR's Labor Day Celebration
Fun for the whole family at Lighthouse Point Park in New Haven. 287-9070.

Sunday in the Park
An annual family fair with games, food, and entertainment in lovely Edgerton Park. 145 Edgehill Road, Hamden. 624-9377.

Annual Labor Day Road Race
Starts at the New Haven Green, downtown. 20K, 5K and 1/2 mile children's run. 481-5933.

Engine 260 Antique Fire Apparatus Show & Muster
Eisenhower Park, North St., Milford. Hand pumpers, steamers, motorized fire engines. 874-2605.

Orange Agricultural Fair
525 Orange Center Road. Fun for the whole family: agricultural exhibits, horse and ox drawing, carriage rally, sheep dog herding, vegetable and flower exhibits, face painting. Live entertainment. 841-2122.

North Haven Agricultural Fair
Fairgrounds on Washington Avenue, North Haven. A midway, great food and entertainment. 239-2668.

Odyssey Greek Festival
St. Barbara Greek Orthodox Church, 480 Race Brook Rd., Orange. Immerse yourself in the Greek culture with music, food, dancing & strolling entertainers. 795-1347.

Fall Festival on the Town Green
Food, music, crafts, rides, business expo and road race in East Haven at the corner of Main Street and Hemingway. 468-3204.

Orange Country Fair
Antiques, entertainment, produce contests & wonderful food at the Country Fair Grounds at 525 Orange Center Road in Orange. 795-6465.

New Haven Fall Antiques Show
New Haven Colisuem, South Orange Street. Exhibitors from the United States and Europe. 772-4200.

October

Stone-Otis House Apple Festival
Farmhouse tours, cider pressing, baked goods, white elephant and fall plants. Corner of Orange Center and Tyler City Roads, West Haven. 795-9466.

WELI Fall Festival and Chili Cook-Off
Radio Towers Park, 495 Benham Street, Hamden. Arts, crafts, family entertainment & great chili. 281-9600.

Pardee-Morris House Harvest Festival
Celebrate in 18th century style with cider pressing, scarecrow stuffing, pumpkin decorating and apple pie baking contest at 325 Lighthouse Road, New Haven. New Haven Colony Historical Society: 562-4183.

Haunted Hayride
Field View Farm, 707 Derby Avenue, Orange. 795-5415.

November

Holiday Fair
High Plains Community Center, 525 Orange Center Road, Orange. Orange Arts and Crafts Guild: 799-8817.

Celebration of American Crafts
Four hundred artists from all over the United States are represented in the annual exhibition and sale of contemporary fine crafts at the Creative Arts Workshop, 80 Audubon Street, New Haven. 562-4927.

Holiday Tree Lighting
On the New Haven Green. 777-8550.

December

Christmas in the Mansion
This 1864 Victorian mansion will be decked to include 50 exhibitors, horse drawn carriage rides, antiques. High Street, Milford. 877-2786.

Toy Train Exhibit
An annual holiday exhibit at the Eli Whitney Museum, 915 Whitney Avenue, Hamden. 777-1833.

Trolley Cars with Santa!
Weekends at the Shore Line Trolley Museum on River Street in East Haven. 467-6927.

"*Let me win*

But if I cannot win

Let me be brave in the attempt"

~*Special Olympics Oath*

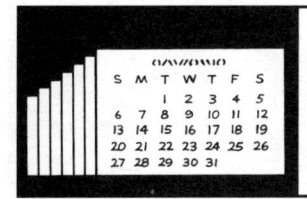

SPECIAL OLYMPICS
1995 World Games

From July 1-9, 1995, Connecticut will host the Ninth Special Olympics World Games—the largest sports event in the world in 1995 and the largest sports event ever held in Connecticut. Over 7,000 athletes from more than 120 nations will participate. Around 500,000 spectators are expected in New Haven, and millions more will watch the Games via international television coverage. The theme for the 1995 Special Olympics is *Sport, Spirit, Splendor*, a phrase which aptly captures the essence of this unique event.

The Opening and Closing Ceremonies will be held at the Yale Bowl, with seating for over 70,000 people. The towns and cities throughout the state are involved in hosting the visiting teams and making them feel at home.

The Special Olympics was founded over 25 years ago, by Eunice Kennedy Shriver, as an international sports organization for people with mental retardation. Today, Special Olympics is one of the largest and most successful sport and volunteer organizations in the world. The mission of the Special Olympics is to provide year-round training and athletic competition in a variety of well-coached, Olympic-type sports for individuals with mental retardation, by providing them with continuing opportunities to develop fitness, demonstrate courage, experience joy and participate in the sharing of gifts, skills and friendships with their families, other Special Olympic athletes, and the community.

Former Connecticut Governor Lowell P. Weicker, Jr., is Chairman of the Board, and Timothy P. Shriver is President of the 1995 Special Olympics World Games Organizing Committee.

Special Olympics World Games Connecticut 1995

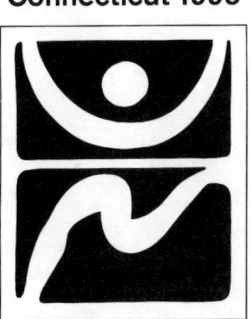

The logo for the 1995 Special Olympics World Games was designed by Peter Good, an internationally-known graphic designer whose studio is in Chester, Connecticut. The logo was inspired by the paper cutouts of great 20th century artist, Henri Matisse.

"What better place? ... A beautiful state, tremendous arenas for sports of all kinds and wonderful volunteers. There will be great thrills in '95 and no shortage of world-class heartstopping competition."

Timothy Shriver, President
Organizing Committee
1995 World Games

Special Olympics World Games
•
New Haven
•
July 1–9, 1995
•
7,000 Athletes
•
120 Countries
•
20 Sports
•
World's Largest Sporting Event

Sport. Spirit. Splendor.

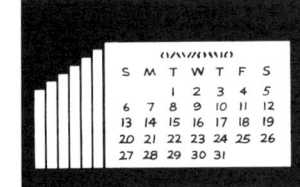

SPECIAL OLYMPICS
1995 World Games

AIRLINE SERVICE

TWEED~NEW HAVEN AIRPORT 787-8283
Service is available to more than 150 domestic and international destinations. Tweed is served by US Air Express [1(800) 428-4322] and United Airlines / United Express [1(800) 241-6522]. Ample on-site parking is $7/day and is 2 minutes from the gate.

Directions: From New Haven and West: I-95N, exit 50, straight to second light. Right on Route #337 (Townsend Avenue), 1.2 miles to light. Left onto Fort Hale Road, then .4 miles to airport entrance. *From East and CT Shoreline*: I-95S, exit 51, .3 miles to light. Left on Route #337 (Townsend Avenue), 1.2 miles to light. Left onto Fort Hale Road, then .4 miles to airport entrance. Good signs.

RAIL SERVICE

Shoreline East .... 1(800) 255-7433
  New Haven to Old Saybrook
Metro North .... 1(800) 638-7646
  New Haven to New York Grand Central
Amtrak .... 1(800) 872-7245
  Boston to Washington, and beyond

FERRY SERVICE

Bridgeport and Port Jefferson
Steamboat Company, Bridgeport 367-3043
  Transporation across Long Island Sound from Bridgeport to Port Jefferson, Long Island, NY

FROM NYC AIRPORTS

Connecticut Limousine .... (800)-472-5466
  Service to and from John F. Kennedy, LaGuardia, and Newark airports.

RENTAL CARS

Airways 776-2377
Avis .... 1(800) 331-1212
Budget 787-1143
Enterprise 789-2252
Hertz .... 1(800) 654-3131
Thrifty .... 1(800) 367-2277

TAXIS

Metro Taxi 777-7777
New Haven Taxi Co. 877-0000
Yellow Cab Co. 777-5555

BUS SERVICE

CT Transit .... (203) 624-0151
  CT Transit operates 30 bus routes in Greater New Haven. Call for fares, schedules and map.

TRANSPORTATION SERVICES

Rideworks .... 777-RIDE or 1(800) ALL-RIDE
  Regional non-profit commuter transportation service for commuters and emploiyers — arranges carpools, vanpools, and bus/train alternatives to driving alone.

GREATER NEW HAVEN
Attractions & Amusements

There are many things to do and see in the 20 communities that make up Greater New Haven. The letters SC, C & S after the admission fee indicate senior citizen, children and student discounts. Similar attractions outside the area are described in the Trips section, pages 30-37.

Attractions

NEW HAVEN BREWING COMPANY
458 Grand Avenue, New Haven   (203) 772-2739
New Haven's only brewery which under new management is growing quite rapidly. Watch them make Elm City Ale, Connecticut Ale, Mr. Mike's lower calorie ale and a variety of other beers and ales. Admission free. Tours are limited to Saturdays for now.

NEW HAVEN VETERANS MEMORIAL COLISEUM
275 South Orange Street, New Haven   (203) 772-4200
A variety of events are scheduled throughout the year including a circus, ice show, antique show, home show, sports events, etc. Ticket prices vary. Open when events are scheduled.

SHORE LINE TROLLEY MUSEUM
17 River Street, East Haven   (203) 467-6927
This registered National historic site contains 103 classic trolleys, including the world's first electric freight loco, world's oldest rapid transit car, rare parlor car, interpretive displays and a trolley ride through the beautiful shoreline woods and wet lands. Admission $4.00 SC & C. Closed in the winter. Closed weekdays in the spring and fall. Open daily in the summer.

WHITLOCK FARM BOOK BARN
20 Sperry Road, off Rt. 69, Bethany   (203) 393-1240
Two barns full of books, maps (over 20,000 of 1860s towns!), prints (many of farm animals), and all sorts of curiosities. Specializing in out-of-the-ordinary books in all fields. Prices average half of normal retail. You'll also find gardens, picnic tables, "cows in the field, goats, and a friendly woodchuck." Admission free. Open daily except Monday, throughout the year.

YALE UNIVERSITY
Visitors Center, 149 Elm Street, New Haven   (203) 432-2300
There are several guided tours daily. This is one of the world's great universities, with many unusual and unique buildings, dating from the 1700s to the present. Open daily. Admission is free except for museums, concerts and some sporting events.

Crafts, Antiques & Flea Markets

BOULEVARD FLEA MARKET
520 Ella T. Grasso Blvd (Rt. 10), New Haven   (203) 772-1447
The oldest flea market in Conn. keeps expanding. Everything from produce to antiques, plenty of new and used junk for sale. Everything is negotiable. $1 parking fee. Open most weekends.

BRANFORD CRAFT VILLAGE AT BITTERSWEET FARM
799 East Main Street   (203) 488-4689
This 85-acre farmstead has been converted into a charming and accessible crafts center. Restored buildings house studios where artists and artisans do their work and sell their crafts. Hand-blown glass, wood sculptures, handmade pottery, and more, with on-going demonstrations by various artisans. Admission free. Open daily except for major holidays.

GUILFORD HANDICRAFTS CENTER
411 Church Street, Guilford   (203) 453-5947
This combination of store, gallery and school is devoted to the creation and enjoyment of fine arts & handicrafts. Admission is free. Open daily, except major holidays.

Cruises & Boat Trips

LIBERTY BELLE CRUISES
Long Wharf Pier, New Haven   1(800) 745-2628 (BOAT)
Cruise season is June to after Labor Day. Brunch cruise, Happy Hour Cruise, Murder Mystery Cruise, Shoreline Cruise, Moonlight Cruise and more. Admission varies. Open daily.

SCHOONER, INC.
60 South Water Street, I-95 exit 42, New Haven   (203) 865-1737
The Quinnipiak is a 91 foot gaff rigged wooden schooner which is available for individuals and group charters. Advanced reservations required. Ticket prices vary based on length of trip.

THIMBLE ISLAND CRUISES
Stony Creek, I-95 exit 54, Route 146, Branford
Take a leisurely boat trip through the Thimble Islands, home to pirates of old, and contemporary cognoscenti of gracious summer living. Typical tours last 45 minutes, with personal narration of the area's unique history. Season is mid-May to early October, and all tours leave from the Stony Creek Town Dock.
Islander, CT. Sea Ventures, POB 3302, Branford   (203) 397-3921
Sea Mist II, 168 Thimble Islands Rd., Branford   (203) 488-8905
Volusnga III, POB 3284, Stony Creek, Branford   (203) 488-9978

Farms & Orchards

BISHOP FARMS & WINERY
500 South Meriden Road, Cheshire   (203) 272-8243
A 200-year-old working farm with apple orchards, cider press, fruit winery and farm animals. Admission is free. Open daily, from March through December.

BISHOP'S ORCHARD
33 Branford Road (Rt. 139), North Branford   (203) 453-6424
During apple harvest season you can pick you own apples. Admission is free. You pay for what you pick and keep. Open daily during apple harvest in late summer and early autumn.

BISHOP'S ORCHARD
1355 Boston Post Rd., Exit 57-I95, Guilford   (203) 453-6424
Pick your own fresh fruits. Gather strawberries in June, blueberries in mid-July, peaches in August, and raspberries and pears from late August until frost; pumpkins and flowers available in October. Admission is free. You pay for what you pick and keep. (There's even a "Sinner's Jar" for conscience-stricken pickers who nibble a bit as they pick; proceeds go to charity.) Open daily, all summer and into the fall. Call for hours and crops available.

Field View Farm
707 Derby Avenue, Orange   (203) 795-5415
The oldest operating dairy farm in Connecticut, run by the same family for 355 years. One of the few places that still sells raw (unpasteurized) milk. Also sells its own pasteurized milk, cream, and homemade ice cream, fresh corn meal, vegetables & flowers. Hayrides by appointment. Admission is free, and the farm is open daily, all year round.

Glendale Farm
Wheeler's Farm Rd., Milford   (203) 874-7203
Pick your own strawberries in June, and tomatoes in August and September. Pay by the pound. Also offers annuals in spring and summer. Admission is free. Open daily, 8am to 6pm in season.

Hindinger Farm
835 Dunbar Hill Road, Hamden   (203) 288-0700
A pick-your-own strawberry farm in June. The rest of the season, it sells local fruits and produce. Admission is free. You pay for the strawberries you keep. Open daily. Closed in the winter.

Jones Tree Farm
Rt. 110 & Israel Hill Road, Shelton   (203) 929-8425
Arbor Day in April begins the year's farm activity. June –August are berry months: harvest your own strawberries and blueberries. Follow with pumpkins, fall produce, corn stalks and free hayrides in October. In December, cut your own Christmas tree or buy one already cut. Admission free. Pay for what you keep.

Julie's Orchard and Farm Market
234 Upper State Street, North Haven   (203) 239-0474
A "pick-your-own" heaven. Thornless blackberries (August), seven types of pears and raspberries (August & September), and 27 apple varieties and pumpkins (late September-October). Hayrides to the orchards. Petting ducks, rabbits and chickens. Free admission. Pay for what you pick and keep. Open daily in season.

Macci Farm
1018 Willard Road (off Rt. 34), Orange   (203) 795-5469
Pick your favorite apples in August, September and early October. Admission is free. You pay for what you pick and keep. Open daily during harvest season.

Maple View Farm
603 Orange Avenue, Orange   (203) 799-6495
Horse-drawn hayrides and wedding coach, pony rides and party barn available year round. Negotiated fees; open by appointment.

Neubig Farms
111 North Hill Road, North Haven   (203) 234-0018
Fall and winter horse-drawn hayrides and sleigh rides. Fees charged. By appointment only.

Pell Farm, North Haven
Middletown Avenue, North Haven   (203) 234-0204
Pick your own strawberries in June. Admission free. You pay for what you pick and keep. Open daily during season.

Rose Orchard
33 Branford Road (Rt 139), North Branford   (203) 488-7996
Pick seasonal fruit, from strawberries and peaches to apples and pumpkins, and pet the friendly goats, lamb, chickens and turkeys. Hayrides available. Admission is free. You pay for what you pick and keep. Open daily, May to December.

Shamrock Farm
621 Lambert Road, Orange   (203) 799-8869
A farm that sells plants, flowers and vegetables. Pick your own raspberries in the late summer. Admission free. You pay for what you pick and keep. Open daily during season.

Shepard's Farm
Litchfield Turnpike (Rt. 69), Woodbridge   (203) 393-0171
A 105 year old dairy farm offering rich farm fresh pasteurized milk, homemade ice cream and yogurt. Admission free. You pay for what you buy. Open daily.

Wayne's Sugar House
89 Cedar Lake Road, North Branford   (203) 488-2549
Wonderful winter outing, watching maple syruping process at a family run sugar house. Gift shop sells syrup and homemade candy. Admission is free. Open weekends in February and March.

Galleries & Arts Activities

Audubon Arts District
Audubon Street off Whitney Ave., New Haven
Arts Council (203) 772-2788
A "cultural mecca" on Audubon Street. This revitalized neighborhood has galleries, schools, bookstores, restaurants and shops. On-going activities are listed in the Arts Council Calendar monthly, available free at their building at 70 Audubon Street, across from Leeney Plaza. Admission free. Open daily.

Madison Gallery
845 Boston Post Road, Madison   (203) 245-7800
Housed in a federal building, it contains six galleries that are dedicated to showing serious works of contemporary artists with emphasis on sculpture, painting and photography. Outdoor sculpture garden. Docent-led "Art Talks" are conducted for each special exhibition. Changing exhibits. Admission is free. Open Wednesday through Saturday.

Historic Sites & Houses

Allis~Bushel House and Museum (c. 1785)
853 Boston Post Road, Madison   (203) 245-4567
A colonial house with unusual corner fireplaces and original paneling, exhibits of china, dolls and toys, costumes and kitchenware. Admission free. Closed Monday, Tuesday and Sunday. Opened only in the summer.

Center Church Crypt
311 Temple Street on the Green, New Haven
Under the Center Church (First Church of Christ). Admission is free. Tours are available by appointment only.

Fort Nathan Hale and Black Rock Fort
Woodward Avenue, New Haven   See page 161.

Grove Street Cemetery
Grove Street at High Street, New Haven
Contains graves of many original settlers of New Haven and Roger Sherman, Eli Whitney, Noah Webster. Admission free. Open daily.

Henry Whitfield House Museum
Whitfield Street, Guilford   (203) 453-2457
Built in 1639. One of the oldest stone houses in America, and the oldest stone house in New England. Now a state museum showing 17th and 18th century furnishings. Also offers a large herb garden. Admission $3, SS & C. Closed Monday and Tuesdays and some national holidays.

GREATER NEW HAVEN
Historic Societies & Museums

HOTCHKISS FARMHOUSE
Waterbury-New Haven Road, Prospect   (203) 758-0185
Built in 1815. Occupied by three generations of the Hotchkiss family. Admission is free. Open only by appointment.

HUNTINGTON HISTORICAL SOCIETY
SHELTON HISTORIC CENTER
70 Ripton Road, Shelton   (203) 925-1803
Wide variety of historic exhibits. Tours of Trap Falls Schoolhouse and Hezekiah Marks House are also given. Admission is free. Closed Sunday through Wednesday.

HYLAND HOUSE (1660)
84 Boston Street, Guilford   (203) 453-9477
A Classic Colonial Style Salt Box Style house with rare furnishings, unusual interior woodwork, three walk-in fireplaces outfitted for 17th century cookery. Admission $2.00, SS & C. Closed Mondays. Open summers only.

JONATHAN DICKERMAN HOUSE
105 Mt. Carmel Avenue, Hamden   (203) 248-6030
A carefully preserved late 18th century farming home. It includes a herb garden with plants used in documented folk medicines. Cider mill being restored. Admission free. Open weekend afternoons in the summer, or by appointments for groups.

LOCK 12 HISTORIC PARK
487 North Brooksvale Road., Chesire   (203) 272-2743
A restored part of the Farmington Canal that ran from New Haven to Massachusetts (1828 - 1847) and then was a railroad. Lock 12 features a museum, lock-keeper's house, helicoidal bridge and picnic area. Free admission; open daily, March through December.

MILFORD WHARF LANE COMPLEX
34 High Street, Milford
The Nathan Clark Stockade House (c.1780) and three buildings that house an outstanding archaeological collection. Admission is free. Open many days on a changing schedule.

OSBORNE HOMESTEAD MUSEUM, DERBY
500 Hawthorn Ave., Derby   734-2513
Former home of Frances Osborne-Kellogg. An elegant Colonial Revival home that has exhibits of the family's arts and antiques, a formal rose and rock garden. Admission is $1. Open Friday, Saturday and Sunday from April through December.

PARDEE~MORRIS HOUSE, NEW HAVEN
325 Lighthouse Road, New Haven   (203) 562-4183
See pages 20-23.

STONE~OTIS HOUSE
Orange Center Road (Rt. 152), Orange   (203) 795-9466
Restored 1830s farmhouse including country store and adjacent blacksmith shop; displays local history. Free admission. Open Sunday afternoons or by appointment, April through October.

THOMAS DARLING HOUSE
1907 Litchfield Turnpike, Woodbridge   (203) 387-2823
An 18th century home in the National Register of Historic Places, home to the Amity and Woodbridge Historical Society. Admission is free. Open Sunday afternoons. Closed November through May.

THOMAS GRISWOLD HOUSE (1774)
171 Boston Street, Guilford   (203) 453-3176
A Colonial Style Salt Box Style house turned into a museum. Displays of costumes, local furniture, farm tools, books and photographs. Restored blacksmith shop. Admission is $1.00; SS & C. Closed Mondays and most major holidays.

WOODS ESTATE
1856 Huntington Turnpike, Trumbull   (203) 377-6620
The former Abraham Nichols house in now a museum. It stands on the site of the first house built in Trumbull in 1820. Free admission. Open Thursday and Sunday. Limited hours.

Museums

BEINECKE RARE BOOK AND MANUSCRIPT LIBRARY AT YALE
121 Wall Street, New Haven   (203) 432-2977
See pages 21 & 262.

CONNECTICUT CHILDREN'S MUSEUM
22 Wall Street, New Haven   (203) 562-KIDS (5437)
See page 23.

ELI WHITNEY MUSEUM
Whitney Avenue at Armory Street, Hamden   (203) 777-1833
The original site of Eli Whitney's gun factory where mass production was invented. Restored and converted to a museum. Admission free. Closed Monday & Tuesday. (See page 23.)

102ND INFANTRY REGIMENT MUSEUM
NATIONAL GUARD ARMORY
290 Goffe Street, New Haven   (203) 784-6851
Hundreds of rare items, from the Civil War to the present. Full size bunker, a Jeep, display of uniforms, weapons, letters, and library. Admission free, scheduled by appointment tours only.

JEWISH HISTORICAL SOCIETY OF GREATER NEW HAVEN
169 Davenport Avenue, New Haven   (203) 787-3183
See page 22.

NEW HAVEN COLONY HISTORICAL SOCIETY
114 Whitney Avenue, New Haven   (203) 562-4183
See page 22.

PEABODY MUSEUM OF NATURAL HISTORY
170 Whitney Avenue, New Haven   (203) 432-5050
See pages 21 & 262.

YALE CENTER FOR BRITISH ART
1080 Chapel Street, New Haven   (203) 432-2800
See pages 20 & 262.

YALE UNIVERSITY ART GALLERY
1111 Chapel Street, New Haven   (203) 432-0600
See pages 20 & 262.

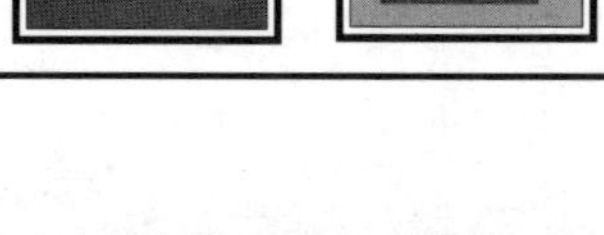

Nature Centers & Environmental Attractions

KELLOGG ENVIRONMENTAL CENTER
500 Hawthorne Avenue, Derby   (203) 734-2513
Offers natural science and environmental programs, special events, evening lectures, children's exhibits, field walks and mini-courses for the public. Admission free. Open daily.

MILFORD POINT BIRD SANCTUARY
1 Milford Point Road off Seaview Avenue, Milford   (203) 259-6305
A true "sanctuary" that is open to the public only for passive nature recreation. Run by the Audubon Society. Admission is free. The Sanctuary is open daily, year round.

WEST ROCK NATURE CENTER
Merritt Parkway at exit 60, New Haven   (203) 787-8016
West Rock is 428 feet high. West Rock Nature Center, at its base, is where rescued animals are treated and released back into the wild, or if unable to fend for themselves, become permanent wards of the park. Typical animals are birds, foxes and racoons. A very pleasant, low-key, small zoo for younger kids. Admission is free. Open daily dawn to dusk, except in bad winter weather.

Parks in Greater New Haven

Note: City Parks in New Haven are described on page 161.

BRADLEY POINT PARK & PROMENADE
On shore, off I-95, exit 42, West Haven   (203) 937-3651
A beautiful place to walk, bike, fly kites on Long Island Sound. Admission free. Open daily.

BROOKSVALE PARK
524 Brooksvale Avenue, Hamden   (203) 243-0440
A 195-acre wooded park with hiking trails, ball fields, picnic areas and a domestic animal petting zoo. Free admission. Open daily.

EAST ROCK PARK
East Rock Rd. & Davis St., New Haven   (203) 787-6086   See page 261.

INDIAN LEDGE & PEQUONNOCK VALLEY PARK
(BMX RACE TRACK)
Whitney Avenue, Trumbull   (203) 452-5060
Admission free, open daily.

NEW HAVEN GREEN
Center of New Haven
Sixteen acres of common ground controlled by a committee of proprietors. The three churches on the green were all built around 1813 and are open to the public. Admission free. Open daily.

SLEEPING GIANT STATE PARK
200 Mt. Carmel Avenue. Hamden
Merritt Pkwy, exit 61. Exit 10 off I-91   (203) 789-7498
A 1,500 acre State Park with 33 miles of hiking trails. Well marked walk up the mountain to an observation tower. Good picnic area, with brick fireplaces. Fishing is permitted in Mill River. Free admission. Sometimes there is a small parking fee. Open daily year round, with staffed Ranger station.

WHARTON BROOK STATE PARK
Wallingford
Off I-91 in Wallingford. Open dawn to dusk. Attractive hiking, lake side beach, and picnic facilites. A great family place.

Sports & Amusement Centers

B & R RIDING STABLES
Roaring Brook Road, Prospect   (203) 758-5031
A 200-acre farm offering guided trail rides for adults and children 8 and older. Fees charged. Open daily; reservations required.

CONNECTICUT SKYHAWKS
Jonathan Law H.S., 20 Lansdale Ave., Milford   (203) 874-2055
A United States Basketball League team. Ticket prices vary. Season is from May to July. Most games start at 7pm.

MILFORD AMUSEMENT CENTER
1607 Boston Post Road, Milford   (203) 877-3229
A "Family Fun Center" featuring miniature golf, batting cages, bumper cars and boats, video games, Kiddieland. Food available in adjoining restaurants. Admission free. You pay for everything you do. Open daily for long hours.

MILFORD JAI~ALAI
311 Old Gate Lane right off I-95, Milford   (203) 877-4211
The world's fastest ball game is played in this large attractive fronton featuring pari-mutual betting. Excellent restaurant and lounges. Also OTB betting. Admission charge. Open daily. Jai-Alia season is May 1 to December 31. OTB open year round.

NEW HAVEN RAVENS, AA PROFESSIONAL BASEBALL
Yale Field, Derby Ave. on Rt. 34, West Haven   1(800) RAVENS-1
New Haven's own AA Eastern League affiliate of the Colorado Rockies. Admission charge. Open all baseball season. (See p. 26)

SPORTS HAVEN
600 Long Wharf Drive, New Haven   (203) 821-3100
The Northeast's newest entertainment complex featuring parimutual wagering. Four giant screens show live thorough-bred, harness and greyhound racing. With a 17 ft. high shark aquarium, game room with high-tech virtual reality games, and several restaurants. Admission and parking charge. Open daily.

THE ONLY GAME IN TOWN
275 Valley Svc. Rd. off I-95 exit 12, North Haven   (203)239-GOLF
The ultimate sports complex built on 20+ acres for the whole family to enjoy. Facilities include a miniature golf course, batting cages, a large exciting go-kart race track and mini go-kart track for young children. Admission is free. You pay for each event. Open daily in good weather. Closed in the winter.

Public Boat Launches in Greater New Haven

Branford River State Launch Site, Route 142, Branford

Branford River Launching Ramp, Goodsell Pt Rd., Branford

Stony Creek Public Dock, Indian Point Road, Branford

Lighthouse Point Park Ramp, Lighthouse Road, East Haven

East River State Launch Site, Neck Road, Guilford

Hammonasset Beach State Launch Site, Meigs Point, Madison

Devon-Milford State Public Ramp, Naugatuck Road, Milford

Housatonic River State Launch Site, Naugatuck Rd, Milford

Milford Launching Ramp, Shipyard Lane, Milford

Lighthouse State Launch Site, Lighthouse Park, New Haven

West Haven Public Boat Ramp, First Avenue, West Haven

LONG ISLAND SOUND
Beaches & Waterfront Parks

The coastline is clearly one of Connecticut's most beautiful and precious natural resources and a source of commerce, recreation and tourism. The greater New Haven area is very fortunate to have many miles of scenic shoreline with numerous beaches and waterfront parks.

Although beaches are technically public property below the mean high water mark, access to the shoreline is somewhat limited because many beaches are privately or municipally owned, and parking is restricted. There is usually a non-resident fee for cars without town stickers. Listed below are beaches available to the public which have reasonable parking and admission fees.

Beaches

HAMMONASSET BEACH STATE PARK
Along the Beach off I-95 exit 62, Madison
(203) 245-2785

This is largest Connecticut shoreline park. There are two miles of beach with facilities for swimming, camping, picnicking, fishing, scuba diving, hiking and boating. Nature center, changing facilities and food concessions, too. Admission is free. Parking fee $4.00 weekends, $2.00 weekdays. Free off season. Open daily.

LIGHTHOUSE POINT PARK AND BEACH
End of Townsend Ave (I-95 exit 46), New Haven
(203) 787-8005

Gorgeous beach, changing rooms, and food concessions, plus nearby ball fields and picnic areas. The Old Lighthouse was built in 1840. The antique carousel has been completely restored and offers rides for a small fee. Admission fee in summer is $3.00 per car on weekends and $2.00 per car on weekdays. Open daily.

MILFORD BEACHES
Milford Parks and Recreation (203) 783-3280

Along the Milford shore are several accessible and lovely public beaches. Gulf Beach is off I-95, exit 39A. Silver Sands State Park is off I-95, exit 35. Improvements for Silver Sands have been delayed by budget restrictions for several years. Currently the beach is very pretty, but the park has no facilities. Walnut Beach is off I-95, exit 34. Admission is free for Milford residents. Non-resident fee is $5. Season passes are $165. Open daily.

WEST HAVEN BEACHES
Off I-95, exit 42, West Haven
West Haven Parks and Recreation (203) 937-3651

Along the West Haven shore are four beaches open to the public: Bradley Point Beach, Sandy Point Beach, Morris Beach and Oak Street Beach. Admission is free for West Haven residents. Non-resident fee is $10, $5 after 4:00pm. Season pass: $150. Open daily.

Pollution of Long Island Sound

Several decades of strong environmental regulation and enforcement have greatly improved the water quality of Long Island Sound, by reducing the discharge of heavy metals and other toxic pollutants into rivers and harbors. Still, much more can be done.

Despite existing regulations, and high public awareness of the problem, millions of gallons of partially treated and raw sewage pour into the Sound every day. During heavy rainstorms, wastes from combined storm and sanitary sewer systems must be shunted past treatment plants. From time to time, this results in beach closures due to high levels of contaminating bacteria in the water.

Bacteria is not the only problem created by sewage. The high level of nitrogen in most sewage throws off the natural balance of the Sound's ecology by stimulating massive growths of algae. The decomposition of the algae depletes the levels of oxygen in the water. Low oxygen levels, or *hypoxia*, threaten fish and other aquatic creatures.

Some coastal sewage plants have already been improved. However, the cost of modernizing all these plants is a long-term, billion dollar undertaking. Other projects are underway to reduce pollution from roads, run-off of fertilizers from farming, draining septic systems, dumps and other sources.

Yale Center for British Art

The Yale Center for British Art, open to the public since 1977, was founded in 1966 when Paul Mellon, Yale Class of 1929, donated his unparalleled collection of British art to the University. The museum collection now includes more than 1,200 paintings; 10,000 drawings; 20,000 prints; 20,000 rare books; and a small representative group of sculptures. It is considered the most comprehensive collection of British art outside of the United Kingdom.

The center has four principal aims: to foster a wider appreciation of British art among students and the general public; to encourage the interdisciplinary use of the collections by social and cultural historians; to support advanced research and develop special programs for Yale undergraduates. The Center contains exhibition and conservation facilities, classrooms, faculty offices, a photograph archive of postmedieval British art, and a reference library of prints, drawings and rare books.

Designed by the late Louis I. Kahn, the internationally acclaimed architect, the beautiful museum building is located across the street from the Yale University Art Gallery.

The Yale Center for British Art is open Tue-Sat, 10 am - 5 pm; Sun 12 noon - 5 pm. Closed Mondays, as well as New Year's Eve and New Year's Day, July 4th, Thanksgiving, Christmas Eve and Christmas Day. Admission is free.

Yale University Art Gallery

The Yale University Art Gallery was founded in 1832, when patriot-artist Colonel John Trumbull donated more than 100 of his paintings to Yale College. The Yale Art Gallery is the oldest and one of the most prestigious university art museums in the country, housing more than 100,000 objects from virtually all schools and periods in the history of art, from ancient times to the present.

Among the gallery's collection are ancient Egyptian and Pre-Columbian artifacts, African sculpture, American paintings and decorative arts, Asian art, Italian Renaissance paintings and works by 19th and 20th century artists such as Van Gogh, Manet, Degas, Picasso, Homer, Hopper, O'Keefe, and Pollack. The Yale Art Gallery features numerous special exhibitions each year and many programs of general interest.

The Gallery is open Tue-Sat, 10 am - 4:45 pm; Sun 2 pm - 4:45 pm. The Gallery is closed during August. Admission is free.

Yale Center for British Art   432-2800
1080 Chapel Street, New Haven

Yale University Art Gallery   432-0600
1111 Chapel Street, New Haven

MUSEUMS & HISTORICAL SOCIETIES
Yale Museums

Peabody Museum of Natural History

Founded in 1866, the Peabody Museum is one of the largest and oldest museums of natural history in the country. It houses a world-famous collection of dinosaur fossils, and the 110-foot-long Pulitzer Prize-winning mural, *The Age of Reptiles*, by Rudolph F. Zallinger.

Among the many prehistoric creatures found in its Great Hall are the original specimens of Brontosaurus and Stegosaurus. The Insect Zoo and the Discovery Room fascinate children, and the museum has a number of programs designed to encourage children of all ages to learn about natural history through hands-on experiences. The museum offers a variety of special events such as tours, films, lectures, workshops and naturalist programs. In addition to the dinosaur collection, other permanent exhibits include mammals, Egypt, Minerals, Plains Indians, Connecticut Birds, Pacific Cultures and Human Origins.

The Peabody is open Mon-Sat, 10 am - 5 pm; Sun 12 noon - 5 pm. Closed New Year's Eve and Day, July 4th, Labor Day, Thanksgiving, Christmas Eve and Christmas Day. Admission is $5 for adults; $3 for senior citizens and children 3-15.

Beinecke Rare Book and Manuscript Library

The Beinecke Rare Book and Manuscript Library at Yale, one of the largest buildings in the world devoted entirely to rare books, contains more than 500,000 volumes and several million manuscripts. The magnificent building is constructed of translucent panels of Vermont marble, cut one and one-quarter inches thick.

An original copy of the Gutenberg Bible, the first Western book printed from movable type, is on permanent display in the library's mezzanine as is Audubon's *Birds of America*. In the center of the library stands a six story glass book tower which houses nearly 4,000 books printed in Europe before 1500. Scholars from all over the world travel to the Library to study its treasures.

Beinecke Rare Book and Manuscript Library is open Mon-Fri, 8:30 am - 5 pm; Sat 10 am - 5 pm. Research access is available only on weekdays. Admission is free.

Peabody Museum   432-5050
170 Whitney Avenue, New Haven

Beinecke Rare Book and Manuscript Library   432-2977
121 Wall Street, New Haven

MUSEUMS & HISTORICAL SOCIETIES
Historical Societies

New Haven Colony Historical Society

The New Haven Colony Historical Society focuses on the study and preservation of materials that document the history of the New Haven Colony from 1638 to the present. The Historical Society pursues this mission through its library, photographic archives, education department, and collections.

Another interesting facility of the Society is the Pardee-Morris House, at 325 Lighthouse Road, where visitors can step back in time to see how a prominent New Haven family lived at the end of the 1700s. The Pardee Morris House is open seasonally.

The Historical Society is open Tue-Fri, 10am-5pm; Sat-Sun, 2-5pm. Admission is free Tuesdays; regularly $2 for adults, $1.50 for students, senior citizens and children over 6. Call for further information and library hours.

Pardee-Morris House

New Haven Colony Historical Society   562-4183
114 Whitney Avenue, New Haven

Huntington Historical Society
Shelton History Center   562-4183
70 Ripton Road, Shelton

Call for hours and program information.

Irish American
Historical Society   468-0426
Venice Place, East Haven

A research facility. Call for hours and information.

Jewish Historical Society   787-3183
169 Davenport Avenue, New Haven

Archival information and various memorabilia documenting the history of the Jewish Community of Greater New Haven. Open Mon-Fri, 9 am-12 noon; closed on major national and Jewish holidays.

Trumbull Historical Society   377-6620
1856 Huntington Tpke, Trumbull

The Museum stands on the site of the first house built in Trumbull in 1820. Open Thursday, 10am-1pm and Sundays 2-4pm.

Ukranian Heritage Center   875-0388
555 George Street, New Haven

Call for hours and programming.

MUSEUMS & HISTORICAL SOCIETIES
More Museums

CT Children's Museum   562-KIDS
22 Wall Street, New Haven

A wonderful place for young children 7 and under to play and learn. Summer Hours: Mon-Fri, 10 am-2pm. School Year Hours: Tue-Thu, 10 am-2pm; Sat-Sun 10 am-4pm. Admission: $3 per person: free for children under the age of 1.

Yale Collection of Musical Instruments   432-0822
15 Hillhouse Avenue, New Haven

This collection contains over 850 European and American Instruments from the 16th to the 20th centuries. Call for further information about its concert series. Open Tue-Thu, 1- 4pm, Sept.-July.

Knights of Columbus Museum and Archives   772-2130
1 Columbus Plaza, New Haven

The Museum displays 500 artifacts, documents and works of art illustrating the history and activities of the Knights of Columbus, as both an insurance and fraternal organization. Call for hours and location; the museum will soon be moving to new quarters at 1 State Street.

Eli Whitney Museum   777-1833
915 Whitney Avenue, New Haven

The museum was established in 1979 on the banks of the Mill River, where Eli Whitney built his musket factory in 1798. It is the cradle of the American Industrial Revolution. The Museum celebrates Whitney's spirit of Yankee ingenuity and features numerous workshops, exhibits, programs, and lectures designed to expand our understanding of technology. The 1816 Barn offers country dances, folk music and summer theater. Open Sun, Wed, Thu, and Fri, 12-5pm; Sat. 10am-3pm. Admission: $1.50 for children 3-18; $2.50 for adults.

Shoreline Trolley Museum   467-6927
17 River Street, East Haven

This museum houses over 100 antique trolleys from 1904-1939. Children love the 3 mile trolley ride. The Museum is a registered National Historic site. Open weekends April -December; every day from Memorial Day - Labor Day, 11 am -5 pm.

Shopping Centers

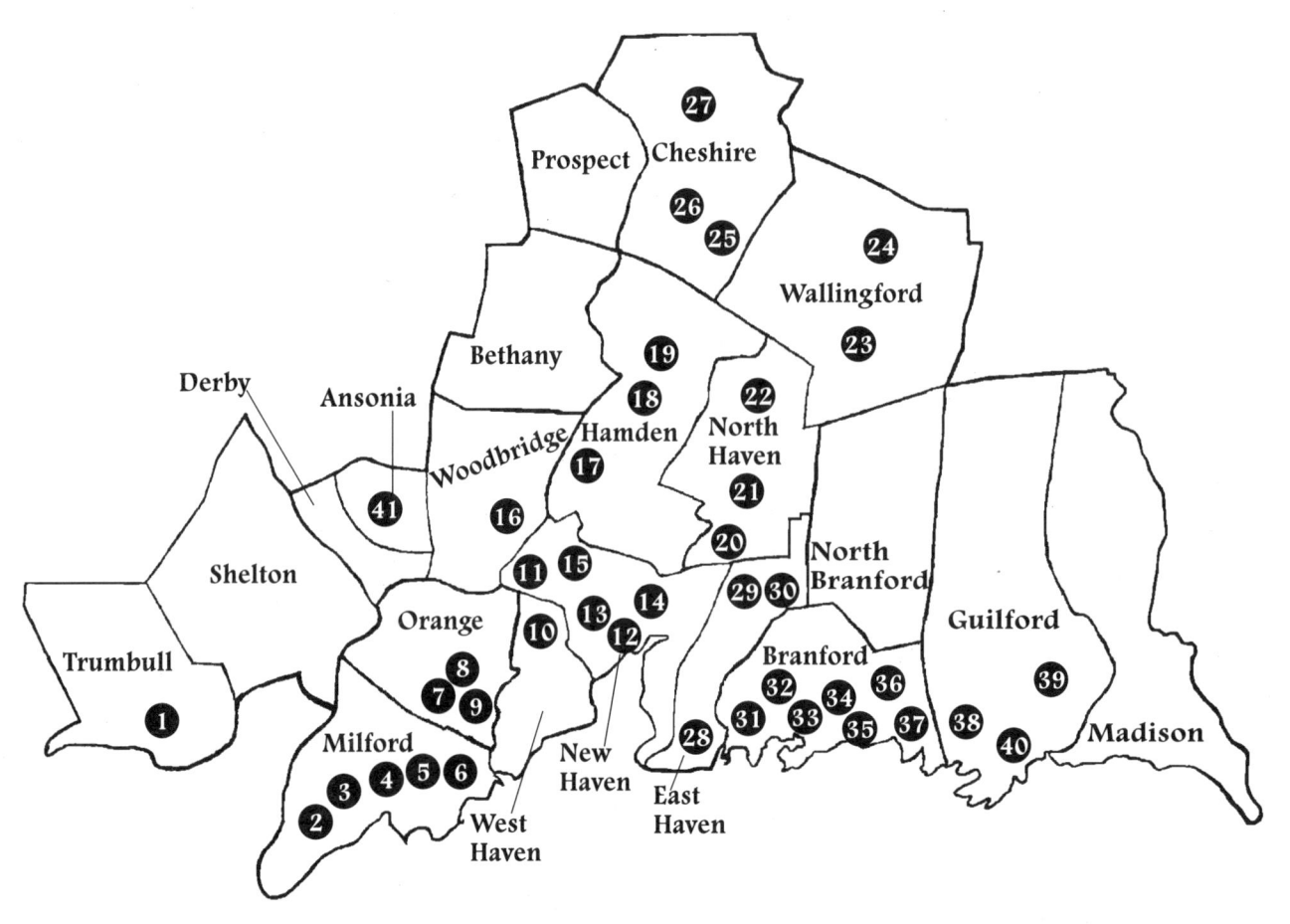

Trumbull
1. Trumbull Mall

Milford
2. Milford Factory Outlets
3. Milford Shopping Plaza
4. Connecticut Post Mall
5. Cosco Plaza
6. Wayside Plaza

Orange
7. 500 Post Plaza
8. Firelite Shopping Center
9. Home Depot Plaza

West Haven
10. West Haven Post Plaza

New Haven
11. Amity Shopping Center
12. Chapel Square Mall
13. Downtown Area Shops
14. Upper State Street
15. Westville Area

Woodbridge
16. New Haven Plaza

Hamden
17. Hamden Plaza
18. Hamden Mart
19. Hamden Mart Extension

North Haven
20. Price Club Plaza
21. North Haven Shopping Center
22. Drazen Shopping Center

Wallingford
23. Wallingford Shopping Plaza
24. Colony Shopping Center

Cheshire
25. Route 10 Shouth Chesire
26. Maple Court Plaza
27. Cheshire Shopping Center

East Haven
28. Trolley Square
29. Foxhaven Plaza
30. Millbrook Shopping Center

Branford
31. Branford Outlet Center
32. Branford Hill Plaza
33. Branhaven
34. Branford Shopping Center
35. 50/95 Shopping Center
36. The Mews
37. Bittersweet Herb Farm

Guilford
38. Shoreline Plaza
39. Lighthouse Square
40. Downtown Guilford

Ansonia
41. Ansonia Mall

A representative list of shopping centers and malls in Greater New Haven

SHOPPING
Bookstores

Afristar
850 Grand Avenue
772-7827

Albertus Magnus Bookstore
Albertus Magnus College
700 Prospect Street
777-2478

Arethusa Book Shop
87 Audubon Street
624-1848

Atticus Book Store
1082 Chapel Street
776-4040

Barnes & Noble
470 Universal Drive, North Haven
234-1805

Barnnett Books
20 N. Plains Industrial Road,
Wallingford
265-2013

Black Cat Mysteries
77 Whitney Avenue
776-6008

Blackprint Heritage Gallery
162 Edgewood Avenue
782-2159

Book Haven
290 York Street
787-2848

The Book Swap
633 Boston Post Road, Guilford
453-6090

Bookstore, Inc.
933-4000

Branford Book and Card Shoppe
1020 Main Street, Branford
488-5975

Breakwater Books
81 Whitfield Street, Guilford
453-4141

Bryn Mar Book Shop
56-1/2 Whitney Avenue
562-4217

The Elements of Life, Ltd.
977 State Street
773-0084

Foundry Book Store
33 Whitney Avenue
624-8282

Foundry Music Co.
102 Audubon Street
776-3650

**Gateway Community
Technical College Bookstore**
865-5614

Golden Thread Book Sellers
915 State Street
777-7807

Lighthouse Book & Gift Shop
118 New Haven Avenue, Milford
874-1119

Nostalgia Shop
1853 Dixwell Avenue, Hamden
288-6860

Penny's Book Shelf
1099 Bridgeport Avenue, Milford,
878-1411

R.J. Julia Book Sellers
768 Boston Post Road, Madison
245-3959

Silver Books
20 N Plains Industrial Rd, Wallingford
269-1861

Sober Camel Recovery Book & Gift
448 Forest Road, West Haven
387-5622

Univ. of New Haven, Book Store
300 Orange Avenue, West Haven
932-7030

Southern CT State Univ. Bookstore
Fitch Street, Hamden
389-8923

Village Green Book Shop
499 Campbell Avenue, West Haven
932-5402

Waldenbooks
2165 Dixwell Avenue, Hamden
248-9625

Waldenbooks
91 Boston Post Road, Orange
795-4430

A Walk In Truth Christian Books
162 Edgewood Avenue
782-2159

Whitlock Farm Booksellers
Sperry Road, Bethany
393-1240

Whitlock's Inc.
17 Broadway
562-9841

Yale Co-op
77 Broadway
772-2200

NEW HAVEN Ravens

When the gates opened at Yale Field on April 14, 1994, the New Haven Ravens ushered in a new era of professional sports in Connecticut. As the record crowd of 6,667 spun the turnstiles, it was obvious that something exciting was taking place. On that day and throughout the summer of 1994, the New Haven Ravens offered excitement and fun, both on and off the field, as they introduced a new form of affordable family entertainment to the New Haven area and the State of Connecticut.

Over 281,000 fans attended Ravens games in 1994 (the 10th highest total in the 71-year history of the Eastern League), for an average of over 4,000 per night.

Although the team is the New Haven Ravens, the entire state got on the Ravens bandwagon. Over 26% of Ravens fans reside in Fairfield County. The Ravens also saw a strong showing from out of state, with fans from New York and Massachusetts appearing frequently on fan surveys.

In September of 1994, the Ravens signed a two-year working agreement with the Colorado Rockies organization that will continue the affiliation through the 1996 season. The Rockies supplied the Ravens with a highly talented team in 1994, with the Ravens earning a spot in the Eastern League playoffs.

New Haven Ravens
63 Grove Street
New Haven 06510

782-3140
1(800)RAVENS-1

Future major league stars shined throughout the season at Yale Field. Ravens pitcher Juan Acevedo was named both the Eastern League's Pitcher of the Year and Rookie of the Year for his outstanding efforts. Acevedo led the league in wins and ERA and was third in strikeouts in 1994. Third baseman Bryn Kosco and pitchers Phil Schneider and Rod Pedraza were named All-Stars during the 1994 season.

The home of this exciting baseball action is historic Yale Field, located on the New Haven/West Haven border in the Yale Athletic Complex. This 67-year-old park went through an extensive facelift before the inaugural season and renovations continue to provide greater fan comfort and enjoyment in all areas of Yale Field.

A night of minor league baseball is not necessarily limited to watching the game. By participating in creative on-field contests, fans provide much of the entertainment themselves.

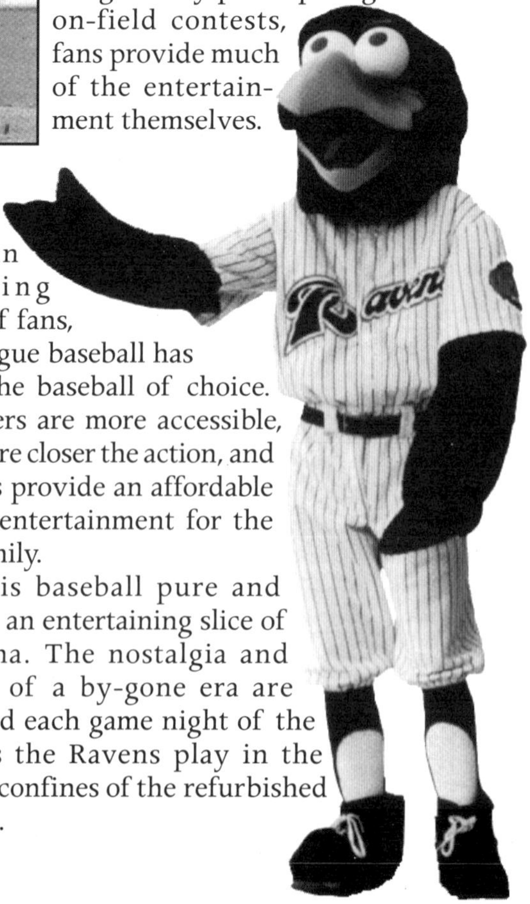

For an increasing number of fans, minor league baseball has become the baseball of choice. The players are more accessible, the seats are closer the action, and the games provide an affordable night of entertainment for the whole family.

This is baseball pure and simple — an entertaining slice of Americana. The nostalgia and intimacy of a by-gone era are recaptured each game night of the season as the Ravens play in the beautiful confines of the refurbished Yale Field.

All photos courtesy New Haven Ravens

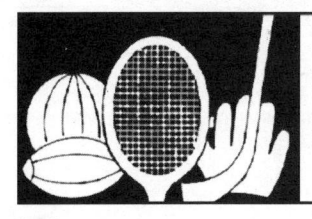

SPORTS
Baseball & Tennis

In 1990, the Volvo International Tennis Tournament, one of the premier professional men's tournaments on the ATP Tour, moved from its home in Stratton Mountain, Vermont, to New Haven. City officials, representatives of Yale and the State wooed Tournament-owner Jim Westhall with a promise to build one of the world's largest tennis facilities.

The 1990 Volvo Tournament, a warm-up for the U.S. Open, was staged in a 12,000-seat temporary tennis facility, the largest ever built. Derrick Rostagno defeated Mark Woodbridge to be crowned New Haven's first tennis champion that year, and construction of the new $18 million, 15,000-seat stadium, featuring a Deco Turf Hard Court, began immediately thereafter.

By early 1991, the Connecticut Tennis Center was completed, and New Haven became home to the third largest tennis facility in the world. The Volvo International has a prestigious list of past champions, including Jimmy Connors, Ivan Lendl, Stefan Edberg and Boris Becker. Big-name players such as André Agassi, Michael Stich, Sergi Bruguera and Michael Chang provide spectators with some of the most exciting tennis in the world.

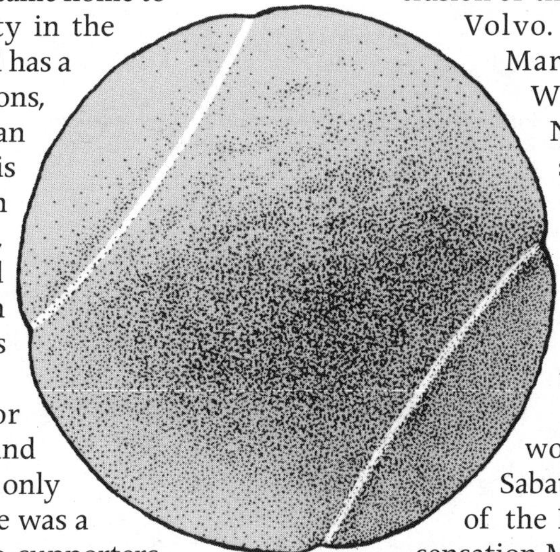

With the enthusiasm for tennis generated by the Volvo and a world-class stadium utilized only one week out of the year, there was a need for another event. Volvo supporters and Connecticut residents were polled to see if there was enough interest to warrant a women's tennis event. Southern New England Telephone stepped in to provide title sponsorship, and tournament promoters Jewel Productions became involved. The SNET Classic, a three-day special event which features top-ranked women professionals on the WTA Tour, was staged only four days after the conclusion of the Volvo. A match between superstar Martina Navratilova and 1993 Wimbledon runner-up Jana Novotna drew the highest single-session attendance ever at the Connecticut Tennis Center. A record 34,528 tennis lovers attended over the three days, the largest crowd ever to see a non-Grand Slam outdoor women's tennis tournament.

Since that first tournament, women players such as Gabriela Sabatini of Argentina, Brenda Schultz of the Netherlands, and Swiss teenage sensation Martina Hingis have headlined at the Connecticut Tennis Center.

Today, New Haven provides tennis lovers with the best players on both the men's and women's tours. It all takes place in the beautiful Connecticut Tennis Center in the Westville section of town, where history is made each August at the Volvo International and the SNET Women's Classic.

When not used for tennis, the conveniently located stadium hosts such exciting events as the Crosby, Stills, Nash benefit concert.

Jewel Productions   772-3838
545 Long Wharf Drive, New Haven

Public Golf Courses in Connecticut

Town	Course	Address	Phone	Price
Avon	Bel Compo Golf Club	65 Nod Rd.	678-1679	$27
Bethany	Woodhaven Country Club	275 Miller Rd	393-3230	$15, 9 Holes
Canton	Canton Public Golf Course	110 Rte 44	693-8305	$13, 9 Holes
Colchester	Chanticlair Golf Course	288 Old Hebron Rd	537-3223	$11, 9 Holes
Coventry	Skungmaug River Golf Club	104 Folly Lane	742-9348	$24
Coventry	Twin Hill Country Club	Rt. 31	742-9705	$24
Danbury	Richter Park Golf Club	100 Aunt Hack Rd	792-2550	$44
East Hartford	East Hartford Golf Club	130 Long Hill St	528-5082	$23
East Lyme	Cedar Ridge Golf Course	18 Drabik Rd	691-4568	$17
Enfield	Grassmere Country Club	130 Town Farm Rd	749-7740	$12, 9 Holes
Fairfield	D. Fairchild Wheeler Golf Club	Easton Turnpike	576-8083	$20
Fairfield	H. Smith Richardson Golf Course	Morehouse Highway	255-6094	$26.50
Farmington	Tunxis Plantation Country Club	87 Town Farm Rd	677-1367	$27
Glastonbury	Minnechaug Golf Course	16 Fairway Crossing	643-9914	$11.50, 9 Holes
Granby	Copper Hill Country Club	20 Copper Hill Rd	653-6191	$10.50, 9 Holes
Groton	Shennecossett Golf Course	274 Plant St	441-0262	$26
Groton	Trumbull Golf Course	119 High Rock Rd	445-7991	$15
Hamden	Laurel View Country Club	310 W. Shepard Ave	288-1819	$23
Hamden	Meadowbrook Country Club	2761 Dixwell Ave	281-4847	$9, 9 Holes
Hamden	Sleeping Giant Golf Course	3931 Whitney Ave	281-9456	$11.75, 9 Holes
Hartford	Goodwin Park Golf Course	1130 Maple Ave	956-3601	$21
Hartford	Keney Golf Course	280 Tower Ave	525-3656	$18
Hebron	Blackledge Country Club	180 West St	288-0250	$26
Hebron	Tallwood Country Club	91 North St	646-1151	$24
Kensington	Timberlin Golf Club	330 Southington Rd	828-3228	$24
Lisbon	Lisbon Country Club	78 Kendall Rd	376-4325	$10, 9 Holes
Litchfield	Stonybrook Golf Club	263 Milton Rd	567-9977	$20
Manchester	Manchester Country Club	305 S. Main St	646-0226	$28
Meriden	G. Hunter Memorial Golf Course	685 Westfield Rd	634-3366	$22
Middlefield	Indian Springs Golf Club	Mack Road	349-8109	$13
Middlefield	Lyman Orchards Golf Club	Rt. 157	349-8055	$31
Milford	Mill Stone Country Club	384 Herbert St	874-5900	$11, 9 Holes
Monroe	Whitney Farms Golf Club	175 Shelton Rd, Rt. 110	268-0707	$37
Moodus	Banner Resort & Country Club	10 Banner Rd	873-9075	$23
Naugatuck	Hop Brook Country Club	615 N. Church St	729-8013	$16
New Britain	Stanley Golf Course	245 Hartford Rd	827-8144	$23
New Haven	Alling Memorial Golf Course	35 Eastern St	946-8013	$24
New Milford	Candlewood Valley Country Club	401 Danbury Rd	354-9359	$27
Norwalk	Oak Hills Park	165 Fillow St	838-0303	$30
Norwich	Norwich Golf Course	685 New London Tpke	889-6973	$27
Orange	Grass Hill Country Club	441 Clark Lane	795-1422	$17
Orange	Orange Hills Country Club	489 Racebrook Rd	795-4161	$30
Pawcatuck	Elmridge Golf Course	229 Elmridge Rd	599-2248	$28
Portland	Portland Golf Course	169 Bartlett St	342-2833	$26.50
Ridgefield	Ridgefield Golf Club	545 Ridgebury Rd	748-7008	$27
Rocky Hill	Rolling Greens Golf Course	600 Cold Spring Rd	257-9775	$13, 9 Holes
Saybrook	Fenwick Golf Course	Maple Ave	388-2516	$12.75, 9 Holes
Simsbury	Simsbury Farms Golf Club	100 Old Farms Rd	658-6246	$25
Somers	Cedar Knob Golf Course	Billing Rd	749-3550	$20
Southington	Pine Valley Golf Course	300 Welch Rd	628-0879	$26
Southington	Pattonbrook Country Club	201 Pattonwood	793-6000	$18
Southington	Southington Country Club	Savage St	628-7032	$23
Stamford	E. Gaynor Brennan Municipal	451 Stillwater Rd	324-4185	$30
Stamford	Sterling Farms Golf Club	1349 Newfield Ave	461-9090	$33
Stonington	Pequot Golf Club	127 Wheeler Rd	535-1898	$24
Suffield	Airways Golf Course	1070 S. Grand St	668-4973	$19
Thompson	Raceway Golf Club	East Thompson Rd	923-9591	$22
Torrington	Eastwood Country Club	1301 Torringford West St	489-2630	$14.50, 9 Holes
Trumbull	Tashua Knoll Golf Club	40 Tashua Knolls Lane	261-5989	$24
Wallingford	Pilgrims Harbor Country Club	Harrison Rd	269-6023	$18, 9 Holes
Waterbury	East Mountain Golf Course	171 E. Mountain Rd	753-1425	$20
Waterbury	Western Hills Golf Course	Park Rd	756-1211	$20
West Hartford	Buena Vista Golf Course	56 Buena Vista Rd	521-7379	$9.75, 9 Holes
West Hartford	Rockledge Country Club	289 S. Main St	521-3156	$25
Windsor	Millbrook Golf Course	147 Pigeon Hill Rd	688-2575	$24
Wolcott	Farmington Hills Country Club	141 East St	879-9380	$11, 9 Holes
Woodstock	Harrisville Golf Course	125 Harrisville Rd	928-6098	$13, 9 Holes
Woodstock	Woodstock Golf Course	Roseland Rd	928-4130	$12, 9 Holes

SPORTS
More Sports...

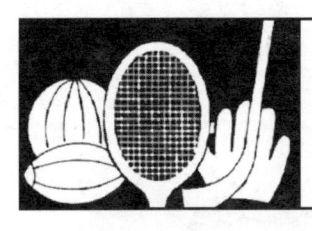

Milford Jai-Alai 877-4211
See page 18.

Connecticut Skyhawks 874-2055
See page 18.

Sports Haven 821-3100
See page 18.

Indoor Professional Soccer 772-4200
Coming soon! Call the Coliseum for details.

Marinas and Yacht Clubs

BRANFORD
Pier 66	Goodsell Pt Rd	488-5613
Goodsell Point Marina	Goodsell Pt Rd	488-5292
Dutch Wharf	Maple St	489-9000
Bruce & Johnson's	S. Montowese Ave	488-8329
Branford Yacht Club	Goodsell Pt Rd	488-9798
Indian Neck Yacht Club	Indian Neck	488-9276
Pine Orchard Yacht Club	Pine Orchard Road	488-2575

EAST HAVEN
Ct Marina	Short Beach Rd	467-1183

GUILFORD
Brown's Boat Yard	Caffinch Island Rd	453-6283
Town Marina	Lower Whitfield St	453-8092
Sachem's Head Yacht Club	Chimney Corner Circle	453-9207
Guilford Yacht Club	Whitfield St	453-9245

MILFORD
Flagship Marina	Bridgeport Ave	874-1783
Milford Harbor Marina	High St	878-2900
Town Dock	High St	(NA)
Spencer's Marina	Rose St	874-4173
Valley Yacht Club	Riverside Dr	877-0077
Milford Yacht Club	Trumbull Ave	878-1271
Port Milford	Rogers Ave	877-7802

NEW HAVEN
Oyster Point Marina	S. Water St	624-5895
City Point Yacht Club	Kimberly Ave	789-9530
Waucoma Yacht Club	Front St	777-9530
New Haven Yacht Club	Cove St	469-9608
New Haven Marina, Inc	Cove St	469-8230

WEST HAVEN
West Haven Yacht Club	First Ave	933-9825
Shiners Cove Marina	Water St	934-2182
West Cove Co-Op Marina	Kimberly Ave	933-3000

40 One Day Trips in Connecticut

1. Arboretum at Connecticut College • *New London*
2. American Clock & Watch Museum • *Bristol*
3. Barnum Museum • *Bridgeport*
4. Beardsley Zoological Gardens • *Bridgeport*
5. Bradley Airport & New England Air Museum • *Windsor*
6. Center for the Arts at Wesleyan • *Middletown*
7. Connecticut Fire Museum • *East Windsor*
8. Connecticut Trolley Museum • *East Windsor*
9. Connecticut River Museum • *Essex*
10. CT Yankee Atomic Power Company • *Haddam Neck*
11. U.S. Coast Guard Academy • *New London*
12. Dinosaur State Park • *Rocky Hill*
13. Discovery Museum & Planetarium • *Bridgeport*
14. Essex Valley Railroad • *Essex*
15. Foxwoods Casino • *Ledyard*
16. Gillette Castle • *East Haddam*
17. Hill-Stead Museum • *Farmington*
18. Historical Museum of Medicine & Dentistry • *Hartford*
19. Mark Twain House • *Hartford*
20. Harriet Beecher Stowe House • *Hartford*
21. Maritime Center • *Norwalk*
22. Mystic Maritime Aquarium • *Mystic*
23. Mystic Seaport Museum • *Mystic*
24. White Flower Farm • *Litchfield*
25. Connecticut River Cruise Boats • *Haddam*
26. New England Carousel Museum • *Bristol*
27. Old Newgate Prison & Copper Mine • *East Granby*
28. Ocean Beach Park • *New London*
29. Prudence Crandall Museum • *Canterbury*
30. Quassy Amusement Park • *Middlebury*
31. Quinebaug Valley Fish Hatchery • *Central Village*
32. State Capital • *Hartford*
33. State Library and Supreme Court Building • *Hartford*
34. Stamford Museum & Nature Center • *Stamford*
35. The Hitchcock Museum • *Riverton*
36. Travelers Tower • *Hartford*
37. SS Nautilus Memorial • *Groton*
38. Wadsworth Athenaeum • *Hartford*
39. Mystic Cruises • *Mystic*
40. Wineries • *Litchfield Area*

CONNECTICUT
40 Day Trips

Here are 40 suggested day trips to places outside of the Greater New Haven area in Connecticut. There are also many places within Greater New Haven to visit that are covered in the Attractions section of this book, starting on page 15. In choosing trips for inclusion, variety and popularity were taken into consideration.

There are three good books about where to go in Connecticut when you want to make the trip within a day and be back at night. (*AAA CT, MA, RI Attractions, Lodgings & Restaurants*; *CT-Off the Beaten Path* by David & Deborah Ritchie; and *CT-An Explorer's Guide* by Barnett D. Laschever & Barbara Beeching). The AAA book is free to AAA members; the other two are available in most books stores).

Days of operation and admission prices were accurate when this book went to press. Telephone numbers are included; *we strongly suggest that you call before you go*. Hours and admission prices are subject to change, and many places have periodic special exhibits.

1. ARBORETUM AND CONNECTICUT COLLEGE
New London • (203) 439-2140

Connecticut College is located on Route #32, north of I-95. The Arboretum contains more than 415 acres of land (in addition to the campus of Connecticut College), with over 300 varieties of trees and shrubs. It is open daily, dawn to dusk. Admission is free.

2. AMERICAN CLOCK AND WATCH MUSEUM
Bristol • (203) 583-6070

100 Maple Street, 2 blocks south of Route #6, in the historic Miles Lewis House. Display includes more than 3,000 clocks and watches dating back to 1590. There is also a recreated Victorian clock shop. Open daily. Closed in winter. $3 admission. SC & C.

3. BARNUM MUSEUM
Bridgeport • (203) 331-9881

820 Main Street. This 3-story museum chronicles the life and achievements of P.T. Barnum, who was from Bridgeport. It presents 3 separate themes: *The Man, Barnum's Bridgeport, Showman to the World*. There is a continuous introductory film. There are often special shows in the 7,000 sq. ft. exhibition wing. Closed Mondays and major holidays. $4 admission. SC, C & S.

4. BEARDSLEY ZOOLOGICAL GARDENS
Bridgeport • (203) 576-8082

A traditional zoo with over 80 animals, many in outdoor settings. There is also a children's zoo and a replica of a New England farm, complete with animals. Pony rides are often available. Open daily, including many holidays. $5 admission plus parking. SC, C & S.

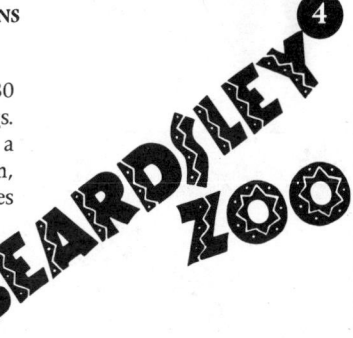

5. BRADLEY INTERNATIONAL AIRPORT/NEW ENGLAND AIR MUSEUM
Windsor Locks • (203) 623-3305

West of I-95, exit 40, off Route #75. Very good signs to airport. Airport is open to visitors, who can go to the observation deck and watch airplanes land and take off. Next door to the airport is the New England Air Museum with displays of vintage planes, modern planes and aviation memorabilia. Open daily; closed on only a few holidays. Airport visit is free. There may be a small charge for the observation deck. Museum $3. SC & C.

6. CENTER FOR THE ARTS AND WESLEYAN UNIVERSITY
Middletown • (203) 347-9411 x2577

Wesleyan is located in the center of Middletown, off Route #9. The Center for the Arts, at 301 High Street, includes two galleries with changing exhibits. The Davidson Art Center focuses on printmaking and photography. The Zilkha Gallery presents contemporary paintings and sculpture. Open daily except Mondays during school year. Restricted openings in the summer. Free admission.

We strongly suggest that you call before visiting any of these places. Hours & admission fees are subject to change, and many have periodic special exhibits.

Abbreviations: SC = Senior Citizen Discount   C = Children Prices   S = Student Discount.   Example SC, C & S

7 — CONNECTICUT FIRE MUSEUM
East Windsor • (203) 623-4732

58 North Road, 1/2 mile east of I-95, at exit 45, behind the CT Trolley Museum. The collection contains antique fire equipment, including some for sleighs (c. 1800s) and a 1955 Zabek pumper. Open daily in the summer, and weekends only in the winter. Admission $1. SC & C.

8 — CONNECTICUT TROLLEY MUSEUM
East Windsor • (203) 623-6540

58 North Road, 1/2 mile east of I-95, at exit 45, in front of the CT Fire Museum. The collection contains trolley cars dating between 1894 and 1947. There is a 3-1/2 mile trolley ride. Open daily in the summer, and weekends only in the winter. Museum admission is free. Unlimited trolley rides cost $6. SC & C.

9 — CONNECTICUT RIVER MUSEUM
Essex • (203) 767-8269

At the foot of Main Street, at the edge of the Connecticut River. Exhibits relate to river steam boats built or used on the Connecticut River. The 1775 submarine *Turtle* was said to have been used in the Revolutionary War, and is claimed to be the first submarine. Closed Mondays and some holidays. Admission $3. SC & C.

10 — CT YANKEE ATOMIC POWER CO.
Haddam Neck • (203) 267-9279

The information and science center is located at 362 Injun Hollow Road 4-1/2 miles southwest of Route #151, on the grounds of Connecticut's first nuclear power plant. Exhibits include hands-on displays about all types of energy, including nuclear power. There are also films. Admission is free. Open daily, except major holidays.

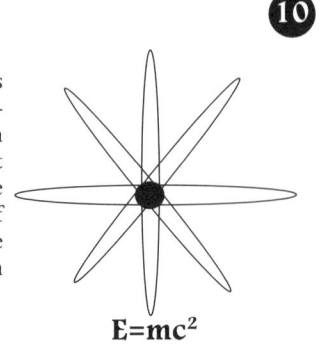

$E=mc^2$

11 — U.S. COAST GUARD ACADEMY
New London • (203) 444-8270

Just north of I-95 on Route #32 (Mohegan Avenue). Very good signs. The cadet corps marches in review most Fridays at 4 p.m. in April, May, September and October. The visitors pavilion shows a multimedia presentation about the academy and the Coast Guard. When in port, the tall ship *Eagle* is open to visitors on weekends. There is a museum in Waesche Hall. Everything is free admission.

12 — DINOSAUR STATE PARK
Rocky Hill • (203) 529-8423

One mile east of exit 23 of I-91, on West Street. A geodesic dome exhibit center covers a sandstone layer in which more than 500 dinosaur footprints have been preserved. Make your own plaster casts of the footprints! (It's best to call in advance for instructions.) Park is open daily year-round. Exhibit center closes Mondays and some holidays. Parking $1. Exhibit center $2. SC & C.

13 — DISCOVERY MUSEUM & PLANETARIUM
Bridgeport • (203) 372-3521

4450 Park Avenue. Set in a 90 acre park, it contains art and science exhibits. Special attractions are the Challenger Learning Center and a planetarium. Closed Mondays. Call for planetarium schedule. Admission $6. SC & C.

14 — ESSEX VALLEY RAILROAD
Essex • (203) 767-0103

The station is located on Railroad Avenue, 1/4 mile west of Route #9 at exit 3. Featured is a 12-mile railroad ride along the Connecticut River. One train daily connects with the riverboat, offering a combined boat and train ride. In the summer, there are five or six trips daily. The schedule is reduced off-season. Train ride: $8.50. Combination ride: $14. SC & C.

15 — FOXWOODS CASINO
Ledyard • (203) 885-3000

The world's most profitable (for the owners) casino is on Route #2, 8 miles west of I-95 exit 92. Very good signs. What started as a Bingo hall run by the Mashantucket Pequot continues to grow and expand into a complete resort and gambling complex. You must be 18 to play Bingo and 21 to get into the casino. Admission is free, but it costs money to gamble. This place never closes.

16 — GILLETTE CASTLE
East Haddam • (203) 526-2336

2.5 miles south of Route #82 and then 1-3/4 miles west. Excellent signs. William Gillette, an actor and playwright most famous for his portrayal of Sherlock Holmes, owned the 24-room castle, built 1914-19. Most rooms are furnished and open for viewing. There is also an interesting outdoor model train display in the park. Open daily including most holidays. Admission $4. SC & C.

INTERSTATE 91
CONNECTICUT
40 Day Trips

17 — HILL~STEAD MUSEUM
Farmington • (203)677-4787

35 Mountain Road, 1/4 mile from the center of Farmington. The art collection includes the work of Mary Cassatt, Degas, Manet, Monet and others. There is a Ming and Ching dynasty porcelain collection. The house itself is a showplace, set on 125 acres. Closed Mondays and major holidays. $6 admission. SC, C & S.

18 — HISTORICAL MUSEUM OF MEDICINE AND DENTISTRY
Hartford • (203) 236-5613

230 Scarborough Street, at Albany Avenue, inside the Hartford Medical Society Building. Exhibits trace the progress of medical technology from the Revolutionary War through today. Unusual medical devices, instruments and medical art work are also displayed. Open weekdays; closed most holidays. Admission is free.

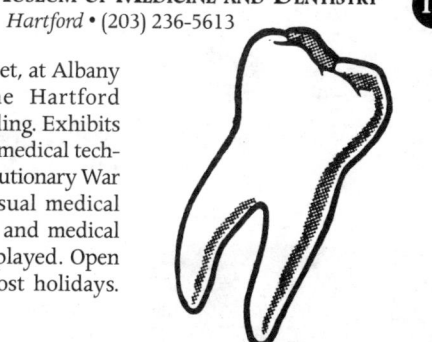

19 — MARK TWAIN HOUSE
Hartford • (203) 493-6411

351 Farmington Avenue. Preserved home of Mark Twain, who lived in Hartford for 17 years. The unusual 19-room Victorian Gothic house, built in 1873, offers wonderful insight into the life of one of America's best-known authors. Open daily in the summer, and frequently in the winter. Closed major holidays. Admission is $6.50. SC & C.

20 — HARRIET BEECHER STOWE HOUSE
Hartford • (203) 525-9317

Farmington Avenue at Forest Street, next-door to the Twain House. Victorian cottage was home of the author of *Uncle Tom's Cabin*, from 1873-96. Displays family and professional memorabilia, period furnishings, historical gardens. Guided tours, gift shop. Open daily in summer, frequently in winter. Closed major holidays. Admission $6.50. SC & C.

HARRIET BEECHER STOWE CENTER
The Harriet Beecher Stowe House and the Stowe Day Library

21 — MARITIME CENTER
Norwalk • (203) 852-0700

South of Exit 16 on I-95, on the Norwalk River at 10 N. Water Street. Very good signs. Restored 19th century factory building houses interactive exhibits about marine history and marine life in Long Island Sound. Large aquarium with over 125 species. Touching tank for children. IMAX theater shows movies on a 6-story-high curved screen that makes everything larger than life. A Maritime Hall has rotating exhibits about ships and the sea. Open most days, except some holidays. Admission to everything except IMAX is $7.50. IMAX is $6. SC&C.

22 — MYSTIC MARINELIFE AQUARIUM
Mystic • (203) 572-5955

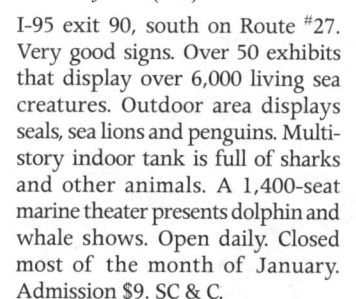

I-95 exit 90, south on Route #27. Very good signs. Over 50 exhibits that display over 6,000 living sea creatures. Outdoor area displays seals, sea lions and penguins. Multi-story indoor tank is full of sharks and other animals. A 1,400-seat marine theater presents dolphin and whale shows. Open daily. Closed most of the month of January. Admission $9. SC & C.

23 — MYSTIC SEAPORT MUSEUM
Mystic • (203) 572-0711

Along the Mystic River, off I-95 at exit 90 on Route #27, 3/4 miles south of I-95. Very good signs. Historic homes, shops and several boats of great historical interest. Three boats (*Charles P. Morgan*, *Joseph Conrad* and *L. A. Duncan*) can be visited. There are many shops, a children's museum, and interesting exhibits. Open daily. Admission is $16. SC&C.

24 — WHITE FLOWER FARM
Litchfield • (203) 567-8789

Located 3.5 miles south off Route #63. The farm contains 8 acres of display gardens, 20 acres of growing fields and a greenhouse with giant tuberous begonias. Peak blooming season is May through September. Open daily, except for a few holiday, from mid April to late October. Admission to the farm is free.

We strongly suggest that you call before visiting any of these places. Hours & admission fees are subject to change, and many have periodic special exhibits.

Abbreviations: SC = Senior Citizen Discount   C = Children Prices   S=Student Discount.   Example SC, C & S

33

25. CONNECTICUT RIVER CRUISE BOATS
Haddam • (203)345-8591

The dock is located on Route #82, across the river from the Goodspeed Opera House. A variety of cruises are available, including a three-hour Murder Mystery Dinner and a weekly trip to Sag Harbor. Dinner cruise is $47.75. Sag Harbor cruise is $22.75. Reservations are required.

26. NEW ENGLAND CAROUSEL MUSEUM
Bristol • (203) 585-5411

95 Riverside Avenue, Route #72. Displays beautiful old hand-carved European and American carousel pieces. Guided tours available. Actual restorations are done on the premises, and can be viewed by visitors. Open daily, year-round. Closed on major holidays. Admission $4. SC & C.

27. OLD NEWGATE PRISON & COPPER MINE
East Granby • (203) 653-3563

Located 3/4 mile west of Route #20, then 1 mile North on Newgate Road. Good direction signs. This old copper mine was used as the first state prison in the U.S. during the Revolutionary War until 1827. The old prison building and underground caverns are open to visitors. Open Wednesday through Sunday, including most holidays. Closed in Winter. Admission $3. SC & C.

28. OCEAN BEACH PARK
New London • (203) 447-3031

South of Exit 83 of I-95. Besides a beach with boardwalk, there is an Olympic-size pool, a playground, a video arcade, an 18-hole miniature golf course and water slides. The park is owned by the City of New London and open to the public. Admission $7 per vehicle weekdays, $9 weekends. Additional fees for some facilities.

29. PRUDENCE CRANDALL MUSEUM
Canterbury • (203) 546-9916

Located on the Canterbury Green at the intersection of Route #14 and Route #169, in an historic 1805 house in which Prudence Crandell ran an academy for young black women before the Civil War. Changing exhibits about women's history. Open Wednesday through Sunday, including many holidays. Admission $2. SC & C.

30. QUASSY AMUSEMENT PARK
Middlebury • (203) 758-2913

Located off I-84 exit 16E or 17W on Route #64. It has a beach and picnic areas, as well as rides and games. Open in summer from 7 a.m. to 9 p.m. daily. Off-season, it is closed many days and hours are shorter. Free entertainment. Parking $3. Entrance to the park is free, but there is a charge for rides and for the beach.

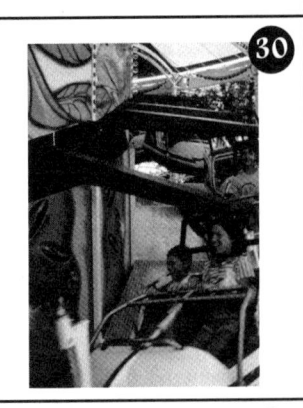

31. QUINEBAUG VALLEY FISH HATCHERY
Central Village • (203) 564-7452

Located 1-3/4 miles northwest of I-395 at exit 89 via Route #14. It is well-marked with signs. This is one of the largest fish hatcheries in the East. Over 600,000 trout are raised here annually in large, round tanks with glass walls to allow viewing. Guided tours are available. Open daily. Admission is free.

32. STATE CAPITAL
Hartford • (203) 240-0222

Located in the center of Hartford, off I-84 exit 48. The building is open for tours weekday and Saturdays. Besides the legislative chambers, there is a vast collection of statues and historical relics. Guided tours start at the west entrance of the modern Legislative Office Building next to the Capital building. Both admission and parking in the garage are free. Closed holidays.

33. STATE LIBRARY AND SUPREME COURT BUILDING
Hartford • (203) 566-3056

Faces the Capitol building on the south side. Besides the actual court, there is a museum of Connecticut History and a Colt firearms collection of firearms and other historical items. Open weekdays; closed on all state holidays. Admission is free.

34. STAMFORD MUSEUM & NATURE CENTER
Stamford • (203) 322-1646

The 118-acre center is located north of the Merritt Parkway exit 35 on Route #137. A variety of exhibits include a complete farm with animals, a "Farmer's Year" Exhibit, a lake with water fowl, and a country store. The museum contains 6 galleries with art and American Indian exhibits. There is a planetarium which usually has shows on Sundays. Open daily; closed most holidays. Admission $4. SC & C.

CONNECTICUT
40 Day Trips

35. THE HITCHCOCK MUSEUM
Riverton • (203) 738-4950

Route #20, Union Church. A fine collection of furniture. Many of the pieces are hand-decorated furniture created by Lambert Hitchcock and other craftsmen in the 1700s and 1800s. The church is made of hand-cut granite. Admission is free, though donations are accepted. The museum is open Thursday through Sunday, January through April.

36. TRAVELERS TOWER
Hartford • (203) 277-2431

1 Tower Square, in the center of Hartford. Home office of a pioneer insurance company. Tours up the 527-foot tower observation deck leave every half hour weekdays in the spring, summer and fall. You must walk up 70 steps. Closed on all holidays. Admission is free.

37. SS NAUTILUS MEMORIAL
Groton • (203) 449-3174

Just outside the submarine base off I-95 at exit 86, then north on Route #12. Self-guided tours of the world's first nuclear-powered submarine include its torpedo room and attack center. The Submarine Forces Library and Museum is at the same location and is open the same hours. Several films are shown regularly. Closed Sunday, Monday and most major holidays. Admission is free.

38. WADSWORTH ATHENAEUM
Hartford • (203) 247-9111

600 Main Street, in downtown Hartford. This is the nation's oldest public art museum. Its collection contains over 45,000 works of art, including paintings, sculpture, and furniture. Guided tours are available on Thursday, Saturday and Sunday. Closed Mondays and holidays. Admission $5. SC, C & S.

Wadsworth Atheneum — Connecticut's Premier Art Museum

39. MYSTIC CRUISES
Mystic

Several companies run cruises from Mystic's Whaler's and Steam Boat Wharves. These wharves are just north and south of the drawbridge in the center of Mystic. They are both off I-95 at exit 90, and are reached by going south on Route #27 and following the signs.

Mystic Whaler Cruises - Ranging from 1 to 5 days, these trips are on ships which are replicas of 19th century schooners and clipper ships. There are also dinner and twilight cruises. Call for schedules and rates. Reservations are required. May 1st to late October. (203) 536-4218

Voyager Cruises - 1, 2 and 3 days cruises aboard the schooner *Voyager*. Call for schedules and rates. Reservations are required. Boats operate between May 1st to late October. (203) 536-0416

40. WINERIES
Litchfield area

Haight Vineyard and Winery, Litchfield. Chestnut Hill Road. 1 mile East of the Litchfield Green on Route #118. Hourly tours. Open daily except major holidays. Admission is free. (203) 567-4045

Hopkins Vineyard Winery, New Preston. Hopkins Road. Open daily in season and weekends rest of year. Admission is free. (203) 868-7954

Digrazia Vineyards & Winery, Brookfield. 131 Tower Road. This is a small winery making specialty wines. Admission is free. (203) 775-1616

We strongly suggest that you call before visiting any of these places. Hours & admission fees are subject to change, and many have periodic special exhibits.

Abbreviations: SC = Senior Citizen Discount   C = Children Prices   S = Student Discount.   Example SC, C & S

New York City

The 10 most popular attractions are: Art Museums (Guggenheim, Metropolitan, Modern Art, Whitney); boat trips around Manhattan; the Bronx & Central Park Zoos; Empire State Building; Museum of Natural History; Rockerfeller Center; Statute of Liberty and Ellis Island; Times Square; Wall Street; and World Trade Center. The South Street Sea Port and the battleship *Intrepid* are also very popular.

New Jersey

Atlantic City was the first place in the east to have Casino gambling. It also has a wide sandy beach with a board walk that seems to go on forever. The Six Flags Great Adventure in Jackson is the largest amusement park in the East.

Boston, Massachusetts

Within three miles are 350 years of history. "Must sees" are: Faneuil Hall; Quincy Market; the *USS Constitution*, the War of 1812 battleship nicknamed "Old Iron Sides"; Freedom Trail; Back Bay; Harvard University; Boston Commons; Bunker Hill; and the Museum of Science and Technology.

Cape Cod • Nantucket Martha's Vineyard

When you cross one of the two bridges that connect the Cape to the mainland, you enter a land of white sand beaches and dunes, cozy restaurants and quaint shops, motels and inns all designed to delight the tourist. The islands of Nantucket and Martha's Vineyard can be reached only by boat or air. They are unique vacation places full of the lore of the sea.

Newport, Rhode Island

Grand restored mansions are open to the public along the breathtaking Cliff Walk. This restored colonial seaport has many fine restaurants and quaint shops. The Touro synagogue, built in 1763, is the oldest in the USA.

Old Sturbridge Village, MA

This is an authentic re-creation of a rural 1830s New England community. Everyone is dressed in authentic 19th century clothes and everything operates as it did over 150 years ago. You leave your car and the present behind as you walk into the past.

Basketball Hall of Fame Springfield, Massachusetts

A state-of-the art museum that features basketball exhibits, memorabilia, interactive video tape monitors and three movie theaters. Visitors also can shoot baskets and test their jumping skills.

Riverside Park Agawam, Massachusetts

This is New England's largest family amusement park. There are over forty rides for all ages including three great roller coasters. Entry to the park which includes all rides is one package price.

Vermont

Vermont is a visual delight. The Green Mountains provide the East's best skiing in the winter and golf in the summer. There are charming farms and quaint villages everywhere. Their maple syrup really comes from trees.

Maine and New Hampshire

The rocky Maine coast with real fishing villages and a vast sparsely populated interior provide great "getaways." Mt. Desert in Acadia National Park is a specially notable attraction. There's wonderful hunting and fishing too. New Hampshire's White Mountains are the highest in the East. A cog railroad goes to the top of Mt. Washington, which has snow on its peak, even in summer.

INTERSTATE 91 OUT-OF-STATE One Day Trips

Distances from New Haven

Albany, NY	135	New York, NY	75
Avon	38	Newport, RI	97
Boston, MA	141	Norwalk	33
Bridgeport	19	Norwich	55
Bristol	28	Old Saybrook	29
Canaan	61	Plainfield	72
Clinton	21	Providence, RI	101
Colchester	44	Putnam	90
Danielson	75	Rockville	52
Derby	10	Sharon	59
Durham	18	Southbury	18
Farmington	32	Springfield, MA	66
Glastonbury	39	Stafford Springs	63
Granby	48	Stamford	40
Greenwich	46	Thomaston	28
Hamden	5	Thompsonville	54
Hartford	36	Torrington	39
Litchfield	36	Voluntown	67
Manchester	41	Waterbury	19
Marlborough	38	Westerly, RI	64
Middletown	25	Westport	29
Milford	9	Willimantic	54
New Britain	26	Windsor Locks	48
New London	46	Winsted	48
New Milford	37	Worcester, MA	101

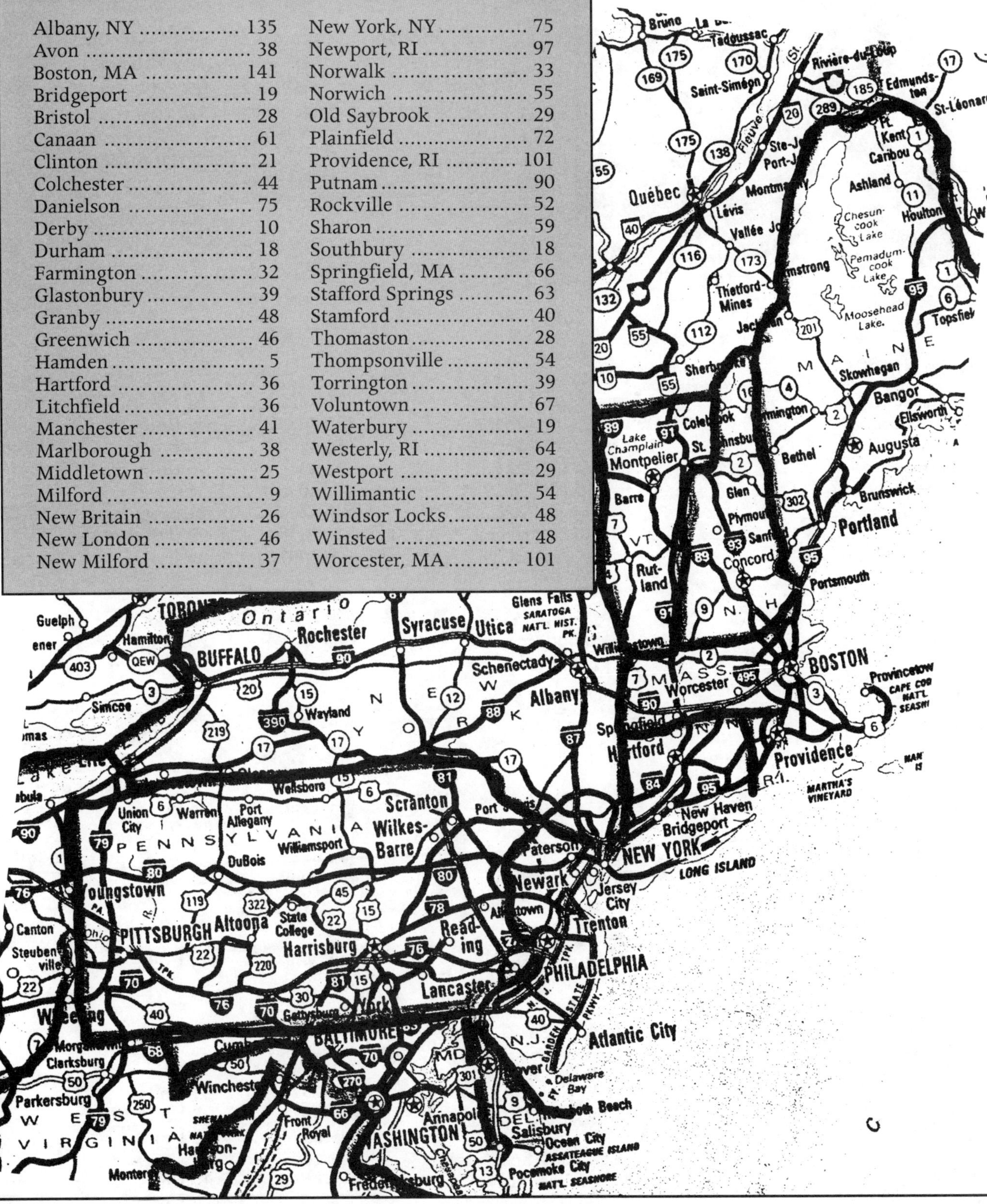

The interior of one of the suites at the Residence Inn, an all-suites modern facility at Long Wharf with spacious livingroom and kitchen in each unit.

Other accommodations in the greater New Haven area are listed by town below.

Branford

Advanced Motel	81 Leetes Island Road	481-4528	28 Units	14 Suites
Branford Econolodge	309 East Main Street	488-4035	52 Units	14 Suites
Branford Motel	470 East Main Street	488-5442	80 Units	30 Suites
Days Inn	375 East Main Street	488-8314	76 Units	2 Suites
Knights Inn	309 E. Main Street	488-4035	52 Units	
MacDonald's Motel	565 East Main Street	488-4381	21 Units	1 Suite
Motel 6	320 East Main Street	483-5828	99 Units	
Ramada Limited	3 Business Park Drive	488-4991	85 Units	30 Suites

Cheshire

Cheshire Welcome Inn	1106 S. Main Street	272-3244	23 Units

East Haven

Holiday Inn Express	30 Frontage Road	469-5321	82 Units	25 Suites

Guilford

B&B at B	279 Boston Street	453-6490	2 Units	
The Cottage on Church Street	190 Church Street	458-2598	1 Unit	
The Guilford Suites	2300 Boston Post Road	453-0123		32 Suites
Tower Motel	320 Boston Post Road	453-9069	15 Units	

Hamden

Days Inn	3400 Whitney Avenue	288-2505	34 Units
Howard Johnson Lodge	2260 Whitney Avenue	288-3831	90 Units

Madison

Crescent Motel	60 Boston Post Road	245-9145	10 Units	
Dolly Madison Inn	73 West Wharf Road	245-7377	11 Units	
Honeysuckle Hill B&B	116 Yankee Peddler Path	245-4574	2 Units	
Madison B&B	318 Boston Post Road	245-0896	3 Units	
Madison Beach Hotel	94 West Wharf Road	245-1404	35 Units	6 Suites
Tidewater Inn	949 Boston Post Road	245-8457	10 Units	2 Suites

LODGING
Hotels & Motels by Town

Milford

Comfort Inn	278 Old Gate Lane	877-9411	120 Units	4 Suites
Devon Motel	438 Bridgeport Avenue	874-6634	35 Units	
Hampton Inn	129 Plains Road	874-4400	148 Units	
Howard Johnson Lodge	1052 Boston Post Road	878-4611	165 Units	3 Suites
Liberty Rock Motel	421 Bridgeport Avenue	874-9936	18 Units	
Mayflower Motel	219 Woodmont Road	878-6854	96 Units	
Milford Inn	345 Old Gate Lane	878-0685	60 Units	
Milford Motel	1015 Boston Post Road	878-3575	50 Units	
Post Motor Inn	1700 Boston Post Road	874-3777	31 Units	
Red Roof Inn	10 Rowe Avenue	877-6060	110 units	1 Suite
Shoreline Motel	735 Boston Post Road	874-9975	28 Units	
Susse Chalet Motor Lodge	102 Schoolhouse Road	877-8588	102 Units	
Turnpike Inn	1083 Boston Post Road	874-3216	16 Units	

New Haven

The Colony Inn	1157 Chapel Street	776-1234	86 Units	6 Suites
Holiday Inn at Yale	30 Whalley Avenue	777-6221	160 Units	
Hotel Duncan	1151 Chapel Street	787-1273	90 Units	
Howard Johnson Long Wharf	400 Sargent Drive	562-1111	153 Units	1 Suite
New Haven Medical Hotel	229 George Street	498-3100	93 Units	
Motel 6	270 Foxon Boulevard	469-0343	58 Units	
Park Plaza Hotel	153 Temple Street	772-1700	300 Units	
Quality Inn & Conference Center	100 Pond Lily Avenue	387-6651	125 Units	2 Suites
Regal Inn	1605 Whalley Avenue	389-9504	80 Units	
Residence Inn by Marriott	3 Long Wharf Drive	777-5337		112 Suites
The Inn at Chapel West	1201 Chapel Street	777-1201	10 Units	
Three Judges Motor Lodge	1560 Whalley Avenue	389-2161	40 Units	

North Haven

Holiday Inn	201 Washington Avenue	239-4225	138 Units	4 Suites

Shelton

Ramada Hotel	780 Bridgeport Avenue	929-1500	155 Units	11 Suites
Residence Inn by Marriott	1001 Bridgeport Avenue	926-9000		96 Suites

Trumbull

Trumbull Marriott	180 Hawey Lane	378-1400	320 Units

Wallingford

Courtyard by Marriott	I-91, Exit 15, Wallingford	284-9400	149 units
Susse Chalet Inn	100 Chalet Drive	284-0001	119 Units
Toll House Motel	North Turnpike Road	269-1677	20 Units

West Haven

Days Hotel	490 Saw Mill Road	933-0344	102 Units	
Debonair Inn	295 Beach Street	934-6373	21 Units	
Econolodge	7 Kimberly Avenue	932-8338	82 Units	5 Suites
Tremont Motor Court	400 Derby Avenue	387-6671	50 Units	
Yankee Motor Inn	370 Highland Street	934-6611	87 Units	

① BRAZI'S
A New Concept IN FAMILY DINING

What's new? Check it out.

201 Food Terminal ~ Longwharf
New Haven, CT 06511   498-2488

② Charthouse

A knock-out location right on the harbor, at City Point. Try Sunday Brunch -- it's fabulous. A great view of Long Island Sound.

100 South Water Street
New Haven, CT 06511   787-3466

③ Tony & Lucille's
Little Italy Dinner Restaurant

Take along a native who knows what to order. Always reliable and good.

150 Wooster Street
New Haven, CT 06511   787-1621

④ HOWARD JOHNSON'S

Same old, same old -- reliable that is.

Sargent Drive
New Haven, CT 06511   865-6181

⑤ BIG TONY'S WATER STREET RESTAURANT

New kid on the block, trying for the major leagues.

145 Water St
New Haven, CT 06511   773-1115

⑥ Mauro's Town Squire Cafe

Reasonable food at reasonable prices.

130 Court Street
New Haven, CT 06511   787-1150

⑦ Frank Pepe
Since 1925
PIZZERIA NAPOLETANA

Is it really #1 in the world? You decide....

157 Wooster St.
New Haven, CT 06511   865-5762

⑧ FRANK PEPE'S PIZZERIA
THE SPOT

Same pizza, you just skip the line. Where the natives go.

163 Wooster St.
New Haven, CT 06511   865-7602

⑨ Sally Pizza

Or is this #1 in the world? A taste test is in order. Be prepared to wait to find out.

237 Wooster Street
New Haven, CT 06511   624-5271

⑩ Tony & Lucille's

The best place to try a calzone. Warning: They are habit-forming.

127 Wooster Street
New Haven   787-1620

NEW HAVEN RESTAURANTS BY LOCATION
Wooster Square, Long Wharf, City Point & Ninth Square

⓫ Consiglio's of New Haven

Where old time Italian families take grandmother and the kids.

165 Wooster Street
New Haven, CT 06511   865-4489

Rusty Scupper ⓬

A superb view of the harbor and a popular Friday night singles scene.

501 Long Wharf Drive
New Haven, CT 06511   777-5711

⓭ Abaté Apizza & Seafood

This is where President Clinton ate -- the Secret Service couldn't secure Pepe's.

129 Wooster Street
New Haven, CT 06511   776-4334

DELMONACO'S RESTAURANT ⓮

Sit in this very European restaurant, and watch all the local politicians in action.

232 Wooster Street
New Haven, CT   865-1109

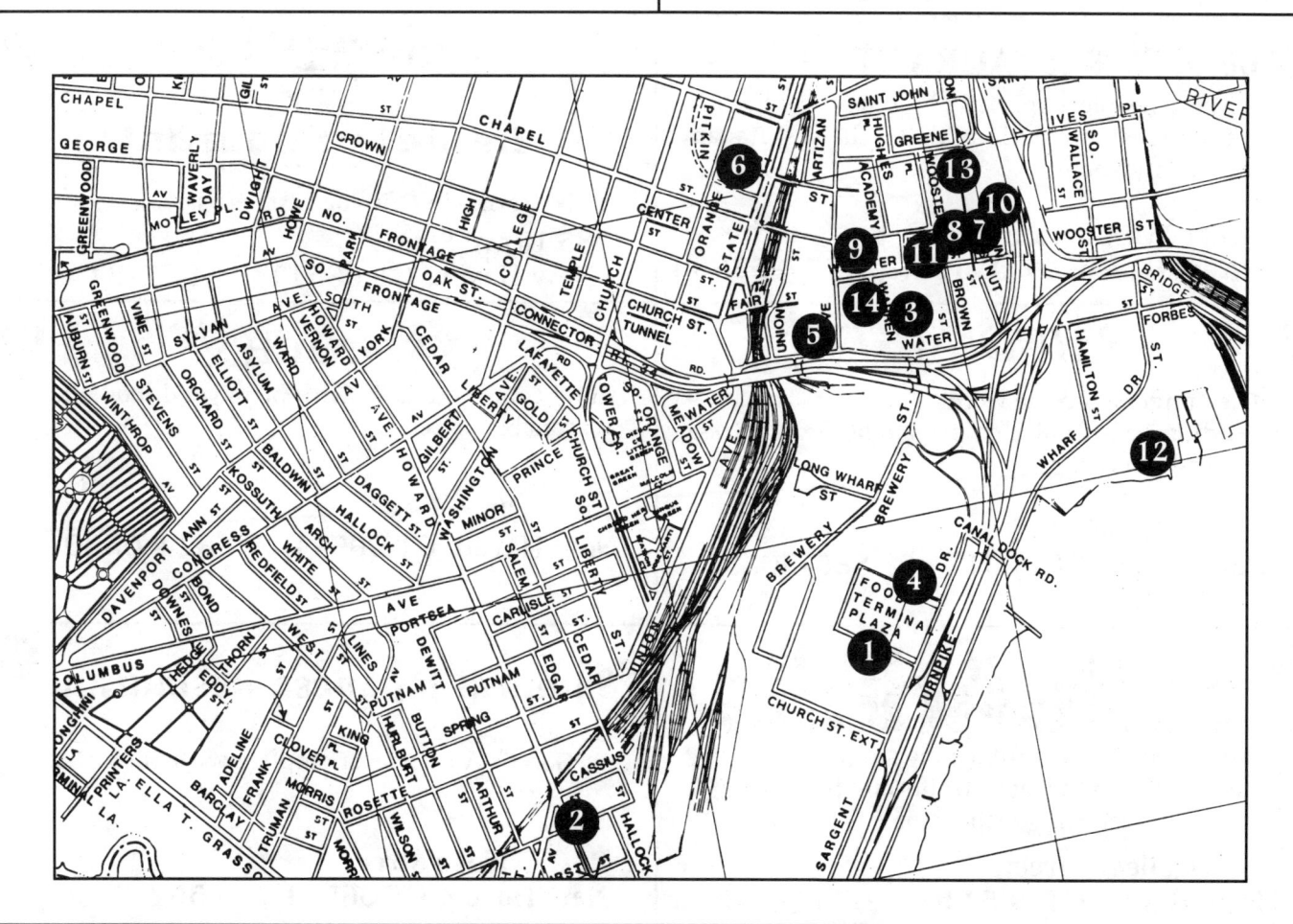

1. Scoozi Trattoria and Wine Bar

An authentic, imaginative cold buffet and original menu.

1104 Chapel Street
New Haven, CT 06511   776-8268

2. CLAIRE'S CORNER COPIA

An institution as much as a restaurant. Great good-for-you salads, baked goods, veggie burgers. Convenient and reasonably priced.

1000 Chapel St
New Haven, CT 06510   562-3888

3. VIVA ZAPATA

Sturdy Mexican.

161 Park St
New Haven, CT 06511   562-2499

4. INDIA PALACE RESTAURANT

***** Advocate 1994 & Connecticut Magazine.

65 Howe Street
New Haven, CT 06511   776-9010

5. SIAM SQUARE THAI

In the basement where the Old Heidelberg used to be.

1151 Chapel Street
New Haven, CT 06511   776-9802

6. RICHTER'S CAFE

More choices of draft beer than you ever saw before.

990 Chapel Street
New Haven, CT 06510   777-0400

7. LEON'S RESTAURANT

Many people, expecially high political figures from Washington, think this is the best Italian food anywhere.

321 Washington Ave
New Haven, CT 06511   777-5366

8. MAMOUN'S falafel restaurant — MIDDLE EASTERN FOODS

Like eating in Cairo or East Jerusalem.

85 Howe Street
New Haven, CT 06511   562-8444

9. SAIGON CITY

They understand the word "hot", but also do "medium" and "mild." It pays to be clear. Prices are medium to high.

1180 Chapel St.
New Haven, CT 06511   865-5033

10. KAVANAGH'S

Long-time landmark, with plain good food and reasonable prices.

1166 Chapel St
New Haven, CT 06511   624-0520

11. caffé Adulis

Spicy food you eat from a big sharing bowl in the middle of the table. Uniformly pleasant service, interesting dishes, some very hot.

254 College Street
New Haven, CT 06511   777-5081

12. Samurai Japanese Restaurant

"Good". *NY Times*. Complete with Sushi Bar.

230 College Street
New Haven, CT 06511   562-6766

NEW HAVEN RESTAURANTS BY LOCATION
College and Chapel, Upper Chapel, & Yale

⓭ Union League Café

Successor to the best restaurant in Connecticut -- it's in a class by itself. A bit noisy (non-acoustical ceilings.) Elegant space, great furnishings. Pricey.

1032 Chapel Street
New Haven, CT 06511   562~4299

⓮ LOUIS' LUNCH

Where the hamburger was invented. Really.

263 Crown Street
New Haven, CT 06511   562~5507

⓯ SPANKY'S RESTAURANT

A truer-than-life renovation of an old White Tower diner. Old time 1950's food. Reminds you of your first convertible -- the one with the fins.

236 Crown Street
New Haven, CT 06511   562~3530

⓰ Bruxelles
Brasserie & Bar

Across College Street from the Shubert, with lots of choices for pre-theatre dining.

220 College St
New Haven, CT 06511   777~7752

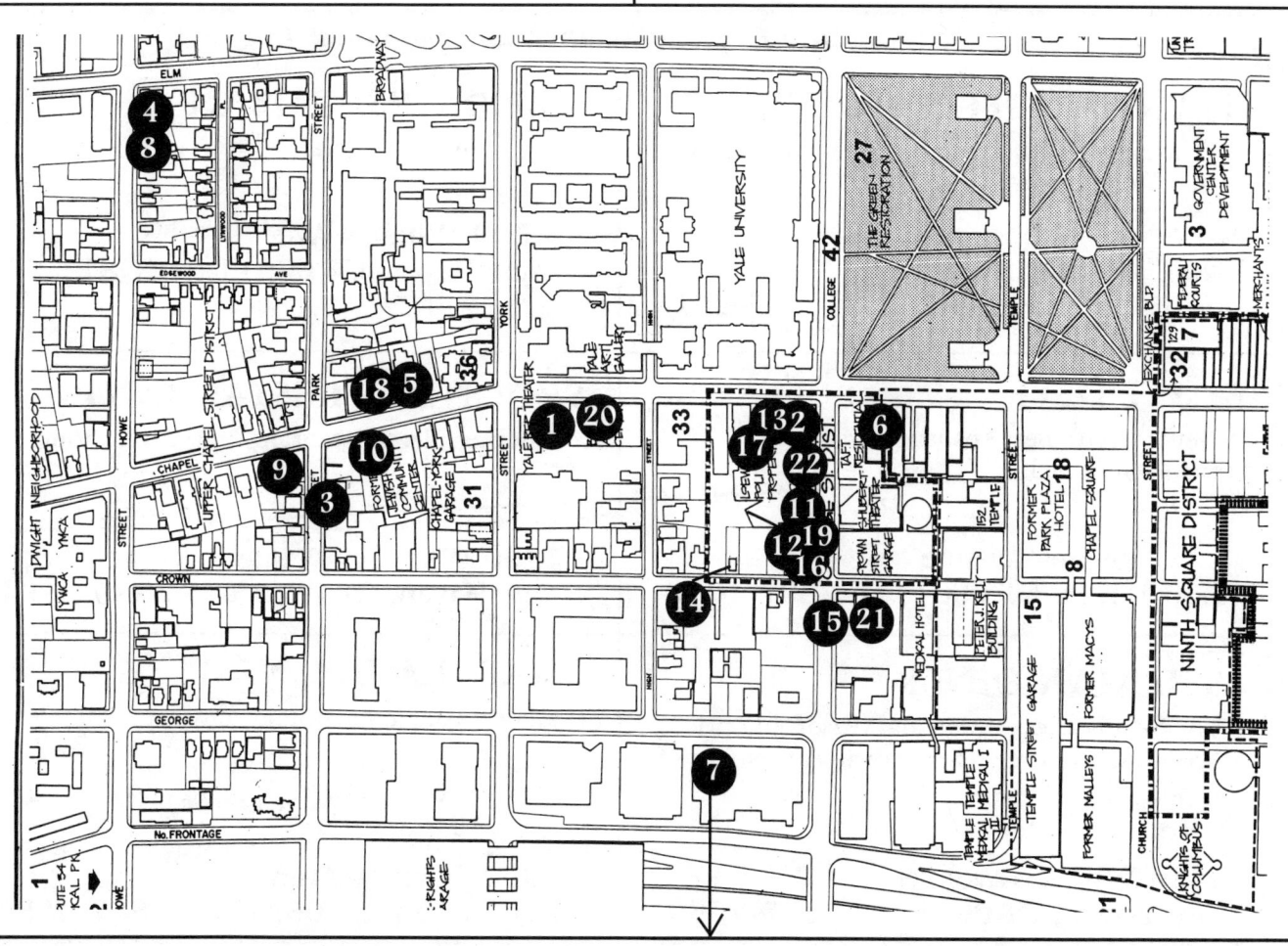

⑰ RAINBOW GARDENS CAFE

A cute place in the Palace Theatre Alley.

1022 Chapel St
New Haven, CT 06511   777-2390

CHARLIE B'S ⑱

A steak, rib and fish house in the Colony Inn Hotel.

1157 Chapel St
New Haven, CT 06511   776-7689

⑲ THE POMEGRANATE

The new fad in food is Med-Rim and they've got it here. Enjoy that hummus.

242 College Street
New Haven, CT 06510   776-3304

ATTICUS RESTAURANT & BOOKSTORE ⑳

Read the latest books as you down the black bean soup. Save room for desserts.

1082 Chapel Street
New Haven, CT 06511   776-4040

㉑ CHALLENGERS SPORTS BAR

Lots of noise, and big TVs. Go team!

230 Crown Street
New Haven, CT 06511   782-2284

THE ANCHOR ㉒

Standard food at reasonable prices.

272 College Street
New Haven, CT 06511   865-1512

For restaurants above, see previous map on p.43

① PERRY'S COFFEE HOUSE

The name is deceiving -- they serve real food too. Good coffee.

896 Whalley Ave
New Haven, CT 06511   397-2811

PEPPINO'S ITALIAN ②

Full course dinners.

1500 Whalley Ave
New Haven, CT 06511   387-2504

③ M & T DELI

New Haven's best Kosher delicatessen. Try the lox and pickles.

543 Whalley Avenue
New Haven, CT 06511   397-1070

SPOONER'S RESTAURANT ④

Another pizza restaurant, but in Westville.

1400 Whalley Avenue
New Haven, CT 06515   389-9894

⑤ ATHENIAN DINER

The food is always good and reasonably priced. Breakfast any time. There are always plenty of people here.

1426 Whalley Avenue
New Haven, CT 06515   397-1556

AKASAKA JAPANESE ⑥

Good sushi and sashimi -- always fresh.

1450 Whalley Avenue
New Haven, CT 06515   387-4898

NEW HAVEN RESTAURANTS BY LOCATION
Whalley Avenue & Westville

❼ EASTERN PEARL SEAFOOD CHINESE RESTAURANT

Not typical -- the one your Chinese friends will take you to.

1307 Whalley Ave
New Haven, CT 06515   397-1688

❽ CHAVOYA'S

A popular full service Mexican restaurant with moderate prices. Not a Taco Belle -- the real thing. *Mensa* meets here Friday Happy Hour.

883 Whalley Ave.
New Haven, CT 06515   389-4730

❾ CAPE CODDER RESTAURANT

A Westville institutions, full menu and moderate prices.

882 Whalley Ave
New Haven, CT 06515   389-8576

❿ 500 BLAKE STREET, INC.

Many people think this is the best Italian spot in town. Definitely not fast food, this is a busy, noisy place. A large, and inventive menu. Not economy class.

500 Blake Street
New Haven, CT 06515   387-0500
                         FAX 387-7578

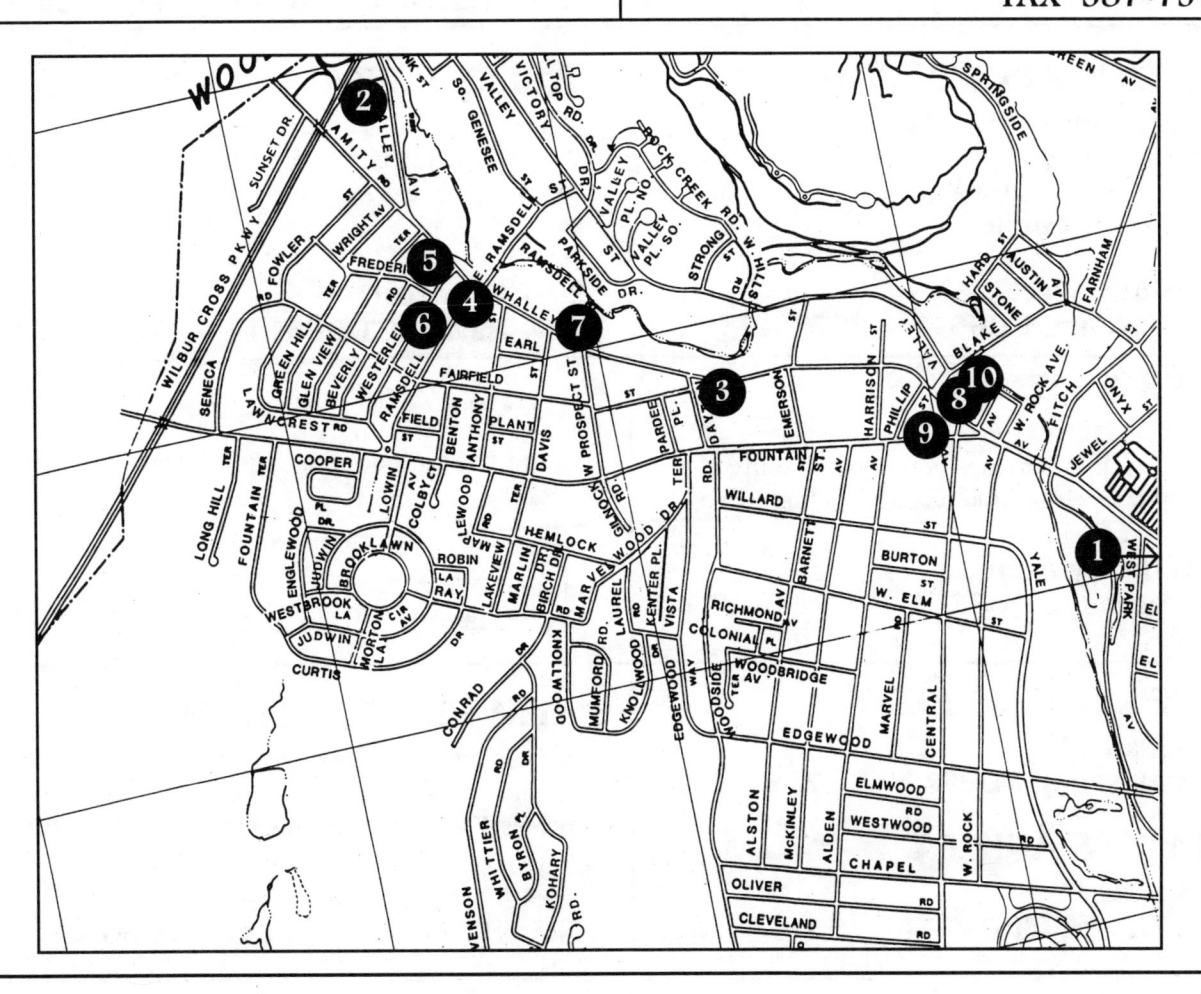

1 CHRISTOPHER MARTIN'S
Good food, quiet dining room and lively bar with music.

860 State Street
New Haven, CT 06511   776-8835

2 GEPPI'S
Big portions of good Italian food in Fair Haven. Try the marinara, or any shrimp dish.

113 Grand Avenue
New Haven, CT 06512   776-0100

3 ARCHIE MOORE'S BAR & RESTAURANT
Excellent food at reasonable prices. Very popular bar and lunch spot. Neighborhood landmark.

188-1/2 State Street
New Haven, CT 06511   773-9870

4 AZTECA'S
This is how the rich eat in Mexico City. Truly gourmet. Priced for special occasions.

14 Mechanic St. (off State)
New Haven, CT 06512   624-2454

5 THAI ORCHID
1027 State St.
New Haven, CT 06511   624-7173

6 J. P. DEMPSEY'S TAVERN
974 State Street
New Haven, CT 06511   624-5991

8 ARIRANG HOUSE
Korean & Japanese Cuisine.
93 Whitney Avenue
New Haven, CT 06511   624-0311

7 MALONE'S TAVERN
758 State Street
New Haven, CT 06511   624-2400

9 MODERN APIZZA PLACE
Authentic brick oven makes what is arguably the best pizza in town, outside of Wooster Street. Try onion, black olive & mushroom -- our personal favorite.

874 State Street
New Haven, CT 06511   776-5306

19 NAPLES PIZZA
A Yale hang-out popular with kids of all ages. Carve your initials in the table top and order a pitcher of beer. Ahh...

90 Wall Street
New Haven, CT 06511   776-9021

10 CLARK'S PIZZA
Good Greek/American food & nice family atmosphere. Great jukebox and Velvet Elvis.

93 Whitney Avenue
New Haven, CT 06511   624-0311

11 AVANTI
Good Italian food in a bright, clean, modern facility.

45 Grove Street
New Haven, CT 06511   777-3234

13 LA FORTUNA'S PIZZA
996 State St
New Haven, CT 06511   772-4239

12 AMATO'S APIZZA
858 State St
New Haven, CT 06511   562-2760

14 PALM BEACH APIZZA
This is where the Italians come to eat and drink. Nothing fancy, just good pizza and food at easy prices. Take the kids and the grandparents too.

384 Grand Avenue
New Haven, CT 06512   865-0353

NEW HAVEN RESTAURANTS BY LOCATION
Upper State, Fair Haven, Whitney Avenue & Grand Avenue

⑮ HAYA'S JAPANESE NOODLE HOUSE

One of New Haven's best kept secrets. Very plain but cheap! Bring your own bottle and try the crab or shrimp dumplings.

1012 State Street
New Haven, CT 06511   787-0535

⑯ Humphrey's EAST
A New Haven Neighborhood Original

175 Humphrey Street
New Haven, CT 06511   782-1506

⑰ Adriana's

A rising star against stiff competition. Try the veal - supposedly the best in town.

771 Grand Ave
New Haven, CT   865-6474

⑱ GENNARO'S RISTORANTE D'AMALFI

Hands down the finest Northern Italian food in Connecticut. No pizza, elegant service. Plan for a long, leisurely meal with serious attention to every detail. Superb desserts. Not for the price conscious.

937 State Street
New Haven, CT 06511   777-5490

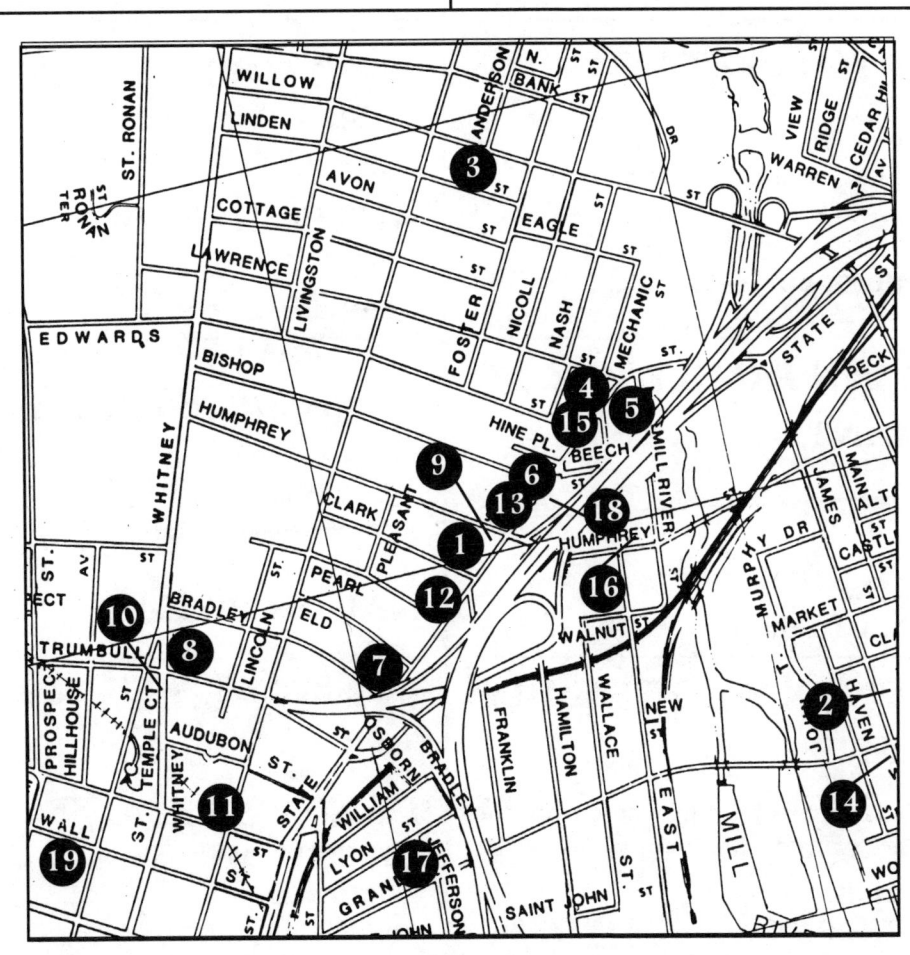

⑤ THE RIB HOUSE

These stick to your ribs, too.

16 Main St.
East Haven, CT 06513   468-6695

⑧ PASTA COSÍ

Pasta Cosí

202 S. Montowese
Branford, CT   483-9397

⑪ KAMPAI JAPANESE
869 W. Main St.
Branford, CT 06405   481-4536

⑬ SU CASA
400 East Main St.
Branford, CT 06405   481-5001

⑮ DOODY'S TOTOKET INN

Elegant dining in rural North Branford. This inn has an attractive and welcoming bar.

465 Foxon Rd.
North Branford, CT 06471   484-0588

⑱ VILLAGE INN FAMILY RESTAURANT

699 Main St.
East Haven, CT 06513   468-7144

㉑ U.S.S. CHOWDER POT FAMILY RESTAURANT

A comfortble family restaurant where even the littlest salts are welcome and happy.

560 E. Main St.
Branford, CT 06405   481-2356

⑥ HAPPY WOK ORIENTAL
633 Boston Post Road
Guilford, CT   453-4936

⑦ DARBAR INDIA
1070 Main St.
Branford, CT 06405   481-8994

⑨ THE DOLLY MADISON INN
73 W Wharf Rd.
Madison, CT 06443   245-7377

⑩ THE BISTRO ON THE GREEN
25 Whitfield St.
Guilford, CT 06437   458-9059

⑫ CAFE LAFAYETTE
725 Boston Post Road
Madison, CT   245-7772

⑭ THE HOLLOW RESTAURANT
58 Academy St.
Madison, CT 06443   245-7928

⑯ GUILFORD TAVERN
2455 Boston Post Rd.
Guilford, CT 06437   453-2216

⑰ ANTHONY'S OF GUILFORD
2392 Boston Post Rd.
Guilford, CT 06437   453-4121

⑲ RONIS PASSION FOR PASTA
899 W. Main St ~ Rte 1
Branford, CT 06405   488-7668

⑳ NAPLES PIZZA
850 Boston Post Rd.
Guilford, CT 06437   453-4759

㉒ DANNY'S EXPRESSO
1060 W. Main St.
Branford, CT   488-5174

GREATER NEW HAVEN RESTAURANTS
East Haven, Branford, Guilford, Madison & North Branford

❶ WEBSTER'S RESTAURANT

Named after the dictionary writer, and designed to look like a private library in a stately home, this is a fine restaurant run by people who care about good food and service.

1114 Main Street
Branford, CT 06405   488-8161

❷ LENNY'S INDIAN HEAD INN

If summer to you is a bowl of steamers, corn on the cob and lobster, head to this big red barn and enjoy! Very casual, and ideal for kids.

205 South Montowese
Branford, CT 06405   488-1500

❸ RIVIERA CAFÉ

Getting all this raves, the little successor to the Back Water (a past local favorite) is doing a surprising amount of out of town and even out of state business. Gourmet all the way.

3 Linden Ave.
Branford, CT   481-7011

❹ WHITFIELD ALLEY

63 Whitfield St.
On the Green
Guilford, CT 06437   458-2226

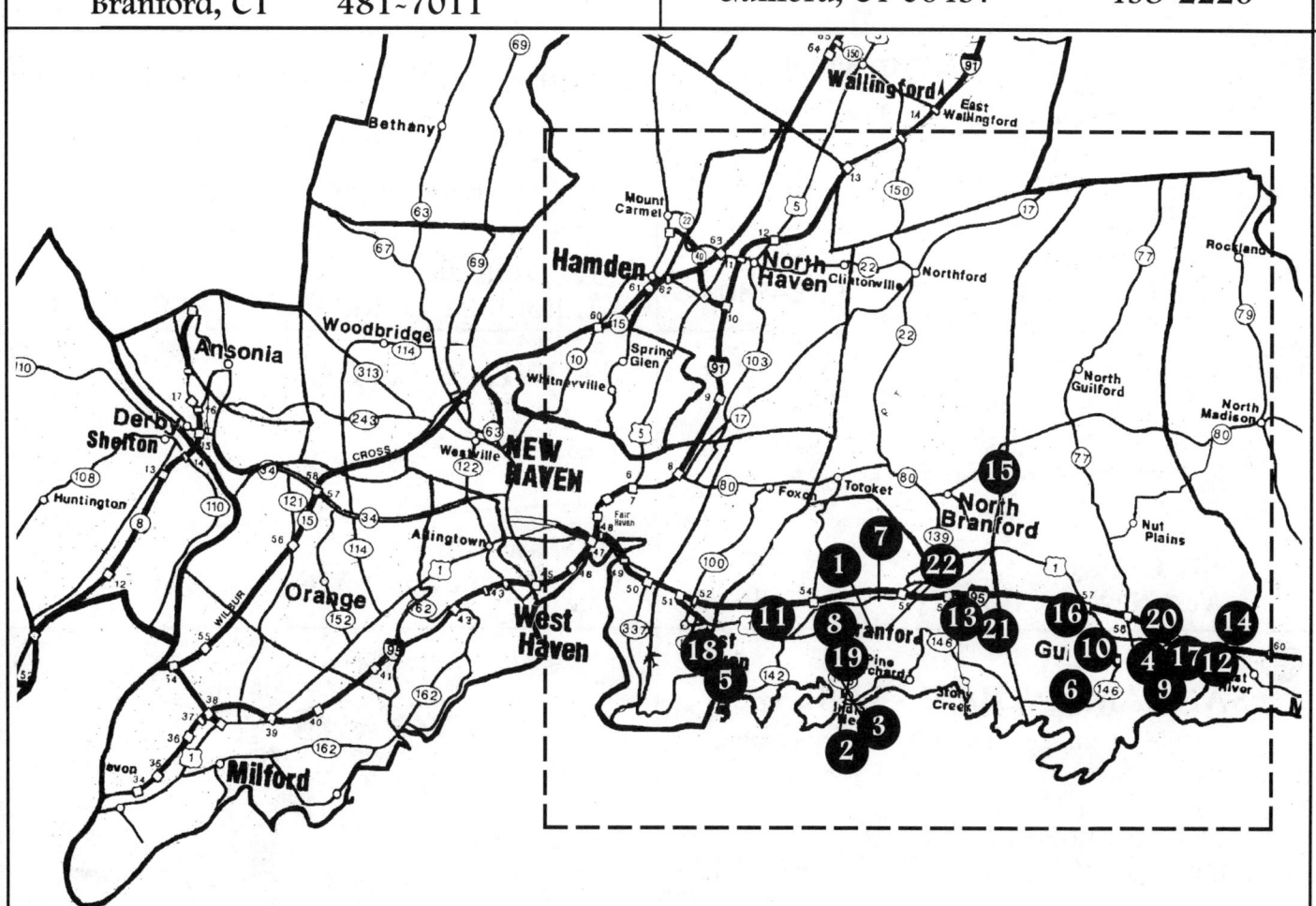

1. The Ship's Wheel

Where the mature folks with good funding go.

471 New Haven Ave.
Milford, CT 06460   874-4626

2. SAVIN ROCK SEAFOOD CO.

The best fish here is fried. Try it!

1157 Campbell Ave.
West Haven, CT 06516   937-1767

3. SILVERBROOK PUB

350 Boston Post Rd.
Orange, CT 06477   795-1059

4. SEAFARER RESTAURANT

Very good seafood.

1651 Boston Post Rd.
Milford, CT 06460   977-2077

13. STEAK & SWORD

1360 Boston Post Road
Milford, CT 06460   878-0691

5. Pilgrim by-the-Sea

45 Seaside Ave.
Milford, CT   878-1113

6. DP DELICIOUS PIZZA

429 Naugatuck Ave.
Milford, CT 06460   878-5097

7. RANDALL'S RESTAURANT

A new one to us -- we'll report on it in the next edition.

236 Platt Ave.
West Haven, CT 06516   932-1806

8. SLOPPY JOSE'S MEXICAN

Not fancy, just good food at fair prices. Formerly just plain ole' Sloppy Joe's.

186 Hillside Ave.
Milford, CT 06460   878-9847

9. ROYAL PALACE

Many people think this is the best Chinese food in greater New Haven. Try the crispy shrimp and the veggie lo mein.

857 Orange Ave.
West Haven, CT 06516   937-8686

10. SYDNEY'S CAFÉ

A good all 'round café.

490 Saw Mill Rd.
West Haven, CT 06516   932-5419

11. SANGAM INDIAN CUISINE

People who like Indian cuisine keep coming back.

157 Boston Post Rd.
Orange, CT   799-8162

12. The Old Fibbers RESTAURANT & TAVERN

15 Factory Lane
Milford, CT 06460   877-0034

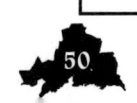

GREATER NEW HAVEN RESTAURANTS
West Haven, Orange, Milford, Trumbull, Ansonia, Derby & Shelton

⑭ BAGEL FACE
BAGEL BAKERY & RESTAURANT

Owned by the Bagel Brothers, Murray and Marvin, who still know how to cook 'em up.

175 Boston Post Rd.,
Orange, CT 06477   795-3549

SAYBROOK FISH HOUSE ⑮

First class fish, reasonable prices.

56 S. Broad Street
Milford, CT 06460   878-2428

⑯ Scribner's Restaurant
"Where Great Food is Just the Beginning"

Fine fish fare.

31 Village Road
Milford, CT 06460   1(800) 828-7019

LUCILLE'S DINER ⑰
Connecticut Post Mall
Milford, CT 06460   874-5385

VALLEY DINER
636 New Haven Ave.
Derby, CT 06418   735-2445 ⑱

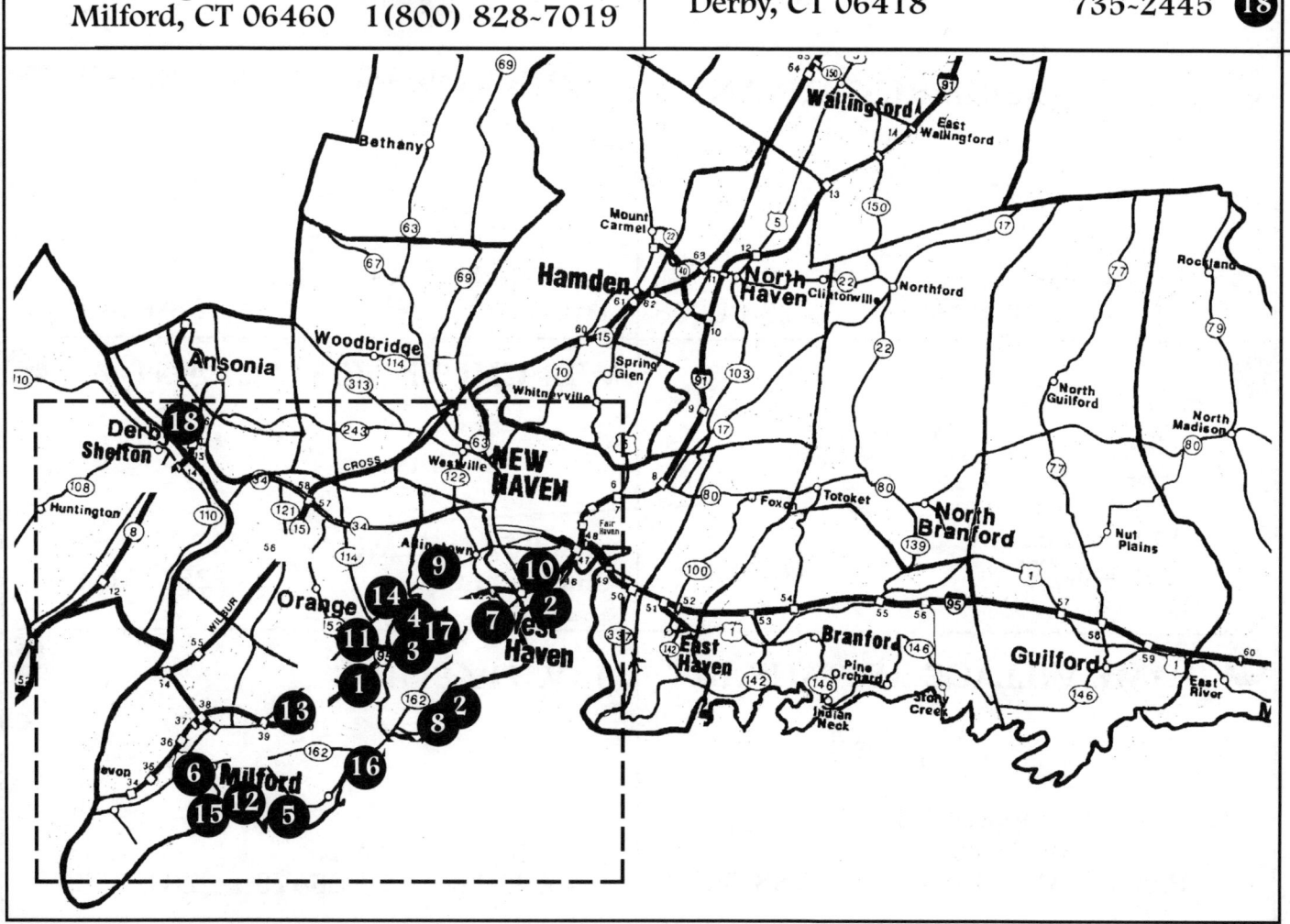

1 Shangri-Lee 大觀園 (formerly Home Village) 965 No. Main St. Cheshire, CT 06410 — 250-8888	**2** RATTLESNAKE BAR & GRILL 1125 Dixwell Ave. Hamden, CT — 498-1948
3 YANKEE SILVERSMITH INN 1033 N. Colony Rd. Wallingford, CT — 269-5444	**4** COLONIAL TYMES 2389 Dixwell Ave. Hamden, CT 06517 — 230-2301
5 WEED'S CAFÉ 1435 Dixwell Ave Hamden, CT — 288-6393	**6** WHITNEY GARDEN 2411 Whitney Ave Hamden, CT — 248-8384
7 J.B. WINBERIE RESTAURANT & BAR 2323 Whitney Ave Hamden, CT 06517 — 288-6608	**8** FOUR CORNERS RESTAURANT 19 Waterbury Rd. Prospect, CT 06712 — 758-6044
9 WING THING 900 Dixwell Ave Hamden, CT — 782-9464	**10** WEI CHUEN RESTAURANT 1869 Dixwell Ave Hamden, CT — 287-0129
11 HOME VILLAGE RESTAURANT Caldor's Shopping Ctr 2380 Dixwell Ave Hamden, CT 06514 — 288-5479	**12** J.W. PEABODY 1955 Whitney Ave. North Haven, CT 06473 — 281-5888

GREATER NEW HAVEN RESTAURANTS
Hamden, No. Haven, Cheshire, Wallingford Prospect, Woodbridge, Bethany

DANTE'S

218 Skiff St.
Hamden, CT 06517   288-5995

THE MUSTARD SEED

4137 Whitney Ave.
Hamden, CT 06517   288-8653

CALLAHAN'S

1270 South Main St.
Cheshire, CT 06410   271-1993

RUSTIC OAK

the RUSTIC OAK

165 Washignton Ave.
North Haven, CT 06473   239-1107

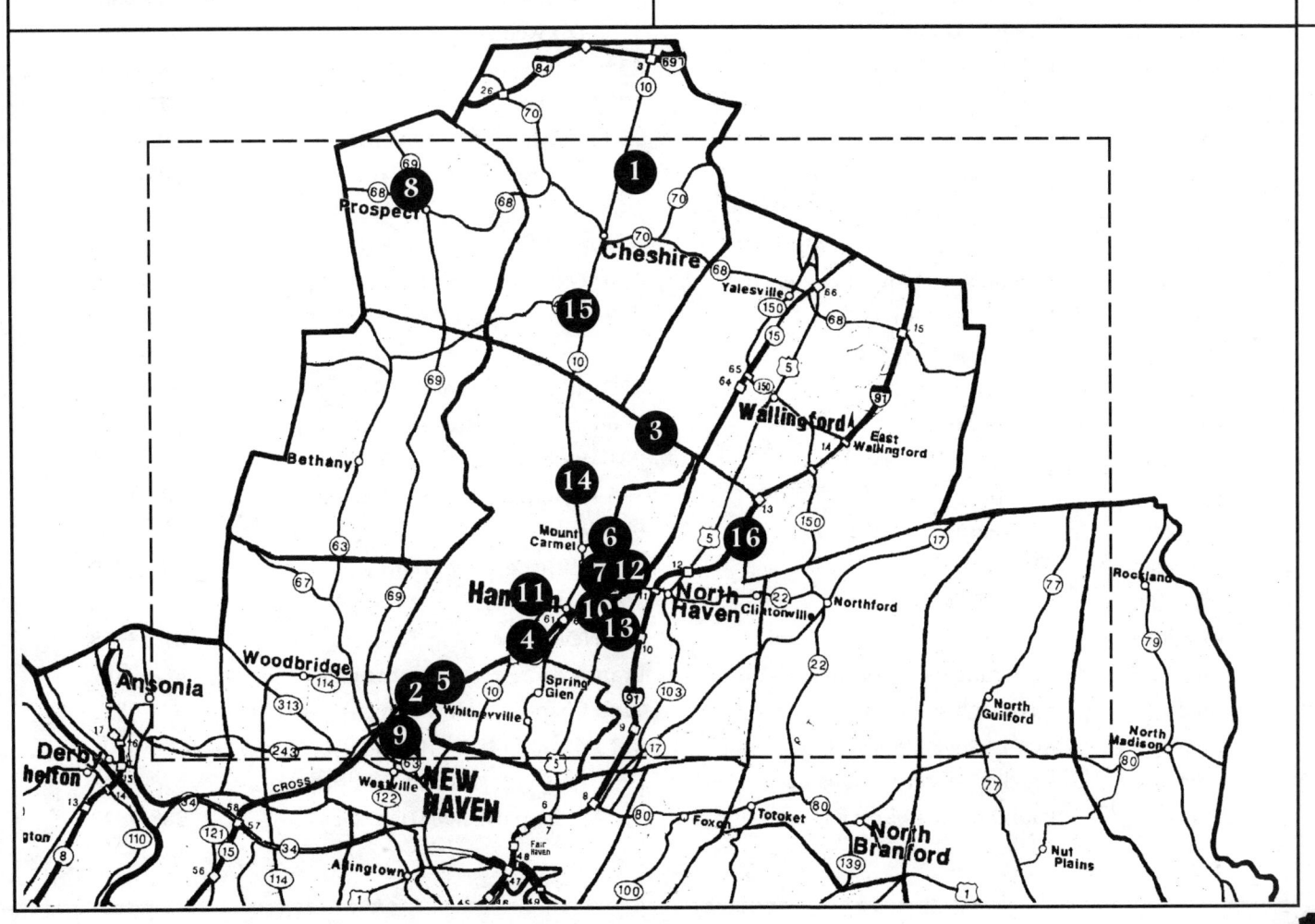

American	Abbott & Cassello's	339 N. Colony Road (Wallingford)	949-9477
American	Allegra's	538 Boston Post rd. (Orange)	795-6985
American	Archie Moore's	188-1/2 Willow St (New Haven)	773-9870
American	Arthur's Bar & Grille	15 Edwards St (New Haven)	498-0551
American	Barbecue Pit	173 Arch St (Hamden)	782-0118
American	Bobby Valentine's Sports Gallery	304 Old Gate Lane (Milford)	878-5262
American	Brickers	229 Bridgeport Ave. (Milford)	878-2220
American	Callahan's	1027 South Main Street (Cheshire)	271-1993
American	Casey's Restaurant	266 College St (New Haven)	624-3903
American	Challenges	230 Crown Street (New Haven)	782-2284
American	Chambers Restaurant	195 Church Street (New Haven)	776-6117
American	Chuck's Steak House	1003 Orange Avenue (WH)	934-5300
American	Claire's Corner Copia	1000 Chapel St (New Haven)	562-3888
American	Clark's Dairy Luncheonette	74 Whitney Ave. (New Haven)	777-2728
American	Clark's Dairy Restaurant	89 Boston Post Road (Orange)	799-0880
American	Colonial Diner	1038 Dixwell Ave (Hamden)	562-9105
American	Colonial Tymes	2389 Dixwell Ave (Hamden)	387-6653
American	Copper Kitchen	1008 Chapel St. (New Haven)	777-8010
American	Dakota J's American Grill	15 Broadway (New Haven)	497-8217
American	Dickerman's Steak House	3307 Whitney Avenue (Hamden)	287-1717
American	Dino's	540 Washington Ave. (No. H)	239-5548
American	Dolly Madison Inn and Restaurant	73 West Wharf Road (Madison)	245-7377
American	Donald's Restaurant & Catering	33-R Old Tavern Road (Orange)	799-7790
American	Down Town Tavern	259 Orange Street (New Haven)	498-1980
American	Friends and Company	11 Boston Post Rd. (Madison)	245-0462
American	Hamden Townhouse	2256 Whitney Avenue (Hamden)	288-8118
American	Here's the Beef	756 Amity Rd (Rte.63) (Bethany)	393-0474
American	Holiday Inn-North Haven	201 Washington Ave. (No. H)	239-4225
American	Humphrey's East Restaurant	175 Humphrey Street (New Haven)	782-1506
American	J.P. Dempsey's Food and Drink	974 State Street (New Haven)	624-5991
American	J.W. Peabody's	1995 Whitney Ave (Hamden)	281-5888
American	Julia's Bakery	185 Boston Post Rd. (Orange)	799-7106
American	Kader's Drive-In Restaurant	315 New Haven Ave. (Milford)	877-8958
American	Katherine's - A Country Bistro	Branford Craft Village (Bfd)	488-9457
American	Kavanagh's	1166 Chapel St (New Haven)	624-0520
American	Kenny Rogers Roasters	111 Boston Post Rd (Orange)	795-8300
American	Knickerbocker Famous Bar	1201 Boston Post Road (Milford)	878-8700
American	Laurel View Country Club	310 W. Shepard Ave (Hamden)	288-2822

RESTAURANTS BY TYPE OF CUISINE

American	Louis' Lunch	261-3 Crown Street (New Haven)	562-5507
American	Mary's Breakfast Club	2400 Foxon Road (No.Bfd)	481-2030
American	Maxis' Alpine Cafe	630 Washington Ave (No. H)	239-1989
American	Meadow Muffins Restaurant	201 Meadow (Branford)	481-4198
American	Millpond Tavern	1565 Middletown Ave (No.Bfd)	484-9316
American	Moon Star Restaurant	2 Commercial Pkwy (Branford)	483-9640
American	My Dad's Place Cafe	313 E Main Street (Branford)	488-6170
American	Noni's Kitchen	1505 Dixwell Avenue (Hamden)	288-3050
American	Rattlesnake Southwestern Grill	1125 Dixwell Ave. (Hamden)	498-1948
American	Richter's Cafe	990 Chapel Street (New Haven)	777-0400
American	Russian Samovar	342 Orange Street (New Haven)	789-1128
American	September's Restaurant	70 Pond Lily Avenue (New Haven)	397-2626
American	Skyline Café	15 Whitney Ave (New Haven)	865-1933
American	Steak Loft	420 East Main Street (Branford)	483-8257
American	The Rustic Oak	165 Washington Ave. (No. H)	239-1107
American	Woodbridge Gathering	9 Lucy Street (Woodbridge)	387-8349
American	Yankee Doodle Coffee Shop	258 Elm Street (New Haven)	865-1074
American	Yankee Silversmith Inn	1033 N. Colony Rd (Wallingford)	269-5444
American	Vinny's Deli	567 Center St (Wallingford)	265-7288
American	Spanky's Restaurant	236 Crown Street (New Haven)	562-3530
American	Star Diner	585 Lombard Street (New Haven)	562-5582
American	Twin Pines Diner Restaurant	34 Main Street (East Haven)	468-6887
American	Water Street Diner	95 Water Street (New Haven)	562-0044
American	West Haven Duchess Dineraunt	706 Campbell Ave (West Haven)	933-9128
American	Athena Diner II	320 Washington Ave (No. H)	239-0663
American	Born In America	4 Brushy Plain Rd #514 (Branford)	483-0211
American	Brickford's	741 No. Colony Rd. (Wallingford)	265-1858
American	Duchess Family Restaurant	240 Boston Post Rd. (Orange)	799-6919
American	Duchess of Dixwell Avenue	2425 Dixwell Ave (Hamden)	248-5941
American	Elm Diner	427 Elm St. (West Haven)	933-9966
American	Friendly Family Restaurant	54 Frontage Rd. (East Haven)	467-3465
American	Friendly Family Restaurant	30 Leetes Island Rd. (Branford)	481-5357
American	Friendly Family Restaurant	445 West Main St. (Branford)	488-6947
American	Friendly Family Restaurant	Cherry Hill Rd (Branford)	488-4264
American	Friendly Family Restaurant	340 Saw Mill Rd. (West Haven)	932-3728
American	Glenwood Drive-In	2538 Whitney Avenue (Hamden)	281-0604
American	Howard Johnson Restaurant	405 Sargent Drive (New Haven)	787-3463
American	Howard Johnson Restaurant	1040 Boston Post Road (Milford)	874-1575
American	Ma's Corner	588 Main Street (Branford)	481-5522
American	Mayflower Diner Inc.	465 Old Gate Lane (Milford)	878-7345

GREATER NEW HAVEN RESTAURANTS BY TYPE OF CUISINE

55

American	Park Place Coffee & Sandwich Shoppe	11 Business Park Dr (Branford)	481-8637
American	Patricia's Restaurant	18 Whalley Ave (New Haven)	787-4500
American	Scott's Landing Restaurant	Tweed-New Haven Airport (East Haven)	468-2996
American	Town Squire Restaurant	130 Court Street (New Haven)	787-1150
American	Chuck E Cheese's	82 Boston Post Rd. (Orange)	799-3200
American	Educated Burger	51 Broadway (New Haven)	777-9198
American	Lou's Lunch	257 Forbes Ave (East Haven)	468-1404
American	Main Street Lunch	556 Main Street (Branford)	481-5847
American	Silverbrook Pub	350 Boston Post Rd (Orange)	795-1059
American	The Rib House	16 Main ST (East Haven)	468-6695
American	Tommy I's - A Place for Ribs	1075 Orange Ave (West Haven)	933-7427
American	Candlelite By the Sea	147 Cosey Beach Ave. (East Haven)	469-1327
American	Chart House Restaurant	100 South Water Street (New Haven)	787-3466
American	Frankies of West Haven	1152 Orange Ave (West Haven)	933-6631
American	Jimmies of Savin Rock	5 Rock St. (West Haven)	934-3212
American	Jimmies of Savin Rock	2100 Dixwell Ave. (Hamden)	288-1808
American	Lee's Fish and Chips	716 Dixwell Ave (New Haven)	787-1194
American	Lenny's Indian Head Inn	205 South Montowese (Branford)	488-1500
American	Pilgrim by the Sea	45 Seaside Ave. (Milford)	878-1113
American	Port of Call Family Restaurant	3 E. Industrial Road (Branford)	481-2076
American	Red Lobster Restaurants	2045 Dixwell Ave (Hamden)	248-0244
American	Rusty Scupper	501 Long Wharf Drive (New Haven)	777-5711
American	Savin Rock Seafood Co.	1157 Campbell Ave (West Haven)	937-1767
American	Saybrook Fish House Restaurant	56 S. Broad Street (Milford)	878-2428
American	Sea Breeze Restaurant	525 Boston Post Rd. (Guilford)	453-6715
American	Seafarer Restaurant	1651 Boston Post Rd. (Milford)	977-2077
American	Seafood Peddler	1950 Dixwell Ave (Hamden)	248-9907
American	Supreme Seafood Restaurant	999 Foxon Road (No. Bfd)	484-2721
American	The Ship's Wheel	471 New Haven Avenue (Milford)	874-4626
American	The Stone House Restaurant	506 Whitfield Street (Guilford)	458-0893
American	Turk's Restaurant	425 Captain Thomas Blvd. (West Haven)	933-4552
American	168 York	168 York Street (New Haven)	789-1915
American	Charlie B's	1157 Chapel St (New Haven)	776-7689
American	Indian River Steakhouse	471 New Haven Ave (Milford)	874-4624
American	New Deal Steakhouse	1651 Boston Post Rd. (Milford)	977-2077
American	New Deal Steakplace	1165 Boston Post Rd (Milford)	877-2077
American	Steak & Sword Restaurant	1360 Boston Post Road (Milford)	878-0691
American	The Gathering	898 Boston Post Rd. (Milford)	878-6537
American	Rainbow Gardens Cafe	1022 Chapel St (New Haven)	777-2390

RESTAURANTS BY TYPE OF CUISINE

Cafe	J.J.'s Cafe	765 Boston Post Rd. (Milford)	878-8086
Cafe	Jonathan Michael's Cafe	1533 Dixwell Ave (Hamden)	248-8808
Cafe	Massimino's Cafe	266 Chapel Street (New Haven)	865-0522
Cafe	Matthew's Tavern (Cafe)	703 Campbell Ave (West Haven)	937-0845
Cafe	Off Sides Café	203 Foxon Rd (No. Bfd)	484-2127
Cafe	Sydney's Café	490 Saw Mill Rd (West Haven)	932-5419
Cafe	Weed's Café	1435 Dixwell Ave (Hamden)	288-6393
Coffee House	Ahh-Some Gourmet Coffee	55 York St. (New Haven)	562-8122
Coffee House	Colombian Connection	2 East Main St (Branford)	483-0645
Coffee House	Common Grounds	1096 Main ST. (Branford)	488-BEAN
Coffee House	Daily Caffe	316 Elm St. (New Haven)	776-5063
Coffee House	Jamaican Gourmet Coffee & Tea	585 Washington Avenue (No.Hvn)	239- 5046
Coffee House	Koffee?	104 Audubon St. (New Haven)	562-5454
Coffee House	Lulu European Coffee House	49 Cottage St (New Haven)	785-9218
Coffee House	Perry's Coffee House	896 Whalley Ave (New Haven)	397-2811
Coffee House	The Coffee Table	486 Orange ST (New Haven)	777-7893
Coffee House	Willoughby's Coffee House	1006 Chapel St. (New Haven)	789-8400
Coffee House	Willoughby's Coffee House	258 Church St. (New Haven)	773-1700
Coffee House	Cafe Europa and Cookie Greetings	99 Audubon Street (New Haven)	821-2011
Chinese	Blessings	45 Howe St. (New Haven)	624-3557
Chinese	China Buffet	117 Washington Ave (No. H)	234-9294
Chinese	China Buffet	2300 Dixwell Avenue (Hamden)	288-2000
Chinese	China Inn	1720 Dixwell Avenue (Hamden)	288-7199
Chinese	China Pavilion	185 Boston Post Road (Orange)	795-3555
Chinese	Dynasty Restaurant	419 Universal Drive North (No. H)	239-6678
Chinese	Eastern Pearl Seafood Chinese Rest.	1307 Whalley Ave (New Haven)	397-1688
Chinese	Formosa Chinese Restaurant	880 Grand Ave. (New Haven)	782-0739
Chinese	Fortune Village	120 N. Main St. (Branford)	481-8888
Chinese	Fortune Village Chinese Restaurant	120 N. Main Street (Branford)	481-3568
Chinese	Great Wall Chinese Restaurant	153 Saw Mill Rd. (West Haven)	931-9873
Chinese	Great Wall Chinese Restaurant	164 Washington Ave. (No. H)	234-2388
Chinese	Great Wall of China	67 Whitney Ave (New Haven)	777-8886
Chinese	Hing Wah	905 Dixwell Ave (Hamden)	562-4415
Chinese	Ho Kin Chinese Kitchen	560 Forest Ave (West Haven)	387-5363
Chinese	Home Village Gourmet Chinese Rest.	2380 Dixwell Avenue (Hamden)	288-5479
Chinese	House of Chao	898 Whalley Ave. (New Haven)	389-6624
Chinese	Hunan Chinese Restaurant	55 Washington Ave (No. H)	239-0396

Chinese	Hunan Wok	142 York St (New Haven)	776-9475
Chinese	Imperial Wok Chinese Restaurant	884 Howard Ave. (New Haven)	776-6699
Chinese	Jade East	9 Connolly Pkwy (Hamden)	288-3581
Chinese	King's Sun Chinese Restaurant	1378 Whalley Ave (New Haven)	389-4114
Chinese	Kingbird Garden	403 Saw Mill Road (West Haven)	933-8565
Chinese	Li's Garden	501 Boston Post Road (Orange)	799-0883
Chinese	Lion City Chinese Restaurant	4 Brushy Plains Rd. (Branford)	481-7474
Chinese	Main Garden	376 Elm Street (New Haven)	777-3747
Chinese	New China	669 Main St (East Haven)	467-2876
Chinese	New China	2100 Dixwell Avenue, (Hamden)	281-1750
Chinese	New Palace Chinese Restaurant	1245 Chapel St (New Haven)	773-0654
Chinese	Number One Chinese Restaurant	937 Foxon Rd (East Haven)	468-8130
Chinese	Pagoda Chinese Restaurant	2 Broadway (No.Hvn)	234-8236
Chinese	Panda House	111 Elm Street (West Haven)	933-2822
Chinese	Panda House	538 Boston Post Road (Orange)	891-8277
Chinese	Pavillion East Chinese Restaurant	146 Amity Rd. (New Haven)	387-3539
Chinese	Peking Garden Restaurant	220 Captain Thomas Blvd (West Haven)	934-7536
Chinese	Royal Palace	857 Orange Ave (West Haven)	937-8686
Chinese	Shangri-Lee	965 No. Main Street (Cheshire)	250-8888
Chinese	Shong Fa Jaing	670 Foxon Rd (East Haven)	468-2066
Chinese	Silver Palace Chinese Buffet	657 Foxon Rd. (East Haven)	466-3389
Chinese	Sing Hee	107 Middletown Ave (No.Hvn)	777-1110
Chinese	Sing-Wah Chinese Restaurant	548 Whalley Ave (New Haven)	387-5225
Chinese	Sunny Garden Restaurant	883 Whalley Ave (West Haven)	389-2117
Chinese	Three Star Chinese Restaurant	3030 Whitney Ave (Hamden)	281-6789
Chinese	Tong Sing Restaurant	1088 Orange Ave (West Haven)	934-6828
Chinese	United China Restaurant	10 Jones Hill Rd (West Haven)	937-8047
Chinese	Wah-Chun Chinese Restaurant	218 Grand Ave (New Haven)	785-1957
Chinese	Wei Chuen Restaurant	1869 Dixwell Ave (Hamden)	287-0129
Chinese	Wei Wei Kitchen	2151 State Street (Hamden)	497-8911
Chinese	Wing Thing	900 Dixwell Ave (Hamden)	782-9464
Chinese	Wong's Chinese Restaurant	521 New Haven Ave (Milford)	877-2242
Chinese	Mt. Fuji Japanese & Chinese Rest.	1245 Chapel Street (New Haven)	773-0654
Chinese	Happy Wok Oriental Restaurant	633 Boston Post Road (Guilford)	453-4936
Continental	Bagdon's	9 Elm Street (New Haven)	777-1962
Continental	Bruxelle Brasserie & Bar	220 College Street (New Haven)	777-7752
Continental	Cafe Lafayette	725 Boston Post road (Madison)	245-7772
Continental	Christopher Martins	860 State St. (New Haven)	776-8835
Continental	Pomegranate	242 College St (New Haven)	776-3304
Continental	Riviera Café	3 Linden Avenue (Branford)	481-7011
Continental	Shawn's	1642 Whitney Ave. (Hamden)	288-5756
Continental	The Bistro	25 Whitfield St. (Guilford)	458-9059
Continental	Union League Café	1032 Chapel Street (New Haven)	562-4299

RESTAURANTS BY TYPE OF CUISINE

Continental	Webster's Restaurant	1114 Main Street (Branford)	488-8161
Continental	Whitfield Alley	63 Whitfield Street (Guilford)	458-2226
Continental	Le Petit Café	225 Montowese Ave (Branford)	483-9791
Delicatessen	Anthony's Sandwich Shoppe	1125 Dixwell Ave.(Hamden)	772-4292
Delicatessen	Chuck's	341 Whalley Ave. (New Haven)	776-6851
Delicatessen	Bagel Connection	61 Grove Street (New Haven)	782-1441
Delicatessen	Bagel Face Bakery & Restaurant	175 Boston Post Road (Orange)	795-3549
Delicatessen	H. Lender & Sons Bakery / Rest.	2400 Dixwell Ave (Hamden)	248-4564
Fast Food	Chapel Square Mall Food Court	900 Chapel Street (New Haven)	773-3437
Greek	New Center Spa Restaurant	340 Main St (West Haven)	934-6762
Greek	Olympia Diner	604 Ella T. Grasso Blvd. (New Haven)	865-6877
Greek	Clark's Pizza	68 Whitney Ave. (New Haven)	776-8465
Greek	Mykonos Greek Restaurant & Pizza	12 Selden (Woodbridge)	387-8889
Indian	Dabar India	1070 Main St. (Branford)	481-8994
Indian	Darbar India	1070 Main St (Branford)	481-8994
Indian	Gandhi Restaurant & Bar	1195 Chapel St. (New Haven)	776-6632
Indian	India Palace Restaurant	65 Howe Street (New Haven)	776-9010
Indian	Royal India	140 Howe Street (New Haven)	787-9493
Indian	Sangam Indian Cuisine	157 Boston Post Rd. (Orange)	799-8162
Indian	Tandoor - The Clay Oven	1226 Chapel St (New Haven)	776-6620

Italian	Antonio's of East Haven	672 Main Street (East Haven)	469-2386
Italian	Avanti	45 Grove Street (New Haven)	777-3234
Italian	Big Tony's Water Street Restaurant	145 Water reet (New Haven)	773-1115
Italian	Carbones of New Haven	100 Wooster St (New Haven)	773-1866
Italian	Consiglio's of New Haven	165 Wooster Street (New Haven)	865-4489
Italian	Danny's Expresso Restaurant	1060 W. Main St. (Branford)	488-5174
Italian	Danny's Expresso Restaurant	594 Boston Post Rd. (Guilford)	453-1813
Italian	Danny's Expresso Restaurant	1834 Dixwell Ave. (Hamden)	777-2309
Italian	Danny's Expresso Restaurant	Capt Thomas Blvd (West Haven)	932-0871
Italian	Danny's Expresso Restaurant	270 Washington Ave. (No.Hvn)	239-6011
Italian	Dante's Restaurant	218 Skiff St (Hamden)	288-5585
Italian	DelMonaco's Restaurant	232 Wooster Street (New Haven)	865-1109
Italian	Diglio's Restaurant	2582 Whitney Avenue (Hamden)	288-0925
Italian	Gaetano's Restaurant	2547 Whitney Ave. (Hamden)	248-5003
Italian	Geppi's Restaurant	113 Grand Ave. (New Haven)	776-0100
Italian	Grazie	1651 Boston Post Rd. (Milford)	977-2077
Italian	La Cusina	128 Bridgeport Ave. (Milford)	874-5300
Italian	Leon's Restaurant	321 Washington Ave (New Haven)	777-5366
Italian	Lorenzo's Rsistorante Italiano	111 Elm Street (West Haven)	932-5846
Italian	Mama Teresa's	962 Boston Post Rd (Milford)	877-5108
Italian	Olive Garden Restaurant	2047 Dixwell Ave (Hamden)	288-9485
Italian	Olive Garden Restaurant	439 Boston Post Road (Orange)	795-8600
Italian	Pasta Così	202 South Montowese Street (Branford)	483-9397
Italian	Pavillion Restaurant	1721 Highland Ave (Cheshire)	272-3584
Italian	Ronis	899 W. Main St - Rte 1 (Branford)	488-7668
Italian	Tony & Lucille's Calzones	127 Wooster Street (New Haven)	787-1620
Italian	Tony & Lucille's Little Italy Dinner	150 Wooster (New Haven)	787-1621
Italian	500 Blake Street Cafe	500 Blake Street (New Haven)	387-0500
Italian	Adriana's Restaurant	771 Grand Ave (New Haven)	865-6474
Italian	Evie's Restaurant	565 Washington Avenue (No.Hvn)	239-1578
Italian	Gennaro's Ristorante d'Amalfi	937 State Street (New Haven)	777-5490
Italian	Gusto Restaurant	255 Boston Post Road (Milford)	876-7464
Italian	Mangia Qua	3 Clifton Street (East Haven)	468-7449
Italian	Noodles Restaurant	504 Old Toll Road (Madison)	421-5606
Italian	Scoozzi Trattoria & Wine Bar	1104 Chapel Street (New Haven)	776-8268
Italian	Sergio's Restaurant & Pizzeria	3860 Whitney Avenue (Hamden)	248-2564
Italian	Sorrento's Restaurant & Pizzeria	244 Skiff Street (Hamden)	288-0447
Italian	Amato's Apizza	858 State St (New Haven)	562-2760
Italian	Bellini's Restaurant	2 Broadway (No.Hvn)	234-2221
Italian	Bertucci's Brick Oven Pizza	550 Boston Post Road. (Orange)	799-6828
Italian	Bimonte's Pizza Castle	2402 Whitney Ave. (Hamden)	288-1686
Italian	Brazi's Restaurant	201 Food Terminal Plaza,(New Haven)	498-2488
Italian	Broadway Pizza	45 Broadway (New Haven)	562-7263
Italian	Brooklyn's Pizza	38 Sawmill Rd. (West Haven)	931-0909

RESTAURANTS BY TYPE OF CUISINE

Italian	Circle Store Pizza	1278 Durham Rd. (Madison)	421-3434
Italian	Dimatteo's Pizza	2100 Dixwell Ave. (Hamden)	288-6655
Italian	Ernie's Pizzeria	1279 Whalley Ave (New Haven)	387-3362
Italian	Est Est Est	1176 Chapel St. (New Haven)	777-2059
Italian	Firehouse Restaurant	1505 State St. (New Haven)	777-9125
Italian	Francesco's Pizza-Deli	279 Boston Post Road (Orange)	795-5844
Italian	Gabriele Restaurant & Pizza	326 Boston Post Rd. (Orange)	799-2633
Italian	Grand Apizza North	448 Washington Ave. (No.Hvn)	239-5786
Italian	John and Maria's Pizzeria	280 Foxon Rd (East Haven)	466-1550
Italian	John's Best Pizza	159 Cherry Street (Milford)	877-7475
Italian	Lombardi's Pizzeria	1874 Middletown Ave (No.Bfd)	484-2535
Italian	Lomonaco's Restaurant	990 W. Main Street (Branford)	481-9990
Italian	Luigi's Pizzeria & Restaurant	920 Foxon Rd (East Haven)	469-7778
Italian	Maria's Pizza	34 Middletown Ave (No.Hvn)	561-7175
Italian	Mike's Apizza & Restaurant	111 Campbell Ave (West Haven)	934-4933
Italian	Minervini's Pizzeria & Restaurant	457 Main Street (East Haven)	467-0017
Italian	Modern Apizza Place	874 State St. (New Haven)	776-5306
Italian	Modestino's Apizza and Restaurant	2151 State St (Hamden)	497-8668
Italian	Modestino's Apizza and Restaurant	867 Jones Hill Road (West Haven)	937-8755
Italian	Naples Pizza & Restaurant	850 Boston Post Road (Guilford)	453-4759
Italian	New Haven Pizza	260 Bull Hill Lane (Orange)	799-6658
Italian	Palm Beach Pizza	384 Grand Ave. (New Haven)	865-0353
Italian	Pasta Fair Restaurant	262 Boston Post Rd (Orange)	799-9601
Italian	Pasta Plus	1020 South Main Street (Cheshire)	272-6165
Italian	Paul and Eddy's Pizza Restaurant	1630 Whitney Ave. (Hamden)	230-9396
Italian	Paul's Apizza	240 Hemingway Ave (East Haven)	466-1915
Italian	Peppino's Italian Rest./Clam Bar	1500 Whalley Ave (New Haven)	387-2504
Italian	Pizza House of North Haven	117 Washington Ave (No.Hvn)	239-9372
Italian	Pizza House Restaurant	89 Howe Street (New Haven)	865-3345
Italian	Rascati's Pizza	330 Main Street (East Haven)	468-6592
Italian	Ristorante Faustini	190 Main St (East Haven)	467-9498
Italian	Rossini's Pizza Restaurant	529 W Main Street (Cheshire)	272-7297
Italian	Salernos Pizza & Subs	106C Boston Post Road (Orange)	799-6004
Italian	Sbarro Italian Eatery	421 Universal Drive (No.Hvn)	234-1048
Italian	Silvio's Restaurant & Pizza	620 Coe Ave (East Haven)	467-1303
Italian	Spooner Restaurant & Pizza	1400 Whalley Ave (New Haven)	389-9894
Italian	Star Pizza Restaurant	1380 Dixwell Ave (Hamden)	288-2626
Italian	Tammaro's Pizza & Italian Restaurant	7 Curtiss Place (West Haven)	933-7393
Italian	Tolli's Apizza Restaurant	410 Main St (East Haven)	468-6554
Italian	Tom's and Pat's Pizzeria & Take Out	9 Prospect Ave (West Haven)	932-5315

Italian	Town Pizza Restaurant	25 Whitney Avenue (New Haven)	865-6065
Italian	Venice Restaurant & Pizza	808 Dixwell Ave (New Haven)	865-0271
Italian	Vesuvio Restaurant & Pizza	1223 Campbell Ave. (West Haven)	934-5577
Italian	Vic's Pizza Restaurant	244 Quinnipiac Ave (No.Hvn)	776-5411
Italian	West Haven Pizza Palace	215 Saw Mill Rd (West Haven)	933-4596
Italian	Whalley Pizza	3250 Whalley Ave (New Haven)	789-8100
Italian	Yorkside Pizza & Restaurant	288 York (New Haven)	787-7471
Italian	Zeko's Pizza & Restaurant	456 Forest Road (West Haven)	389-9777
Italian	Zuppardi's Apizza	179 Union Ave (West Haven)	934-1949
Italian	Anthony's of Guilford	2392 Boston Post Rd. (Guilford)	453-4121
Japanese	Ashiya Japanese Restaurant	400 Derby Ave (West Haven)	389-9839
Japanese	Hama Japanese Restaurant	1206 Dixwell Ave. (Hamden)	281-4542
Japanese	Haya's Japanese Noodle House	1012 State Street (New Haven)	787-0535
Japanese	Hayama	199 Boston Post Rd (Orange)	795-3636
Japanese	Kampai Japanese Restaurant	869 W. Main St (Branford)	481-4536
Japanese	Samurai Japanese Restaurant	230 College St (New Haven)	562-6766
Japanese	Sanhsia	2279 Boston Post Road (Guilford)	453-2988
Japanese	Yoshida Japanese Restaurant	439 Boston Post Road (Milford)	874-0475
Korean	Seoul Restaurant	341 Crown Street (New Haven)	497-9634
Mexican	Aunt Chilada's	3931 Whitney Avenue (Hamden)	230-4640
Mexican	Azteca's	14 Mechanic Street (New Haven)	624-2454
Mexican	Chavoya's	883 Whaley Ave (New Haven)	389-4730
Mexican	El Amigo Felix	8 Whalley Ave. (New Haven)	785-8200
Mexican	El Bohio Ltd	690 Washington Ave (New Haven)	562-2182
Mexican	El Charro	262 Grand Avenue (New Haven)	498-7354
Mexican	El Torero	1698 Boston Post Rd. (Milford)	878-7734
Mexican	Hot Tamales	555 Campbell Ave (West Haven)	934-2829
Mexican	Il Forno Restaurant	765 W. Main Street (Branford)	488-0573
Mexican	Jalapeno Heaven	40 North Main Street (Branford)	481-6759
Mexican	Margaritas Mexican Restaurant	377 E. Main St (Branford)	483-7557
Mexican	Sloppy Jose's Mexican Restaurant	186 Hillside Ave (Milford)	878-9847
Mexican	The Taco Maker	500 Foxon Blvd (New Haven)	468-8535
Mexican	Viva Zapata	161 Park St (New Haven)	562-2499
Mideastern	Caffé Adulis	254 College Street (New Haven)	777-5081
Mideastern	Mamoun's Falafel Restaurant	85 Howe Street (New Haven)	562-8444
Misc	Parthenon Diner	374 East Main Street (Branford)	481-0333
Misc	Tropical Krust	240 Kimberly Avenue (New Haven)	865-6588

RESTAURANTS BY TYPE OF CUISINE

Oriental	Bon China Buffet	25 Frontage Road (East Haven)	467-6649
Oriental	Great Wall Restaurant	508 Old Toll Road (Madison)	421-4240
Oriental	Arirang House	93 Whitney Avenue (New Haven)	624-0311
Oriental	Miya Japanese Restaurant	68 Howe Street (New Haven)	777-9760
Pizza	Di Nicola's Pizzeria	931 Campbell Ave (West Haven)	937-1299
Pizza	Giovanni's Pizzeria	1612 Dixwell Ave (Hamden)	288-3886
Pizza	Giulio's Pizza and Restaurant	126 Middletown Avenue (No.Hvn)	239-3515
Pizza	Grand Apizza	111 Grand Ave. (New Haven)	624-7646
Pizza	Pepe, Frank - Pizzeria Napoletana	157 Wooster St (New Haven)	865-5762
Pizza	Pepe, Frank - The Spot	163 Wooster St (New Haven)	865-7602
Pizza	Sally's Pizza	237 Wooster Street (New Haven)	624-5271
Pizza	Delicious Pizza Restaurant	429 Naugatuck Avenue (Milford)	878-5097
Pizza	DePalma's Apizza	440 Main Street (East Haven)	469-1988
Pizza	La Fortuna's Pizza Restaurant	996 State Street (New Haven)	772-4239
Pizza	Mario's Pizzeria and Riostorante	56 Fairview Avenue (Hamden)	782-9191
Pizza	Naples Pizza & Restaurant	90 Wall Street (New Haven)	776-9021
Pub	280 Pub	284 East Main Street (Branford)	488-4337
Pub	Darson's Pub Eatery	543 Whalley Ave (New Haven)	397-1070
Pub	Hennessey's Pub	285 George St. (New Haven)	777-9961
Pub	Malone's Tavern	758 State Street (New Haven)	624-2400
Seafood	Abate Apizza & Seafood	129 Wooster Street (New Haven)	776-4334
Seafood	Cape Codder Restaurant	882 Whalley Avenue (New Haven)	389-8576
Seafood	Captains Galley	19 Beach Street (West Haven)	932-1811
Seafood	Chart House Restaurant	100 South Water Street (New Haven)	787-3466
Seafood	Chowder Pot Family Restaurant	560 E. Main St. (Branford)	481-2356
Seafood	Coral Reef Restaurant	1212 Main Street (Branford)	488-5573
Seafood	Scribner's Restaurant	31 Village Road (Milford)	878-7019
Soulfood	Mom's South Style Soul Food	1337 Chapel St (New Haven)	624-1023
Soulfood	Moody's Fish & Chips & Soul Food	614 Winchester Ave (New Haven)	865-2994
Soulfood	Soulfood Seafood	352 Whalley Ave (New Haven)	787-4831
Sports Pub	Triple Play Sports Bar & Restaurant	113 Water Street (New Haven)	787-9944
Syrian	Aladdin Syrian Restaurant	260 Crown St (New Haven)	777-5660
Thai	Bangkok Garden Restaurant	172 York St (New Haven)	789-8684
Thai	Cha-Da Thai	1151 Chapel St. (New Haven)	776-9802
Thai	Siam Square Thai Restaurant	1151 Chapel Street (New Haven)	776-9802
Thai	Thai Orchid	1027 State Street (New Haven)	624-7173
Vietnamese	Saigon City	1180 Chapel St. (New Haven)	865-5033

RESTAURANTS & NIGHT CLUBS
Area Night Clubs

The following is a list of night clubs in the Greater New Haven area. If you are interested in live music you should call them or check the newspapers to see what is appearing.

Bar	254 Crown Street	495-8924
Boppers of New Haven	239 Crown Street	562-1957
Challenges	230 Crown Street	782-2284
Demery's on Crown	216 Crown Street	776-4446
The Great Gatsby at the Palms	261 College Street	776-3316
Kavanagh's	1166 Chapel Sreet	624-0520
Malcolms Jazz and Dance Cafe	71 Whitney Avenue	772-4773
Maxl's Alpine Cafe	630 Washington Avenue, North Haven	239-1989
Newt's Cafe	362 Whalley Avenue	562-0801
The Nile Club	365 Crown Street	865-0166
Phoenix Rising Club	85 St. John Street	865-3911
Reflections Cafe	127 Fitch Street	387-9791
Seven Eleven Club	572 Winchester Avenue	776-5691
Toad's Place	300 York Street	624-8623
Tune In	29 Center Street	772-4310
Wallabies	425 Washington Avenue, North Haven	239-6042

ARTS GUIDE

Frances T. Clark
Executive Director

The Arts Council of Greater New Haven
772-2788
70 Audubon Street • New Haven, CT 06511

Five Symphony Orchestras. Two regional theaters that routinely send plays to Broadway. A community music school with lessons in every instrument and over 50 student ensembles. A famous touring ballet. Two world famous art museums. An art school with courses for every age and interest. These are just some of the enormous cultural resources you can find in this small city.

There is something for every artistic interest, taste and level of participation. If you are a trained singer, dancer or actor, you can audition for the many professional choral, dance and theater groups that perform in the area's excellent theatrical and performance spaces. For people who prefer to practice art in their spare time, there are dance clubs, community and little theater groups, poetry societies and numbers of fine exhibition spaces where you can show your work.

Yale University's four professional art schools, the City's proximity to New York, a supportive city government and corporate community, a school system that values and educates in the arts, together with a long history of educated and appreciative audiences all add up to make New Haven the Cultural Center of the State of Connecticut.

The Arts Council of Greater New Haven, founded in 1964, is a metropolitan art service organization that promotes, coordinates and advocates for all the arts in the region. It is a membership organization of artists, patrons, arts organizations and corporations.

The Council publishes the area's only monthly arts news and events magazine, *New Haven Arts*; operates a Business Volunteers for the Arts program; and develops audiences through such programs as the Alliance for Architecture, Singles and the Arts and its Small Space Gallery.

Working in partnership with the City of New Haven over a 25 year period, the Arts Council took the leadership in the development of Audubon Street as a vibrant Center for the Arts. The Council continues to work closely with the City of New Haven, the Greater New Haven Chamber of Commerce and community groups such as Vision for a Greater New Haven in order to develop, maintain and promote the area's lively art scene.

We hope you will read the next 30 pages with wonder, joy, and a resolve to take part as audience and participant in the many artistic activities that New Haven has to offer.

Cheever Tyler
President

Frances T. Clark
Executive Director

The Arts Council is supported by its members as well as grants from the Connecticut Commission on the Arts, the New Haven Foundation and Executive Partner, the Knights of Columbus.

Cheever Tyler
President

ARTS GUIDE
New Haven Theater History

New Haven is a city whose very name evokes the finest in dramatic arts. In the consciousness of the general public, the City's association with the theater stems largely from its historical role as the try-out stage for many of the great Broadway plays of this century. Though "bombing in New Haven" has become a well-worn expression of failed efforts and fizzled expectations, the city is, in fact, renowned for launching smash hits.

Since the latter part of the 19th century, New Haven has been one of the major theatrical centers of this country: the home to playwrights and producers; the school of actors, directors, designers and technicians; the stage on which many of this century's greatest plays have been first produced.

Long after the "try-out" circuit ceased to function, New Haven continues to provide the setting for new voices and dramatic developments in the nation's—indeed, in the world's—theater.

Four institutions in particular have earned New Haven's reputation as a world-class theater town. The Long Wharf Theatre, the Yale Repertory Theatre, the Yale School of Drama, and the Shubert Performing Arts Center, though by no means the only theatrical players in town, have each made significant contributions to the shape of the theater arts today.

The Shubert

Since the Shubert opened on December 11, 1914, with *The Belle of Bond Street*, the Theater has hosted more than 3,000 productions, including 300 world and 50 American premieres. As New York's try-out site, the Shubert earned its title, "The Birthplace of the Nation's Greatest Hits," staging nearly 200 shows that later opened in New York.

Oklahoma, *South Pacific*, *The King and I*, *My Fair Lady*, and the *Sound of Music*, were all born at the Shubert. Marlon Brando (in the premiere of *Streetcar Named Desire*), Humphrey Bogart, Katherine Hepburn, and Clark Gable, to name only a few, first came to critical acclaim on the Shubert stage. To this day, big-name stars of stage and screen play the Shubert each season.

Today, the Shubert is an entertainment magnet to the New Haven area as the theater which hosts the best of Broadway and acclaimed touring productions of opera, music and dance.

In addition to the countless fine plays staged in its history, the Shubert Performing Arts Center hosts other events, such as the Alvin Ailey American Dance Theater's performance of Dwight Rhoden's Frames, *with Michael Thomas and Renee Robinson.*

The Yale School of Drama

Until 1924, Yale University did not have a department dedicated solely to teaching dramatic literature and theater. Having filled that gap by establishing a Drama Department, the University enrolled its first drama students in the fall of 1925. At the same time, Yale began construction of the University Theatre, a 654-seat proscenium house, and associated theater and classroom space, and hired the famous George Pierce Baker from Harvard as its first department head. The Department's mission to provide quality theater education while paying particular attention to the art of the playwright was amply rewarded by the achievements of its graduates.

In 1955, under Dean F. Curtis Canfield, the Department came into its own and was reorganized as a separate school within the University: the Yale School of Drama. Wendy Wasserstein, A.R. Gurney, John Guare and Christopher Durang are among the illustrious playwrights who were once students at the Yale School of Drama.

Stars of stage, screen and television who are School of Drama alumi include: Paul Newman, Meryl Streep, Stacy Keach, Sigourney Weaver, Charles Dutton, John Turturro, Henry Hamlin, Ken Howard and Daniel J. Travanti.

(continued on next page)

(continued from previous page)

Directed by Lloyd Richards, the world premiere of August Wilson's The Piano Lesson *at the Yale Rep starred Starletta DuPois and Tommy Hollis.*

The Yale Rep

The Yale Repertory Theatre was founded by Yale School of Drama Dean Robert Brustein in 1966. The Theatre, which was formed in the former Calvary Church building in the heart of downtown New Haven, created a unique laboratory of learning for drama students, combining the theoretical groundwork of the classroom with the eminently practical professional experience of the living stage. Under the direction of Dean Brustein, the Yale Repertory Theatre produced works by classical writers of the dramatic cannon, as well as premieres by contemporary writers, such as Jules Feiffer, Terrence McNally and Michael Feingold.

Lloyd Richards became the Dean and Artistic Director in 1979, ushering in a new era in American theater. During his 12-year tenure, the "Rep" premiered all of the plays of August Wilson as well as many of the plays of Athol Fugard.

The late Jessica Tandy and Hume Cronyn were regulars at Long Wharf Theatre. In 1977, they appeared in The Gin Game.

Ma Rainey's Black Bottom, Fences, The Piano Lesson, Two Trains Running, Master Harold and the Boys, The Road to Mecca—all are plays which owe their existence to the collaborative efforts of the playwrights, Lloyd Richards and the Yale Repertory Theatre.

The present Dean and Director, Stan Wojewodski, Jr., has continued the tradition of innovation and excellence established by his predecessor.

Long Wharf Theatre

Founded in 1965, the Long Wharf Theatre has emerged in its relatively brief history as a major player on the international stage. Now entering its 31st season, the Long Wharf Theatre has two fully-equipped stages.

In the 30 years since it opened its doors, the Theatre has mounted more than 200 full productions, many of which have gone on to Broadway or Off-Broadway runs. Plays that were launched from the Long Wharf stage have received Pulitzer Prizes and New York Drama Critics Circle Awards, as well as innumerable Tony and Obie Awards and nominations.

The success of the Long Wharf Theatre is a direct result of community support. Board members and others raise money, help with productions, house and feed actors and form a continuous loyal audience, joined regularly by people who travel from New York and Boston to enjoy its shows.

Artistic director Arvin Brown has seen many of his productions go on to Broadway and London in his 28 years at Long Wharf. His range, from Shakespeare to contemporary drama, attracts many fine actors who want to work with the repertory company of this internationally-renowned theatre.

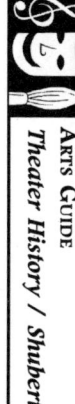

ARTS GUIDE
Shubert Performing Arts Center

SHUBERT NEW HAVEN

Since its opening in 1914, the Shubert Theater has staged nearly 200 shows that later opened on Broadway, earning the Shubert the title "Birthplace of the Nation's Greatest Hits." Today, the Shubert Performing Arts Center has evolved into the region's foremost entertainment center, offering a variety of performances in Broadway, Opera, Dance, Cabaret and Family Entertainment.

Located in the heart of historic New Haven, the Shubert Theater is surrounded by inviting restaurants, boutiques, museums, the landmark New Haven Green and Yale University. The Shubert Theater is also used by corporations, civic and community organizations for special performances, business and social functions.

Caroline Werth is the President and Chief Executive Officer of the Shubert.

Clockwise from upper right: Jerry Lewis; Tommy Tune in Bye Bye Birdie; *Karen Ziemba and James Brennan surrounded by Showgirls in Gershwin's musical comedy,* Crazy for You.

Shubert Performing Art Ctr 624~1825
Caroline Werth, President and CEO
247 College Street

The Shubert… "Birthplace of the Nation's Greatest Hits"
* Prior to Broadway   ** American Premiere   *** World Premiere

1914-15
The Belle of Bond Street
The Miracle Man
Shakespearean Repertory
Quality Street
The Blue Bird
Peg O' My Heart
The Girl from Utah

1915-16
Pygmalion
Major Barbara
The Princess Pat
*** Robinson Crusoe, Jr.
The Only Girl
Justice
The Passing Show of 1915
The Little Minister
Ziegfeld Follies of 1915
Our Mrs. McChesney
* The Passing Show of 1916

1916-17
Very Good Eddie
Mile-A-Minute Kendall
* Love O' Mike
* Eileen
Sarah Bernhardt & Company

1917-18
Sarah Bernhardt & Company
*** Doing Our Bit
*** Over the Top
The Copperhead
Oh, Boy
*** Sinbad
*** Rock-A-Bye-Baby

1918-19
Oh Lady! Lady
Seventeen
The Passing Show of 1918
Leave It to Jane
Maytime
Hamlet

1919-20
*** The Passing Show of 1919
Shakespearean Repertory
* My Golden Girl
** Poldekin
Bab

1920-21
Clarence
*** The Passing Show of 1921
Apple Blossoms
Smilin' Through

1921-22
Abraham Lincoln
Lightnin'
The Emperor Jones
George White's Scandals (Third Edition)
Dulcy

1922-23
*** Greenwich Village Follies (4th Ed.)
*** The Passing Show of 1922
* Rose Bernd
Liliom
Shakespearean Repertory
Sherlock Holmes
Blossom Time
Anna Christie
The Merry Widow

1923-24
* George White's Scandals (5th Ed.)
*** Greenwich Village Follies (5th Ed.)
*** The Stepping Stones
Bombo
Sally
Hamlet
The Moscow Art Theatre
Stella Dallas
Zander the Great
Balieff's Chauve Souris
(The Bat Theatre of Moscow)
Romeo & Juliet
*** The Dream Girl

1924-25
*** Old Man Minick
Wildflower
Quarantine
Seventh Heaven
Rose Marie
The Swan
I'll Say She Is

1925-26
*** The Vagabond King
What Price Glory
Desire Under the Elms
The Student Prince
No, No Nanette
Kid Boots

1926-27
The Cradle Song
* Dracula
The Constant Wife
Oh, Kay
The Merchant of Venice
Broadway
George White's Scandal of 1926
The Desert Song
The Letter
Saturday's Children
Hit the Deck
Countess Maritza
Escape

1928-29
*** Machinal
Paris Bound
The Trial of Mary Dugan
The Shanghai Gesture
The Kingdom of God
Coquette
*** The Sky Rocket
A Connecticut Yankee
The Lady from the Sea
Blackbirds
Cyrano DeBergerac

1929-30
** Rope's End
Animal Crackers
Diamond Lil
** Berkeley Square
* Waterloo Bridge
* Strike Up the Band
Strange Interlude
*** Nine Fifteen Revue
*** Ripples
The Little Show
The Chocolate Soldier
Uncle Vanya
The Tavern
New Moon

1930-31
* Mr. Gilhooley
Death Takes a Holiday
The Vinegar Tree
Ruth Draper (Character Sketches)
Street Scenes
Strictly Dishonorable
* The Wonder Bar
Simple Simon
*** The Third Little Show
The Admirable Crichton

1931-32
Three's a Crowd
* The Laugh Parade
Fine and Dandy
The Merchant of Venice
Hay Fever
*** Smiling Faces
The Fatal Alibi

1932-33
The Cat and the Fiddle
Camille
Abbey Theatre, Dublin
Mourning Becomes Electra
The Green Pastures
* Gay Divorce
Of Thee I Sing

1933-34
Music in the Air
Alice in Wonderland
Design for Living
*** Jezebel
*Dark Victory
Biography
The Barretts of Wimpole Street
Candida

1934-35
Roberta
Abbey Theatre, Dublin
Ah, Wilderness!
As Thousands Cheer
Ziegfeld Follies
Dodsworth

1935-36
*** Paths of Glory
Bitter Sweet
Othello
Romeo & Juliet
** Love on the Dole
3 Men on a Horse
Tobacco Road

1936-37
Boy Meets Girl
* Stage Door
The Children's Hour
* Red, Hot, and Blue!
Ethan Frome
Othello
* Jane Eyre
Brother Rat
Idiot's Delight
Dead End
The Great Waltz

1937-38
Victoria Regina
Tovarich
You Can't Take It with You
*** Between the Devil
King Richard II
Room Service
* On Borrowed Time
Julius Caesar
Brothers Ashkenazi
*** I Married an Angel
Yes, My Darling Daughter

1938-39
*** Leave It to Me
White Oaks
*** The Boys from Syracuse
*** Stars in Your Eyes
One Third of a Nation
*** The Philadelphia Story
I'd Rather Be Right
The Women
Our Town

1939-40
*** Too Many Girls
No Time for Comedy
*** The Time of Your Life
*** DuBarry Was a Lady
Kiss the Boys Goodbye
*** Two on an Island
*** The Fifth Column
Mamba's Daughters
Margin for Error
A Night at the Folies Bergère
Hamlet
*** Higher and Higher
The Little Foxes
*** Louisiana Purchase

1940-41
*** George Washington Slept Here
*** Panama Hattie
Twelfth Night
Elmer the Great
Hellza Poppin
Old Acquaintance
The Male Animal
* Claudia
There Shall Be No Night
The Man Who Came to Dinner

1941-42
*** Best Foot Forward
Arsenic and Old Lace
Hold on to Your Hats
The Doctor's Dilemma
Blithe Spirit
Macbeth
Banjo Eyes
My Sister Eileen
Watch on the Rhine
Private Lives
Without Love

1942-43
* The Skin of Our Teeth
Junior Miss
Angel Street
* Harriet
*** Oklahoma!
The Corn Is Green

1943-44
Kiss and Tell
Othello
Uncle Harry
Life with Father
Porgy & Bess

* The Voice of the Turtle
* Over 21
The Cherry Orchard
* Jacobowsky and the Colonel
Rosalinda

1944-45
* I Remember Mama
Sons O' Fun
A Bell for Adano
Dear Ruth
Catherine Was Great
*** Carousel
A Doll's House

1945-46
Carib Song
The Tempest
* Billion Dollar Baby
The Joyous Season
Pygmalion
* Lute Song
*** Born Yesterday
10 Little Indians
The Late George Apley
*** St. Louis Woman
State of the Union
*** Call Me Mister
*** Annie Get Your Gun
* Around the World

1946-47
Carmen Jones
The Duchess of Malfi
Come On Up
The Magnificent Yankee
*** All My Sons
*** John Loves Mary
*** Brigadoon
Bloomer Girl
Up in Central Park
Anna Lucasta
The Iceman Cometh

1947-48
*** Allegro
Man & Superman
*** A Streetcar Named Desire
Lady Windermere's Fan
Sweethearts
* Make Mine Manhattan
*** Mister Roberts
The Glass Menagerie
The Red Mill
The First Mrs. Fraser

1948-49
*** Love Life
* Edward, My Son
*** Light Up the Sky
Commend Decision
Harvey
*** The Big Knife
*** South Pacific
Media
Shakespearean Repertory

1949-50
Finian's Rainbow
*** Regina
As You Like It
*** The Happy Time
Lend an Ear

1950-51
Affairs of State
*** Call Me Madam
I Know My Love
* Bell, Book & Candle
The Consul
Death of a Salesman
*** The King and I
*** A Tree Grows in Brooklyn

1951-52
St. Joan
Kiss Me Kate
The Rose Tattoo
* Gigi
Pal Joey
The Member of the Wedding

1952-53
The Shrike
Gentlemen Prefer Blondes
Don Juan in Hell
*** The Fifth Season
*** Wonderful Town
*** Camino Real
I Am a Camera
The Fourposter

ARTS GUIDE
Shubert *Wall of Fame*

1953-54
*** Tea & Sympathy
*** The Teahouse of the August Moon
*** Sabrina Fair
Time Out for Ginger
*** The Prescott Proposals
John Brown's Body
* The Caine Mutiny Court Martial
** The Confidential Clerk
Staleg 17
Guys and Dolls
*** The Pajama Game

1954-55
*** Reclining Figure
* On Your Toes
** The Living Room
** Witness for the Prosecution
*** Plain & Fancy
*** The Desperate Hours
*** Damn Yankees
Kismet

1955-56
* A View from the Bridge
*** The Chalk Garden
*** No Time for Sergeants
*** A Hatful of Rain
*** Pipe Dream
The Boy Friend
* Red Roses for Me
** Fallen Angels
*** My Fair Lady
Can-Can
Bus Stop

1956-57
*** Girls of Summer
*** Bells Are Ringing
* Long Day's Journey into Night
*** Visit to a Small Planet
Fanny
*** Ziegfeld Follies
*** The First Gentlemen
*** New Girl in Town

1957-58
*** Copper and Brass
** Time Remembered
Middle of the Night
** The Rope Dancers
*** The Dark at the Top of the Stairs
Cat on a Hot Tin Roof
*** Sunrise at Campobello
The Happiest Millionaire
The Diary of Anne Frank
* The Visit

1958-59
** A Touch of the Poet
** Once More with Feeling
*** The Pleasure of His Company
* The Cold Wind and the Warm
Look Back in Anger
Romanoff & Juliet
*** Redhead
** A Raisin in the Sun

1959-60
* The Warm Peninsula
*** The Sound of Music
*** Fiorello
J.B.
* A Loss of Roses
*** The Andersonville Trial
Dear Liar
** Duel of Angels

1960-61
*** Tenderloin
*** Advise & Consent
*** Under the Yum-Yum Tree
* Period of Adjustment
*** All the Way Home
The World of Suzie Wong
*** Mary, Mary
*** The Happiest Girl in the World
*** Far Country
Once Upon a Mattress
The Music Man

1961-62
*** Milk and Honey
** The Caretaker

** A Shot in the Dark
The Tenth Man
Gypsy
Nine O'Clock Revue
** Take Her She's Mine
A Taste of Honey
*** New Faces of 1962
* No Strings
*** A Funny Thing Happened on the Way to the Forum
Irma La Douce

1962-63
*** Never Too Late
I Can Get It for You Wholesale
*** She Loves Me
Carnival

1963-64
* Barefoot in the Park
* One Flew Over the Cuckoo's Nest
Black Nativity
*** Nobody Loves an Albatross
*** Dylan
The Royal Shakespeare Company
The National Repertory Theatre
*** Any Wednesday
*** High Spirits
Beyond the Fringe
A Man for All Seasons
*** Fade out, Fade in
Luther
Who's Afraid of Virginia Woolf?

1964-65
*** Do I Hear a Waltz?
From the Second City
* The Roar of the Greasepaint, the Smell of the Crowd
*** Flora the Red Menace
Oliver
After the Fall

1965-66
The Owl and the Pussycat
Kismet
*: Hostile Witness
*** Wait Until Dark
The Deputy
Ivanov
The Subject Was Roses

1966-67
Man of La Mancha
On a Clear Day You Can See Forever
*** The Star-Spangled Girl
The Fantasticks
A Delicate Balance
Half a Sixpence
Luv
Marat De Sade
The Odd Couple

1967-68
How Now Dow Jones
Stop the World I Want to Get Off
*** Plaza Suite
The Homecoming

1968-69
*** Zorba
Fiddler on the Roof
Hello, Dolly!
The Cactus Flower
Mame
*** 1776

1969-70
The Price
I Do! I Do!
George M
*** Last of the Red Hot Lovers
Hadrian VII

1970-71
*** Two by Two
*** The Gingerbread Lady
Dear Love
*** And Miss Reardon Drinks a Litte
Hair
Butterflies Are Free

1971-72
Jesus Christ Superstar
*** The Prisoner of Second Avenue
Company
Purlie
Promises, Promises

1972-73
No Sex Please, We're British
The Effects of Gamma Rays on Man-in-the-Moon Marigolds
** The Sunshine Boys
Sleuth
No, No Nanette
Grease

1973-74
*** Godspell
*** The Good Doctor
Two Gentlemen of Vietnam
** Noel Coward in Two Keys
That Championship Season

1974-75
*** God's Favorite
Don Juan in Hell
The Major Show
Clarence Darrow

1975-76
Sammy Cahan/Words & Music
A Matter of Gravity
Who's Afraid of Virginia Woolf?

1976-1983
The Shubert is Closed

1983-84
While the Shubert Slept
Master Harold and the Boys
Evita
Joseph and the Amazing Technicolor Dreamcoat
Jerry's Girls
Grease
Fiddler on the Roof
Chicago
Baby
Annie

1984-85
Brighton Beach Memories
One Mo' Time
Guys and Dolls
Macbeth
Candida
Take Me Along
'Night Mother
Sugar Babies
Dracula
Taking My Turn

1985-86
Camelot
42nd Street
Tap Dance Kid
Great Expectations
Dreamgirls

1986-87
Biloxi Blues
** The Lord of the Rings
Arsenic and Old Lace
A Funny Thing Happened on the Way to the Forum
Cats
Singin' in the Rain
My One and Only

1987-88
Broadway Bound
Mama I want to Sing
La Cage Aux Folles
Cats
Big River
I'm Not Rappaport
Cav/Pag
Tango Argentina
* Macbeth
** Elvis

1988-89
The Mystery of Edwin Drood
Nunsense
La Traviata
Anything Goes
Me and My Girl
South Pacific
Tosca
As You Like It
Cabaret
Highlights of Verdi and Puccini
Into the Woods

1989-90
Carmen
Les Miserables
Rumors
Driving Miss Daisy
Sarafina
Die Fledermaus
The King and I
Romeo and Juliet
The Unsinkable Molly Brown
The 75th Anniversary Gala
Rigoletto

1990-91
Oklahoma
Lend Me a Tenor
Ballet Folklorico de Mexico
Don Giovanni
Africa Oye!
Peter Pan
** Ziegfeld
A Chorus Line
The Heidi Chronicles
Romeo and Juliet
Dance Theater of Harlem
Madama Butterfly
M. Butterfly
Grand Hotel
Faust

1991-92
My Fair Lady
Les Miserables
Il Trovatore
Meet Me in St. Louis
L'Elisir D'Amore
Tru
Buddy
Lettice and Lovage
Bye-Bye Birdie
American Indian Dance Theater
Glasnost Ballet
The Nutcracker
La Boheme
Music of Andrew Lloyd Webber

1992-93
Brigadoon
Sweet Honey in the Rock
Ballet Folklorico de Mexico
City of Angels
The Nutcracker
Guys and Dolls
Cavalleria Rusticana e I Pagliacci
Lost in Yonkers
Hearts for Life
Mummenschanz
Evita
Lucia Di Lammermoor
The Will Rogers Follies

1993-94
Chinese Magic Revue
Camelot
Mel Torme, Cleo Laine, and John Dankworth
Bolshoi Dance Ensemble of 50
The Secret Garden
The Sound of Music
Hungarian State Folk Ensemble
Echoes of Africa
Roberta Flack
Madama Butterfly
The Sisters Rosensweig
Alvin Ailey American Dance Theater
Jerry Lewis
The Canadian Brass
Porgy and Bess
Crazy for You
Paul Hall Contemporary Dance Theatre

LONG WHARF THEATRE

Left-to-right, top-to-bottom:
Ada Lester (Pamela Payton-Wright) advises her daughter Pearl (Lucinda Jenney) about her future in Tobacco Road, *from a novel by Erskine Caldwell.* Akili Prince as Young Mickey and Neal Huff as one of his best friends, Billy, argue in Michael Henry Brown's gripping portrayal of gangs, truth, loyalty and friendship, The Day the Bronx Died. *Elizabeth Wilson and Richard Venture in a scene from George S. Kaufman and Edna Ferber's* Dinner at Eight. *Dr. Harry Hyman (Ron Silver) tries to uncover the mystery behind Gellburg's (Amy Irving) sudden paralysis in Arthur Miller's* Broken Glass. *Rex Robbins, Charles Cioffi, Allen McCullough, Joyce Ebert, Richard Spore, Frank Converse, and Maryann Plunkett in Arthur Miller's* The Crucible. *Richard Dreyfuss and (on table) John Lithgow in Rod Serling's* Requim for a Heavyweight. *An accident-prone Derek Meadle, played by Anthony Heald, displays his latest catastrophe to a befuddled St. John Quartermaine (Remak Ramsay) in the American premiere of* Quartermaine's Terms. *Kelly Neal as the Prince (left) makes Luis A. Laporte, Jr. as Alexander (right) yield to a new gang leader Troy Winbush as Odd Job (center) watches in a scene from* The Day the Bronx Died. *William Swetland and Geraldine Fitzgerald in a scene from* Ah Wilderness!. *Al Pacino in* American Buffalo.

Photo credits: Gerry Goodstein (*Requiem for a Heavyweight*); William B. Carter (*American Buffalo* and *Quartermaine's Terms*); T. Charles Erickson (*BrokenGlass, The Crucible, The Day the Bronx Died* and *Dinner at Eight*); others courtesy Long Wharf Theatre.

ARTS GUIDE
Long Wharf Theatre

Long Wharf Theatre was founded in 1965 and opened its doors with a production of Arthur Miller's *The Crucible*. The first year's budget was $294,000 and the theater played to over 30,000 patrons. Now entering its 31st season, Long Wharf is an organization of international renown with a $4.2 million budget, 14,000 subscribers, and an annual audience exceeding 120,000.

In the past 30 years, Long Wharf Theatre has mounted more than 200 full productions, over 20 of which have transferred to Broadway or Off-Broadway runs—including *Travels with My Aunt, Broken Glass, All My Sons, American Buffalo, Quartermaine's Terms* and *Ah, Wilderness!*. Many of the plays that premiered at Long Wharf are being performed today throughout the world.

Long Wharf's theatrical achievements have received international recognition. Two plays first produced at Long Wharf, *The Shadow Box* and *The Gin Game*, received Pulitzer Prizes. Long Wharf productions of *The Changing Room, The Contractor,* and *Streamers* received New York Drama Critics Circle Awards for Best Play. Long Wharf has also received many Tony Awards and nominations, Obie Awards for Ensemble Performance, the Margo Jones Award for production of new works, a special citation from the Outer Critics Circle, and the 1978 Tony Award for Outstanding Regional Theater.

In 1993, the world premiere of Susan Kim's stage adaptation of Amy Tan's *The Joy Luck Club* was presented in China in a collaboration between Long Wharf Theatre and the Shanghai Peoples Art Theatre, culminating a two-year international theater exchange program.

While premieres, transfers, and awards tend to make headlines, Long Wharf's reputation ultimately rests on the work seen season after season at its New Haven home—fresh and imaginative revivals of classics and modern plays, rediscoveries of neglected works and a variety of world and American premieres.

With its Newton Schenck Stage (487 seats) and its more intimate Stage II (200 seats) playing to an audience averaging 90% of capacity, Long Wharf reaches a large Connecticut audience in addition to those out-of-state theater-goers who also count on Long Wharf to continue to fulfill its artistic vision: the presentation of plays of character which examine the human condition and spirit.

Tony Lo Bianco and Saundra Santiago in Arthur Miller's A View from the Bridge, directed by Arvin Brown.

Stockard Channing and Richard Dreyfuss appear in Peter Nichols' A Day in the Death of Joe Egg.

A continuity of vision and leadership has contributed to Long Wharf's success. Arvin Brown has been associated with the Theatre since its inception. Executive Director M. Edgar Rosenblum joined Brown in 1970 to manage Long Wharf's business affairs and production operations.

Long Wharf Theatre   787-4282
Arvin Brown, Artistic Director
222 Sargent Drive

Palace

September 18, 1984 was a theater night when even the most sophisticated New Haven theater goer could not recall a more electrifying theater evening in New Haven. Those lucky few who years before had attended the opening of *My Fair Lady* and *Oklahoma* on the same street as the refurbished Palace Theater claimed they were equally thrilled by the performance of Marvin Hamlisch and Peter Alden whose one night concert received five standing ovations.

The night really belonged to Joel Schiavone whose dream had turned the run-down upper Chapel-College street area into the glamorous rebuilt Shubert Alley with two legitimate theaters flanked by new stores and fine restaurants.

When Hamlish asked the audience that included Gov. William O'Neill and Mayor Biagio Dilieto and a host of other New Haven theater supporters—including the Wiffenpoofs (who sang in the lobby during intermission)—to suggest the title of a song that he could improvise, members of the audience shouted out "Joel's the Greatest," "Mr. Schiavone You're Damn Good" and "The Schiavone Rag." Hamlisch obliged to all these requests.

Marvin Hamlisch on Opening Night

Joel Schiavone had successfully supervised the $30 million dollar restoration of the College Street theater district. For ten years, he risked his capital and reputation on the idea that New Haven could again have the finest theater in the United States. The reopening to the Palace Theater was the successful culmination of his dream.

Today the Palace Theater is being managed by a New York theatrical management firm which is in the process of developing the Palace's 1995-1996 entertainment season.

Palace Performing Arts Ctr   789~2120
246 College Street

University Theatre

A Department of Drama was founded in the Yale School of Fine Arts in 1924 through the generosity of Edward S. Harkness, who graduated from Yale in 1897. In 1925, George Pierce Baker brought to Yale his famous playwriting course and workshop that he had originated at Harvard. The first students were registered in the fall of 1925 while the University Theater was under construction, and the first Master of Fine Arts in Drama was conferred in 1931.

In 1955, by a vote of the Yale Corporation, the Department was reorganized as a separate professional school with jurisdiction over the administration of the Master of Fine Arts in Drama. In 1966, the School of Drama extended the policy instituted in 1927, of granting certificates to those students who had completed the three-year program without having the normal prerequisite bachelor's degree, allowing actors and designers to continue training at the School and Repertory Theatre after receiving a certificate, and eventually to earn an MFA degree. The policy of continuing in residence to earn the MFA was discontinued in 1979.

The Yale Repertory Theatre was founded by the School of Drama in 1967 to facilitate a closer relationship for faculty and students between training and the practicing professional theater.

The two main stage facilities of the Yale School of Drama are the University Theatre on York Street and the Yale Repertory Theatre on Chapel Street. In addition to these two outstanding facilities, the School of Drama also uses Vernon Hall on Park Street as a cabaret theater and rehearsal space, and the Drama School Annex on Park Street for playwrights' workshops, rehearsal space and classrooms. The Yale University Library, in the University Theatre building on York Street, operates a Drama Library of almost 30,000 volumes.

In addition to its own productions, the University Theatre hosts a number of Yale Rep performances, such as The Marriage of Figaro/Figaro Gets a Divorce, *an adaptation by Eric Overmyer of a work by Beaumarchais and Ödön von Horváth.*

University Theatre   432-1212
222 York Street

ARTS GUIDE
Other New Haven Theatres

The Yale Repertory Theatre was founded by the Yale School of Drama in 1966 to facilitate a closer relationship for faculty and students between training and the professional theater. In 1991, Stan Wojewodski, Jr. assumed the role of Dean and Artistic Director of both the Yale School of Drama/Yale Repertory Theatre.

The Rep constructs its vision by deliberately juxtaposing freshly re-imagined classics with new writing for the stage, providing an environment in which theater professionals and conservatory students become engaged in the exchange of ideas vital to the creation of new works of art.

In 1991, the Rep received the Tony Award for Outstanding Regional Theater and, in 1992, it was awarded the Jujamcyn Theaters Award, which honors a theater that has made an outstanding contribution to the greater theater community.

The Yale Repertory Theatre is easily accessible with an elevator and special seating locations for patrons in wheelchairs. The theater is equipped with an infrared listening system and special sign language-interpreted performances are available.

Sarah Knowlton, Nicky Paraiso, Amy Brenneman, David Chandler and Alessandro Nivola appear in a scene from Bertolt Brecht's Saint Joan of the Stockyards, *directed by Liz Diamond.*

Alexandra Gersten appears in a scene from George F. Walker's Escape from Happiness.

King Edward the Second (Byron Jennings) vows to avenge the death of Gaveston as his supporter, Spencer (Sean Haberle), looks on in Marlowe's Edward the Second.

Yale Repertory Theatre   432-1570
Stan Wojewodski, Jr., Artistic Director
Chapel and York Streets

75

Act-I Players

Act-I Players is a non-profit organization that produces original works for and by inner-city youth about issues that affect their lives—AIDS, suicide, drugs, gangs—Through plays and skits, workshops, conferences, dance, entertaining and educating. Act -I accepts original scripts.

Act-I sponsors a "free" drama, dance, and playwriting after-school support group for grades 7-12. The group performs in schools, health fairs, and other community events. Academic tutoring is also offered.

Act-I Jr. offers introductory drama and dance workshops for grades K-2, including A-Team, Express Yourself, I Can Do It–Yes I Can, and Show and Tell.

Act-I Players	**288-4422**
Tony Moss, Director	
P.O. Box 2083, New Haven 06521	

Humanities Touring Group

The Humanities Touring Group (HTG) has its origin in a class project begun at Sacred Heart University in 1986. Professors Claude McNeal and Piotr Gzowski wrote and produced a script *The Greeks: In the Beginning* in order to bring the Humanities to their students in a multi-media production structured like the musical theater. An immediate hit, it succeeded in arousing students' interest, causing them to delve deeper into the classics on their own.

In 1987 HTG was founded and incorporated. Since then, the program has been eminently successful performing for more than 20,000 students from approximately 185 schools in Connecticut and New York. In April 1991, HTG held the successful premiere of *The Renaissance Era: Europe Awakens*, the second production in its planned trilogy, *The Great Eras of Western Culture*. HTG will premiere *The Modern Era: The Age of Technology* in 1995, completing the trilogy.

Humanities Touring Group	**268-3909**
Claude McNeal, Director	
41 Wauneta Road, Trumbull	

New England Actors' Theatre, Inc.

Founded in August of 1992 by professional actor Jerry Prell, NEAT provides residents of Connecticut and Southern New England quality educational programs, classes, workshops and seminars in the performing arts. NEAT's mission is to broaden public awareness of the communicative value of the performing arts by providing and maintaining an artistic and educational resource and to contribute to and further enrich the community through the establishment of a repertory theatre company. Workshops and seminars for teens and adults are taught by experienced professionals. NEAT's Summer Arts Performing Arts Workshop is a special four-week program for grades 6-9 which takes place on the campus of the Wightwood School in Branford.

NEAT produces 3-6 plays a year, many of them new works by local writers and also stages new interpretations of theater classics. Most courses and all productions are presented at New Haven's Educational Center for the Arts.

New England Actors' Theatre	**458-7671**
Jerry Prell, Director	
160 Little Meadow Road, Guilford	

Nutmeg Players

A shoreline community theater group, Nutmeg Players strives to stimulate and encourage interest in theater arts, not only through productions, but also by participation in area town events, workshops, and annual performing arts scholarships offered to qualified high school seniors. Since 1963, the Players have been entertaining audiences with well-known musicals, comedies and dramas as evidenced by the group's strong and ever-increasing subscriber support. In 1980, an annual One-Act Drama Festival was added to the season of three mainstage productions with each year's winner representing NPI in Connecticut and regional competitions. Although theater is the main focus for the Nutmeg Players, social activities are also planned throughout the year. Members receive a monthly newsletter. Performances are held at Clinton's Andrews Memorial Town Hall Theater, which is handicapped accessible.

Nutmeg Players	**388-3932**
Bobbie Gelinas-Wight, Membership Chair	
P.O. Box 100, Guilford 06437	

Orange Players

The Orange Players Association, on the stage since 1974, is a non-profit organization dedicated to the enrichment of theater in the community through encouragement of participation in all aspects of the production of quality theatrical productions. The organization is made up entirely of volunteers who take part in all aspects of the production of its plays.

Each year, the Orange Players stage at least two major productions. Musicals are performed in the Summer and a comedy or drama is staged each Spring. A popular Children's Cabaret and other small shows take place at the beginning of each season.

Orange Players	**789-0723**
High Plains Community Center	
Orange Center Road, Orange	

Something Players

The Something Players is thought to be New Haven's oldest continuously producing community theater. Its spirited and dedicated members produce four plays a year, often including a musical. New plays, most often by company members, have found a forum here, together with works by well-known playwrights of comedies and dramas.

Housed in winter at the Black Box Theatre at Church of the Redeemer, and in summer at the Eli Whitney Barn, the players welcome new members, especially those willing to participate behind the scenes

Something Players	**776-2025**
Robert Sandine, Director	
188 Livingston Street	

ARTS GUIDE
More Theater

The Little Theatre

The Little Theatre forms a remarkable endpiece to one of the most notable streets in New Haven. Its shape, scale and placement offer a fitting and subtle, yet substantial, closure to Lincoln Street. The Theatre itself relates well to both the residential buildings on either side of Lincoln Street to the north, as well as to the larger brick carriage houses converted to architectural offices and a residence on its immediate block. As originally constructed, The Little Theatre is a fine example of the English (or Modern) Free Style movement of architecture.

Historically, The Little Theatre Guild was one of the most popular and largest volunteer organizations in New Haven, having almost 1000 adult and 130 child members in 1930. Its organizers were primarily associated with Yale University and lived on the residential streets adjacent to the site of The Little Theatre. The building represented a permanent home for the Guild, which had been producing plays in various New Haven church and other halls since its organization in 1921. The Little Theatre was built in 1924 for $34,000 ($25,000 of which was raised by sale of stock and subscriptions to the public). As the home of the Yale Play-craftsmen, The Little Theatre became a founding base for the societies that became the Yale Dramat.

The Little Theatre Guild was part of the national Little Theatre movement of the 1920s. It spawned non-professional theatre groups and small theatres in cities across the country. The movement was credited with fostering the talent of such noted American playwrights and producers as Eugene O'Neill, George S. Kaufman, Elmer Rice, Maxwell Anderson and Robert E. Sherwood. As a community activity, it drew not only those who wanted to act, but artists to design and create scenery and costumes. It is clear from the memorabilia and records of the Little Theatre Guild that many volunteers devoted hours of work.

The Little Theatre Guild had introduced the little theatre movement to New Haven through its play production; today the Little Theatre belongs to the Educational Center for the Arts and is used by them for theater classes and productions. After school hours, ECA rents the Theatre to theater production groups and community organizations.

Educational Center for the Arts

ECA is a part-time, regional public high school program for students who are talented in the literary, performing, and visual arts. ECA actively seeks students with potential or demonstrated talent from a diversity of cultural backgrounds, experiences and interests in the arts. Students are selected through a competitive audition/interview process and receive credit at their local high school for work completed at ECA. Ninety-nine percent of our graduates go on to further study of the arts in either university or arts training programs.

The ECA faculty is comprised of practicing, professional artists who work with students in collegiate level courses or projects designed to help them achieve a balance between the development of their technical skills and of their imagination and critical skills.

ECA Theatre School offers tuition-based courses for adults and older students in topics related to the performing arts. These evening courses are taught by area professional artists.

The Arts Hall, The Little Theatre and rehearsal studios which make up ECA's facilities are available for rent to the arts community for rehearsal and performances. The Arts Hall is a black-box theatre seating 180; The Little Theatre is a proscenium theatre seating 200.

The Educational Center for the Arts is housed in the former Temple Mishkan Israel on Audubon Street. The Spanish Rennaisance edifice is the work of the New York firm of Brunner and Tryon.

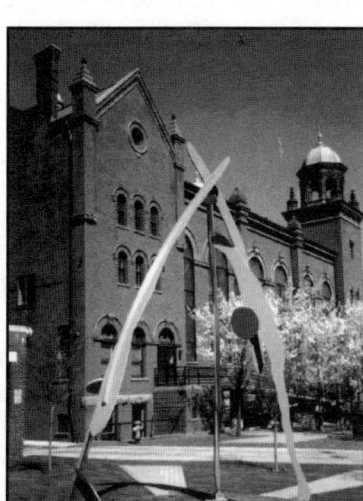

Educational Center for the Arts   777-5451
Robert D. Parker, Director
55 Audubon Street

ARTS GUIDE
More Music Groups

Orchestra New England

Orchestra New England (ONE) was founded in 1974 as the Yale Theater Orchestra, adopting the name Chamber Orchestra of New England in 1975. In 1985, the "Chamber" was dropped from the name to emphasize the Orchestra's versatility. Early in its history, ONE began to establish itself as one of the most innovative and critically acclaimed orchestras in the Northeast, recording its first album of premieres for CBS Masterworks immediately following its very first concert.

Each year, the Orchestra performs a subscription series of concerts in its hometown of New Haven, but that is only the tip of the iceberg. In recent seasons, ONE has averaged as many as 50 performances annually throughout New England and the Northeast. The Orchestra's subscription concerts are presented at Yale's acoustically superb Battell Chapel and are regularly broadcast on Connecticut Public Radio. ONE has also been heard over the Voice of America and National Public Television. During the summer months, Orchestra New England tours the area with exciting pops concerts, many of them sponsored by local corporations and community groups.

James Sinclair, one of the world's outstanding scholars and champions of the music of Charles Ives, has been the music director of Orchestra New England since its founding. His versatility in delivering superb performances in styles ranging from the Baroque to pops has driven the remarkable success of ONE. Maestro Sinclair has served as music director for four PBS television documentaries, including the Peabody Award-winning film about Ives, *A Good Dissonance Like a Man*.

Orchestra New England   934-8863
1124 Campbell Avenue, West Haven

Connecticut Chamber Orchestra

The Connecticut Chamber Orchestra was established under its present name in 1962 following two seasons of concerts at Town Hall in New York City. Conductor Stone moved the orchestra's home operation to New Haven, where it became the first professional chamber orchestra in Connecticut, with hundreds of concerts to its credits, tours throughout New England, New York, and other eastern cities. In 1979 the Orchestra initiated its own "Celebrated Artists Series," featuring internationally acclaimed soloists. The success of these concerts resulted in invitations for the Orchestra to appear in New York City's Carnegie Hall on two occasions.

Since 1970, the Young Artists Concerts have continued with corporate support. The Orchestra's Choral and Band Festivals, held at Woolsey Hall, are augmented with an all High School Orchestral Concert at Sprague Hall, with the aggregate number of participating youth exceeding 800 and with an audience of approximately 3500 in attendance.

The Orchestra's shows for elementary age children, both in New Haven and Bridgeport, have attracted thousands of children over the years. The Connecticut Chamber Orchestra has performed in several European countries and Mexico, where it was sponsored by the U.S. State Department.

During the past summer the Orchestra performed in Spain for several concerts. Future plans include a tour of Greece and Turkey.

Connecticut Chamber Orchestra   387-1376
Sayard Stone, Music Director and Conductor
P.O. Box 1166, New Haven 06505

For over forty years, the New Haven Chorale has enriched the cultural life of greater New Haven, with professional performances of a broad range of choral music. Modeled after Robert Shaw's famous Collegiate Chorale in New York, the Chorale was initiated by Alden Hammond in the fall of 1950.

A landmark in the Chorale's early history was the 1955 performance of an all-Mozart program at the Metropolitan Museum of Art in New York City.

The Chorale produces three major concerts annually, featuring masterworks of classical and contemporary choral literature, sung *a cappella*, with symphonies such as the New Haven Symphony Orchestra and Orchestra New England, and with chamber ensembles. The Chorale's 90 voices are drawn from the New Haven region through auditions, held at the beginning of each season.

The New Haven Chorale   787-1887
P.O. Box 1897, New Haven

ARTS GUIDE
New Haven Symphony
100 Years of Music

Founded in 1894 by immigrant-entrepreneur and music lover Morris Steinert, the New Haven Symphony Orchestra is the fourth oldest orchestra in the United States.

Each season, the Symphony performs seven classical concerts at Woolsey Hall. Van Cliburn, Leontyne Price, Rudolph Serkin, Glenn Gould, Arthur Rubinstein, and Yo-Yo Ma represent only a small sampling of the celebrated artists who have performed with the Symphony throughout its century of excellence. In January 1994, as part of its Centenary season, the Symphony performed at Carnegie Hall with soprano Jessye Norman. The jubilee performance led the New York Times music reviewer to exclaim that the New Haven Symphony Orchestra was "...a big league band, at home in a big-league setting."

In its review of the New Haven Symphony Orchestra's Carnegie Hall premiere on January 21, 1994, The New York Times called the Symphony "...a big-league band, at home in a big-league setting."

Over its long life, the Symphony has demonstrated its spirit of responsibility by providing a variety of cultural, educational and social events to the community-at-large in a series of outreach programs. In 1932, for example, the New Haven Symphony initiated its first Young People's Concert for elementary school age students. A Pop Series, launched in 1945, now also comprises the Valley Pops Series, which plays in neighboring towns of the Naugatuck Valley. In 1965, the Symphony first offered free summer concerts on the New Haven Green and has since expanded its outdoor concert territory to include towns such as Hamden, Branford, North Haven, and West Haven.

Today, with help from generous corporate funding, the Symphony enriches the musical lives of 10,000 school-age children every year. The Symphony also exposes preschool children to the whole orchestra at Kinder Konzerts, during which children sit near the performers as they tell their musical story.

During the spring of 1995, the Symphony initiated its first Family Concert Series at the Shubert with two Sunday afternoon performances in the spring. Each performance is preceded by an Instrument Petting Zoo, an opportunity for children to feel and play the instruments that they will hear.

As the NHSO has grown, its has aged with grace and style, enriching the lives of those in our community. Its devotion to its musical art and its unwavering pledge to enlighten future generations should bring the New Haven Symphony Orchestra continued success well into its second century.

MICHAEL PALMER
Musical Director / Conductor

NHSO performed on the Green in celebration of their anniversary.

New Haven Symphony   865-0831
33 Whitney Avenue

ARTS GUIDE
More Music Groups

The **Chancel Opera Company** of Connecticut is a *gemütlich* repertory company of professional and talented amateur adults and children performing operas by Susan Bingham. The company presents sermon-length devotional operas based on Scripture in Reformed Jewish or Christian worship services, and longer fairy tale and fable operas which are often used as fund-raisers. The group produces one major opera per year to benefit the Downtown Evening Soup Kitchen. *Susan Bingham, Director. 277 Willow Street, New Haven 06511. Tel: 562-0634*

Chestnut Hill Concerts presents world-class chamber music to the Connecticut Shoreline. Artistic Director Ronald Thomas, uses groups of players that represent years of musical growth and experience, resulting in performances that are more seasoned and musically thought out than that of the typical summer chamber music performance. Chestnut Hill continues to build a lasting, self-perpetuating audience through taped recordings of its concerts, which are broadcast on both public and private radio. *Margie Kreschollek. P.O. Box 183, Guilford 06437. Tel: 457-1148*

The **Connecticut Gay Men's Chorus** performs on a regular concert schedule throughout the state. Founded in 1986, the non-profit volunteer group strives for excellence in choral music while presenting a varied repertoire of traditional, popular, and Broadway selections. Three regular concert series are planned annually with a holiday concert in December, a fully staged cabaret revue in March, and a gay pride concert in June. *Winston Clark, Director. P.O. Box 8824, New Haven 06532. Tel: 777-2923.*

The **Elm City Girls' Choir** was established in 1993 by its conductor, Thomas Brand. The 32 members represent 21 schools and 10 towns of residence in Southern Connecticut. *Thomas Brand, Director. 63 Forest Hill Road, North Haven 06473. Tel: 248-6232.*

The **Galvanized Jazz Band** has been performing at the Millpond Tavern in Northford since 1971. Performances include music for listening and dancing and feature a different trombonist each week. The jazz is hot and the air is clean, because smoking and non-smoking seating is provided. Delicious snacks, salads, soups, sandwiches, and full meals are available in the Tavern room where the Band performs. *Fred Vigorito, Director. 20 Ledgeview Lane, Guilford 06437. Tel: 453-5916.*

Gamelan Jagat Anyar ("Gamelan of the New World") is an ensemble of musicians dedicated to learning and performing the traditional and contemporary gamelan music of Bali, Indonesia, using gongs, drums, bronze xylophones, cymbals and bamboo flutes. The full ensemble consists of 25 players. Music is taught and memorized in the traditional rote manner. *Michael Tenzer, Director. 143 Elm Street, New Haven 06520. Tel: 432-2985.*

The Greater New Haven Community Chorus is a non-auditioned chorus whose goal is to offer an enjoyable and educational singing experience to the community while providing quality performances for its audiences. Under the experienced baton of Ronald D. Konetchy, Chorus members perform two major programs performed at such locations as Yale's Sprague Hall, Church of the Redeemer, Center Church on the Green, and Battell Chapel. *Ronald D. Konetchy, Director. P.O. Box 351, New Haven 06502. Tel: 624-1979.*

Rozmarin, a small group of instrumentalists and singers based in New Haven, brings the vibrant harmonies and rhythms of East European village music to American audiences. Folklorists as well as performers, the group has done extensive field research in Eastern Europe, collecting and learning songs rarely heard in the U.S. Rozmarin performances combine varied singing styles, authentic folk costumes, and dance. *Barbara Andrews. P.O. Box 593, New Haven 06503. Tel: 287-9090.*

The **United Church on the Green** presents many musical concerts each year in its 1815 meeting house. The cornerstone of its concert program is the United Church Choir, a semi-professional chorus of 30 singers, which performs major choral masterworks in several concerts each year accompanied by New Haven's finest orchestral musicians. Each fall and spring a four-week series of concerts is presented Wednesdays at noon, featuring a variety of performers. The church's 41-stop tracker-action pipe organ, built in 1967, is heard several times each season in solo concerts. *Mark Brombaugh, Director of Music. 323 Temple Street, New Haven 06511. Tel: 787-4195.*

The **Yale University Bands** have a long history of insolence and elegance. Records show that the first appearance of a band at Yale was in the year 1775, when Yale sophomore Noah Webster and a militia band of Yale students accompanied George Washington to Cambridge. They found it "not to their liking," and returned one week later. From those humble roots have sprung the Yale University Bands.

The Yale Concert Band performs at Yale's Woolsey Hall as well as off campus. Known for its performance of traditional and unusual music in a variety of settings, the band has collaborated with such guest artists as Walter Cronkite, Benny Goodman, and Max Roach. Repertoire consists of the entire range of wind music, from chamber pieces to larger ensemble music, including marches, suites, popular band music.

The Yale Jazz Ensemble is a standard 18-piece big band that performs in Yale's Morse Recital Hall and off campus. Repertoire ranges from the classic swing tunes of the '40s to more contemporary charts. *Thomas C. Duffy, Director. P.O. Box 209048, New Haven 06520. Tel: 432-4111.*

ARTS GUIDE
Neighborhood Music School

Neighborhood Music School was founded in 1911 to provide high quality music instruction to all, regardless of ability to pay. The 78-year history of the school has its roots in the settlement house movement at the beginning of this century. It began as part of a neighborhood ministry at St. Paul's Church in Wooster Square, which addressed the social, educational and medical needs of the immigrant population. NMS has evolved into a fully-accredited community music school, providing quality instruction in music and dance for 1200 children and adults from the entire greater New Haven community.

The Neighborhood Music School occupies its own building on Audubon Street in New Haven, with branches in Guilford, the Hill neighborhood, and at Hopkins in the Westville section of New Haven. In September 1995, a new branch will open in the Fair Haven Community Learning Center.

The School's curriculum focuses on individual and group instruction, theory, and ensemble playing. The curriculum ranges from movement classes for infants and toddlers, to a music-oriented nursery program, continuing on through dance offerings at all levels, jazz and electronic music studies, and classes designed specifically for adults. Neighborhood Music School also offers a comprehensive Suzuki music program in many instruments.

Neighborhood Music School is wheelchair accessible, and offers "Music for Special Needs" to children and adults. A five-week summer program includes individual music instruction, plus the Audubon Arts Theater and Summer Day Camps.

The school's mission is summed up in the words of Clarence A. Grimes in ***They Who Speak in Music: The Story of the Neighborhood Music School***:

"As long as there are people in the low income brackets who need and love music; as long as there are people who believe in and have faith in cultural values; the need for and the importance of the (musical education) services given by the Neighborhood Music School will remain."

School hours are Monday-Friday 8:30am to 9pm and Saturdays 8am to 4pm. Sundays 11am-4pm.

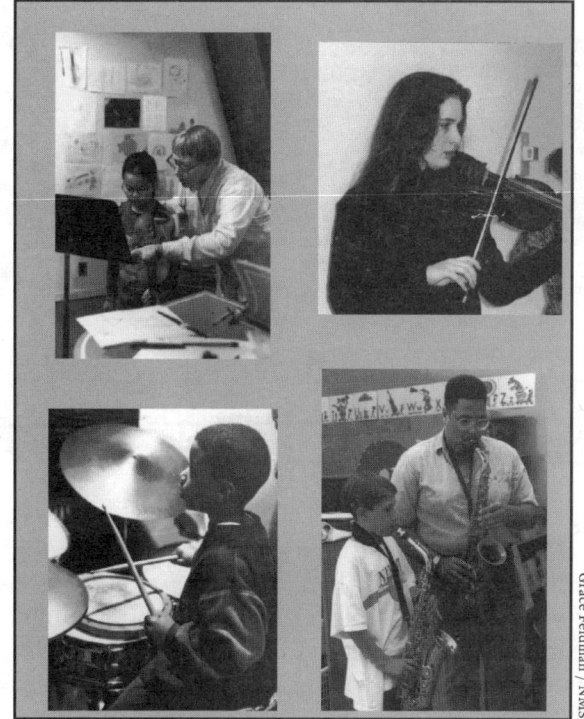

Neighborhood Music School 624-5189
Robert Eberle, Director   FAX 772-3566
100 Audubon Street

ARTS GUIDE
Creative Arts Workshop

Creative Arts Workshop (CAW) is a strategically-located, non-profit community arts center on the Audubon arts street in downtown New Haven. It was founded in 1960 as a learning center for both professional and amateur artists alike. From the outset, it has had a dual commitment: to excellence in visual arts education, and to service to the New Haven community. Today CAW offers a wide range of classes in fine arts and crafts in its own three-story building, with fully-equipped studios for everything from metal sculpture to jewelry, painting to pottery. It also has a handsome gallery space, with high ceilings and glass frontage.

Nearly 3,000 adults and young people are enrolled annually in over 300 courses offered by the school during four terms, including a summer session. Classes are open to students at all levels of experience. Some fifty to sixty professional artists, drawn from the local community, to serve as the instructors, and encourage their students with a commitment to the very highest standards. The CAW Program for Young People includes a variety of classes for children ages two to twelve, as well as classes which are especially designed for teens.

CAW also maintains an active exhibition program in its two-story Susan M. Hilles Gallery, with a series of shows. These arts exhibitions are related to the school's educational programs, including some which are held annually: two student shows, a faculty show, and The Celebration of American Crafts. The Workshop is committed to keeping tuition fees as low as possible and provides tuition assistance to students with financial need.

Gallery hours are Monday through Friday, 9am to 5pm, and Saturday, 9am to noon. The building's facilities are accessible to the disabled. Ongoing classes include basketry, book arts, ceramics, drawing, graphic arts, jewelry, media arts, painting, photography, print-making, sculpture, weaving, and the Young People's Program. There are also workshops of one to two days and up to a week on special topics of interest. Members are entitled to discounted class fees. Discounted parking is available at Audubon Court Garage next door.

Creative Arts Workshop   562-4927
Susan Smith, Director
80 Audubon Street

ARTS GUIDE
ARTSPACE ~ Erector Square Gallery & John Slade Ely House

ARTSPACE

A Center for Visual, Literary, and Performing Arts

A regional arts center, ARTSPACE is the place where new work in the visual, literary and performing arts finds a home. These works, by and for a diverse multi-cultural constituency, are showcased in an exciting, accessible gallery on the first floor of the Community Foundation/Arts Council Building on Audubon Street.

Gallery hours are Tuesday through Saturday, 11am to 5pm with unusual and exciting exhibitions changing monthly. *Writers Network*, a mentoring and peer reading program, meets on the first Wednesday of each month, from 7pm to 9pm. *Network of Visual, Literary and Performing Artists* meets on the third Wednesday each month, from 7:30pm-9pm. *Coffeehouse* is held on the fourth Friday of the month, from 8pm to 11pm.

Major programs include: "Jazz at ARTSPACE"; the Summer Arts for Youth (S.A.Y.!) mentoring program; "Art for ARTSPACE" (in March); the annual art auction; the Small Theater Festival (in April); New Arts Festival (in June); a variety of exhibitions and performances from juried competitions in the visual arts, choreography and musical composition.

For information about membership, an update on performing arts events, or any of ARTSPACE's programs, please call (203) 772-2377.

ARTSPACE   772-2377
Barbara Webster, Director   FAX 782-2070
70 Audubon Street
55 Audubon - ARTSPACE at ECA

---

erector square GALLERY

The Erector Square Gallery was established in 1986 as a not-for-profit gallery to exhibit works by contemporary American artists. Exhibits vary monthly and include paintings, drawings, prints, photography and sculpture. The gallery is handicapped accessible.

Hours: Wednesday through Saturday, 1 to 4pm.

Erector Square Gallery   865-5055
Joan P. Appicelli, Director
315 Peck Street, Building #20

The John Slade Ely House is a non-profit center for artistic and humanitarian activities in the greater New Haven area. Including eight galleries on its two floors, the John Slade Ely space houses the exhibits and classes offered by New Haven's oldest art clubs, the New Haven Paint and Clay Club and the Brush and Palette Club.

From September to June, Ely House sponsors exhibitions of works by contemporary artists, showing both individual artists and groups primarily from Connecticut or the greater New Haven area.

Lectures and special events are also sponsored by the Ely House. All exhibits are free and open to the public.

John Slade Ely House   624-8055
Carla Bengston, Director
51 Trumbull Street

ARTS GUIDE
Yale Center for British Art

YALE CENTER FOR BRITISH ART

The Yale Center for British Art was designed by Louis I. Kahn.

The Yale Center for British Art houses the most comprehensive collection of British paintings, prints, drawings, watercolors, and rare books outside of Great Britain. Displayed in sky-lit galleries designed by American architect Louis I. Kahn, paintings by Hogarth, Gainsborough, Reynolds, Stubbs, Constable, and Turner, among others, provide an unparalleled visual history of life in Britain since the reign of Henry VII. The collection, together with the Reference Library, Photo Archive, and the Prints and Drawings Study Room, affords faculty, students, and members of the general public a rare opportunity for research.

The Center mounts four to six temporary exhibitions a year. These exhibitions interpret the collection and often bring together loans from other institutions as well as private collections. The work of contemporary British artists is also featured. The museum offers tours, lectures, films, concerts, and children's programs. Admission is free.

Hours: Tuesday-Saturday, 10am to 5pm; Sundays noon to 5pm. Closed Mondays, New Year's, July 4th, Thanksgiving, Christmas Eve, and Christmas Day. Reference Library/Prints and Drawing Study Room: Tuesday-Friday, 10am to 5pm.

Mrs. Abington as Miss Prue in Congreve's 'Love for Love,' 1771. Sir Joshua Reynolds (1723-1792), Artist.

Yale Center for British Art   432~2800
1080 Chapel Street   FAX 432~9695

Hadleigh Castle, 1829. John Constable (1776-1837), Artist.

ARTS GUIDE
Yale University Art Gallery

The Yale University Art Gallery is the oldest university art museum in North America. Since its founding in 1832, when John Trumbull gave more than 100 of his paintings to Yale, the collections have grown to approximately 100,000 objects from around the world dating from ancient Egyptian times to the present day.

Highlighted in YUAG's renowned collection are superb works by Van Gogh, Manet, Monet, Picasso, Homer, and Eakins, as well as the distinguished Société Anonyme collection of early modernist art. There are notable collections of Etruscan and Greek vases; early Italian paintings; Chinese paintings, ceramics, bronzes, and textiles; as well as a comprehensive collection of 30,000 master prints and drawings.

The Yale University Art Gallery's collection of American paintings and decorative arts is one of the finest in the world. In addition to its permanent collection, the Art Gallery maintains a rigorous schedule of special exhibitions and educational programs. It is also a center for scholarly research in the history of art and in museum training for both Yale's graduate and undergraduate students.

The museum occupies two adjacent structures. The main building, completed in 1953, was designed by the distinguished American architect Louis I. Kahn. His first important public commission, and the first of four art museums he would design, the Art Gallery has been acclaimed for its significance to the history of contemporary American architecture. While it was the first modern-style building on the campus, Kahn's Art Gallery harmonizes with the older structures, such as Edgerton Swartwout's Art Gallery of 1928, in the Italian Gothic style, to which it is connected on the first and third floors.

Yale University Art Gallery   432-0600
Susan Vogel, Director   FAX 432-7159
1111 Chapel Street at York

Discobolos, by Robert Cronin (c.mid-1980s)
Leeney Plaza, Audubon Court

Ode V, metal sculpture by James Rosati (1988)
Long Wharf Maritime Center, Long Wharf Drive

Lighthouse Point Carousel, in East Haven
by Charles I.D. Looft & C. Carmel (1911)

Department of Cultural Affairs   946-7821
Lauren D'Alessandro, Director
New Haven City Hall, 165 Church Street

On High, metal sculpture by Alexander Lieberman (1979)
% for the Arts Program, Federal Building Plaza, Orange Street

ARTS GUIDE
Public & Outdoor Art

Gallows & Lollipops, by Alexander Calder
Beinecke Plaza, Wall Street

Modern Head, by Roy Lichtenstein
on Sachem Street at Hillhouse Avenue

Roots, by Sosivu Caldwell
at Dixwell Community House

Flight, by John Lippincott (1969)
Tweed New Haven Airport, East Haven

BARBARA FELDMAN & DANCERS

From its inception in 1981, Barbara Feldman and Dancers, Inc., has worked with dancers, composers, designers, and musicians to develop original dance works and to bring performances and workshops to diverse audiences throughout New England. The company presents its New Haven performances at ARTSPACE-at-ECA and in the ARTSPACE Dance Studio. A member of CONN-TOURS, Barbara Feldman and Dancers is available for master classes, workshops, performances, residencies and commissioned events. Special arrangements can be made for school and college programs. Well-known for its collaborative spirit, BF&D has been the recipient of numerous grants in support of its creative work during its past 14 years.

Barbara Feldman & Dancers   387-0774
Barbara Feldman, Director
P.O. Box 3060, New Haven 06515

Dancers In Concert, Inc.

Dancers In Concert, Inc. is a non-profit company organized in August 1992 and composed of nine women who range in age from 17-51. Led by artistic directors and choreographers, Sally Cohn and Susan McLain, the company has performed for the past three summers on Martha's Vineyard, winters in Hamden, New Haven, and most recently Skidmore College. They have, along with their own repertory, included historical pieces in their programs by choreographers Anna Sokolow, Mary Wigman, and Isadora Duncan.

Dancers In Concert, Inc.   624-4477
Sally Cohn and Susan McLain, Directors
100 Reservoir Street, Hamden

Mary Barnett/In Good Company

Mary Barnett/In Good Company is a professional dance/theater company and producing organization, established in 1989, with a two-fold mission: to further Barnett's sophisticated artistic vision while supporting and creating performance opportunities for other emerging and established artists from New York and New England. The Company's works have been produced by Jacob's Pillow, the New England Foundation for the Arts, ARTSPACE, Real Art Ways, the Avignon France Art Exchange, the Morningside Dance Festival, the Mulberry Street Theater, and The Field in NYC and Pearl Productions in Boston. Quarterly performances featuring a diverse pool of out-of-town guest artists are held at ECA on Audubon Street in New Haven. Mary Barnett/ In Good Company is available for touring engagements, & workshops.

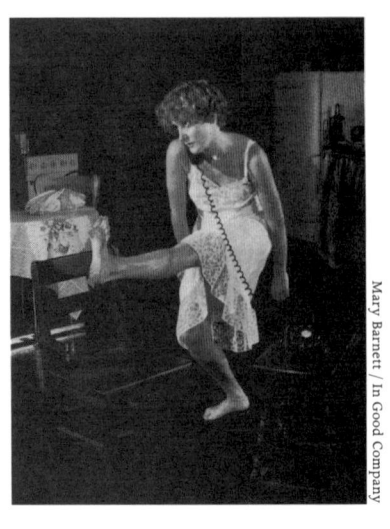

Mary Barnett / In Good Company

Mary Barnett/In Good Company   245-3090
Mary R. Barnett, Artistic Director
Laura Wiley, Managing Director
24 Wildwood Avenue, Madison

Contra dances in New Haven are held throughout the fall and winter at either St. Paul's Church, or the Arbeiter Maenner Chor, on the campus of the University of New Haven; dances are held, usually, on the first, third, and last Saturday of the month, from 8pm to 11pm. Beginner's session starts at 7:20pm. For more information, a complete schedule, or directions call: 776-1812.

New Haven Country Dancers   393-3464
Bill Fischer, Director
312 Litchfield Turnpike, Bethany

New Haven International Folk Dancing began at Yale over twenty years ago. Now it meets at the New Haven Medical Assn.,362 Whitney Avenue, on the second and fourth Friday of each month.

Enjoy a wide range of dances from around the world—sample the dances of Greece, Hungary, Macedonia, Israel, Bulgaria, Sweden, etc. Many of the dances are done in a circle or line, others are couple dances. Beginners and seasoned dancers alike will enjoy the variety and haunting beauty of the accompanying ethnic music.

New Haven Int'l Folk Dancing   248-1046
Marjorie Drucker, Contact
78 Elihu Street, Hamden 06517

ARTS GUIDE
Dance Schools & Societies

New Haven Ballet

New Haven Ballet has been providing quality dance education for both the serious and casual student since 1985. From its offices at 70 Audubon St., the New Haven Ballet conducts classes at ARTSPACE and ECA in the Audubon Street Arts district and at its extension studios in New Haven and Madison.

The school offers a comprehensive curriculum in classical ballet for ages 7 - 17 in addition to pre-ballet programs for ages 4-7 and adult classes for ages 18 and above.

The New Haven Ballet offers Afro -Modern and Jazz as well during the school year and additional dance forms during its Summer Dance Camp in July. Among the performing opportunities the ballet provides for its members are an annual Nutcracker, a year-end school performance, a full-length ballet such as Coppelia, and other collaborative projects with local artists.

Intermediate and advanced students are eligible for the New Haven Ballet Ensemble, the student performing company. Extension programs include the Neighborhood Scholarship Program for inner city children, and the Dance Program for Hopkins School and Choate Rosemary Hall.

The New Haven Ballet is staffed by Artistic Director Noble Barker, Managing Director Harriet Reilly, and the Madison Branch Director Allyson Barker as well as fully experienced and professional instructors and accompanists.

Office hours are Monday through Friday from 10am to 5pm, and Saturdays from 9am to 2pm.

New Haven Ballet	782-9038
Nobel Barker, Artistic Director	
70 Audubon Street	

Royal Scottish Country Dance Society, New Haven Branch

Scottish country dancing is a delightful and invigorating social experience for all ages. Jigs and reels and graceful strathspeys are danced to fiddle band or accordion music. Scottish dancing is similar to American contra and English country dancing, involving sets of several couples. There is no need to bring a partner, and new faces are always welcome. A class for all levels is held on Tuesday evenings at 7:30pm. Each Tuesday includes instruction and social dancing. There is an Intermediate/Advanced class on the 2nd and 4th Thursdays of the month (call to confirm). Demonstrations of Scottish Country Dancing are available upon request.

Royal Scottish Country Dance	777-4025
Mary Kate Adami-Sampson, Contact	
P.O. Box 8842, New Haven, 06532	

Starship Dance Theater

Starship Dance Theater, founded in 1988 by Joyce DiLauro, is a community-based dance theater dedicated to bringing dance to the Shoreline communities. The core of the Theater is its performing ensemble. This company of dancer/actors ranges in size from six to twelve, and ranges in age at present from 9 to 17. Performers rehearse weekly with Joyce DiLauro, choreographer and Kim Herard, dance teacher, and Megan Brown Geist, acting coach. Each September, Starship holds auditions, and the ensemble performs year round to audiences in varied spaces from school cafeterias to nursing homes.

Another focus of Starship is an annual springtime major performance. A cast of approximately 60-100 youngsters performs on a stage or in a community building for an audience primarily of children and young adults. The staff consists of parents and community volunteers.

Starship Dance Theater	457-0822
Joyce DiLauro, Director	
Route 80, Guilford	

ARTS GUIDE
Miscellaneous Arts Programs

Yale Summer Programs

Yale Summer Programs is a college-level summer school offering courses for Yale College credit. Among them are courses in art, including drawing, painting, and graphic design. There is a six-week writing program featuring courses in fiction, non-fiction, and a course in screenwriting and playwriting. This year there are also nine evening courses. Summer Program also sponsors a series of three lectures by famous writers, open to the New Haven public, free of charge. All classes are held in handicap-accessible facilities. For further information or a catalogue call 432-2430.

Yale Summer Programs	432-2430
Penelope Laurans, Director	FAX 432-2434
246 Church Street, Suite 101	

Center for Independent Study

The Center for Independent Study is a forum for intellectual and creative effort, providing mutual encouragement, advice, and criticism in order to support standards of professional excellence. CIS publishes a newsletter to facilitate networking and to provide useful information on such subjects as grants opportunities, conferences and calls for papers. The Center organizes study groups for people of particular interests to meet and discuss their work. CIS also sponsors conferences on subjects of interest to independent scholars, such as translation, biography, and photography. Members use the CIS affiliation to apply for grants and fellowships. About half of the members are in scholarly fields, and half are creative writers or artists. CIS offers local independent scholars a link to a nationwide network of similar organizations. A pioneer in the independent scholarship movement, CIS is now in its 17th year of offering an intellectual community to scholars and artists who work independently.

Center for Independent Study	562-7945
Diane Joy Charney, President	
Box 203193, New Haven, 06520	

Vital Elements Productions, Inc.

The Vital Elements are a group of people who are dedicated to the fine arts. Their goal is to help expose new and unknown talent. They have begun to explore the many aspects of the fine arts. The company was founded in June of 1976 by current president, Liston Filyaw (playwright and performer), Leroy Thomas, and Ronald Clarke. The Vital Elements are comprised of actors, dancers, singers, musicians, models, writers, and designers. There is a small nucleus of performers.

Workshops meet every week on Wednesday and Thursday evenings from 7pm to 10pm. They include Drama, Music (contemporary and gospel choral), Modeling, and Personal Growth Basics. The Vital Elements have worked, created, and learned together resulting in fashion shows, plays, and concerts. Sometimes the group blends all three elements in a Showcase. The company's pride is that half of our works are original plays, choreography, and designs. Weekly rehearsals/workshops are held at the Keefe Community Center, 11 Pine St. (corner of George St. & Dixwell Ave), Hamden.

Visual Elements Productions	782-0112
Liston N. Filyaw, Director	or 946-8592
P.O. Box 58, New Haven, 06501	FAX 946-8587

Ukrainian Heritage Center

The Ukrainian Heritage Center, founded in 1984, is a focus for the cultural heritage of St. Michael's Ukrainian Catholic Church parish. It is a superb resource for anyone with an interest in Eastern European art, design and history, and displays treasures from antique regional costumes to decorated Easter eggs. 3000 volumes in the Ukrainian and English library include works of noted authors and poets. A large photograph collection dates back to early 1900. The Center is open on Saturdays and Sundays from 9am to 1pm and by appointment.

Ukrainian Heritage Center	288-7637
Roman Hezzey, Director	
79 Blue Trail, Mt. Carmel, 06518	

ARTS GUIDE
More Museums & Galleries

Field Museum For Creating Visual Art

The Field Museum For Creating Visual Art was opened in May 1992 as a place "to preserve and promote our human ability to transform (abstract) natural life into ideas and ideals; to teach experience of abstract art as visualizing (imagining) means into meaning, thereby practicing (co-creating) the work of art as part of the work (and joy) of life, and (thereby) learning (that the) mind is the primary tool in making anything." The museum is open to the public from 1 to 5pm Saturdays and Sundays.
Field Museum for Creating Visual Art, 140 Water Street, Guilford, Phone: 453-5750 Robert Bryden, Director.

Paul Mellon Arts Center

Set on the campus of Choate Rosemary Hall, the PMAC sponsors an annual series of student and guest artist performances. All events are open to the public, and a subscription is available for reduced ticket prices. Programs include theater, dance, mime, and all forms of music. An art gallery features new exhibits approximately every six weeks. Open daily from 10am to 10pm. Box office is open week days from 10 to 11:30am and 12:30pm to 4:30pm and one hour prior to performances.
Paul Mellon Arts Center, PO Box 788, Wallingford, 06492 Ph: 697-2398 FAX: 697-2396, Terrence Ortwein, Director.

Inner Space Gallery at Erector Square

The Inner Space was established in 1991 as a not for profit gallery in the Erector Square Management Office to exhibit works by artists who lease studio space at the Erector Square Complex.

Shows vary month to month and include drawings, paintings, prints, photography and sculpture.
Inner Space Gallery, 315 Peck Street, Building #24, Phone: 865-5055, Joan P. Appicelli, Director.

Gallery 12

Gallery 12 is a cooperative gallery of local artists dedicated to producing fine contemporary crafts. The gallery gives us control over the way in which our work is sold, and also allows us more interaction with customers; new member interviews are held every two months. Hours are Tuesday - Saturday 10am to 5:30pm, Sunday noon to 5pm.
Gallery 12, 29 Whitfield Street, Guilford, 06437, Phone: 458-1196 Wendy Lewis, Director.

Bohemia

Bohemia carries a unique selection of handcrafted gifts, featuring some of Connecticut's most talented artisans, plus an extensive selection of clothing, accessories and gifts from around the globe. Monthly exhibits feature paintings, drawings, graphics, photography, mixed media, and sculpture. Art openings consist of entertainment, poetry readings, and refreshments. Call or visit to be included on the mailing list. If you are an artist, handcrafter, poet, or musician, we would be interested in meeting with you. Please call for an appointment. Store hours are Monday through Friday 11am to 6pm, and Saturdays 11am to 5pm.
Bohemia, 992 State Street, Phone: 624-2409, Denise Logan, Kathryn Evans & Cara Malovolti.

North Haven Art Guild

The North Haven Art Guild, organized in 1966, maintains its art studio-- Studio 27 Gallery -- which holds monthly non-profit exhibitions to promote the arts and community enjoyment of them, including a high school art show, Women in the Arts, and a spring show of members work, Black Art Month, and a Xmas arts and crafts show are annual events.
Studio 27 Gallery, 27 Broadway, North Haven, 06473, Phone: 239-0048, Mary Lou Fiore, Director.

York Square Cinema Gallery

The York Square Cinema Gallery is an independently curated and funded exhibition space in the lobby of York Sq., located on Broadway. The art exhibition space functions as a forum for innovative and avant-garde painting, photography, and mixed-media artwork, showing a wide range of local and regional artists. Since 1988, it has been curated by Johnes Ruta, art activist and writer.
York Square Cinema Gallery, 22 Willard Street, Phone: 387-4933, J. Ruta, Director.

Art Haven West

Art Haven West, a father/daughter owned and managed studio facility, was renovated in 1988 above the old Peck Bindery. AHW specializes in deluxe but affordable workspaces for visual and performing artists and art-related businesses. All spaces are secure, handicapped-accessible, and open 24 hours. Free parking. Spaces shown by appt.

Art Haven West, 14 Gilbert Street, West Haven, 06516, Phone: 932-1220, Karen Andrews, Director.

Educational Center for the Arts

ECA is a part-time, regional public high school program for students who are talented in the literary, performing, and visual arts. ECA actively seeks students with potential or demonstrated talent from a diversity of cultural backgrounds, experiences and interests in the arts. Students are selected through a competitive audition/interview process and receive credit at their local high school for work completed at ECA. 99% of our graduates go on to further study of the arts in either university or arts training programs.

The ECA faculty is comprised of practicing, professional artists who work with students in collegiate level courses or projects designed to achieve a balance between the development of technical skills and the development of the imagination and critical skills. The Arts Hall, The Little Theatre and rehearsal studios are available for rent to the arts community for rehearsal and performances.

Educational Center for the Arts, 55 Audubon, Phone: 777-5451, FAX: 495-7111, Robert D. Parker, Director.

Dancers In Concert, Incorporated

Dancers In Concert, Inc. is a non-profit company organized in August 1992 and composed of nine women who range in age from 17 to 51.

Led by artistic directors and choreographers, Sally Cohn and Susan McLain, the company has performed for the past three summers on Martha's Vineyard, winters in Hamden, New Haven, and most recently Skidmore College. They have, along with their own repertory, included historical pieces in their programs by choreographers Anna Sokolow, Mary Wigman, and Isadora Duncan.

Dancers In Concert, Inc., 100 Reservoir St., Hamden, 06517, Phone: 624-4477, Sally Cohn & Susan McLain, Directors.

"The Morris Dancers", Wood cut, c.1730s

Music and Movement Center

Music and Movement Center offers music classes for parents and children, ages 1 to 5, called *Music and Me*. It is a ten-week semester, 45-minute weekly class. They work with a large variety of instruments and move to music using scarves and parachutes. They are playful, mindful of the children taking small steps in their musicality and social integration. There are fall, winter, spring, and summer sessions in the communities of Milford, Hamden, North Branford, and Wallingford on weekdays and also on Saturdays.

Music and Movement Center also offers singing, chanting, and drumming classes for adults, Mondays and Thursdays, 7:30pm to 9pm. No musical experience required.

Groups are limited to twelve people. Participants are led in simple exercises of toning, singing, rhythm, and ensemble work.

Music and Movement Center, 415 Central Avenue, Phone: 387-8390, Marcia Nelken, Director.

ARTS GUIDE
Arts Commissions & Councils

West Haven Council of the Arts

The West Haven Council of the Arts was organized in 1974 to expand and enrich cultural and artistic activities in West Haven. The Council promotes art exhibits and demonstrations, circulating art collections, drama, poetry, music, and activities like the annual Halloween Haunted House. It has sponsored special events such as photography exhibits, lectures, filmfests, art lessons, band concerts, and choral sings.

In June, 1995, the Council is sponsoring the *Twenty-First Annual West Haven Cultural Arts and Crafts Show* on the West Haven Green, which will attract exhibitors from throughout New England.

In June, 1987, the West Haven Council of the Arts dedicated its new John C. Ireland Bandstand on the Green in West Haven.

West Haven Council of the Arts, P.O. Box 17594, West Haven, 06516, Phone: 937-3669, Gloria V. Freland, Director.

Hamden Arts Commission

The Hamden Arts Commission develops and presents a wide variety of culturally diverse programs, and also serves as the information center for community arts activities.

Annual events include Hamden's popular Saturday Afternoon Family Entertainment Series that offers quality, affordable programs for parents and children to share.

Connecticut arts agencies have recognized the Hamden series as "one of Connecticut's great success stories." The Salute to Young Artists gives recognition to high school students from Hamden who have shown outstanding talent in the arts. The free bimonthly "Hamden Arts Calendar" publicizes arts and cultural activities in Hamden. The office is open daily, 8:30am-4:30pm.

Hamden Arts Commission, 2901 Dixwell Ave., Hamden, 06518; Phone: 287-2546, Barbara Stickle, Director.

Prospect Arts Association

Prospect Arts Association (PAA) is a non-profit Town of Prospect organization. The group was formulated to help enrich the community with artistic and cultural activities and has adopted the following objectives:

1. To further interest in arts and humanities in the Prospect community and surrounding area.

2. To promote fellowship and exchange of ideas among active artists, craftpersons, and patrons throughout Connecticut.

3. To encourage appreciation of all forms of art and cultural humanities by means of educational programs, exhibits, workshops, lectures, musical and theatrical productions.

All proceeds from membership and fundraisers will benefit future programming and scholarships for local high school students.

Prospect Arts Association, 14 Brighton Road, Prospect, 06712; Phone: 758-5141, Stefany Coviello, President.

Shoreline Alliance for the Arts, Inc.

The Shoreline Alliance for the Arts was founded in 1980 to stimulate and promote the artistic and cultural climate in the shoreline region. In collaboration with the Guilford, Parks and Recreation Department, the Alliance presents July Sunday Concerts on the Green, including a special children's program.

All facilities used for any of the above activities have access for the handicapped. In addition, the Alliance acts as a service organization with a great deal of networking for individuals and other community and arts organizations.

Under the Umbrella, the newsletter published three times a year, has a page devoted to the activities of over 20 affiliate member arts organizations as well as an arts calendar.

Shoreline Alliance for the Arts, POB 1430, Guilford, 06437, Ph: 453-3890, FAX: 458-2753 Ann B. Christensen, Director.

Guilford Art League

The Guilford Art League was founded by a group of artists in 1947 to promote and stimulate interest in the visual arts, and to learn and benefit from association with one another. Artists living within 25 miles of Guilford are eligible for membership after being accepted in two Guilford Art League juried shows. The annual juried show is held in April. In addition, Guilford Art League members are eligible to show their work on the Green during the Guilford Handcraft Center Annual Expo.

Guilford Art League, 31 Rockledge Drive, Madison, 06443, Phone: 245-4397, Henry Ferris, Director.

The Guilford Handcraft Center

In 1962, The Guilford Handcraft Center was founded as an organization dedicated to the preservation of The American Craft Heritage. They have continued that commitment and expanded our goals to include education in and appreciation for contemporary crafts and fine arts. Both adults and children may discover or further develop their aesthetic potential through classes in painting, drawing, pottery, sculpture, jewelry, basketry, weaving, glasswork and metal-smithing. Scholarships are available. Ten free exhibits annually in the Mill Gallery and the Loft Gallery feature both nationally renowned and emerging artists. The gift shop celebrates the traditional origins and contemporary innovations of American Craft.

Guilford Handcraft Center, 411 Church Street, Guilford, 06437, Ph: 453-5947, FAX: 453-6237, F. Hubbard, Director.

Kaleidos Art

Kaleidos Art is a multi-cultural arts organization founded by Jamaican-born artist Victor Smith of New Haven. Kaleidos Art's goals are: 1) To provide a support group for artists who find themselves out of mainstream arts arenas on the local level; 2) to provide artists of color and others with an open forum to share styles and techniques and to help provide some direction; 3) to provide public awareness and/or education concerning individual and ethnic art styles; and 4) to provide galleries, schools, etc., with ongoing sources of artistic styles encompassing all backgrounds to promote universal art appreciation.

Kaleidos Art, 168 Frank Street, Phone: 787-9632, FAX: 787-6509, Stewart Kelley, Director.

New Haven Paint & Clay Club, Inc.

The New Haven Paint and Clay Club is one of the oldest art associations in the country, founded in 1900. Active members may enter two works in the annual juried spring show, which draws entries from artists all over New England and New York. The New Haven Paint and Clay Club also sponsors an annual active members' exhibit and special programs, as well as administering the Elizabeth L. Greeley Scholarship fund for high school students.

New Haven Paint & Clay Club, 75 Washington Ave., Hamden, 06518, Phone: 288-7677, James Parsons, President.

Meet the Artists and Artisans

Meet the Artists and Artisans was established by Denise Morris-Curt in 1962 to provide a showcase for visual artists on public property, so that they may discuss, display and demonstrate their creative endeavors. Painters, sculptors, carvers, photographers, have been discovered by the public and many museum directors attend these shows. Graphic artists in 1993 were chosen by the Metropolitan Museum and Smithsonian at the Milford Green show in May.

Meet the Artists and Artisans, 41 Green Street, Milford 06460, Phone: 874-5672, Denise Morris-Curt, Director.

New Haven Camera Club

The New Haven Camera Club is an active group sponsoring programs and activities designed to meet the needs of both beginners and advanced amateur photographers. Members have a wide range of interests, encompassing virtually all aspects of photography: color slides, both black and white and color prints, nature, portraits, contemporary techniques, etc.

Along with its scheduled meetings, the NHCC also conducts small workshops and field trips, both day and weekend trips, throughout the year. These offer members the chance to socialize, have fun, and sharpen their photographic skills.

The NHCC meets on the second and fourth Monday of each month, September through May.

New Haven Camera Club, 75 Washington Ave., Hamden 06518, Phone: 288-7677, James Parsons, President.

ARTS GUIDE
Arts Organizations

Calligraphers' Guild of New Haven

The Calligraphers' Guild of New Haven is devoted to increasing knowledge and appreciation of fine lettering.

Founded in 1987, the Guild includes professional calligraphers, graphic designers, teachers, sign-makers and artists. Program meetings are held on the third Monday of the month (7:30-9:30pm, Sept. - May) at the John Slade Ely House, 51 Trumbull Street, New Haven. Topics range from demonstrations of lettering to lectures on the book arts and modern type design, and meetings are free and open to the public.

The Guild also sponsors occasional one and two-day workshops. Each June the members mount an exhibit of their work at the Ely House. This non-juried show gives the community an opportunity to see a wide variety of lettering both of a fine art and a commercial nature.

The Guild also serves as a resource pool, providing speakers and teachers to local schools and non-profit organizations. Group projects are undertaken regularly, such as a book, *The Voice of the Pen*, and an annual calendar.

***Calligraphers' Guild of New Haven**, P.O. Box 2099, Short Beach, 06405, Phone: 488-8836, Pamela LaRegina, President.*

City Spirit Artists, Inc.

City Spirit Artists, Inc. is a non-profit organization committed to bringing the arts to people who have less access to them owing to socio-economic or physical limitations, and to expanding economic opportunities for artists. City Spirit Artists was founded in 1976 as part of a bicentennial project of the National Endowment for the Arts. Incorporated in 1979 and a recipient of the prestigious Connecticut Commission on the Arts Award in 1984, City Spirit Artists continues to be a vital and responsive community resource with growing support from private and public funding sources. CSA designs, develops, and coordinates Artists-in-Residence programs serving the elderly, incarcerated, mentally and physically handicapped, teens at risk, homeless, socio-economically disadvantaged, and other special populations.

***City Spirit Artists**, 850 Grand Ave., Phone: 773-1777, Virginia W. Eicher, Director.*

Media Arts Center

The Media Arts Center is a not-for-profit video production/electronic graphics facility providing artists, independent producers, and non-profit organizations with professional video and graphics services and equipment at below-market rates. In March 1995, MAC began a new era with Educational Center for the Arts, meeting the future head-on as the marriage of video and computers revolutionizes creative possibilities.

They also offer a wide range of affordable courses and workshops covering all aspects of our resources. The Media Arts Center is generally open from 10am to 5pm weekdays.

***Media Arts Center**, 70 Audubon Street, Phone: 782-3675, FAX: 495-7111, Jim Gehrer, Facilities Manager.*

The Arts Council of Greater New Haven
Annual Arts Awards Winners

RECIPIENTS OF THE ARTS COUNCIL ARTS AWARDS

Ann Lehman	Brian Alden
Jane Willoughby	Deborah Weaver
Elizabeth Kubler	Elizabeth Greeley
Robert Leeney	Afro-American Cultural Center at Yale
The Connecticut Savings Bank	Erector Square Gallery
Daniel Kops, Sr.	Amy Seham
Long Wharf Theatre	Armtek Corporation
Hilda Levy	James Patania
Connecticut Ballet Company	Roz Schwartz
Angela Bowen	Larry Ferrell
Renaissance Theater Company	Neighborhood Music School
Chamber Orchestra of New England	Janet Saleh Dickson
Murry Sidlin	Arvin Brown
Creative Arts Workshop	First Constitution Bank
Mary Hunter Wolf	Sherry Knight
Paul Rutkovsky	Polly Lada-Mocarski
Laetitia Pierson	Ruth Lapides
Lloyd Richards	Cheever Tyler
Mary Boyle	Shared Programming - So. CT Library
Ann Cowlin	Bill Brown
Anne Mauro	Jeff Burnett & Nikila Cole
Ruth Resnick	Bob Gregson
So. New England Telephone	Ann Langdon
Jack Smith	United Illuminating
Artists Working in New Haven	Bill Brown
The Bank of New Haven	Bill Derry
Dwight Andrews	Mary Kordak
Conte Arts Magnet School	Humanities Touring Group
Educational Center for the Arts	Chapel Square Mall/Rouse Corp.
C. Newton Schenck, III	Colleen Coleman
Janice Forman	Robert Parker
Norman Harrower	Herbert Pearce
Carol Penney	Edgar Rosenblum
Peter Kimmerlin	

History

New Haven History

Introduction

This short history of New Haven starts with the Native American Indians who had been living here for many hundreds of years, and ends in 1995 when this book went to press. It tries to highlight interesting people, places, and events.

A great deal of the material is based on previous histories written by Rollin G. Osterweis, Floyd M. Shumway, Richard Hegel, Mark Minnenberg and Doris B. Townshend. Their books present in-depth coverage of New Haven's fascinating history.

Additional materials and illustrations were taken from other books listed in the bibliography.

Explanation of Population Icons

At the top of each right hand page there are two icons, shown below. The first one indicates the population of the City of New Haven; the second one refers to the population of Greater New Haven, including the City of New Haven. Yale students were not included in the population figures before 1950.

City of New Haven

Greater New Haven Communities
(including New Haven)

Where the Connecticut Indians Lived

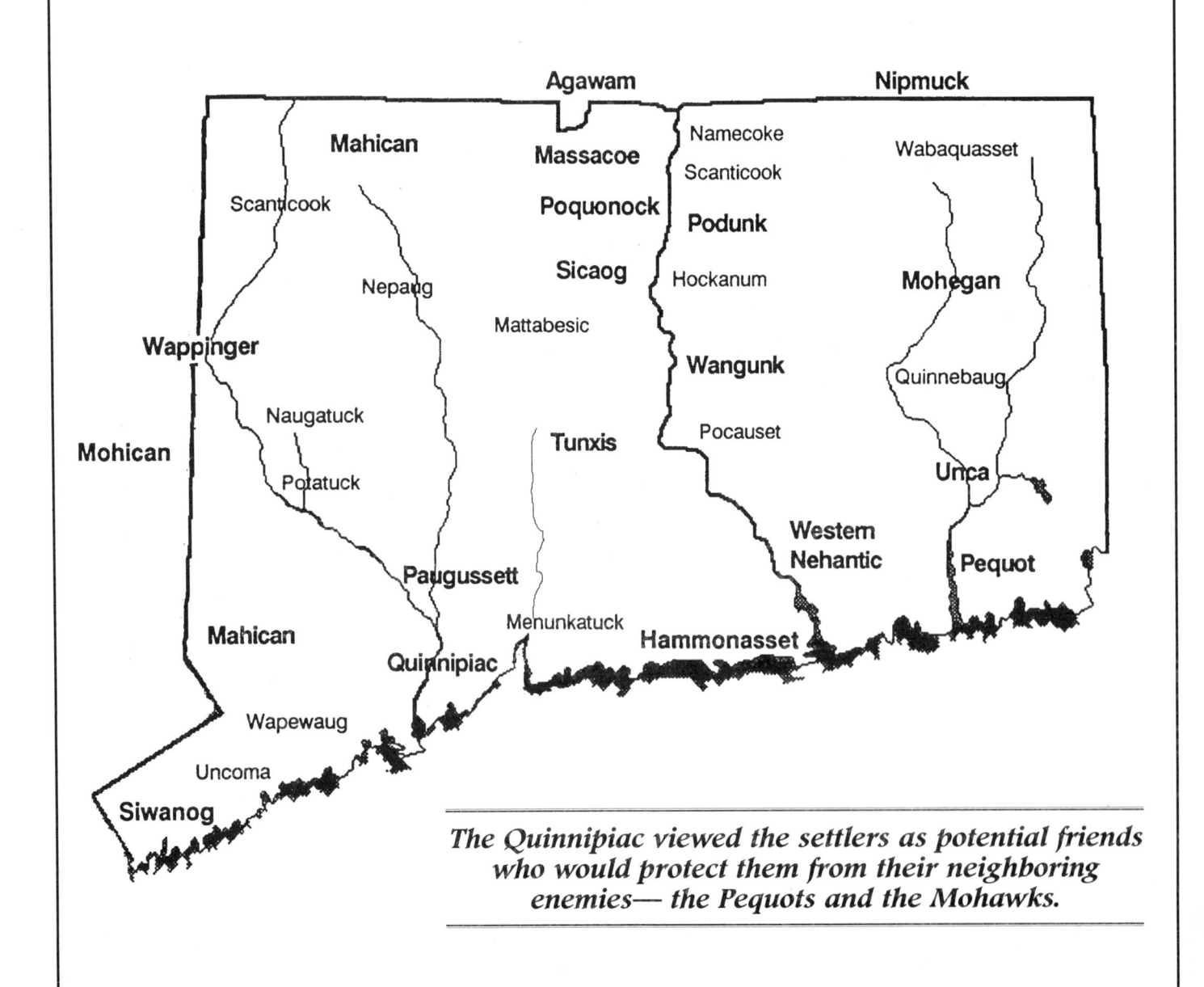

Agawam, Nipmuck, Mahican, Namecoke, Wabaquasset, Scanticook, Massacoe, Scanticook, Poquonock, Podunk, Nepaug, Sicaog, Hockanum, Mohegan, Mattabesic, Wappinger, Wangunk, Quinnebaug, Naugatuck, Pocauset, Tunxis, Mohican, Potatuck, Unca, Western Nehantic, Paugussett, Pequot, Menunkatuck, Mahican, Hammonasset, Quinipiac, Wapewaug, Uncoma, Siwanog

The Quinnipiac viewed the settlers as potential friends who would protect them from their neighboring enemies— the Pequots and the Mohawks.

98

NEW HAVEN HISTORY ~ 1638
Native Americans & Explorers

Population: 🐾 fewer than 100 Indians 🗺 fewer than 200 Indians

When the settlers arrived at New Haven in 1638, they were not the first people to visit or live here. The first residents of New Haven and the surrounding area were Native Americans, whom Columbus misnamed Indians, who had been here for many hundreds of years.

New Haven and the lands extending east to Madison belonged to the Quinnipiak (or Quinnipiac) Indians, who were lead by Momauguin. Lands to the North belonged to a small tribe lead by Montowese. These small tribes lived in fear of the large fierce tribe living to the north, called the Pequots, and the Mohawks who lived further west. The Pequot Indians around New Haven viewed the new English settlers as potential friends who would protect them from their enemies. From these two Indian chiefs, the lands now called New Haven, East Haven, Branford, North Branford, North Haven, Wallingford, Cheshire and parts of Orange, Woodbridge, Bethany, Prospect and Meriden were purchased.

The local Indians were broad-faced plain people with a tawny, almost reddish skin. Both sexes dressed in soft hides and leather moccasins that allowed them to travel quietly. They grew maize, which was the staple of their diet. They also hunted and fished. Lobsters were so plentiful in Long Island Sound that the Indians used them to fertilize their corn.

The Indians moved onto about 1,200 acres of land near what is now Morris Cove and East Haven. They lived there for over 40 years, peacefully selling their land piece by piece. Eventually, they all moved away or died.

In 1614, Adrian Block, a Dutch sea captain employed by the Dutch East India Company, was the first to record significant details about a visit to New Haven aboard his 49 foot ship *Onrust*. He called what he found "Roudeberg" from the "Red Palisades", and stayed several weeks while making a chart of the area. It is interesting to note that he came from New York, an already well-established settlement, on a ship he and his crew bought after their previous vessel caught fire off New York.

Soldiers from Massachusetts had been coming to Connecticut for several years in the early 1600s to explore and fight the Pequot Indians. In 1637, Captain Israel Stoughton visited the mouth of what is now called the Quinnipiac River. He reported back to Theophilus Eaton, a businessman in Boston who had recently arrived from England, that he thought it was an excellent place to establish a colony. In the fall of 1637, an advance party of seven men arrived in New Haven from Boston. They lived in New Haven during the winter. One died and the remaining six greeted John Davenport and his 500 followers when they arrived in New Haven in the spring of 1638.

An Indian Chief, c. 1620s

Important Dates

Pre~1638	New Haven was inhabited by several small Indian tribes.
1614	Adrian Block was the first European to record details of a visit to the area.
1637	Seven advance settlers arrived in New Haven from Boston.
1638	John Davenport and 500 followers arrived in the spring.

Brockett Map of 1641

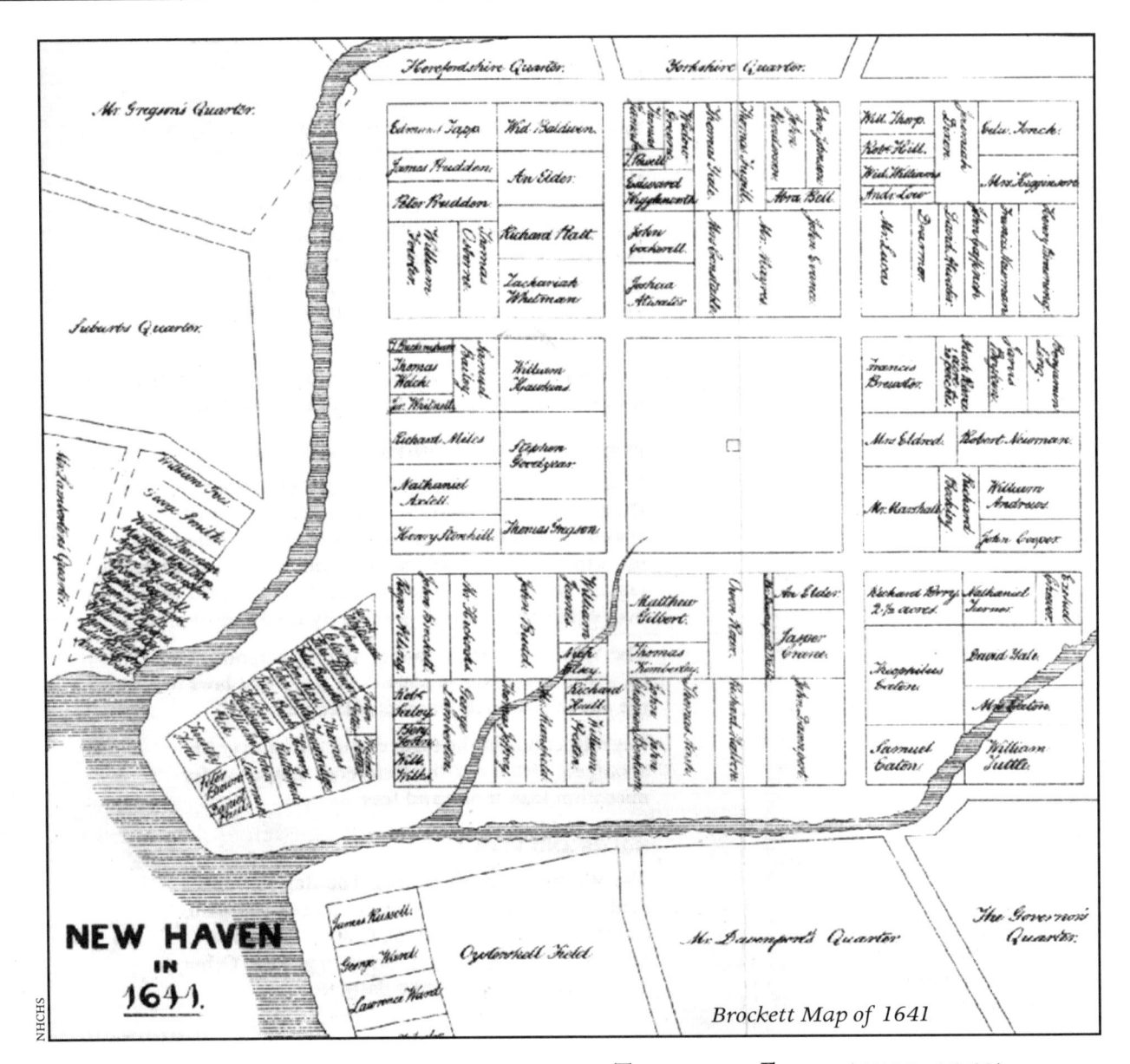

JOHN DAVENPORT (1597~1670)

Became a London Puritan minister in 1624 and found himself in disagreement with the Church of England. He arrived in Massachusetts in 1637 with his wealthy friend Theophilus Eaton, and their group of followers. They wanted a colony of their own with a good harbor. Davenport and Eaton arrived in New Haven (then called Quinnipiak), purchased land from the Indians, and formed their own government based on the Bible. They drew up the "Six Fundamental Orders," and seven men were elected as Founders of the new church-state form of government.

THEOPHILUS EATON (1590-1658)

His father baptized John Davenport in Coventry, England, and he was Davenport's childhood playmate. Deputy Governor of Eastland Company, the commercial agent of James I to Denmark and the agent of Christian IV of Denmark in London. Original patentee of Massachusetts Bay Company. A man of wealth, and a Puritan. Governor of Connecticut around 1645.

Theophilus Eaton's House in New Haven

NEW HAVEN HISTORY 1638 ~ 1660
First Settlers at New Haven

Population: about 500 settlers ♦ about 500 settlers and 200 Indians

The settlement of New Haven in 1638 was led by John Davenport, who was the Vicar of St. Stephens in London. In 1633, William Laud was appointed Archbishop of Canterbury by King Charles I. He accused Davenport, who was a Puritan, of being a threat to the Church of England. Davenport fled to the Netherlands for safety. John Cotton, a friend of Davenport, who loved his life in Boston, urged him to come live there.

Davenport returned to England for a short period of time and organized a group of Puritans with the help of Theophilus Eaton, a wealthy merchant friend and zealous Puritan. They arrived in Boston in June 1637. At first, they planned to settle near Boston, but after some consideration decided that they wanted to be on their own.

They had heard glowing reports about a harbor at the mouth of the Quinnipiak River. They joined a group from Hertfordshire, England, led by the Reverend Peter Prudden. The two groups consisted of about 500 well-to-do people with ample supplies. They sailed from Massachusetts Bay on March 30, 1638 and arrived in New Haven on April 24. The group sought two things: religious freedom and wealth. To secure title to the land, they paid the local Indians "...twelve coats of English trucking cloath, twelve alcumy spoons, twelve hatchetts, twelve hoes, two dozen of knives." What really made the Indians sell the land was the promise of protection from their Indian enemies.

Even the first crude buildings were nicely designed. Within a few years, they were replaced with substantial buildings built with materials imported from England. Theophilus Eaton's house was very large, and Davenport's house was even larger, with thirteen fireplaces and many apartments. These were rich people who brought ample cash with them and were able to buy whatever they needed.

Life and power centered around the Church. Only Church members could vote. The first Meeting House was 2,500 square feet in size, and was completed in 1640 at a cost of £500.

In 1640, the Quinnipiak settlement was renamed New Haven. By this time, a complete government was organized controlled by the "Seven Pillars of the Church." It included a magistrate and four deputies, a General Court, and a legislative and judicial assembly. By 1641, the population had increased 60% to almost 1,000 people.

In 1646, a "Great Shippe" laden with local provisions worth £5,000 set sail for Europe. Its loss was devastating both economically and personally to the people of New Haven. It shattered New Haven's hopes of becoming an international trading port.

The first meeting house was completed in 1640.

Important Dates

1638	On April 24, John Davenport and about 500 settlers arrived at Quinnipiak (New Haven) to form a permanent settlement.
1640	Name of Quinnipiak changed to New Haven.

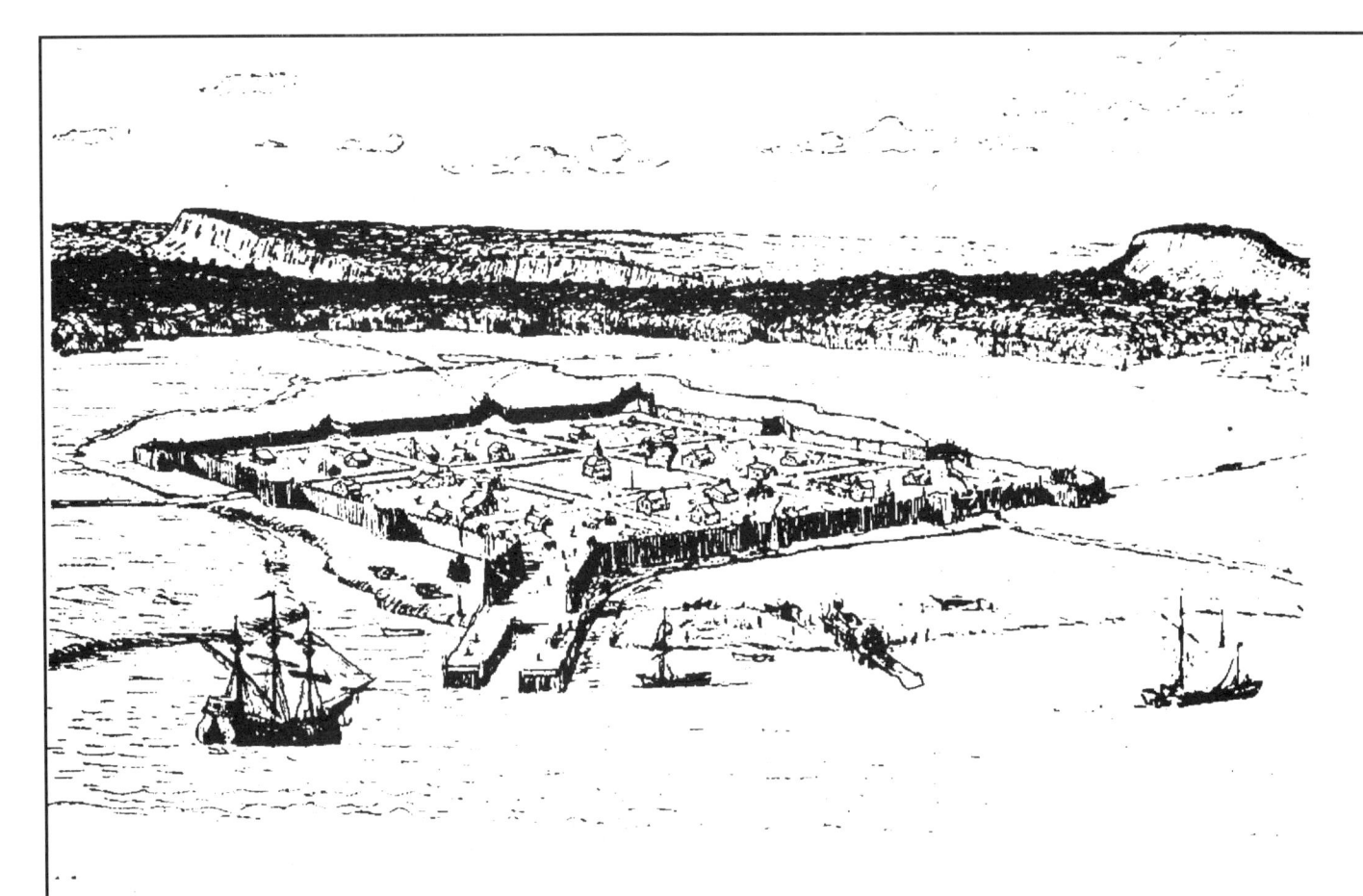

How New Haven looked in 1689 when fortified against attack during King Philip's War.
From Charles Hervey Townshend, *The Quinnipiack Indians*, New Haven, 1900.

The Regicides

King Charles I of England was the reason the Puritans and others left England in the early 1600s. In 1649, he was dethroned, convicted of treason, and beheaded. Eleven years later, his son Charles II became King.

Connecticut wanted to pledge its loyalty to the King and sent John Winthrop to England with their petition of loyalty. The King responded with the Charter of 1662 which established Connecticut as a separate government from Massachusetts.

Charles II sought vengence for his father's death. Fifty-nine men had signed his father's death warrant. He executed ten of them and imprisoned nineteen others for life.

Judges' Cave on West Rock

Colonel Edward Whalley and his son-in-law Colonel William Goffe were officers in the Cromwellian army and members of the High Court of Justice which had tried and convicted Charles I. They fled from England to Boston when Charles II became King.

They lived in Boston until Charles' other officers arrived with warrants for their arrest. They left in 1661 and moved into Davenport's spacious house in New Haven. The king's men followed in hot pursuit *(drawing at left)*. Davenport hid the Regicides ("king killers") in a cave on the top of West Rock. They were joined by John Dixwell, another Regicide, and for nearly three years they stayed in hiding with Micah Tompkins in Milford.

In 1664, they were vigorously hunted and they again they hid, this time in Judges' Cave on West Rock *(photo above)*. They were never caught by King Charles II's men.

Dixwell Avenue, Whalley Avenue, and Goffe Street are named after the three Regicides.

NEW HAVEN HISTORY 1661 ~ 1689
Regicides & Hopkins

Population: ~700 ~900

By the middle of the 1660s, the local economy had switched from trading to farming, with a small iron mining operation near Branford. The Puritan religious control was very strict. On the Sabbath (Sunday), labor, travel, cooking, bed-making, shaving and even kissing your children were prohibited.

In England, however, Puritanism had collapsed and Charles II was King. New Haven's status as an independent colony was in jeopardy. In 1661, Edward Whalley and William Goffe, judges who had signed the death warrant of King Charles I, came to New Haven to hide from the English soldiers searching for them.

One of the institutions that had deteriorated was the school system. It was revived in 1660 with the starting of a Grammar School soon to be funded with money from the estate of Edwards Hopkins, a wealthy merchant who was governor of Connecticut between 1640 and 1654. It became Hopkins Grammar School.

In 1665, New Haven became part of Connecticut Colony. Joining Connecticut had the advantage for New Haven of greater political stability. It also made available the hinterlands to provide products for export.

In 1667, New Haven sponsored the village of Wallingford and, as was the custom, then managed it until 1672 when it was big enough to be allowed by the State to establish its own government. At about the same time Milford started Derby the same way.

John Davenport was completely distraught by the forced union of the independent New Haven Colony and the Connecticut Colony. In 1667, he left New Haven to become the minister of Boston's First Church. Davenport's departure put New Haven's Puritan Church into a state of collapse. It took 20 years to hire Reverend James Pierpont as his replacement.

In 1673, about 85 families left New Haven together to settle in New Jersey, where they hoped to better preserve their old ways of Puritanism. The Utopia that Davenport and Eaton had envisioned had failed to materialize.

Old Hopkins Building, corner of High and Wall Streets in New Haven.

In many ways New Haven had become a sleepy town with few major problems. King Philip's War, between the settlers of Massachusetts, Rhode Island and Connecticut, and the Indians, changed this. By 1675, the settlers, especially in Massachusetts, were pushing their way into Indian territory.

When his father died, King Philip (whose Indian name was Metacom) became chief. He organized the Indian tribes to resist the settlers' expansion. The war consisted of many raids on the settlements of the Colonies. These resulted in counter raids by the Colonial militia. It was a fierce war and dozens of towns were devastated.

New Haven lived in constant fear of being raided by the Indians. They decided to surround the town with a large wall called a palisade, fortified the meeting house and re-established the night watch. The people were so worried about being invaded that the men brought their arms with them to Sunday worship services. Over 600 settlers were killed (one-sixth of the total male population of New England). Finally the settlers destroyed the Indians' crops and wore the Indians out, thus ending the conflict. The Indians were no longer able to stand in the way of the New England settlers' expansion into their lands.

Important Dates

1660	Hopkins Grammar School founded.
1661	Regicides came to New Haven to hide from King Charles II.
1665	New Haven became part of the Connecticut Colony.

The New Haven Green

The history of the New Haven Green dates back to 1638 when the first settlers landed. Before they started to build, they carefully planned the layout of their new city. The basic layout consisted of nine squares surrounding a central green of publicly owned land. Technically, the Green is owned and controlled by a self-perpetuating group first called "The Free Planters," then "The Committee of Proprietors of the Common and Undivided Lands in New Haven," and today by "The Proprietors." Their title to this land is very strong, as it predates both the Connecticut and U.S. Constitutions. It is probably one of the few pieces of land in the country that cannot be taken by condemnation for public use. However, this has never actually been tested in the courts.

The Green has been used to graze cattle, to train soldiers, and as a burial ground. It has also been the site of a meeting house, the state capital building, a grammar school, court house, prison, and various other buildings.

The only buildings that remain are the three churches, all of which were built between 1812 and 1815. They all face Temple Street, which runs through the center of the Green, between Elm and Chapel Streets. The other two sides are bounded by Church and College Streets. The Green is about 17 acres in size.

Trinity Church (Episcopal) is on the corner of Chapel and Temple Streets. It was designed by Ithiel Town and is a good example of Gothic Revival Style.

The United Church (Congregational) is on the corner of Elm and Temple Streets. It was designed by David Hoadley and is Federal Style.

Between these two churches is the Center Church. It has a crypt in its basements containing some of the graves that were removed from other parts of the Green. It is Georgian Style and was designed by Asher Benjamin and Ithiel Town.

Two other structures on the Green are the World War I Memorial Flag Pole, designed by Douglas Orr in 1928, and Bennett Drinking Fountain, in a plaza on the corner of Chapel and Church Streets. It was designed by John Ferguson Weir in 1907.

In 1987, Alfred W. Van Sinderen, who had recently retired as President of Southern New England Telephone, organized The Foundation for the New Haven Green, Inc. This group raised over $4,000,000 and completely restored the Green. The Foundation repaved the streets and walks, planted new grass and trees, installed new lighting, rebuilt Bennett Plaza and the fountain, and restored the granite and iron fence that encloses the entire Green. The Foundation also relocated and replaced the transportation waiting areas, and established an endowment for perpetual care of the Green.

William Giles Mason's representation of the New Haven Green in 1800.

NEW HAVEN HISTORY 1690 ~ 1749
Co~Capital / Yale Founded

Population (1724): 1000   1300

In 1690, New Haven had become a small community containing about 150 houses built around the Green. By this time clapboard had become the most popular building material for houses. There was a fortified wall surrounding the whole town to provide protection from the Indians and the French. There was still only one church with the Rev. James Pierpont as minister. The harbor had several docks. The dream of being an international port with direct trade with Europe had ended. The few ships in the harbor were engaged only in coastal trade, mostly with Boston, New York and Philadelphia.

Long Island Sound was still full of fish, oysters, clams and lobsters. Farming was becoming more important in the area.

After King Philip's War, things settled back to normal. By the turn of the century, many changes were taking place in the political machinery. In 1701, the first Justices of the Peace were elected. That same year, the Superior Court was established.

In 1701, the legislature decided to make New Haven the co-capital of Connecticut along with Hartford. The legislature met twice a year, in May in Hartford and in October in New Haven. At this time, New Haven did not have a capital building, so the lower branch of the legislature met in the meeting house and the upper house in Mr. Miles' tavern, which was located at what is now the corner of Chapel and College Streets. A state house was built in 1719.

England and France were at war almost continuously from 1690 to 1763. Fortunately for New Haven, it was never invaded. Men and money were sent to Massachusetts and New York to help them defend themselves from the French.

England thought the best way to secure the help it needed from New Haven and other settlements in Connecticut was to put the militia under the control of New York's Governor Fletcher. After much wrangling, Connecticut was able to keep control of its militia. They did agree to send 120 men to serve under Governor Fletcher during the wars.

Oystering in New Haven

New Haven has a rich and varied history, and oystering has been a central part of it since people first came to the shores of the harbor.

The Quinnipiac Indians were among the earliest of those who gathered oysters for food. When Europeans settled here in the 1600s, they soon realized that oysters were plentiful, tasty, and easy to obtain. Today, in spite of the poor environmental quality of the water, oysters are still cultivated and harvested for market, although not in the same quantities as in the past.

New Haven Harbor is ideal for oysters because of its shallow water, clear bottom, and the mixture of fresh water from the Quinnipiac and Mill Rivers with the salt water of Long Island Sound. These estuary waters are perfect for oysters to spawn (lay eggs).

The tiny oyster larvae are free-swimming for their first few weeks, before they drop to the bottom and seek a hard surface to which to attach and begin growing a shell. At this stage, the young oysters, called "spat" or "set," can never again move about.

By the mid-1800s, the natural oyster beds were nearly depleted, and people began cultivating oysters by laying clean shells on the harbor bottom to create better beds for young oyster to set. Mature adult oysters were spread over these oyster beds during the spawning season, and the resulting larvae would set on the beds.

Today, only one oyster company, Tallmadge Bros., works the New Haven Harbor beds. These oysters, after growing to market size, must be transported to cleaner waters for several weeks before they are pure enough for consumption. Once in clean water, an oyster will filter pollutants that have been collecting in its body.

The "sharpie", a sailboat specifically for gathering oysters, was invented in the mid-1800s in New Haven.

Important Dates

1701	New Haven co-capital with Hartford.	1718	Collegiate School moved to New Haven.
1701	First justices of the peace were elected.	1718	Collegiate School renamed Yale College.
1700	Collegiate School founded.	1727	Great Earthquake on Ocober 27.
1701	Collegiate School chartered in Saybrook.		

The First Postal System

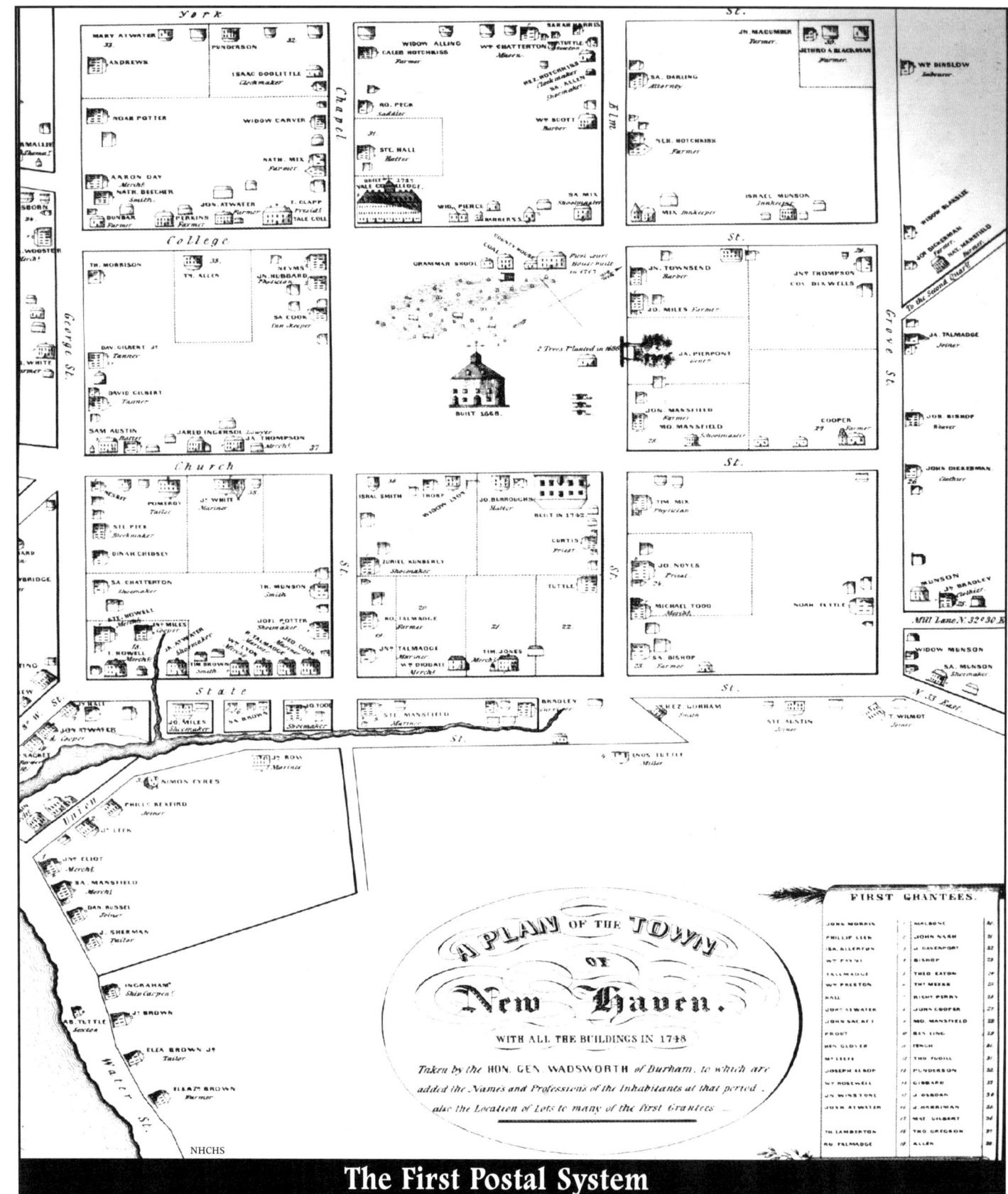

An informal postal system connecting New Haven with the communities between Boston and New York started almost immediately after New Haven was settled. Travelers would take mail and small packages for others either as a favor or for pay.

In 1672, the first official postal system was established between New York and Boston (a distance by land of 300 miles). The post rider left New York on the first of each month and from Boston on the fifteenth. On a good day, the riders covered 30 to 40 miles. Therefore, you could send a letter anywhere between Boston and New York and receive a reply in 30 days.

NEW HAVEN HISTORY 1750 ~ 1773
Puritans Lose Control

Population: 1,500 6,000

Substantial changes were taking place in New Haven. In the 1740s, a religious revival, the Great Awakening, challenged the old Puritan religious leadership. Many citizens, inspired by English Evangelist George Whitfield and his American colleague, Jonathan Edwards, broke away from the First Church to form their own congregation, Center Church. Others joined the Church of England and formed Trinity Church (Episcopal). By 1760, the total control of New Haven by the Puritans had come to an end.

During the Seven Year War (1765-1763), New Haven's militia fought in the Lake George area of New York and in Canada. New Haven sailors also served in the Caribbean.

Roger Sherman, a wealthy, well-known merchant moved from New Jersey to New Haven. He obtained the contract as the commissary officer for all the Connecticut Colonial forces. This again made New Haven Harbor an important transportation center.

During the winters of 1757 and 1758, British troops were housed in Milford (at Milford's expense).

This was a period of rapid growth for New Haven. New wharves were built, a post office was constructed and in 1755, Connecticut's first weekly newspaper, the *Connecticut Gazette*, was founded.

In 1765, Jared Ingersoll became the English stamp Act collector in New Haven. He met bitter opposition. New Haven became a leader in the opposition to the Stamp Act, which was repealed in 1776 only to be followed by even harsher taxes.

View of New Haven from 1786 woodcut used as the masthead for the New Haven Chronicle.

Important Dates

1754	Post Office built.
1755	Connecticut's first weekly newspaper the *Connecticut Gazette* was founded.
1756	Seven Year War began.
1763	Stamp Act repealed.
1766	Treaty of Paris provided for the expulsion of the French from North America.

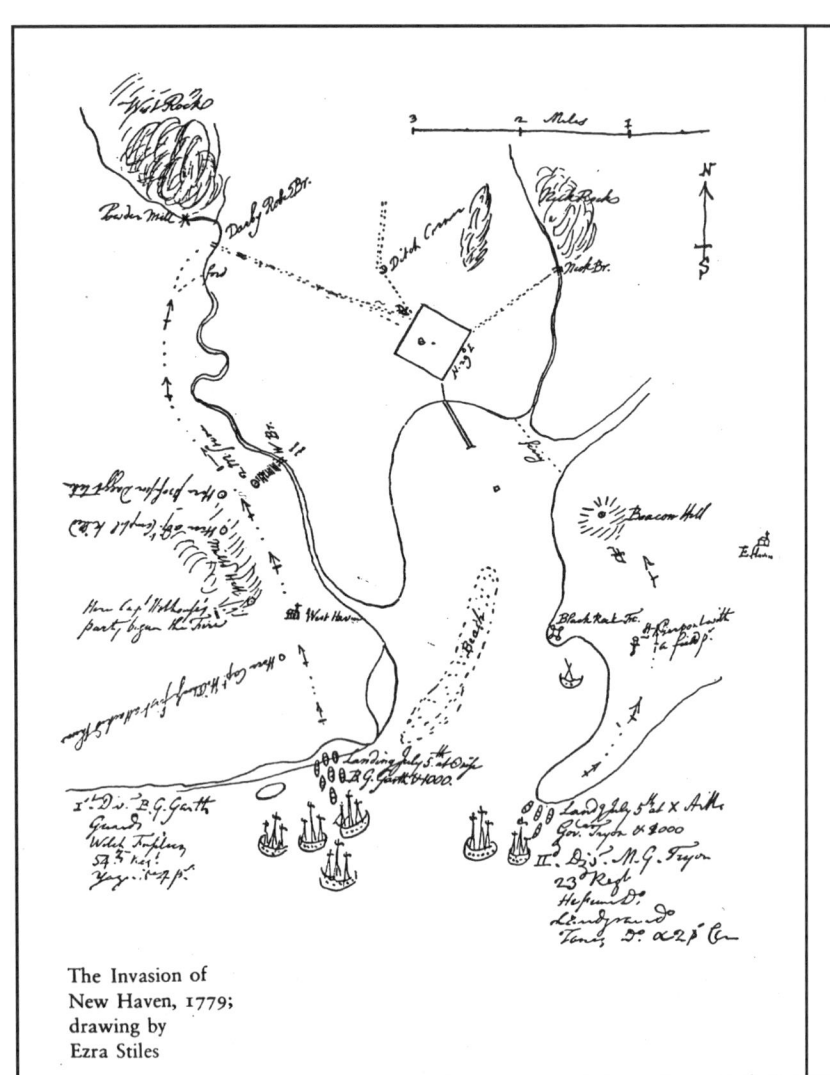

The Invasion of New Haven, 1779; drawing by Ezra Stiles

Roger Sherman (1721-1793)

Merchant. Served as Commissary for colony forces; brought New Haven Harbor to new life as transportation center. At the Constitutional Convention in Philadelphia, offered the "Connecticut Compromise," which resulted in our two-chamber legislature with representation based on population in the House of Representatives and equal representation for each state in the Senate. First mayor of New Haven. Only man to sign all four basic documents of American government: the Articles of Association, Declaration of Independence, Articles of Confederation and the United States Constitution.

General David Wooster

His expertise in the Seven Year War led to his appointment as Major General in the Connecticut Militia during the Revolutionary War. He was one of the "New Lights in Politics and Religion" with Roger Sherman, Benedict Arnold, James Hillhouse and Samuel Bishop. Killed in 1777 in the Battle of Ridgefield.

Benedict Arnold (1741-1801)

One of New Haven's most active West Indies merchants. On April 22, 1775, marched north with 50 members of New Haven's Footguards 2nd Company. Hero of the Battle of Saratoga. In 1780, was accused of attempting to betray West Point as a spy.

Nathan Hale (1755-1776)

"I only regret that I have but one life to lose for my country."

Graduate of Yale College, 1773. Classmate of James Hillhouse. Served as Captain during the American Revolution. Captured and hanged by the British. Known as the Martyr-Spy of the American Revolution.

NEW HAVEN HISTORY 1774 ~ 1783
War Heroes & Traitors

Population (1774): 8000　9200

New Havener Hezekiah Sabin, Jr. petitioned the Connecticut legislature in 1775 for permission to form the "Second Company of the Governor's Guards." Permission was granted and the Foot Guard Company was formed with Captain Benedict Arnold in charge.

On April 21, 1775, two days after the Battle of Lexington and Concord, Massachusetts, where the British troops landed, a town meeting was held in New Haven to decide what to do to aid the patriots. Roger Sherman was elected chairman, but in spite of his strong feelings that aid should be sent, he could not get enough votes to authorize the sending of troops.

Benedict Arnold took things into his own hands and together with about fifty members of the Foot Guard company marched north to join the fight against the British. Before leaving, he went to the New Haven Selectmen and, through his lieutenant, demanded the keys to the powder house which contained the supplies and ammunition that he needed. The Selectmen gave him the keys. The Company was said to have the best uniforms and best equipment of any American Foot Guard Company. This event is reenacted annually on the New Haven Green on Powder House Day.

George Washington visited New Haven on July 2, 1775, on his way to Boston to take command of the new American Army. Accompanied by three officers, he stayed overnight in Beers' Tavern and left the following morning. Many people gathered to bid Washington "godspeed," and three New Haven militia companies escorted him to the highway with much fanfare.

Roger Sherman was one of the drafters and an original signer of the Declaration of Independence.

Benedict Arnold, New Haven's first war hero, rose to the rank of Major General after leading several important battles until he was injured. The leg he lost at the Battle of Saratoga was the only part of him buried with honor. After attempting to turn West Point over to the Redcoats, he turned traitor and became a British officer. He then participated in the attack on New London in 1781. He died in London after the War, a tragic figure.

Nathan Hale, a young Yale graduate, became Connecticut's most cherished war hero. He became an American spy, playing the part of a Dutch schoolmaster. He was just 21 when he was caught and hanged by the British. His immortal last words were, "I only regret that I have but one life to lose for my country."

Major General David Wooster went to Yale and married the daughter of Yale President Thomas Clap. He was killed leading the Connecticut militia from New Haven in pursuit of the British who had just sacked Danbury. Wooster Street and Wooster Square Park, built in 1824, are named in his honor.

The British invaded New Haven on July 5, 1779. They arrived in a fleet of 48 ships with over 3,000 soldiers. They made a two-pronged attack with landings on the east shore of the harbor and Savin Rock on the west shore. Captain James Hillhouse and Colonel Hezekiah Stabin, Jr. led the weak opposition. The British did a lot of drinking on the West Haven green and near Fort Hale park, and then in New Haven where they found large stores of rum. This gave many New Haveners time to pack their belongings and leave town before the British arrived.

The British stayed in New Haven only one day. They did not burn New Haven as they did Norwalk and Fairfield soon afterwards, probably because of resistance forming in the outskirts. Another possibility is that a deal was made to let them leave without a fight. Just 27 Americans and nine Redcoats died in the invasion.

When Cornwallis surrendered at Yorktown on October 17, 1781, the war was effectively over. There were big celebrations in New Haven and each of the surrounding communities.

Important Dates

1775	On April 22, Benedict Arnold and 50 New Haveners demanded and received keys to the powder house, took arms and marched to Massachusetts to fight the British.
1775	George Washington visited New Haven on July 2.
1779	British invaded New Haven with over 3,000 men on July 5.

Eli Whitney

In 1792, Eli Whitney invented the cotton gin, which had a major impact on Southern cotton and the Yankee mills that made cloth from the cotton. Like many great inventions, once the idea was figured out it seemed very simple to copy. Eli Whitney's cotton gin design was stolen and people made unauthorized copies. In spite of patents, he made very little money from the invention. His own cotton gin factory was destroyed by fire in 1795.

In 1798, Eli Whitney had his second great idea. Musket production at that time was under 1,000 per year. Muskets were being made by skilled craftsmen, one at a time.

Whitney convinced the new federal government to give him a contract for 10,000 muskets to be produced in two years. He designed power (water) driven machines for turning metal into guns. Since these machines made *parts* rather than whole guns, he actually invented the concept of removable, interchangeable parts. It took him over 10 years to produce the 10,000 guns, because it took longer to make the machines than he had anticipated. The Whitney factory was run by relatives for almost 100 years before it was sold to the Winchester Arms Company, which went on to become New Haven's largest industrial employer.

Whitney's Cotton Gin

"Olde New Haeven"

Trinity Episcopal Church, First Congregational Church ("Center Church"), and United Congregational Church

"Olde New Haeven" by Tony Falcone depicts the Green in his "imaginistic" style: realistic renderings combining elements of the past and the present to produce a timeless image."

NEW HAVEN HISTORY 1784 ~ 1824
Eli Whitney & James Brewster

Population (1784, size of town reduced): 3,500 15,000

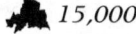

The end of the Revolutionary War was the beginning of the transformation of small sleepy New Haven, dependent upon shipping, agriculture and a small University, into an important eastern industrial city.

On the Hamden boarder was Eli Whitney's gun factory, which was a small city in itself: in addition to the industrial buildings, it had a school and houses for its workers and their families.

John Cook started a carriage shop in 1794, which was small but quite successful. The most successful carriage factory in the United States was operated by James Brewster near Wooster Square. He is credited with the invention of the assembly line, where there was a separate position in the factory for each operation performed in the construction of a carriage.

Brewster started manufacturing carriages in New Haven in 1810. He was the first northern manufacturer in the United States to send a panelled carriage to the South. Among his many notable customers were Presidents Andrew Jackson and Martin Van Buren.

JAMES BREWSTER (1788~1866)

Leading New Haven industrialist. Opened his famous carriage factory—the first of its kind in the country—on Wooster Street. Made carriages for Presidents and other prominent men of the time.

Established 1846.
SAMUEL K. PAGE, SUCCESSOR TO HENRY HALE & CO.,
Carriage Manufacturer.

Rockaways, Cabriolets, Victorias, Visa-Vis, Four and Six Seat Rockaways, Broughams, Coupes, Coaches, Coupelets, Landaulets and Landaus.

60 and 62 Franklin Street, New Haven, Conn.

ESTABLISHED 1859.

M. ARMSTRONG & CO.,
Manufacturers of
FINE CARRIAGES.
SPECIALTIES:
Landaus, Coaches, Coupes, Broughams, Victorias and Hansom Cabs.

MANUFACTORY AND REPOSITORY.
433 Chapel Street, - New Haven, Conn.

Important Dates

1784	Connecticut granted New Haven, North Haven, Hamden and Woodbridge charters with borders. Roger Sherman was elected first mayor of New Haven.
1798	Eli Whitney began manufacturing firearms in Whitneyville plant.
1809	Fort Hale was built near Black Rock Fort to protect New Haven from the British.
1814	Despite the British blockade of New Haven, all three churches on the Green were completed within a two year period.
1815	First steamboat, the *Fulton*, came to New Haven from New York City.

Mendi Warrior Cinqué (above)
Amistad Monument next to City Hall (left)

The Amistad

About 50 African Mendi Warriors, together with their young handsome chief Cinqué, had been captured in Africa by Spanish slave traders. They were taken to Cuba and sold. Their two Cuban plantation owners were in the process of moving them on the Spanish schooner *Amistad* from one Cuban location to another.

The Mendi mutinied, killed the captain and cook, and allowed the crew to flee. They were trying to make the Cubans sail them back to Africa, but the Cubans tricked them by changing course during the night. Eventually they ended up off Montauk Point at the end of Long Island. Here they were intercepted and captured by a United States Coastal Patrol boat. The boat was taken to New London and then moved to New Haven in September 1839, because New Haven had a United States District Court. The Mendi were charged with murder and piracy.

The Mendi were imprisoned in the county jail, located on Church Street. This attracted a great deal of attention from the antislavery movement, and did much to transform the Northern impression of black slaves to that of Africans who had been taken from their native land and forced into a life of merciless captivity.

One of the problems faced by the court was the fact that the Mendi did not speak a language that anyone understood, so it was impossible to get their version of what happened.

Yale professor Josiah Willard Gibbs, a talented linguist, was hired to solve the problem. He went from ship to ship in New Haven and New York looking for someone who understood the Mendi language. He finally located a young man from Sierre Leone who acted as the translator.

The case attracted national attention, especially in New York, and a large defense team was organized which included John Quincy Adams as an advisor.

It took three years for the courts to rule that the Mendi had been kidnapped into slavery in violation of Spanish law and that they were free-born Africans. The Courts ordered them to be taken back to Africa rather than to Cuba, where the plantation owners claimed they should be forced to go.

New Haven and the Railroad

Joseph Sheffield, a prominent New Haven banker, bought controlling stock of the Farmington Canal and, in 1844, before he laid a single track, formed the New York-New Haven Railroad.

The canal had failed for a variety of reasons, including the fact that it leaked. Sheffield emptied out the water and laid track for his trains. Then, he laid 69 miles of track between New York and New Haven. On December 27, 1848, the first trip between these two cities by rail was completed. A typical trip took three and a half hours.

Sheffield moved on to Chicago where he made millions developing that area's railroads. He returned to New Haven and endowed the Sheffield Scientific School, which later merged with Yale.

NEW HAVEN HISTORY 1825 ~ 1859
Prosperity & Expansion

Population (1830): 10,018   20,000

New Haven enjoyed a period of substantial growth in the 35 years prior to the Civil War. It was sparked by the success of Eli Whitney in the mass production of guns, a golden age of shipping and the fast-growing carriage manufacturing business.

The Amistad affair brought the remote anti-slavery issue closer to home. There was a significant wave of immigration and the population quadrupled during this period. By 1860, there were 4,500 houses in New Haven, 30 churches and one synagogue. It was also common for women to work in the factories.

In 1834, Charles Goodyear invented a process for vulcanizing rubber. This was the beginning of the modern tire and rubber goods industry. "India Rubber," commonly used at the time, had the disadvantages of becoming soft and sticky when warm, and hard and brittle when cold. It was also easily torn and punctured. Goodyear's vulcanization process eliminated these problems. Goodyear patented his process and licensed it to Leverett Candee, who started a manufacturing company with over 1,000 employees.

In 1825, most machinery was driven by water power. By 1860, steam had become the major power source in most of the large factories. The New Haven Gas Company started to provide service in 1848. By 1859, there were many gas street lights and 1,500 New Haven homes had gas lights.

In 1855, Benjamin Silliman, Jr.'s Pennsylvania "rock oil" experiments, commissioned by a group of New Haven oil entrepreneurs, led directly to the first great oil boom.

In 1858, Eli Whitney Blake (Eli Whitney's nephew) was on a committee in charge of building a two mile road from New Haven's center to Westville. The biggest problem facing road and railroad builders at this time was obtaining a sufficient supply of crushed rocks, which had to be crushed by hand with sledge hammers. Blake devised a rock crushing machine which had a significant impact on improving transportation nationally. That, in turn, led to the faster development of the suburban communities.

CHARLES GOODYEAR (1800~1860)
Developed vulcanization process for manufacture of rubber boots and shoes. Process was first used by Leverett Candee, a Connecticut native and Goodyear's first patent licensee.

ELI WHITNEY BLAKE (1795~1886)
Invented the stone crusher and sledge hammer around 1858, which made road building much easier. Stimulated business by making the transportation of goods and materials better and less expensive. Established the country's first domestic hardware factory which made locks and bedstead castors.

Eli Whitney Blake's Rock Crusher

Important Dates

1828	Noah Webster completed *The American Dictionary*.
1839	Railroad opened between New Haven and Meriden.
1840	Railroad from New Haven reached Hartford.
1845	Henry Austin designed the Egyptian-style gates to the Grove Street Cemetery.
1846	First gas lights.
1851	New Haven to New York railroad completed. Trip took a little over three hours.

City Hall 1863

NEW HAVEN HISTORY 1860 ~ 1865
The Civil War

Population (1860): 35,535 55,400

In March of 1860, Abraham Lincoln came to New Haven while he was campaigning for the Republican nomination for President of the United States. It is reported that he drew a huge crowd when he spoke at Union Hall, which was located on the corner of Chapel and Union Streets.

The city's elm trees had reached their peak and many streets were completely covered with a canopy of elm branches. New Haven was called the "Elm City." A variety of problems beset the elm trees and today only the name and a few old elm trees remain.

The Civil War started in 1861. It resulted in many New Haven men being enlisted or drafted. Several thousand New Haven soldiers and sailors were seriously wounded; 420 were killed. This was about one percent of the population of 40,000 men, women and children.

Captain Edwin S. Hitchcock and his Seventh Regiment were the first Union troops to invade South Carolina in 1861. Hitchcock was later killed in the battle of James Island. Brigadier General Alfred Howe Terry and Rear Admiral Andrew Hull Foote were well-known local war heroes.

New Haven was a major supplier of war materials throughout the Civil War. As a result it grew by 10,000 people during this short period of time.

Civil War soldiers assemble on the Green near the corner of Church and Chapel Streets.

Important Dates

1860	Abraham Lincoln visited in March to campaign for Republican presidential nomination.
1861	Two horse-drawn railroads began operation from Westville and Fair Haven to downtown New Haven.
1861	The New Haven Water Company started pumping water from Lake Whitney.
1862	First sewer system started with sewerage flowing untreated into the rivers leading to Long Island Sound.
1862	Joseph B. Sargent moved his hardware company from New Britain to New Haven. It rapidly grew into one of New Haven's major industries.
1863	The New Haven City Hall, designed by Henry Austin, was completed.

Above:
State House on New Haven Green, 1855. Handcolored wood engraving by William Roberts.

Above:
The New Haven Yacht Club's boathouse was located in the area that is today's Waterside Park. It was at the end of a long dock near Tomlinson Bridge.

Right:
The first telephone directory published by the predecessor to today's Southern New England Telephone Company.

LIST OF SUBSCRIBERS.
New Haven District Telephone Company.

OFFICE 219 CHAPEL STREET.

February 21, 1878.

Residences.	Stores, Factories, &c.
Rev. JOHN E. TODD.	O. A. DORMAN.
J. B. CARRINGTON.	STONE & CHIDSEY.
H. B. BIGELOW.	NEW HAVEN FLOUR CO. State St.
C. W. SCRANTON.	" " " " Cong. ave.
GEORGE W. COY.	" " " " Grand St.
G. L. FERRIS.	" " " " Fair Haven.
H. P. FROST.	ENGLISH & MERSICK.
M. F. TYLER.	NEW HAVEN FOLDING CHAIR CO.
I. H. BROMLEY.	H. HOOKER & CO.
GEO. E. THOMPSON.	W. A. ENSIGN & SON.
WALTER LEWIS.	H. B. BIGELOW & CO.
	C. COWLES & CO.
Physicians.	C. S. MERSICK & CO.
Dr. E. L. R. THOMPSON.	SPENCER & MATTHEWS.
Dr. A. E. WINCHELL.	PAUL ROESSLER.
Dr. C. S. THOMSON, Fair Haven.	E. S. WHEELER & CO.
	ROLLING MILL CO.
Dentists.	APOTHECARIES HALL.
Dr. E. S. GAYLORD.	E. A. GESSNER.
Dr. R. F. BURWELL.	AMERICAN TEA CO.
Miscellaneous.	*Meat & Fish Markets.*
REGISTER PUBLISHING CO.	W. H. HITCHINGS, City Market.
POLICE OFFICE.	GEO. E. LUM, " "
POST OFFICE.	A. FOOTE & CO.
MERCANTILE CLUB.	STRONG, HART & CO.
QUINNIPIAC CLUB.	
F. V. McDONALD, Yale News.	*Hack and Boarding Stables.*
SMEDLEY BROS. & CO.	CRUTTENDEN & CARTER.
M. F. TYLER, Law Chambers.	BARKER & RANSOM.

Office open from 6 A. M. to 2 A. M.
After March 1st, this Office will be open all night.

NEW HAVEN HISTORY 1866 ~ 1885
Post Civil War New Haven

Population (1870): 50,840   68,051

After rapid growth and economic expansion during the Civil War, there was a national depression, which began in 1873 and lasted almost 10 years. New Haven did not suffer as much as many other parts of the country because of its strong diversified manufacturing and good transportation, which included direct connections to New York and Boston. This was followed by another long period of economic expansion.

In 1872, J. Pierpont Morgan, a Hartford native, national financier and wheeler-dealer, purchased the New York & New Haven railroad line and combined it with the New Haven & Hartford railroad line to form the New York, New Haven and Hartford Railroad. Eventually, Morgan purchased over 300 railroads, trolley lines and steamship companies serving the region, and amassed a vast financial empire.

Until 1881, when a single time zone was created, New Haven, New York, Boston and Hartford each operated on different times, making railroad scheduling difficult.

Yale University emerged during this period as a major economic factor in the city. Between 1870 and 1900, Yale's student population increased from about 800 to almost 3,000 students.

Though hurt by the loss of Southern business during the Civil War, the carriage building industry had a strong comeback in the late 1880s. New Haven's James Brewster was the country's best-known carriage maker. By the turn of the century, carriage-building was made nearly obsolete by the emerging automobile industry.

In 1888, Eli Whitney III rented the Whitney Armory to the Winchester Arms Company, where they began making .22 caliber rifles. The John M. Marlin gun factory was established in 1870.

The H. B. Ives Company, founded in 1876, made mortise bolts. Today it makes a variety of hardware.

Alexander Graham Bell demonstrated the telephone in New Haven on April 27, 1877. By January 15, 1878 George W. Coy, the telegraph office manager, had organized the country's first telephone company by stringing wire between eight subscribers. They were connected through the world's first telephone switchboard. By February 1887, there were 50 subscribers and the first telephone directory was published. By April 1878, 200 homes and businesses had phone service. By 1900, the company served 20,000 customers.

The Bigelow Company was founded in 1861. It moved to River and Lloyd Streets in 1870, where it is still in business today, making large steel boilers. Another company still in business at its original location is the A.W. Flint Ladder Company on Chapel Street, which was started in 1880.

The Henry C. Thompson Company, which manufactured industrial saw blades, was founded in 1876 in Branford.

The world's first telephone switchboard, made by George W. Coy.

Important Dates

1873	New Haven ceased being the co-capital of Connecticut.
1874	The new county courthouse was opened.
1878	On January 15, George W. Coy started the first telephone company, today's SNET.
1881	The New Haven Yacht Club was founded.
1882	Knights of Columbus founded on February 2.

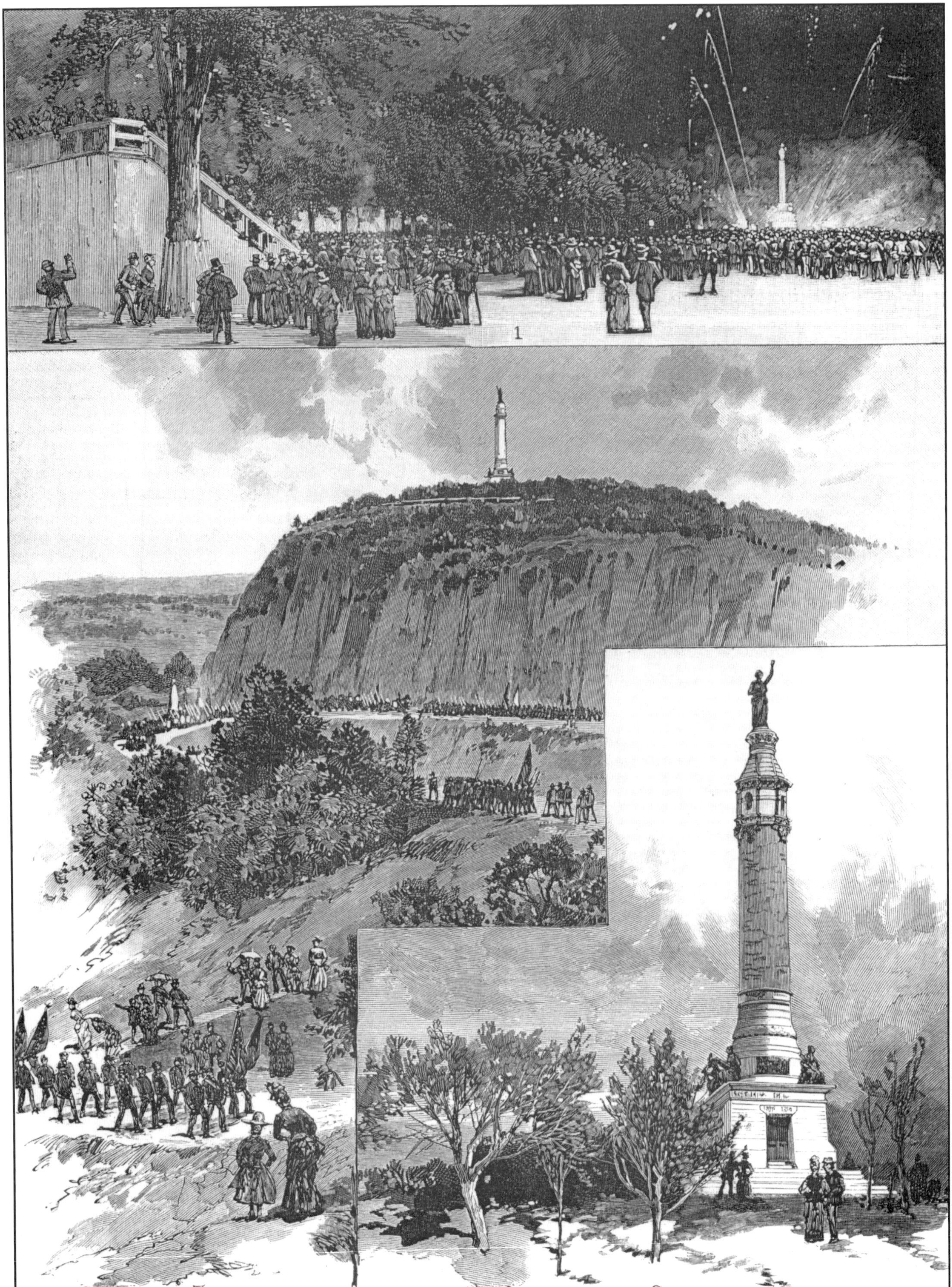

Author's collection

NEW HAVEN HISTORY 1886 ~ 1899
Industry and Shipping

Population (1890): 86,045   102,075

Shipping again became important, and in 1887 the harbor was dredged to a depth of 20 feet at mean low tide. The new channel is still used today. The eastern breakwater was completed in 1888. New Haven and West Haven both had a thriving ship-building industry.

By 1890, New Haven was clearly established as an industrial city. Electricity was beginning to replace steam as the primary source of industrial power. It had also become a hub for rail and maritime trade. Street cars were numerous, connecting every area to the downtown, built around the Green, and extending to the harbor.

The harbor had been dredged and the breakwaters were completed, permitting deep draft boats to load and unload safely. The oyster industry had reached its peak, with oystering operations at both City Point and Fair Haven.

This period began the decline of the beautiful elm trees which gave New Haven its "Elm City" name. First they were attacked by canker worms, then elm leaf beetles and, in 1893, a major storm destroyed many of them. The final blow was Dutch Elm disease.

Southern Connecticut State University was started on Howe Street in 1896 as a normal school for the training of teachers.

By 1890, there were over 250 factories in the Greater New Haven area. Many of the laborers were immigrants. By 1900, 28 percent of the New Haven population was foreign-born. The tide of foreign immigration continued until it was cut off by World War I. It was replaced by an influx of people from the South and other parts of the country who came to work in local factories booming with war material orders.

The largest factory in greater New Haven was the Winchester Repeating Arms Company, located in Newhallville. Other arms makers were Marlin Fire Arms, Strong Fire Arms, and Whitney Fire Arms Company. At the turn of the century, there were still about 35 carriage companies and a dozen hardware manufacturers. Sargent & Company was the largest.

Facing Page:
June 17, 1887
Dedication of the 110' Soldiers' and Sailors' Monument on East Rock as depicted in sketches by Charles Graham, reproduced in the June 25, 1887 edition of Harper's Weekly. *(1) Display of Fireworks. (2) The Monument. (3) The Procession ascending East Rock.*

Right:
Union Station at the corner of Chapel and Union Streets.

Important Dates

1887	Present harbor created by dredging to a depth of 20 feet at mean low tide.
1888	**The first of the three breakwaters was constructed in New Haven Harbor.**
1889	Historic state capital, designed by Ithiel Town and located on the Green, was razed.
1893	Electricity was used for street lights and to run trolley cars.
1898	Spanish American War began. It ended in 1900.
1899	Cornelius T. Driscoll elected first Irish mayor of New Haven.

New Haven First...

New Haven has been the home of an incredible number of inventions, innovations and "firsts" which have had tremendous impact on the way people live. The scientific, artistic, educational, technical, and commercial ingenuity of New Haveners is unparalleled by any community of comparable size.

These people and their inventions have changed the world in ways both big and small and, in doing so, have done much to make **New Haven First and Foremost.**

Agricultural Experimental Station
•••••
University-affiliated art gallery
Yale University Art Gallery
•••••
Automatic Fire Sprinkler System
•••••
Automobile self-starter
John Petrie, 1900
•••••
Chemotherapy for Cancer
•••••
Clinical use of Penicillin
•••••
Daily college newspaper
Yale Daily News
•••••
Complete dinosaur
•••••
Corkscrew - Philos Blake, 1850
•••••
Electric elevator
•••••
Erector set - A.C. Gilbert
•••••
Fine Arts school as part of university
•••••
First assembly line
James Brewster's
Wooster Square Carriage Factory
•••••
Forestry School
•••••
Hamburger - Louie's Lunch

Power Woodcarving Machine
HEZEKIAH AUGUR (1791~1858)
Invented the wood carving machine which he patented in 1840. This made economical, elaborately-carved furniture available to the general public.

Stone Crusher
ELI WHITNEY BLAKE (1795~1886)
Invented the mechanical stone crusher and mechanical sledge hammer in 1858, making road building easier, and stimulating business by making the transportation of goods and materials better and less expensive.

Revolver
SAMUEL COLT (1814~1862)
In 1836, he invented the first revolver. It was manufactured by the Eli Whitney Armory in Whitneyville.

Telephone Switchboard & Directory
GEORGE W. COY
In 1878, while the local manager of Franklin Telegraph Company, he strung wires between 8 locations and developed the first telephone switchboard. His company was absorbed by the Connecticut District Telephone Company, organized by Morris F. Tyler; it later became the Southern New England Telephone Company.

First Corset Factory
ISAAC STROUSE
Just before the outbreak of the Civil War, he began to make sewed corsets. Prior to that time, corsets were woven abroad. In 1862, he associated with Max Adler and four years later they formed the Strouse-Adler Company.

Lattice Truss Bridge
ITHIEL TOWN (1784~1844)
Engineer and architect best known for design of the "Town Bridge," a covered wood bridge over the Mill River near the Eli Whitney Gun Factory. It was based structurally on a lattice truss, which supported a longer span than conventional bridges. He patented this design which became the standard for bridges in the U.S. and Europe for the next 70 years. Also designed the Trinity Church, one of the first Gothic Revival structures in America. In 1828, he designed the Third Congregational Church. His own home, a Greek Revival mansion, was at the foot of Hillhouse Avenue.

Football
WALTER CAMP (1859~1925)
Football's founder at Yale. He was Yale player and coach from 1876 to 1910. He revolutionized what had been a game comprised of rugby and soccer, and is known as the "Father of Modern Football." His inventions included the forward pass, the series of downs, the scrimmage line, the quarterback position, and the All-American team. The Walter Camp Foundation Dinner, a gala event held in New Haven every February, brings to New Haven football's college and professional all-stars for a charity basketball game and formal dinner. Camp's name graces the Walter Camp Gateway outside the Yale Bowl and Lapham Field House.

Lexicographer Noah Webster

A.C. Gilbert's Erector Set

Ithiel Town's Truss Bridge over Mill River

... and Foremost

Dictionary
NOAH WEBSTER (1758~1843)
Moved to New Haven in 1798. Held elected offices of Alderman and State Representative. In 1807, he began to compile his American Dictionary of the English Language; it was published in 1828 and sold over 40,000,000 copies.

Frisbee
YALIES & FRISBEE PIE CO.
Some ingenious Yale students found a way to recycle the metal pie plates used by the Frisbee Pie Company. They discovered that when thrown, the plates hovered, which made passing them an interesting game. Later, someone made similarly shaped plastic disks and the Frisbee was born.

Vulcanized Rubber
CHARLES GOODYEAR (1800~1860)
In 1839, he was trying to find a way to treat rubber to prevent it from melting and becoming sticky when hot, and hard and brittle when cold. He had mixed many chemicals with rubber, but none had worked. By accident, he dropped a mixture of rubber and sulphur on the stove. The resulting cooked product had the desired properties.

Knights of Columbus
REV. M.J. MCGIVNEY
In 1882, led a group of lay-Catholic men who formed the Knights of Columbus. New Haven is still the home of this international fraternal service organization, with over 1.5 million members. It is also the world's largest insurance company.

Painless Dentistry (Laughing Gas)
DR. JOSEPH SMITH
Started using nitrous oxide (laughing gas) on patients whose teeth he was extracting. The procedure was so popular that in one month in 1863 he pulled 1,785 teeth.

Ice Making Machine
ALEXANDER C. TWINING (1801~1884)
Inventor of the ice making machine. Was a civil engineer for New York-New Haven Railroad.

Cotton Gin and Interchangeable Parts
ELI WHITNEY (1765~1825)
Inventor of the cotton gin. His innovative gun factory made New Haven a major arms-manufacturing center. Called by some the inventor of mass production or the father of the Industrial Revolution, in 1798 he introduced interchangeable parts at his Whitney Armory. The Whitney Arms Company was bought by Winchester Arms Company in 1888.

Winchester Rifle
OLIVER WINCHESTER
Founded the New Haven Arms Company in 1847. Started as a shirt manufacturer. In 1857, he was producing 100 dozen shirts per day with 300 employees in the factory and 3,700 people working in their homes. Served as director of Volcanic Repeating Arms, formed in 1856. He reorganized it in 1858, and renamed it Winchester Repeating Arms in 1861.

Heart-Lung Machine

•••••

Infusion Pump to treat diabetes

•••••

Intensive Care Unit for Newborns

•••••

Lobster roll

•••••

Lollipop - Bradley-Smith Co.

•••••

Machine tools
drop hammer, turret lathe, screw machine
Elisha K. Root

•••••

Medical diploma

•••••

Milking machine

•••••

Modern submarine
David Bushnell

•••••

Mortised locks
Blake Bros., 1835

•••••

Ph.D. degree

•••••

Phrenic Nerve Stimulator
to aid paraplegics to breathe

•••••

Pizza (Apizza) in U.S.
Frank Pepe

•••••

Planned city in the U.S.

•••••

Precision press
Dr. Charles Howland-Sherman

•••••

Prepaid postage envelope

•••••

Rubber footwear factory

•••••

Scientific publication in U.S.
American Journal of Science, 1818

•••••

Wooden, sulphur matches
Thomas Sanford & Edward Beecher

•••••

Treatment of burns with donor skin

•••••

Urban Renewal Project

Oliver Winchester

122

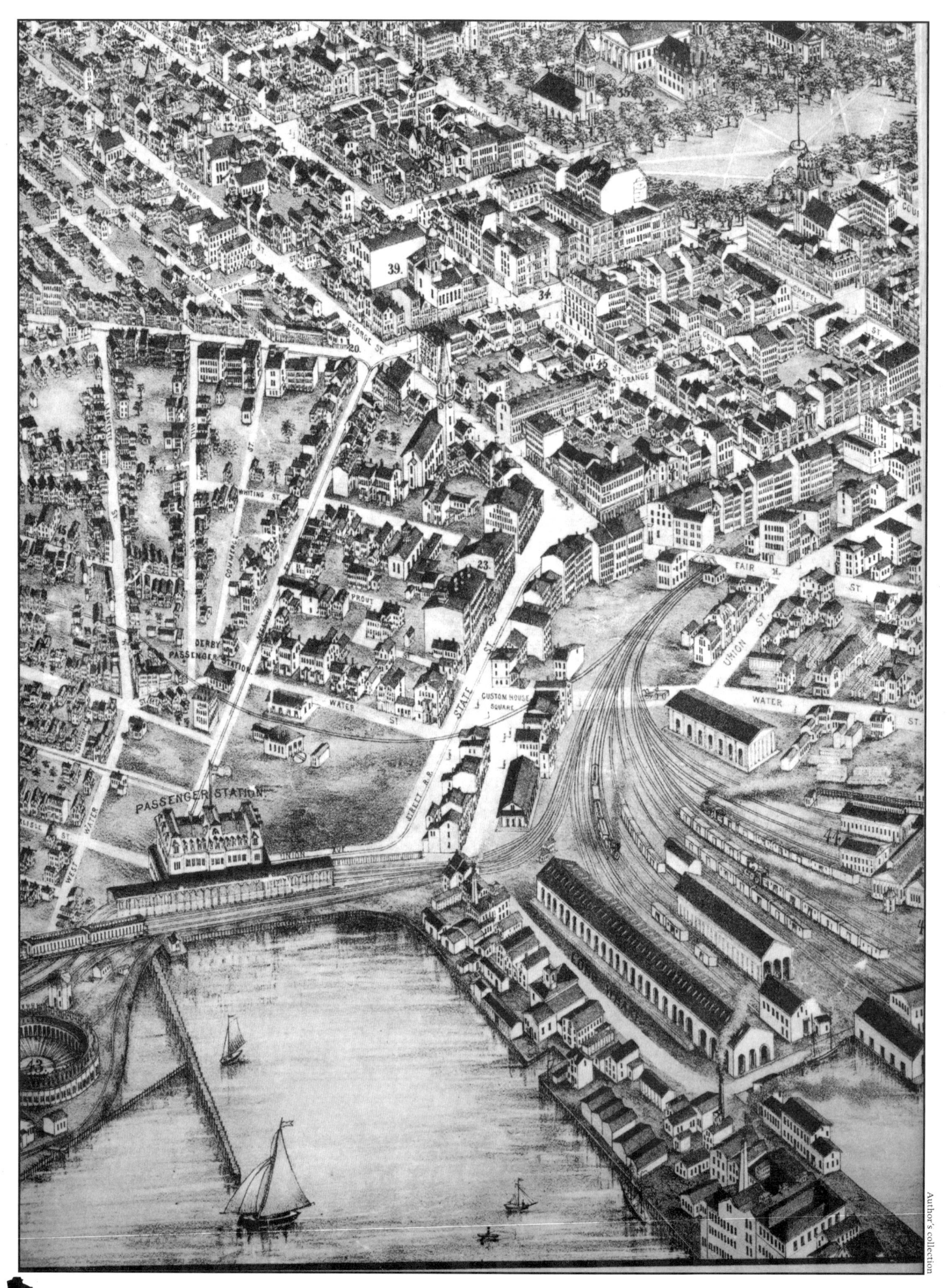

NEW HAVEN HISTORY 1900 ~ 1919
World War I

Population (1910): 133,605 145,130

The corner of Church and Chapel Streets became the center of downtown New Haven. Almost every streetcar passed this corner on its way to its destination. Many of the existing downtown buildings were built in this period, but the two major department stores, the Edward Malley Company and Gamble Desmonds, both on Chapel Street, no longer exist. The present public library was built in 1908. Union Station was finished in 1918. Other existing downtown buildings built in this period are the Court House facing the Green (1909), Old Post Office and Court (1913) and the Taft Hotel (1911). Some of Yale's finest buildings were constructed during this period, including Woodbridge Hall (1901), Woolsey Hall (1901), and the Yale Bowl (1914).

As headquarters for the New York, New Haven and Hartford Railroad, New Haven was clearly a railroading community. Every train coming into New England stopped in New Haven, either at the Union Station or the Cedar Hill freight yards. In 1911, the railroads employed 34,767 employees, a majority of them in New Haven. It had 26,100 passenger cars operational in Connecticut alone and moved 84 million passengers annually.

In 1914, New Haven Mayor Frank J. Rice almost got stranded in Germany as the war started. The city was soon swamped with munitions orders, and a major housing shortage developed due to the influx of workers to Winchester, where 15,000 were employed.

Connecticut's Second Division was sent to the Mexican border to fight Francisco Villa and then to patrol the railroad to prevent sabotage. In 1918, they joined the "Yankee Division" in France, where they fought bravely and suffered many casualties.

In 1918, there was a devastating flu epidemic. In 1919, on November 11, the war was over. The troops returned home six months later, only to engage in one of New Haven's worst "town" versus "gown" fights, complete with rock-throwing. The soldiers were called "tin soldiers" and the Yalies "slackers."

For New Haven, the war really ended with the visit of Generalissimo of the Allied Armies, Marshal Ferdinand Foch, who received an honorary degree from Yale.

Above:
Acting Mayor John Murphy, Governor Everett S. Lake with Marshal Ferdinand Foch, Supreme Allied Commander during World War I, who came to New Haven after the War to receive an honorary degree from Yale.

Right:
Colonel Isaac Ullman, political boss of New Haven's Republican party, from 1899 to the early 1920s.

Facing Page:
New Haven in 1879. Segment of print drawn and published by D.H. Bailey & J.E. Hazen.

Important Dates

1900	Philippine Insurgency. It ended in 1902.
1914	Yale Bowl completed.
1915	World War I begins. It lasted until 1919.

On Wednesday, September 21, 1938, a hurricane whipped through the New England states. It was the worst natural disaster in the area's history.

Above:
John Murphy, born in New Haven in 1878, became the Democratic Mayor of New Haven in 1932 when the Great Depression was at its worst. He had been President of the New Haven Labor Council and minority leader of the Board of Aldermen. He served seven terms until 1945, guiding New Haven through the Depression and World War II. He was defeated by Republican challenger William Celentano.

Left:
One of Southern New England Telephone's four major buildings in New Haven, this art deco building is located at the corner of Church and Wall Streets.

NEW HAVEN HISTORY 1920 ~ 1939
Fabulous 20s/Great Depresssion

Population (1930): 162,612   233,656

New Haven, like the nation, experimented with prohibition, women's suffrage, vast increases in the number of automobiles, and lots of leisure time with money available to enjoy it.

Retailing began a change that was eventually to put an end to most locally owned and operated stores. National retail chain stores started to dominate the food business, with supermarkets, variety stores (then called "five and ten cent stores"), appliances and clothing. Another development affecting retailing was the spread of installment credit buying.

Nowhere was the anti-liquor law held in more contempt. All forms of alcohol were widely available, both to be served and to be taken home. This is contrasted with the active promotion of the women's suffrage movement that took place at the same time.

By 1925, there was an expansion of trolley and railroad transportation. In 1921, the newly formed Community Chest raised $460,000. The New Haven Foundation, today the Community Foundation for Greater New Haven, was started in 1928.

The banking industry was also flourishing. In 1927, the Union and New Haven Trust Company finished their 13-story Colonial Revival office building on the corner of Church and Elm Streets.

Yale University entered into a program to create 10 residential colleges, and restructure the university to follow the organization of Oxford and Cambridge in England. They hired James Gamble Rogers from New York to coordinate the expansion program. It was primarily funded with enormous gifts from the Edward S. Harkness and John William Sterling families. Yale buildings built in the 1920s included Jonathan Edwards, Calhoun, Pierson, Davenport and Trumbull Colleges, Payne Whitney Gymnasium, the Hall of Graduate Studies, Sterling Law Building, Sterling Memorial Library and William Harkness Hall. The rest of the original 10 colleges were finished in the 1930s.

The stock market kept going up. Yale started buying more property and taking it off the tax rolls. In spite of the fact that Yale has made major contributions to the New Haven economy, its tax free status is still questioned by most "townies" who feel it raises everyone else's taxes.

The Roaring Twenties ended in October 1929, when the stock market crashed. This was the same week Albie Booth, Yale's most famous football player, led Yale to a smashing victory over Army.

For three and a half years, the country and New Haven reeled from the devastating effects of the Great Depression. Banks closed; rich families became poor, losing their businesses and real estate; and a large percentage of the workforce was unemployed.

The turning point was the inauguration of President Franklin D. Roosevelt in 1933. Because of its large industrial base, which included Bigelow Steam Boiler Company, Greist Manufacturing, the National Folding Box Company, Winchester, Seamless Rubber, Marlin Firearms, Sargent, Geometric Tool, Berger Brothers and many smaller companies, New Haven's recovery outpaced the rest of the nation.

Yale grew rapidly in the 1930s, using the Depression as an opportunity to purchase choice downtown properties at bargain-basement prices.

By the end of the Thirties, the economy was well on its way to full recovery and the city was once again gearing up to be a major supplier of war materials.

In 1936, there was a big celebration for Connecticut's 300th anniversary and in 1938, a great tercentenary citywide celebration for New Haven.

Important Dates

1925	Albertus Magnus College was founded.
1927	New Haven Airport opened.
1929	Stock market crashed ending the "Fabulous Twenties."
1930	The "Great Depression" began and lasted almost 10 years.
1936	300th anniversary of Connecticut was celebrated.
1938	300th anniversary of New Haven was celebrated.
1939	Nazi armies invade Poland.

Left:
Generalissimo Josef Stalin waves to some of the marchers in Moscow's May Day Parade on May 1, 1947, while Marshal Semion Budenny twirls his mustache preparatory to greeting the paraders from atop Lenin's Tomb in Red Square.

Below:
After Allied troops invaded Europe on "D Day" 1944, President Franklin Delano Roosevelt told the nation that "Americans have all worked together to make this day possible."

Below:
General Douglas MacArthur returns to the Philippines in 1945.

NEW HAVEN HISTORY 1940 ~ 1950
WWII & Postwar New Haven

Population (1940): 160,605   246,436

By, 1940 it was clear to most Americans that Hitler had to be stopped and that only through direct American intervention was that going to be accomplished. Unlike the wars that followed, WWII had broad popular support. Many people in New Haven either fled Europe themselves or had ancestors who had fled to freedom. However, they maintained connections to their homelands, and what Hitler and the other Axis countries were doing was intolerable.

Most New Haveners did not have direct Oriental connections, so the Japanese agression seemed more remote. All of that changed on December 7, 1941 when the Japanese launched a sneak attack on Pearl Harbor. The attack caused massive destruction to the American Navy.

The result was the prompt declaration of war on both the Japanese and the Hitler-led German and Italian Axis Powers. The United States then proceeded to marshall its tremendous productive capacity to wage a war that would ultimately defeat the enemy.

Many New Haven factories ran 24 hours a day. Women entered the workforce in record numbers to replace men between the ages of 16 and 38 who were drafted into the Army. It was common for both men and women to work 12 hours a day. There were few families in New Haven without a relative in the service.

Food and gasoline rationing, price controls, blackouts and air raid practice all became part of everyday life. A flag with a blue star was hung in the window of houses with a man or woman in the service. A gold star in the window indicated that a soldier had been killed. Metal was needed for the war effort and the trolley tracks were torn out of the streets.

The end of the War in 1945 produced a massive public celebration. In post-war New Haven, the economy remained prosperous, filling the pent-up demand for consumer goods and services that were unobtainable during the austerity of the war years.

The end of World War II brought many changes to the greater New Haven area. Good roads and an abundance of automobiles made it possible to live in the suburbs and easily get to work or shopping. Developers seized upon the opportunity and homes by the thousands were constructed throughout the area. Many industries and offices also took advantage of the suburbs: industrial and office parks sprang up in many communities. Shopping centers and malls attracted modern stores, many nationally-owned or franchised. Other retailers located stores along the highways where parking was easy.

This suburban growth contrasted with the urban blight that had been building up over the years. Many areas of New Haven had large numbers of buildings that were over 50 years old. Multi-story industrial buildings were no longer efficient and the run-down residential buildings either needed major renovations or to be razed. Downtown retailing was having a hard time competing with the new stores in the suburbs. The population of New Haven, for the first time in 300 years, stopped growing, while the greater New Haven suburbs continued to grow rapidly.

Mayor William Celentano was elected in 1946. He saw the need to revitalize the blighted areas of the city, and set the stage for the urban renewal programs of the 1960s.

Important Dates

1941   Japanese sneak attack on Pearl Harbor on December 7 brought the U.S. into WWII.
1945   Germany and Japan surrendered, ending World War II.
1946   William Celentano, an Italian funeral director, elected mayor of New Haven.
1949   New Haven Harbor channel dredged to a depth of 40 feet to allow large oil tankers and freighters to dock and unload. The fill was used to create the Long Wharf industrial and commercial area.
1950   Levi Jackson, a New Havener, was elected Yale's first African-American football captain.

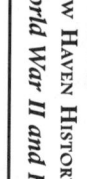

The City Planning Commission was created in 1913, but did not hire professional help until 1941. They hired Maurice Rotival, a well-known city planner, in 1942. He developed proposals which were used in 1953 when the Chamber of Commerce produced a "Ten Point Program" to implement his recommendations.

The money problems that stood in the way of the proposed plans were solved by Henry Wells, a Yale political science professor who was a Democratic Alderman and member of the City Planning Commission. He saw the new Title I federal program as the magic money source and convinced the Board of Alderman and Republican Mayor William Celentano to create a redevelopment agency in 1951. Under Mayor Celentano, redevelopment moved slowly ahead, and in 1952, he approved the razing of the 15-acre slum on Oak Street, without the funds to actually do the job.

In 1953, Richard Lee became Mayor as a result of his campaign promise to do something about the terrible condition of downtown New Haven. He served eight terms as Mayor, from 1953 to 1969. Redevelopment of New Haven was begun by Celentano, but it was Lee who had the big dream. He took a vague plan and turned New Haven into the nation's redevelopment model. Lee sought to stem the flight of the middle class from the city to the suburbs, eliminate the rapidly expanding slums, rebuild the downtown area and stimulate the overall economy of the city.

Before becoming Mayor, Lee was a city hall newspaper reporter and later director of Yale's News Bureau. He attracted to his administration a group of enthusiastic young professionals led by Edward Logue, Redevelopment Director. Logue returned to New Haven in 1953, practicing law here while he worked with the Democratic party.

Lee organized a broad base of community support in the form of a 4,000 member Citizens Action Committee, a coalition of business professionals, community leaders and representatives of Yale.

Yale President A. Whitney Griswold conferring an honorary Doctor of Laws upon U.S. President John F. Kennedy.

Long Wharf Pier

The original settlers of New Haven were attracted here by the harbor and envisioned making it an international seaport. The first blow to this dream was the "Phantom Ship" which was lost at sea in 1646. It caused great economic loss to its New Haven investors.

Because the harbor waters are shallow, it was decided to construct a long wharf out into the harbor from which to load and unload ships. By the early 1880s, it had grown into a long wooden structure upon which shops, taverns, warehouses and offices were constructed, as well as loading and unloading facilities. It grew to over half a mile in length.

In 1796, shipping had again become profitable. An active trade developed where ships went very far south in the Atlantic Ocean and hunted seals. The furs were taken to China where they were traded for silk cloth and chinaware. A New Havener, Ebenezer Townsend, again attempted a large shipping venture. He sent the *Neptune*, captained by Daniel Green, age 30, on a three year voyage. The first stop was the South Atlantic to gather seal furs. Then the ship went on to China by way of Hawaii and traded the furs for chinaware and cloth. The three year voyage ended successfully and Townsend made over a quarter of a million dollars profit, which was a huge amount of money at the time, when the average skilled worker made $4.00-$5.00 per week and meat was 6 cents per pound.

The foreign shipping embargo of 1807 and the War of 1812 disrupted this lucrative trade triangle. Seals became scarce because of over-hunting. China also became saturated with trade from all over the world and profits shrunk.

In 1810, construction started to convert Long Wharf from a wooden structure into one built of stone. It eventually became 3,480 feet long (about 11 football fields), making it the longest pier in the United States.

The Farmington Canal was planned to help promote the shipping business. It was started in 1825 and reached the Massachusetts border in 1829. It connected to another canal and ended in Northhampton, Massachusetts. The canal caused real estate to boom along its edges, but it was never very financially successful. In 1847, the canal was closed and the water replaced with railroad tracks.

Today, only a small section of the long wharf remains. The oil tankers and freighters dock on wharves at the mouth of the Quinnipiac and Mill Rivers. Long Wharf is now the headquarters for the harbor sightseeing boat *Liberty Belle*.

NEW HAVEN HISTORY 1951 ~ 1969
Mayor Richard C. Lee

Population (1960): 152,048   342,296

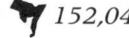

The physical transformation of New Haven started in 1956, with the acquisition of hundreds of slum properties in the path of proposed construction of the Oak Street Connector. Sufficient property was acquired by the State to extend the road to Ella T. Grasso Boulevard, but today it ends at High Street.

In 1958, the Connecticut Turnpike (I-95) was opened and in 1960 the Oak Street Connector (Route 34) provided direct access into downtown New Haven from Interstate 95.

The most dramatic redevelopment project was the rebuilding of downtown New Haven from Chapel Street south between Church and Temple Streets, across the connector, all the way south to Union Station, and east and west along both sides of the highway (Route 34).

Rogers Stevens, a well-known Broadway producer, was the principal developer. His project, completed in 1965, included the office tower facing Chapel, the Rouse-operated shopping mall, a 300-room hotel and two large department stores occupied by Macy's and Edward Malley's—a store with a 100-year history in the city, whose original building had been razed to make way for the new development.

Along the north side of the connector, a new Community Services building was completed in 1965. The dramatic Veterans Memorial Coliseum arena, with its 2,400-car overhead garage, opened in 1969. It was designed to harmonize with the Knights of Columbus World Headquarters nearby. Four residential apartment towers were also constructed along the north side of the highway.

On the south side of Route 34, Tower One and Tower East Elderly Housing were built in 1969, Lee High School in 1964 (now an office building), Church Street South Housing in 1969, and several new buildings in the Yale-New Haven Hospital complex.

At the same time, a very different type of redevelopment was taking place in the Wooster Square area. Here the emphasis was on restoring run-down Victorian era buildings to their former glory. New housing, the Conte Community Center and blocks of commercial and industrial buildings east of I-91, which bisects the neighborhood, were added.

Mary Hommann and Jim Skerits, a landscape architect, spearheaded the project. In the long run, Wooster Square may be the most successful of the many redevelopment projects simultaneously taking place in the Hill, Dixwell and Fair Haven neighborhoods in the 1960s.

During the 16 years of the Lee administration, the federal government spent over $130 million on New Haven redevelopment projects. While all this building and demolition were taking place, human services were not being neglected. With $5 million dollars in support from the Ford Foundation, Community Progress Incorporated was established as an anti-poverty program. Led by Mitchell Sviridoff, former head of the Connecticut AFL-CIO union, it spent over $20 million dollars on a variety of experimental approaches to job training, education, housing and child care.

In spite of all that was done to remake New Haven in the 1950s and 1960s, by the end of the 1960s some New Haveners felt that excess priority had been given to real estate development and not enough to human services.

Important Dates

1953	**Richard C. Lee became Mayor of New Haven.**
1958	**Connecticut Turnpike I-95 completed.**
1959	**Oak Street Connector (Route 34) opened, linking I-95 to High Street and downtown.**
1965	**Rogers Stevens completed Church Street development, including Macy's, Malley's, the Chapel Square Mall, Park Plaza Hotel and 900 Chapel Street office building.**

Ribbon-cutting ceremony at the new Arts Council-Community Foundation Building in 1994. C. Newton Schenck III (left) applauds former New Haven Mayors Richard C. Lee, Biagio DiLieto, Frank Logue, and John Daniels.

Mayor Lee decided not to run for re-election in 1969. The Democratic party was in firm control of New Haven, tightly ruled by Arthur Barbieri and John Golden. The nomination was given to Realtor Bartholomew F. Guida who had been President of the Board of Aldermen based on seniority and his reputation for independence. He served three terms as Mayor, and is best remembered for standing up to Yale when it tried to develop another residential college on Whitney Avenue. He died shortly after leaving office in 1975.

Frank Logue served as Mayor from 1976 to 1979. During his administration, the Robert Giamo Federal Office building on Orange Street, Temple Medical Center, and Teletrack were completed.

The new City Hall project was begun, including plans to raze the old City Hall. Preservationists led by Vincent Scully, a Yale professor specializing in the history of art and urban centers, tried to save it. A compromise resulted in the facade of the old City Hall being preserved and incorporated into the new Government Center. Teletrack was constructed near the harbor and the G & O Manufacturing operation was successfully saved for greater New Haven by its subsequent move to a new plant in North Haven.

Mayor Logue was followed by Biagio "Ben" DiLieto, the popular former Police Chief, who took office in 1980 and served 5 terms. During the 1980s, the theater district on College Street was revitalized, and the historic Hotel Taft was converted into apartments, under the guidance of expert urban developer Joel Schiavone. The Shubert Performing Arts Center and Palace Theater were reopened, bringing to eight the number of legitimate theaters in New Haven: Long Wharf & Stage II, the Shubert, the Palace, Yale Repertory Theatre, Yale University Theater, and E.C.A. at both the Lincoln Theater and the Audubon Arts Center.

John Daniels beat John DeStefano in the Democratic primary, and in November 1990 became the first black Mayor of New Haven. He served for two terms. He faced a national economic downturn, the closing of several old New Haven banks by the FDIC, a high dropout rate in the schools, increasing drug problems, a high rate of infant mortality and a projected $12 million deficit in the New Haven budget. During his administration, Yale agreed to make voluntary payments for city services it received. The "Fighting Back" program grew from initial planning into a full-fledged anti-drug and crime program.

NEW HAVEN HISTORY 1970 ~ TODAY
Revitalization Continues

Population (1990: 130,474 503,712

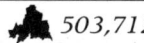

Near the Yale Campus between Orange and Temple Streets is one of New Haven's newest and most exciting revitalized areas. The Audubon Arts Center Complex was completed in 1994. It contains the Neighborhood Music School, Creative Arts Workshop, Educational Center for the Arts (ECA), Artspace, and the Community Foundation for Greater New Haven/Arts Council building. In the same area is the new Audubon Court condominium, and two modern office buildings.

The harborfront revitalization continues south of I-95 with the completion of two large Maritime office buildings, and a parking garage, and the rehabilitation of the harbor port and Vietnamese War Memorial. Long Wharf is home to the charming sightseeing boat, *Liberty Belle*.

The north side of I-95 has become vibrant with the Perelli Armstrong Office Building, Howard Johnson's and Marriott Residence Inn, Gateway Community Technical College, Southern CT Water Authority, *New Haven Register* and *Advocate* plants, renovated One Long Wharf, and a magnet school in the former Boys' Club building.

Science Park in the Newhall neighborhood is transforming run-down, unused industrial buildings into a modern complex of industrial and research facilities. Yale's active support of Science Park allows renting industries to use Yale faculty and students to support their operations. These industries also use Yale's research facilities.

The East Shore community remains vital. Tweed-New Haven Airport is expanding, and Lighthouse Park now enjoys a beautifully restored historic carousel near its fine public beach.

Fair Haven Heights is attracting people who are willing to renovate its many historic buildings. Fair Haven's Quinnipiac Water Front has been revitalized and progress is being made against the slums which have plagued this neighborhood since WWII.

Wooster Square is a successful redevelopment project. This 1950s slum is now the site of new commercial and industrial buildings, a vibrant Wooster Street—pizza headquarters of the world—and an established historic district around the Wooster Square Park. Grand Avenue is stabilizing and work has begun to address the problems of the large deteriorating public housing project in the northeast corner of the neighborhood.

The slums of Upper State Street and Cedar Hill have been converted into a thriving restaurant and shopping area. Its success is spreading to the adjoining residential area, where substantial renovations are taking place.

The Dixwell neighborhood, one of the poorest in New Haven, is benefiting from the re-opening of the Dixwell Plaza commercial area and grass roots

Important Dates

1970	A blast set off in front of Ingalls Rink on May 2 triggered riots that lasted for days. There was much property damage, especially in the Hill neighborhood. The National Guard restored law and order.
1971	Allegheny Air airplane crashed into three cottages next to Colony Beach club and killed 28 people.
1984	On July 10, a tornado swept across Prospect Street hill and into Hamden wrecking hundreds of homes.
1984	Palace Theater opened on September 9 with the musical "Gigi," followed by a spectacular performance by Peter Allen and Marvin Hamlisch.
1985	Hurricane Gloria hit on September 27, causing extensive property damage, especially along the shore. It took weeks to clear downed trees and restore electrical power in many areas.
1989	John Daniels beat John Destanfano in the Democratic primary on September 13 and went on to become the first black Mayor of New Haven.
1992	Yale's $165 million Children's Hospital completed.
1993	John DeStefano beat John Daniels in Democratic primary and went on to become Mayor.
1995	Ninth Square Phase I fully funded.
1995	New Haven hosts the Special Olympics World Games, the largest sporting event in the world.

support from its many churches, which are playing an active role in solving the neighborhood's many problems. Small housing projects are replacing boarded up slum properties, but a high concentration of very poor families continues to cause many serious social problems.

The benefits of the expanding Southern Connecticut State University are being felt in the Beaver Hill and West Hills neighborhoods. Westville Shopping area has established itself as a restaurant and antiques center, which supports a variety of other retail activities. The large Westville neighborhood contains the new Connecticut Tennis Center and other expanded Yale sports facilities. The hill on Forest Road is the home of expanding Hopkins School, which has recently purchased the last large available tract of vacant land in the area.

The expansion of the Hospital of St. Raphael has helped the Dwight-Edgewood-West River neighborhood to halt the deterioration of its housing stock. Strong neighborhood associations are also helping, but there are still significant problems to be solved.

The north side of the Hill neighborhood is benefiting from the expanding Yale-New Haven Hospital medical complex. Many run-down houses have been replaced with modern cooperatives and public and private housing developments. The closed-down Lee High School and Prince School are now successful office buildings. The city has built new schools and a library in the neighborhood, and Hill Health Center is a model community health provider. In spite of what has been accomplished, many buildings remain boarded up, and there is still a high rate of crime and a serious drug problem.

City Point has re-established its maritime identity with a large harbor-oriented condominium project, a shorefront restaurant, a marina and its magnet Sound School.

Downtown New Haven has gone through a series of changes since the completion of the initial re-development phase in the 1960s. Suburban competition proved too much for the two department stores, who were handicapped by a mall design that, in hindsight, was poor. The hotel ran into a series of problems and finally closed. Many long-time businesses have closed their doors. Recently, ownership of the mall, the closed department stores and the hotel has been transferred to a foundation established by the Chamber of Commerce. Plans are already underway to re-open the hotel and revitalize the area.

On a brighter note, the Theater District attracted new restaurants and night clubs into the area. Chapel Street northwest of College benefited from the district and its proximity to Yale. The merchants founded the successful Upper Chapel Street Association. The management of the Palace Theatre has recently been taken over by a New York theater management company.

East of Church Street, an urban development program (UDAG) called "Ninth Square" became fully funded with help from Yale, after many years of delay. It is now nearing completion.

The Green at the very center of town has been completely restored, at a cost of over $4 million, raised by a foundation led by Alfred Van Sinderen (former SNET President). They also raised an endowment to insure the future maintenance of the Green. Government Center on Church Street is complete, incorporating the preserved and restored original front of the Old City Hall clock tower.

Today the city continues its economic renewal. Yale has made a new commitment to the future of New Haven. Older industries are being replaced with expanding education, health care, communications, transportation, and high tech research facilities. Under Mayor John DeStefano, elected in 1993, a new era of voluntary citizen cooperation is emerging. Citizens are participating in the Citizens' Vision Committee and many other community initiatives.

In July 1995, New Haven hosts the Special Olympics World Games and two tennis tournaments, and plans are already underway for an International Festival of Arts & Ideas in the summer of 1996.

City of New Haven
Downtown Development Projects 1990 to Present

Projects	Cost (Millions)	Year of Completion
Century Tower	50.0	1990
Arts Council/Community Foundation	3.0	1990
Exchange Building Renovation	6.0	1990
Chapel & York Garage	7.0	1990
Bank of Boston	6.0	1990
Yale Psychiatric Institute	11.6	1990
Perelli Office Expansion	2.0	1990
Ives Memorial Library Expansion	17.0	1990
New Haven Green Restoration	5.0	1991
Veterans Memorial Coliseum Renovation	25.0	1992
84 Trumbull Street Mormon Center	2.5	1992
Children's Museum	1.3	1992
Children's Hospital	165.0	1992
Brady Memorial Lab	8.5	1992
Connecticut Mental Health Center	4.0	1993
Yale Parking Garage #5	10.0	1993
129 Church Street Renovation	9.0	1994
Government Center	94.0	1994
Church Street South Improvements	1.7	1995
Luce Center	5.0	1995
Arena Block-Development Site	1.2	Under Construction
Ninth Square - Phase I	102.0	Under Construction
Art & Architecture Rehabilitation	11.0	Under Construction
Auto Tote	6.0	Under Construction
Boyer Center for Molecular Medicine	29.0	Under Construction
Yale Press Expansion	4.0	Under Construction
Yale Power Plant Interconnect	15.0	Under Construction
Yale Medical Library Expansion	6.0	Under Construction
Cross Campus & Sterling Libraries	1.0	Under Construction
Yale Law School Renovation	10.0	Under Construction
Sifka Center for Jewish Life (Yale Hillel)	3.0	Under Construction
TOTAL COST	**$621.8 Million**	

NEW HAVEN HISTORY
Hillhouse Avenue

Hillhouse Avenue, originally called Temple Avenue, now in the heart of Yale University, was described by Charles Dickens in 1868 as the most beautiful street in America.

The street was developed by James Hillhouse, who came to New Haven in 1761. He was a graduate of Yale College and Yale Law School. He was a Captain in the Governor's Foot Guard when they tried to defend New Haven from the British invasion in 1779. Hillhouse became a U.S. Senator, and was a good friend of George Washington.

He was active in the real estate market in New Haven, helping many people buy and sell property. In 1792, he laid out a 150-foot-wide Avenue on the south end of his large farm, which extended from Grove Street north across Prospect Hill. He sold lots on this new avenue to New Haven's richest citizens.

Ithiel Town, an architect and engineer who became world famous for inventing the Town Bridge, and his partner, Alexander Jackson Davis, designed and built four of the original mansions. At the top of the Avenue they built *Sachem's Wood*, the home of the Hillhouse family for many years, until it was razed in 1942 according to the instructions in the will of Isaphene Hillhouse, who did not want the house occupied by anyone other than a member of the Hillhouse family. Town also built his own house, the Skinner House and the Prichard House.

James Hillhouse planted elm trees and oak trees all over the Avenue and his farm. He was the driving force behind the planting of elms throughout New Haven. The elm trees grew very tall and formed canopies over the streets, resulting in New Haven's names "City of Elms" and "Elm City." Few elms have survived, but some of the large oaks on Prospect Hill were probably planted by the Hillhouse family.

Elizabeth Mills Brown, in her wonderful book *New Haven: A Guide to Architecture and Urban Design* laments the razed buildings, changed colors and poor alterations to the houses on Hillhouse Avenue.

In spite of the truth of her statements, this two-block street still presents a unique opportunity to gaze back across time to the lives of the "rich and famous" of New Haven in the 1800s. The old Farmington Canal (without water) and the site of the founding of the Knights of Columbus are also here.

Walking Tour of Historic Hillhouse Avenue

On the following three pages, the buildings are not in numerical order; rather, the walking tour begins on the right side of the street at #1 and continues north, across Trumbull Street to Sachem. The tour then turns southward along the left side of the Avenue, ending with #2, opposite the point where it began.

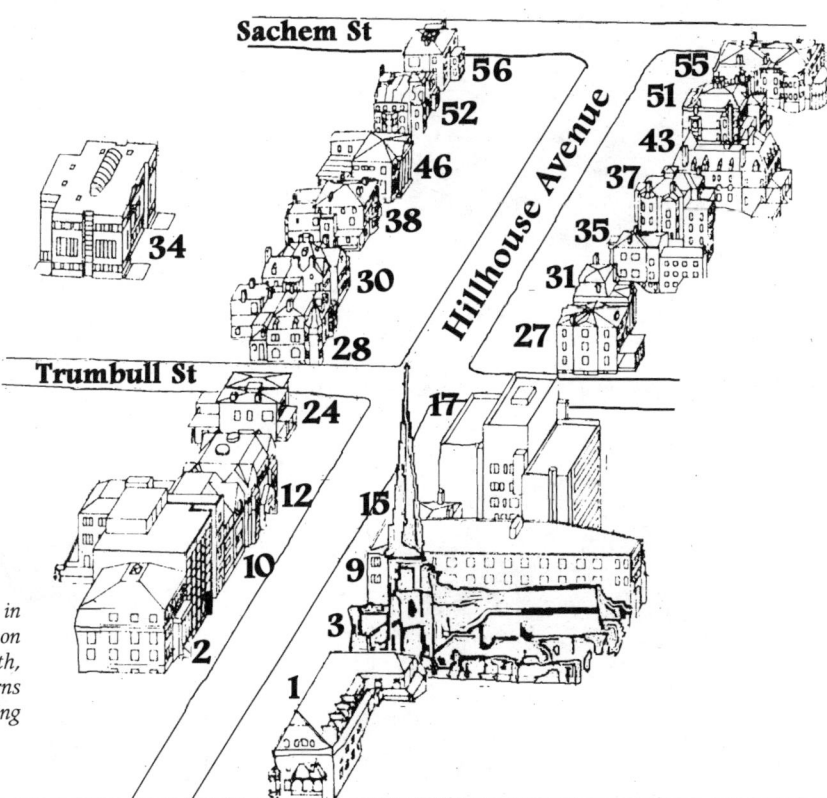

133

#1 Built in 1888, designed by Clarence H. Stilson, the building at 131 Grove Street was known as Cloister Hall, and was occupied by the Book and Snake Society. In 1917, the three-story addition was added and the address became 1 Hillhouse Avenue. Given to Yale in 1933 in memory of William W. Skiddy, PH.B. 1865, a founder of Book and Snake and Wyllys E. Dowd, Jr., PH.B. 1900, its long-time secretary. Now used for Undergraduate Career Services.

#3 St. Mary's Church and Priory were built in 1870, designed by James Murphy of Providence. The new steeple was recently donated by the Knights of Columbus to celebrate their founding there in 1882.

#9 Designed by Charles C. Haight with an Indiana limestone facade, Mason Laboratory was built in 1911. Gift of William S. Mason, PH.B. 1888, and George G. Mason, PH.B. 1888. Extensively remodeled in 1967 to provide facilities for the Department of Mechanical Engineering and Applied Science.

#15 Designed by W.H. Allen, and built in 1894-5 as the Alpha Delta Phi House, the building was bought by Yale in 1930. Today it houses the Collection of Musical Instruments.

#17 Designed by Westermann and Miller of New York, the Yale University Health Services building was constructed in 1969 next to the old bed of the Farmington Canal.

#27 George Fisher House was built in 1865 by the Reverend Professor George Park Fisher (Mrs. Fisher was a sister of Mrs. Benjamin Silliman, Jr.). Purchased by Yale in 1935, it is late Italian Villa Style, and is now used by the Economic Growth Center.

#31 Abigail Whelpley House was built between 1800 and 1827. It may have been moved here from another site. Its original Federal Style was changed to 2nd Empire Style by the addition of a Mansard roof, designed by Henry Austin in the 1860s. Some of the additional design elements were later removed, giving the house its present appearance.

#35 Mary Prichard House was built in 1836 by Nelson Hotchkiss and Ira Atwater by order of Alexander J. Davis. It is Greek Revival style with tall Corinthian columns. Now used as the Yale Provost's house.

#37 *Built for John S. Graves in 1866 and purchased before it was complete by Tredwell Ketcham. Purchased in 1921 by Yale, and now used by the Department of Economics.*

#43 *Henry Farnam House is now the Yale President's House. It was built in 1871, designed by Russell Sturgis of New York. Mr. Farnam gave the house to Yale to be used as the President's house after the life-use of his son Professor Henry Walcott Farnam, B.A. 1874, who died in 1933. It was remodeled in 1937 by Kimball & Husted and used continuously by Yale Presidents since then.*

#51 *James Graves House was built in 1862, and purchased in 1924 by Yale. It was apartments from 1946 to 1956. It is now used by the Department of Anthropology and the Council on Archaeological Studies.*

#55 *Peletiah Perit House, built in 1859 for Peletiah Perit, B.A. 1802, was designed by Sidney Mason Stone. Purchased by Yale in 1931. Its style is called Renaissance Revival.*

#56 *Elizabeth Apthrop House, built in 1837, was designed by Alexander J. Davis. Originally used as a "Young Ladies Seminary." Given to Yale in 1877 by Frederic W. Stevens, B.A. 1858. Now part of the School of Management.*

#52 *John Pitkin Norton House was built in 1848, designed by Henry Austin in the Italian Villa Style. In spite of many changes that spoil the original design, it is still a interesting house. National Historic Landmark. Purchased by Yale in 1923. Now part of the School of Management.*

#46 *Aaron Skinner House was built around 1839 by Hon. Aaron Nichols Skinner, B.A. 1823, who was Mayor of New Haven for four terms. It is Greek Revival Style and was designed by Alexander J. Davis as a boys' boarding school. An addition in the 1850s was designed by Henry Austin. National Historical Landmark.*

#38 *Henry F. English House, built in 1892, was designed by Bruce Price of New York. It was the last private house built on Hillhouse Avenue. It has been extensively remodeled inside to make Yale offices, and is now used as Yale's Undergraduate Admissions Office.*

#34 *Luce Center, completed in 1995. New home of the Luce Center for International and Area Studies. Named for Henry Luce, founder of Time, Inc., and given to Yale.*

#30 *Built by Edwin S. Wheeler, M.A. HON 1886. Remodeled by Lewis H. English in 1908. Purchased by Yale in 1954. Now used by the Cowles Foundation for Research in Economics.*

#28 *The Charles Farnam House was built on the site of a house built for James Hillhouse that was later moved. Built in 1884, designed by either J. Cleveland Cady and/or Russell Sturgis, Jr. An 1898 addition was designed by Leoni Robinson. Purchased by Yale in 1920; now used by the Yale Department of Economics.*

#24 *James Dwight Dana House, built in 1849 designed by Henry Austin. A good example of Austin's Italian Villa Style, it is a National Historic Landmark. Built for Professor James Dwight Dana, it stayed in the Dana family until 1962 when it was purchased by Yale. Next to the Old Farmington Canal, it is now used by the Department of Statistics.*

#12 *Leet Oliver Hall was built in 1908, designed by Charles C. Haight. Gift of Mrs. James Brown Oliver in memory of her son, Daniel Leet Oliver, 1908 S. It is Collegiate Gothic Style, built of Indiana limestone, and is now used by the Department of Mathematics.*

#10 *Dunham Laboratory, built in 1912, was designed by Henry G. Morse as the Dunham Laboratory of Electrical Engineering, a gift of Austin C. Dunham, B.A. 1854. The addition was built in 1958, designed by Douglas Orr. The building houses the Department of Engineering and Applied Sciences, Psychology laboratories and Mathematics offices.*

#2 *Kirtland Hall was built in 1902, designed by Kirtland Kelsey Cutter. It is Neo-Renaissance Style and constructed of East Haven brownstone, with Longmeadow sandstone and terra-cotta trim. A gift of Lucy H. Boardman in memory of her Uncle Jared Porter Kirtland, M.D. 1815. Used as office space for the Department of Geology from 1904 to 1963, it now houses offices of the Department of Psychology.*

All photos author's collection

GREATER NEW HAVEN COMMUNITIES
Introduction

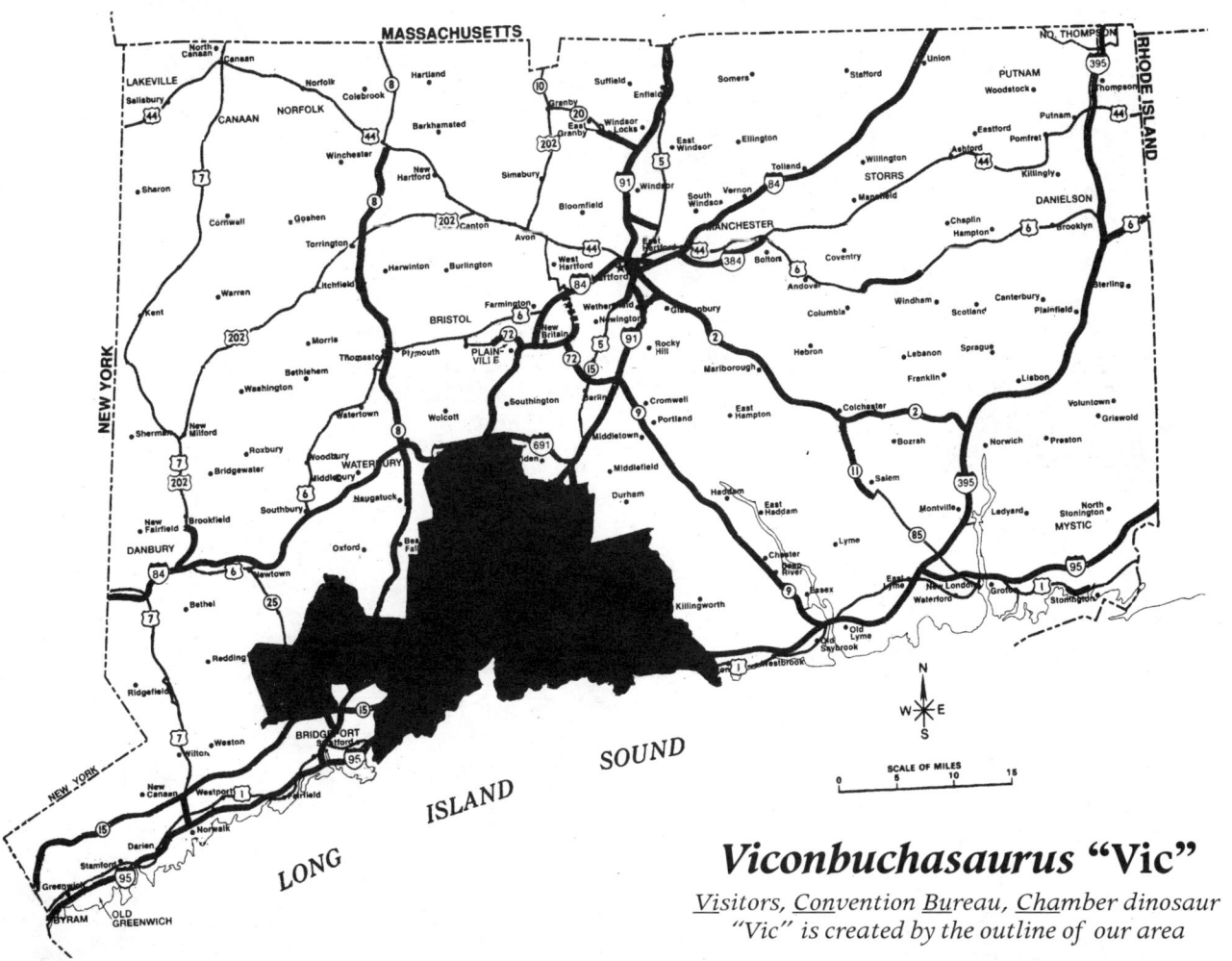

Viconbuchasaurus "Vic"
<u>Vi</u>sitors, <u>Con</u>vention Bureau, <u>Cha</u>mber dinosaur "Vic" is created by the outline of our area

The communities in this book include what is considered to be "Greater New Haven" by the Greater New Haven Association of Realtors, the Greater New Haven Convention and Visitor's Bureau and the Greater New Haven Chamber of Commerce.

1. ANSONIA
2. BETHANY
3. BRANFORD
4. CHESHIRE
5. DERBY
6. EAST HAVEN
7. GUILFORD
8. HAMDEN
9. MADISON
10. MILFORD
11. NEW HAVEN
12. NORTH BRANFORD
13. NORTH HAVEN
14. ORANGE
15. PROSPECT
16. SHELTON
17. TRUMBULL
18. WALLINGFORD
19. WEST HAVEN
20. WOODBRIDGE

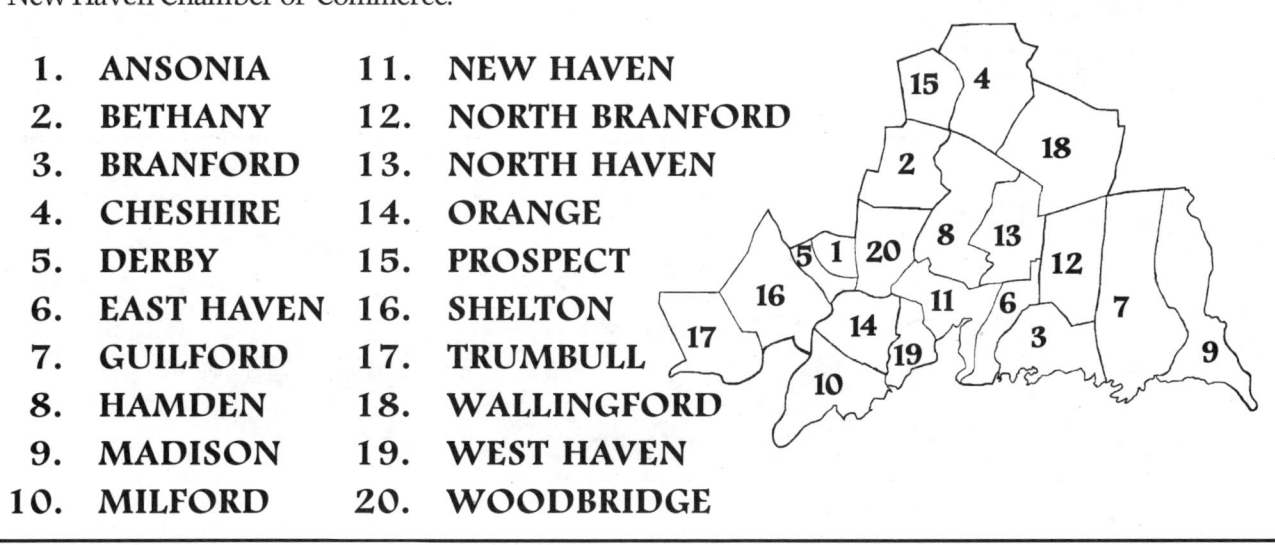

GREATER NEW HAVEN COMMUNITIES
Ansonia

Separated from Derby, Incorporated 1889

Population 100 years ago: 10,342

"Settled in the mid~1600s as a part of Derby, today Ansonia is a small industrial city with a rich heritage. The Copper City has been a center for manufacturing since the 1800s."

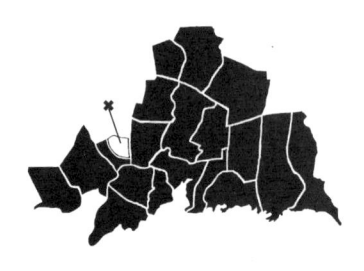

Thomas Hallihan
Mayor

*City Hall
253 Main Street
Ansonia 06401
Telephone 736-5900*

VITAL STATISTICS

Population	18,403
Per Capita Income	$21,687
Median Household Income	$34,181
Cost of Education Per Pupil	$6,410
Teacher:Pupil Ratio	1:22

MAJOR EMPLOYERS

Ansonia Copper & Brass	380
Farrel Corporation	165
Latex Foam Products, Inc.	150
Great County Bank	105
Hershey Metal Products, Inc.	75

POINTS OF INTEREST

Ansonia Nature and Recreation Center	736-9360
General David Humphreys' House	735-1908

Ansonia is an industrial town on the banks of the Naugatuck River. Originally a part of Derby, it was split off and incorporated in 1889. It has a total area of 6.2 square miles. The Town of Ansonia was first developed in 1845 by copper and brass manufacturer Anson G. Phelps. Around the same time, English immigrants William Smith and William Wallace set up a small brass mill which grew into Ansonia's largest industry.

Ansonia Town Hall

Built in the early 1700s, General David Humprheys' house is Ansonia's most historically important landmark. General Humphreys became one of the most important figures in the Revolutionary War, serving as an aide to General Washington.

Typical Property Sales or Listings .... *Residential Median Sales Price: $123,500*

18 Riggs Street
3 Bedrooms, 2 Baths
$100,000

15 Hemlock Drive
3 Bedrooms, 1 Bath
$125,000

3 Catalina Drive
3 Bedrooms, 2 Baths
$185,000

GREATER NEW HAVEN COMMUNITIES
Bethany

Population 100 years ago: 550 *Separated from Woodbridge, Settled 1717, Named 1762, Incorporated 1832*

VITAL STATISTICS

Population	4,608
Per Capita Income	$22,722
Median Household Income	$57,316
Cost of Education Per Pupil	$7,928
Teacher:Pupil Ratio	1:14

MAJOR EMPLOYERS

Uniroyal Chemical	(NA)
Laticrete International Inc.	(NA)

POINTS OF INTEREST

Bethany Airport Golf	393-0485
Sommersett Farm	393-2821
Whitlock Farm Book Barn	393-1240
Windy Hills Farms	393-3179
Woodhaven Country Club	393-3230

John Ford
First Selectman

Town Hall
40 Peck Road
Bethany 06524
Telephone 393-2100

"Bethany is a small town that combines all the splendor of a country atmosphere with the ease of accessibility to metropolitan areas. Trees, farmland, and horses come to mind when one thinks of Bethany."

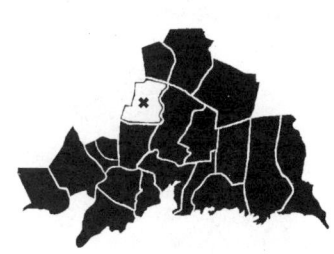

Bethany Town Hall

Before 1638, Bethany was occupied by the Naugatuck and Paugusset Indians. In 1664, Alexander Bryan of Milford bought the Lebanon Swamp from Nehantund, a Naugatuck Indian, for 30 shillings. He is the earliest landowner of record in Bethany. In the early 1700s, the Naugatuck and Paugusset sold more of their land.

In 1784, the General Assembly incorporated the Bethany parish as a separate entity from Woodbridge. In 1914, the present town hall was built on Amity Road. The first road was paved in 1918. In 1920, the population reached an all-time low of 411. Bethany Field (airport) opened in 1923. The State Police Barracks were constructed in 1939.

Typical Property Sales or Listings .... *Residential Median Sales Price: $189,700*

181 Beacon Road
3 Bedrooms, 2 Baths
$180,000

38 Lebanon Road
4 Bedrooms, 2.5 Baths
$205,000

68 N. Humiston Drive
4 Bedrooms, 2.5 Baths
$240,000

GREATER NEW HAVEN COMMUNITIES
Branford

Settled as part of New Haven 1639, Named 1653 *Population 100 years ago: 4,460*

Its exquisite location on Long Island Sound makes Branford the quintessential small shoreline town. Known for its easy pace of living, superlative beaches, gourmet seafood restaurants and its Blackstone Memorial Library, it offers year-round and summer residents easy access to the cultural life of New Haven.

Judy Gott
First Selectwoman

Town Hall
1019 Main Street
Branford 06405

Telephone 488-8394

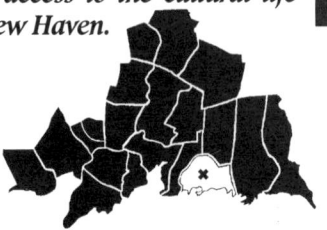

VITAL STATISTICS

Population 27,603
Per Capita Income $22,642
Median Household Income $56,593
Cost of Education Per Pupil $7,654
Teacher:Pupil Ratio 1:13

MAJOR EMPLOYERS

Coatings Technology .... (NA)
Echlin, Inc .... (NA)
Turbine Components .... (NA)
Milford Products, Corp. .... (NA)
Harco Labs .... (NA)
Sero of New Haven .... (NA)

POINTS OF INTEREST

Branford Craft Village at Bittersweet Farm ... 488-4689
Harrison House 488-5771

In 1638, the New Haven Colony traded "eleven coats of trucking cloth and one coat of English cloth made in the English fashion" to the Mattabesec Indians for land known as Totokett (Tidal River). The first permanent settlement was established in 1644 when people from Wethersfield came to Totokett, later renamed Branford after the town of Brentford, Middlesex County, England.

The Sound provided many of the settlers with a livelihood in shipbuilding and coastal trade. Industry began in 1655 when the first iron furnace in Connecticut was set up and operated at Lake Saltonstall.

Yale College was founded here in 1701, when ten ministers met and made a contribution of books.

In 1852, upon completion of the railroad, industrialization flourished. Two leading manufacturing firms were founded during this era: the Malleable Iron Fittings Company in 1854, and the Branford Lock Works in 1862.

The twentieth century has brought some changes to Branford, but much of its historical heritage remains.

Among the most notable structures in the center of town is the James H. Blackstone Memorial Library.

Typical Property Sales or Listings .... *Residential Median Sales Price: $162,500*

5 Spice Bush Lane
4 Bedrooms, 3 Baths
$186,500

37 Pawson Terrace
2 Bedrooms, 2 Baths
$220,000

57 Island View Avenue
5 Bedrooms, 4.5 Baths
$500,000

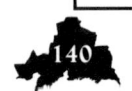

GREATER NEW HAVEN COMMUNITIES
Cheshire

Population 100 years ago: 1,929 *Separated from Wallingford, Named 1724 (New Cheshire), Incorporated 1780*

VITAL STATISTICS

Population	25,684
Per Capita Income	$23,204
Median Household Income	$58,250
Cost of Education Per Pupil	$7,516
Teacher:Pupil Ratio	1:13

MAJOR EMPLOYERS

Airpax	(NA)
Bendix Cheshire Corp.	(NA)
Bloomingdales By Mail	(NA)
Bozzuto	(NA)
Holgrath Corporation	(NA)
FIP Corp.	(NA)
Olin Corporation	(NA)
Consolidated Industries	(NA)

POINTS OF INTEREST

Bishop Farms	272-8243
Farmington Canal Linear Park	272-2743
Lock 12 Historical Park	272-2743

Cheshire's Town Hall

Edward O'Neill
Town Manager

Town Hall
84 South Main Street
Cheshire 06410
Telephone 271-6660

Despite tremendous industrial and commercial growth for four decades, Cheshire has been able to maintain its rural character. The town still has thousands of acres of open space, and a very active agricultural sector.

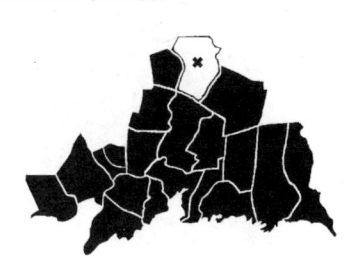

Settled in 1695 as Wallingford "West Farms," this area obtained status as the village of New Cheshire in 1723. It was incorporated as a town in 1780. Cheshire became famous for its agricultural productivity and light manufacturing. Copper and minerals were mined here in the 1700s and 1800s. The Farmington Canal was completed through town in 1825.

Cheshire is renowned for the Episcopal Academy, now Cheshire Academy, founded in 1794 by Samuel Seabury, first Episcopal bishop of Connecticut.

The Congregational Church was completed in 1827 based on a design by David Hoadley, noted architect of New Haven. Among famous hostelries were Beach Tavern, the Wallace and Munson Hotels, and the Waverly Inn.

Among its famous sons are Governor Samuel A. Foot; Amos Doolittle, early silversmith and engraver; landscape artist John Frederick Kensett; Lambert Hitchcock, maker of popular chairs bearing his name; and Commodore Robert Hitchcock.

Typical Property Sales or Listings .... *Residential Median Sales Price: $189,900*

1865 Marion Road
3 Bedrooms, 2 Baths
$120,000

71 Bayberry Road
3 Bedrooms, 1 Bath
$124,700

195 Mountainbrook Drive
4 Bedrooms, 2.5 Baths
$276,500

GREATER NEW HAVEN COMMUNITIES
Derby

Incorporated 1890 *Population 100 years ago: 5,964*

"Derby is a small, close-knit city not far from attractive suburban communities. Derby has a rich history which dates back over 300 years from its shipbuilding days to its modern position as a commercial and residential center."

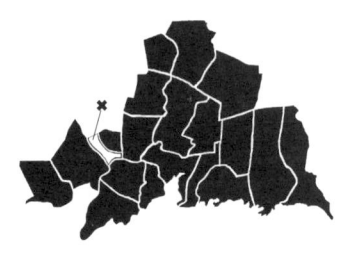

Alan R. Schlesinger
Mayor

City Hall
35 Fitch Street
Derby 06418
Telephone 734-9203

VITAL STATISTICS

Population	12,199
Per Capita Income	$22,738
Median Household Income	$35,808
Cost of Education Per Pupil	$7,330
Teacher:Pupil Ratio	1:20

MAJOR EMPLOYERS

Griffin Hospital	1,150
Farrel Corporation	150
Derby Cellular Products	125
Derby Savings Bank	125
Derby Nursing Center	100
Lifetouch National Studios	100

POINTS OF INTEREST

Osborne Homestead Museum	734-2513
Osbornedale State Park	(NA)

The history of Derby goes back to 1667, when Edward Wooster, a wolf hunter, received permission to start a plantation, conditional upon his ability to find a suitable minister. Wooster was made constable.

In 1675, John Hulls and Joseph Hawkins appeared before the General Court and declared that a minister had been engaged and that £100 had been spent on a house for him. They claimed that 12 families had already settled and eleven more were prepared to come.

The original boundaries extended from Milford and New Haven to Woodbury and Mattatuck (Waterbury).

Derby City Hall

Typical Property Sales or Listings .... *Residential Median Sales Price: $119,300*

124 New Haven Avenue
3 Bedrooms, 1 Baths
$105,000

2 Danielle Court
2 Bedrooms, 1.5 Baths
$165,900

8 Bellview Drive
3 Bedrooms, 2 Baths
$169,000

GREATER NEW HAVEN COMMUNITIES
East Haven

Population 100 years ago: 955 *Separated from New Haven, Founded 1657, Named 1707, Incorporated 1785*

VITAL STATISTICS

Population	26,760
Per Capita Income	$16,389
Median Household Income	$47,253
Cost of Education Per Pupil	$7,519
Teacher:Pupil Ratio	1:25

MAJOR EMPLOYERS

Thermatool Corp.	100
K-Mart	85
Waldbaum's	70
Mathog & Moniello Inc.	70
Pathmark	70

POINTS OF INTEREST

1707 Cemetery	(NA)
Old Stone Church	(NA)
Shore Line Trolley Museum	467-6927

"East Haven is a community of nearly 26,500 people. We are proud to offer full municipal services ... and a quality, expanding education system boasting eight elementary schools, a middle school and a high school"

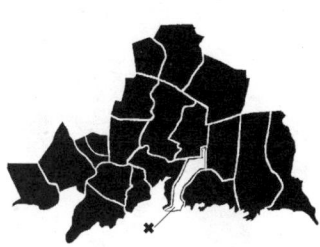

Henry Luzzi
Mayor

Town Hall
250 Main Street
East Haven 06512
Telephone 468-3204

This area, once known as East Farms, was purchased by Rev. John Davenport and Theophilus Eaton in 1638. It was obtained from a pair of Indian Sachems, Momaugin and Mantowese.

In 1639, Thomas Gregson, the first landowner, purchased Solitary Cove, now Morris Cove. The first Connecticut ironworks—and the third in the New England colonies—was located in 1655 by Lake Saltonstall, formerly named Lonotononket, then known as Iron Works Village.

Jacob Heminway, the original Yale student, served as the first pastor of the Congregational Church. In 1774, the Old Stone Church was erected; its first minister was Nicholas Street. This area was invaded in 1779 by British General William Tryon. During the Revolutionary War, Lafayette camped on the Green, revisiting it in 1824. In 1881, Fair Haven, Granniss Corners, and Morris Cove were ceded to New Haven. The Roosevelt Turkey Oak, a gift from President Theodore Roosevelt, was planted on the Green in 1908.

The initial town meeting (1785) named Isaac Chidsey First Selectman. The town became a city during the 1970s under Mayor Francis W. Messina.

East Haven's Town Hall is a handsome Federal style building located on Main Street.

Typical Property Sales or Listings *Residential Median Sales Price: $100,900*

1 Mansfield Grove
2 Bedrooms, 2 Baths
$105,000

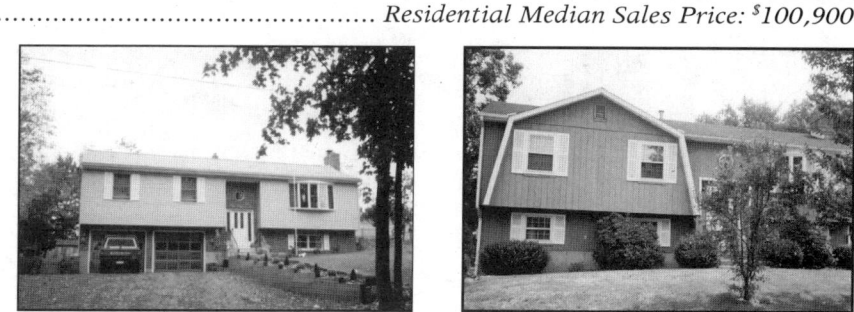

70 Silver Sands Road
3 Bedrooms, 2 Baths
$150,000

13 Timberland Drive
3 Bedrooms, 3 Baths
$176,000

GREATER NEW HAVEN COMMUNITIES
Guilford

Settled 1639, Named 1643 *Population 100 years ago: 2,780*

"Guilford is a unique town full of history and heritage. The town green is a recreational and social center. Guilford has the largest collection of antique houses in New England, and as a result, history can be seen everywhere you look."

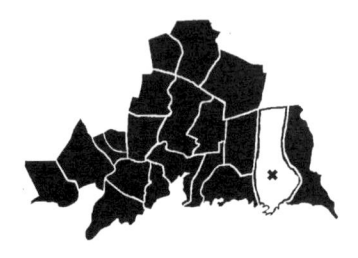

Edward J. Lynch
First Selectman

*Town Hall
31 Park Street
Guilford 06437
Telephone 453-8015*

VITAL STATISTICS
Population 19,848
Per Capita Income $24,583
Median Household Income $56,115
Cost of Education Per Pupil $7,280
Teacher:Pupil Ratio 1:12.2

MAJOR EMPLOYERS
Moroso Performance Products .... (NA)
Clinipad .... (NA)
Shoreline Newspapers .... (NA)

POINTS OF INTEREST
Guilford Handcrafts Center 453-5947
Hyland House 453-9477
Thomas Griswold House 453-3176
Whitfield House Museum 453-2457

This town, the seventh oldest in Connecticut, was founded in 1639 by an oppressed but optimistic band of English Puritans. Henry Whitfield, a minister in Ockley, near London, and about 40 others, formed a joint stock company to sail across the Atlantic.

In a deed of sale dated September 29, 1639, the Whitfield Company purchased the lands between Stony Creek and East River from the Squaw Shaumpishuh, Sachem of the local Menuntuck Indian tribe. In the fall of 1641, the settlers purchased from the Indians the land beyond East River, including most of what became East Guilford, now Madison.

Two good harbors and two tidal rivers assured Guilford's success in shipping and West Indian trade during the 18th century. John Beattie's granite quarries at Leete's Island employed as many as three hundred workmen and supplied stone for the pedestal of the Statue of Liberty. Famous sons of Guilford include William Leete, an early Connecticut Governor; Fitz-Greene Halleck, one of the noted Knickerbocker Poets; and Abraham Baldwin, a signer of the Constitution and Senator from Georgia.

THE OLD STONE HOUSE
Built as a stronghold, meeting hall and minster's house, this is the oldest stone house in New England.

Courtesy Town of Guilford

Typical Property Sales or Listings .... *Residential Median Sales Price: $194,300*

538 Long Hill Road
3 Bedrooms, 2 Baths
$160,000

621 Nortontown Road
4 Bedrooms, 2.5 Baths
$252,000

27 Sachems Head
5 Bedrooms, 5 Full Baths, 3 Half Baths
$1,100,000

GREATER NEW HAVEN COMMUNITIES
Hamden

Population 100 years ago: 3,882 *Separated from New Haven, Incorporated and Named 1786*

VITAL STATISTICS

Population	52,434
Per Capita Income	$19,383
Median Household Income	$41,814
Cost of Education Per Pupil	$8,772
Teacher:Pupil Ratio	1:19

MAJOR EMPLOYERS

Quinnipiac College	435
SNET	390
Arden House	295
Travelers Insurance	250
Lafayette American Bank	175
United Illuminating Company	150
Whitney Manor	150
Hamden Health Care	120
ACES	110
Amphenol	105
AAA Connecticut Motor Club	100

POINTS OF INTEREST

Eli Whitney Museum	777-1833

"The people of Hamden, more than anything else, are why Connecticut Magazine ranked us among the top four large towns in the state. I am very proud of our accomplishments and am honored to be mayor of such a wonderful town."

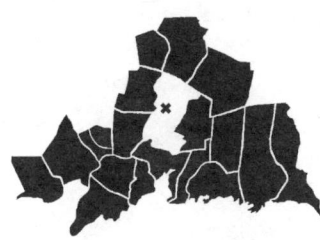

Lillian Clayman
Mayor

*Memorial Town Hall
2372 Whitney Avenue
Hamden 06518*

Telephone 287-2650

Hamden's Eli Whitney Museum is located on Whitney Avenue near the covered bridge and the waterfall at the foot of Lake Whitney.

Incorporated in 1786, the town of Hamden was originally part of New Haven. It was named for John Hampden, a noted English statesman.

In 1798, at the foot of Lake Whitney, inventor Eli Whitney pioneered the use of interchangeable parts in the manufacture of arms for the United States Government. He was also responsible for the creation of the American concept of assembly line production.

The first truss bridge in the United States constructed after the patented design of Ithiel Town, eminent architect, was erected in Whitneyville in 1823. Town used Whitney's concept of standard interchangeable parts to create the Town Truss, making it less expensive than any other truss.

The Farmington Canal, 1825–1848, traversed the entire length of Hamden and evidence of it still exists in the Mount Carmel area.

Typical Property Sales or Listings .... *Residential Median Sales Price: $125,400*

16 Apple Tree Lane
3 Bedrooms, 2 Baths
$138,000

435 Westwoods Road
3 Bedrooms, 3 Baths
$176,000

1021 Ridge Road
4 Bedrooms, 2.5 Baths
$340,000

GREATER NEW HAVEN COMMUNITIES
Madison

Incorporated and Named 1826 *Population 100 years ago: 3,162*

Madison is located at the eastern side of greater New Haven area and has a year-round population of nearly 16,000 residents. Families locate to Madison because of the quality of life that is offered by its location and its superior school system."

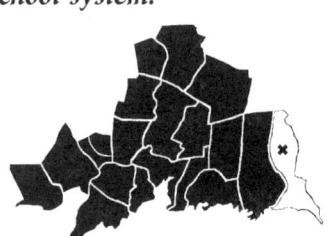

Thomas Rylander
First Selectman

Madison Town Campus
8 Campus Drive
Madison 06443

Telephone 245-5602

VITAL STATISTICS

Population	15,485
Per Capita Income	$29,334
Median Household Income	$61,871
Cost of Education Per Pupil	$7,543
Teacher:Pupil Ratio	1:13

MAJOR EMPLOYERS

Garrity Industries .... (NA)

POINTS OF INTERESTS

Allis-Bushnell House and Museum	245-4567
Hammonasset Beach State Park	245-2785
Madison Gallery	245-7800

Madison was incorporated and named in 1826. It is the site of Hammonasset Beach State Park, Connecticut's largest waterfront park. It features sand beaches, camp sites, and many services.

Madison was a favorite "watering spot" during Victorian times for people from New York and Boston who were summer residents. It still enjoys a surge of tourism in the summer, due to the exceptional resources of this state park.

One of the oldest houses in Madison is the Allis-Bushnell House, built in 1785. It is now occupied by the Madison Historical Society, and is open in the summer months as a museum of local history.

Madison Town Campus

Typical Property Sales or Listings .... *Residential Median Sales Price: $162,500*

137 Cottage Road
3 Bedrooms, 2 Baths
$135,000

93 Blakeman Road
4 Bedrooms, 2 Baths
$212,500

4 Bedrooms, 2.5 Baths
$369,900

GREATER NEW HAVEN COMMUNITIES
Milford

Population 100 years ago: 5,276 *Settled 1639, Named 1640*

VITAL STATISTICS

Population	49,938
Per Capita Income	$19,099
Median Household Income	$44,142
Cost of Education Per Pupil	$7,898
Teacher:Pupil Ratio	1:18

MAJOR EMPLOYERS

Bic Corporation	910
Schick Div. of Warner-Lambert	605
Milford Hospital	600
Subway Franchise World Headquarters	500
Automatic Data Processing	230
Alinabal Inc.	215

POINTS OF INTEREST

Silver Sands State Park .... (NA)

Frederick L. Lisman
Mayor

City Hall
110 River Street
Milford 06460
Telephone 783-3201

"Milford enjoys an abundance of natural and created areas of beauty ~ including a deep harbor, a long green and many historic landmarks ~ together with superb recreational areas and excellent educational facilities."

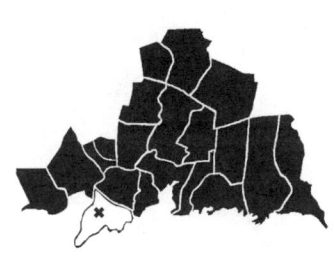

Memorial (or Founder's) Bridge, built in 1888–89 of granite blocks, memorializes the founders of Milford.

Milford was settled in 1639 as an independent colony by a congregation of English Puritans led by Rev. Peter Prudden. Land was purchased from Ansantawae, a Sachem of the Paugusset Indians. The area (originally named Wepawaug) was renamed in November 1640.

Among the Regicides responsible for the trial and execution sentence of English King Charles I, were William Goffe and Edward Whalley, who were sheltered here from royal authorities between 1661 and 1664.

A group led by Robert Treat of Milford founded Newark, New Jersey, in 1666. Milford Resident Rev. Samuel Andrew served as rector of Yale College from 1707 to 1719 and instructed the senior class in his home here.

Early industries included shipbuilding, oystering, seed growing, the manufacture of carriages, boots, shoes, straw hats, and brass and bronze fabrication.

Noted early residents included Connecticut governors Robert Treat, Jonathan Law, and Charles Hobby Pond; colonial lawyer Jared Ingersoll; Revolutionary leaders Charles Pond and Jehiel Bryan; explorer Peter Pond; and inventors George W. Coy, Frank Sprague and Simon Lake.

Typical Property Sales or Listings .... *Residential Median Sales Price: $142,700*

31 Barbara Drive
3 Bedrooms, 1 Bath
$126,000

99 Judith Drive
4 Bedrooms, 1.5 Baths
$226,000

117 Milford Point Road
5 Bedrooms, 2.5 Baths
$530,000

GREATER NEW HAVEN COMMUNITIES
North Branford

Incorporated 1831, Named 1739 *Population 100 years ago: 2,753*

"North Branford is a growing suburban community with many expanding commercial and industrial resources. North Branford offers outstanding municipal services and an excellent educational system."

Joanne Wentworth
Mayor

*Town Hall
2 Colonial Drive
North Branford 06471
Telephone 488-2637*

VITAL STATISTICS
Population	12,996
Per Capita Income	$19,408
Median Household Income	$50,798
Cost of Education Per Pupil	$6,646
Teacher:Pupil Ratio	1:18

MAJOR EMPLOYERS
Fire Lite Alarms	280
Tilcon Connecticut	150
Evergreen Woods	70
Prime Technology	70

POINTS OF INTEREST
Quinnipiac River State Park .... (NA)

This region was opened for settlement in the 1690s as the Third Division of the Town of Branford, originally called by the Indian name Totokett. The North or Second Ecclesiatical Society and the Third Society, later named Northford, were incorporated in 1831, as the Town of North Branford.

Early ministers Jonathan Merick, Samuel Eells and Warham Williams, graduates of Yale College, provided leadership and encouraged education. Colonel William Douglas served under General George Washington during the Revolutionary War and was buried at Northford.

North Branford was noted for its thriving farms and mills, producing wheat and silk in the 18th century. In the 19th century, common pins, horseshoe nails, desiccated coconut, greeting cards, and tinware were manufactured. Trap rock has been quarried here since 1914. In 1933, Lake Galliard reservoir was constructed.

North Branford was designated in 1971 as an All American City for its citizens' public spirit.

North Branford Town Hall

Typical Property Sales or Listings .... *Residential Median Sales Price: $152,500*

207 Valley Road
3 Bedrooms, 2 Baths
$159,900

47 Oxbow Lane
3 Bedrooms, 2 Baths
$180,000

32 Hunter Hill Road
4 Bedrooms, 3.5 Baths
$340,000

GREATER NEW HAVEN COMMUNITIES
North Haven

Population 100 years ago: 4,728 *Incorporated 1831, Named 1768*

VITAL STATISTICS

Population	22,247
Per Capita Income	$21,335
Median Household Income	$49,148
Cost of Education Per Pupil	$8,054
Teacher:Pupil Ratio	1:18

MAJOR EMPLOYERS

U.S. Surgical Corporation	3,215
Blue Cross Blue Shield of Connecticut	2,325
Pratt Whitney Aircraft Group	1,850
Stop & Shop Companies	900
Northeast Graphics	500
Marlin Firearms Company	400
Circuit Wise	365
SNET	335
O.F. Mossberg & Sons, Inc.	285
ACES	285
M.D. Health Plan	235

POINTS OF INTEREST

The Only Game in Town	239-GOLF

North Haven Town Hall

Anthony Rescigno
First Selectman

Town Hall
18 Church Street
North Haven 06473
Telephone 239-5321 ext 760

"A safe, attractive and family-oriented community with outstanding municipal services, an excellent educational system and a dose of traditional New England town charm, North Haven remains a prime location for residential and business growth."

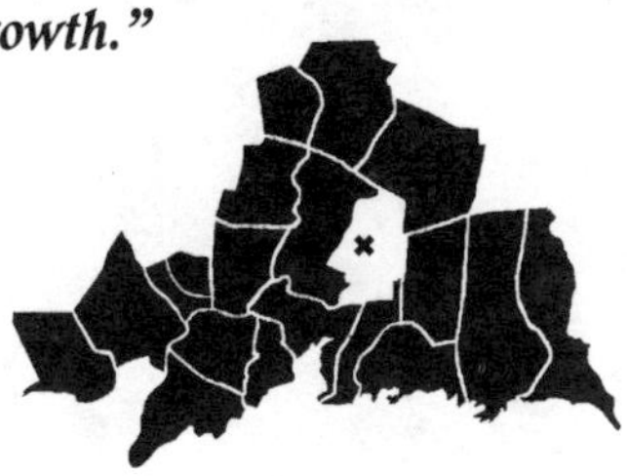

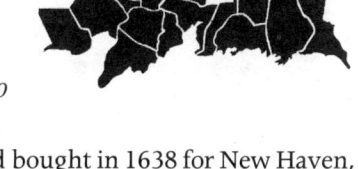

Part of the Indian land bought in 1638 for New Haven, North Haven was incorporated in 1786. The center was settled in 1670 by the Humiston, Thorpe, and Blakeslee families. A separate parish was formed in 1716.

The Reverend James Pierpont gave the Green as land for a meetinghouse, burial ground, and drill field. In the old cemetery lie veterans of the Revolutionary War, including Sergeant Jacob Thorpe, killed at East Haven in 1779. The Reverend Benjamin Trumbull, patriot and historian, lived here from 1760 to 1820. Ezra Stiles, President of Yale (1778-95), and Hobart B. Bigelow, Governor of Connecticut (1881-83) were born here. Theophilus Eaton, a founder of New Haven, opened a brickyard here in 1640. Bog iron was also mined near Pool Road after 1656.

What began as a humble farming village soon became home to small manufacturing enterprises, heralding present-day North Haven, a thriving industrial and residential town.

Typical Property Sales or Listings .... *Residential Median Sales Price: $149,500*

165 Garfield Avenue
2 Bedrooms, 1 Bath
$110,000

36 Bowling Green Drive
4 Bedrooms, 2.5 Baths
$195,500

190 Spring Road
4 Bedrooms, 3.5 Baths
$240,000

GREATER NEW HAVEN COMMUNITIES
Orange

Separated from Milford & New Haven, Incorporated and Named 1822 Population 100 years ago: 4,537

The town of Orange is a suburban residential community with a strong focus on its citizens and their needs. People are attracted to Orange by its convenient location. Lakes, rivers and forests give the community a graceful rural setting.

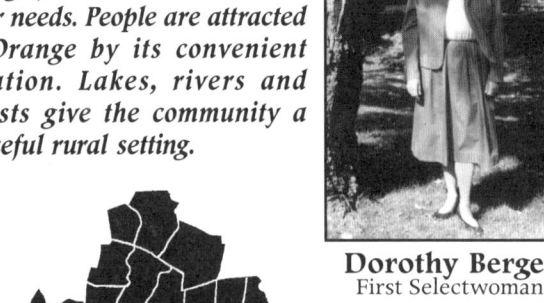

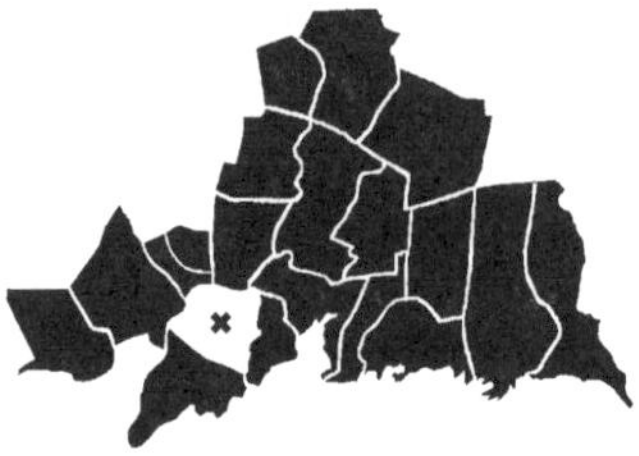

Dorothy Berger
First Selectwoman

*Town Hall
617 Orange Center Road
Orange 06477
Telephone 891-2122*

VITAL STATISTICS
Population 12,830
Per Capita Income $26,860
Median Household Income $62,021
Cost of Education Per Pupil $9,326
Teacher:Pupil Ratio 1:11

MAJOR EMPLOYERS
Muelhens Inc. 250
SNET 235
Sears 180
Rexham Corporation 155
Olive Garden 150
Home Depot 145
General Accident 140
Peak Electronics 115
Pez Candy 100
Sam's Club 100

POINTS OF INTEREST
Otis House Historic Society 795-3106

The rural community of Orange was originally a northern part of Wepawaug. It was purchased from the Paugusett Indians in 1639 by the Reverend Peter Prudden's Milford Colony, which became part of the New Haven Colony in 1643.

The area was settled shortly after 1700 and was known as Bryan's Farms. In 1804, the Ecclesiastical Society of North Milford was chartered here.

The town of Orange was incorporated on May 28, 1822, combining lands from North Milford and the adjacent parish of West Haven.

Orange was named after William, Prince of Orange, in appreciation for benefits received from him by the Connecticut Colony.

The Derby Turnpike was the first major highway in Orange. The toll house, shown together with Everett's Tavern at right, was a regular sight for travelers through the area in the mid-1880s.

Typical Property Sales or Listings .... *Residential Median Sales Price:* $218,800

129 Indian River Road
2 Bedrooms, 1 Bath
$132,000

458 Burning Tree Drive
3 Bedrooms, 2.5 Baths
$252,900

252 Heartland Terrace
4 Bedrooms, 2.5 Baths
$422,500

GREATER NEW HAVEN COMMUNITIES
Prospect

Population 100 years ago: 445 *Separated from Cheshire & Waterbury, Incorporated 1827*

VITAL STATISTICS

Population 8,000
Per Capita Income $22,869
Median Household Income $53,737
Cost of Education Per Pupil $7,163
Teacher:Pupil Ratio 1:18

MAJOR EMPLOYERS

Oliver's Supermarket 40
Foam Plastics of New England 40

POINTS OF INTEREST

Town Green .... (NA)
Civil War Monument .... (NA)

Robert Chatfield
Mayor

*Town Hall
86 Center Street
Prospect 06712
Telephone 768-4461*

"Although Prospect is a small town, it is characterized by great spirit. Volunteerism is the backbone of our community, with a focus on our young people, in scouting and sports. Our town offers an opportunity for strong connection to our neighbors."

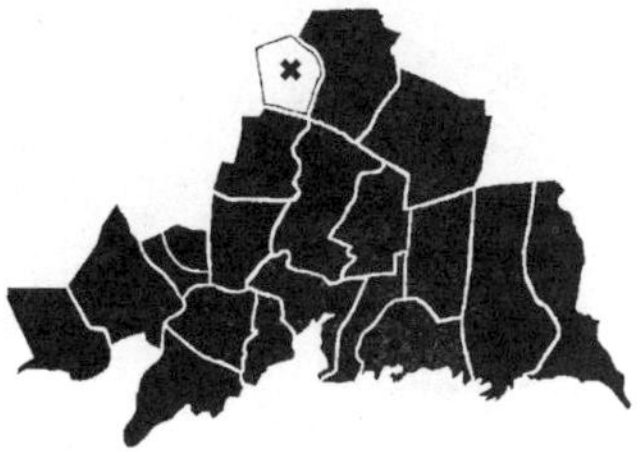

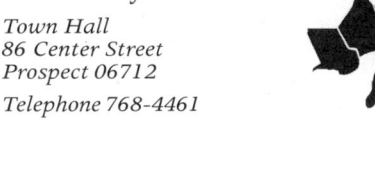

The little hilltop town of Prospect has often been called the best small town in the state. It is located between Waterbury and Cheshire. Prospect is 950 feet above sea level, the highest point in the county, and receives lots of snow, even in relatively dry winters.

The town is located around a central Green, which makes for many charming New England scenes, especially around Christmas time. Visit the Green and the Civil War Monument, and take a step back in time to an easier, calmer, and more peaceful era.

Typical Property Sales or Listings .... *Residential Median Sales Price: $137,000*

9 Putting Green Lane
3 Bedrooms, 2 Baths
$206,000

3 Bedrooms, 2 Baths
$249,900

3 Bedrooms, 2 Baths
$259,900

GREATER NEW HAVEN COMMUNITIES
Shelton

Incorporated 1789 *Population 100 years ago: 3,487*

Shelton's accessibility continues to promote its economic growth. Shelton is alive with community spirit, pride, volunteerism and a concern for the preservation of the land.

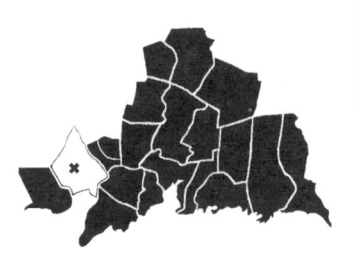

Mark Lauretti
Mayor

*Town Hall
54 Hill Street
Shelton 06484
Telephone 924-1555*

VITAL STATISTICS
Population	36,000
Per Capita Income	$21,739
Median Household Income	$49,837
Cost of Education Per Pupil	$6,976
Teacher:Pupil Ratio	1:18

MAJOR EMPLOYERS
Moore & Munger, Inc. .... (NA)

POINTS OF INTEREST
Indian Wells State Park	(NA)
Plumb Memorial Library	924-1580
Pine Rock Park	(NA)

"Pumpkin People" at a Fall event in Shelton

Shelton Town Hall

Typical Property Sales or Listings .... Residential Median Sales Price: $186,100

44 Maltby Street
2 Bedrooms, 2 Baths
$95,000

186-88 Division Avenue
3 Bedrooms, 2 Baths
$125,000

30 Fairmont Place
4 Bedrooms, 2.5 Baths
$228,000

GREATER NEW HAVEN COMMUNITIES
Trumbull

Population 100 years ago: 1,453   *Separated from Stratford, Incorporated 1797*

VITAL STATISTICS

Population	32,360
Per Capita Income	$32,900
Median Household Income	$60,634
Cost of Education Per Pupil	$7,477
Teacher:Pupil Ratio	1:20

MAJOR EMPLOYERS

Sikorsky Aircraft	500
Physicians Health Services	415
Pitney Bowes	385
Golf Digest	380
St. Joseph's Manor	365

POINTS OF INTEREST
(in Bridgeport)

The Barnum Museum	331-9881
Beardsley Zoo	576-8082
The Discovery Museum	372-3521

David Wilson
First Selectman

Town Hall
5866 Main Street
Trumbull 06611

Telephone 452-5005

What was once small village on the edge of Colonial civilization is now a vibrant community of over 32,000, on the western edge of the greater New Haven area. Today, Trumbull offers its residents a peaceful place to settle, close to urban centers.

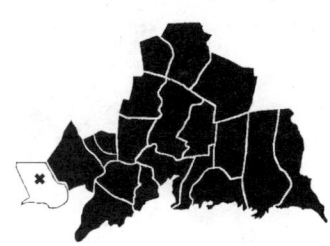

Trumbull was once part of an area known as Pequonnocke or Cubheag, now known as Stratford. Stratford retained its original boundaries from 1639 until 1789, when land was taken to form other communities. The land was surveyed around 1670, but it was 20 years before the first family actually moved on to this land.

A grant for a sawmill was given to James and Edmund Lewis and Ebenezer Curtis in 1702, and in 1704, John Williams and John Seeley were permitted the use of a gristmill on the Pequonnock River.

The General Court granted "village privileges" for the new village of Unity. Families from the Stratfield section of Fairfield began to settle on the Western edge of Unity, and soon formed the society of Long Hill.

In 1744, Long Hill and Unity joined to become North Stratford. In 1797, the name was changed to Trumbull, and new town lines were drawn.

Trumbull Town Hall

Typical Property Sales or Listings .... *Residential Median Sales Price: $187,900*

| 3 Bedrooms, 1.5 Baths | 3 Bedrooms, 3 Baths | 4 Bedrooms, 2.5 Baths |
| $147,900 | $299,000 | $449,000 |

GREATER NEW HAVEN COMMUNITIES
Wallingford

Settled and Named 1670   *Population years ago: 6,585*

"Wallingford is a 325 year old New England town ideally located in the center of the state. A community with spirit and pride, Wallingford is a vibrant, progressive town with an excellent school system. It is a great place to live."

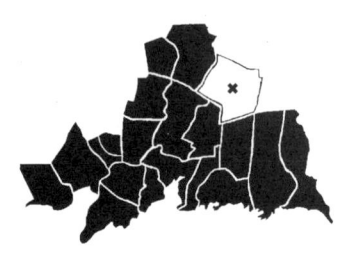

Wm. Dickinson, Jr.
Mayor

Town Hall
45 South Main Street
Wallingford 06492
Telephone 294-2070

VITAL STATISTICS

Population	40,822
Per Capita Income	$18,231
Median Household Income	$42,783
Cost of Education Per Pupil	$6,931
Teacher:Pupil Ratio	1:14

MAJOR EMPLOYERS

Allegheny Ludlum Steel	(NA)
Bristol Myers	(NA)
C&K Unimax Inc.	(NA)
Cytec Industries	(NA)
Duracell Inc.	(NA)
Dataproducts New England	(NA)
Jefferson Federal	(NA)

POINTS OF INTEREST

Parson House	(NA)
Wharton Brook State Park	(NA)

This territory was purchased by the New Haven Colony in 1638 from Montowese, son of an Indian Sachem. It was names after Wallingford, England, and was settled in 1670 by planters from New Haven and Stratford. Its boundaries originally encompassed present-day Cheshire, Meriden and part of Prospect.

From 1766, the "True Sons of Liberty" order was formed in the town. A native son, Dr. Lyman Hall, was a signer of the Declaration of Indepedence. Originally agricultural, the town has made a lasting name for itself through the development of the silverware industry.

Wallingford's town green, or "Parade Ground," is as old as the community itself. During the 1800s, local industrialists built stately homes along Main Street and a commercial district along Center Street. The town green became a central park for the bustling urban center.

Wallingford Town Hall

Typical Property Sales or Listings   *Residential Median Sales Price: $146,400*

27 Brookvale Drive
4 Bedrooms, 2 Baths
$118,000

4 Grieb Road
4 Bedrooms, 2.5 Baths
$206,950

916 Clintonville Road
4 Bedrooms, 2.5 Baths
$229,900

GREATER NEW HAVEN COMMUNITIES
West Haven

Population 100 years ago: 6,374

Incorporated 1921, Named about 1720

VITAL STATISTICS

Population	54,021
Per Capita Income	$15,810
Median Household Income	$35,723
Cost of Education Per Pupil	$6,610
Teacher:Pupil Ratio	1:15

MAJOR EMPLOYERS

U.S. Veterans Hospital	2,000
Bayer Pharmaceuticals	1,400
Sikorsky Aircraft	400
University of New Haven	395
Lenders Bagel Bakery	300
Enthone-OMI, Inc.	195
West Haven Nursing Center	160

POINTS OF INTEREST

Bradley Point Park	(NA)
Savin Rock	(NA)

H. Richard Borer
Mayor

City Hall
355 Main Street
West Haven 06516
Telephone 937-3510

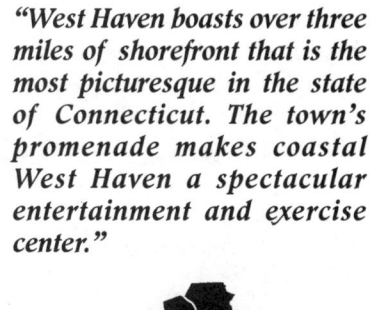

"West Haven boasts over three miles of shorefront that is the most picturesque in the state of Connecticut. The town's promenade makes coastal West Haven a spectacular entertainment and exercise center."

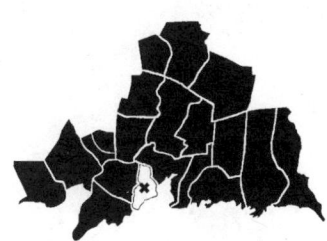

Its amusement park did much to make Savin Rock a prime seaside resort area for many years.

West Farms (West Haven) recorded its first household in 1648. Part of the originanal New Haven Colony, West Farms became the separate parish of West Haven in 1719.

West Haven and North Milford joined in 1822 to form the Town of Orange. The rural sections of Orange separated in 1921 when the residential part, West Haven, became Connecticut's youngest town.

In 1961, West Haven was incorporated as a city and adopted a mayor-council form of government. By this action, one of the oldest settlements became the newest municipality in Connecticut.

For many years, West Haven's Savin Rock was a popular seaside resort. With resort hotels, an amusement park, and dance pavilions which hosted big-name stars, "The Rock," with its rickety wooden roller coaster, was Connecticut's grandest seaside park. Today, this area is a lovely stretch of beach.

Typical Property Sales or Listings ..... *Residential Median Sales Price: $88,400*

597 Jones Hill Road
3 Bedrooms, 2 Baths
$84,900

65 Seaview Avenue
3 Bedrooms, 2.5 Baths
$152,000

5 Woodruff Street
5 Bedrooms, 1 Full & 2 Half Baths
$340,000

GREATER NEW HAVEN COMMUNITIES
Woodbridge

Separated from New Haven & Milford, Incorporated and Named 1784 *Population 100 years ago: 926*

"Woodbridge is a beautiful community of approximately 8,900 people. Hiking trails, a wonderful library and excellent schools help make it a lovely place to live. The town's community-minded residents take an active role in the life of Woodbridge."

Nan Birdswhistell
First Selectwoman

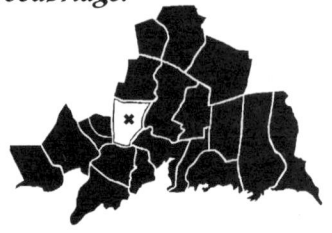

Memorial Town Hall
11 Meetinghouse Lane
Woodbridge 06525
Telephone 389-3400

VITAL STATISTICS

Population 8,900
Per Capita Income $38,008
Median Household Income $70,670
Cost of Education Per Pupil $8.274
Teacher:Pupil Ratio 1:18

MAJOR EMPLOYERS

Research Publications, Inc. 155
Plastics Forming Co., Inc. 60
Frank Perrotti and Sons, Inc. 60
Connecticut Bank of Commerce 55
Bailey, Moore, Glazer, Schaefer & Proto 35

POINTS OF INTEREST

Jewish Community Center 387-2522
Clark Memorial Library 389-3433
West River Complex 389-3446

The town of Woodbridge consists of portions of the colonial jurisdictions of New Haven and Milford. Founded in 1738 as the Parish of Amity, it was incorporated in 1784 and named after the first parish minister, the Reverend Benjamin Woodbridge, who served from 1742 to 1785.

The first meetinghouse was built in 1740 on the town green and met the needs of the community until 1832, when it was replaced by the present building, dedicated on January 1, 1833.

The early economy was largely agricultural, but there were several small factories, producing such items as corkscrews, cement, candlesticks, clocks and spinning wheels. Some of the earliest friction matches in this country were made in Woodbridge.

The decline of farming and improved transportation after 1900, together with the natural beauty and topography of the land, have contributed to its growth and distinction as a residential community.

Woodbridge Memorial Hall

Typical Property Sales or Listings .... *Residential Median Sales Price: $283,600*

46 Hallsey Lane
3 Bedrooms, 2.5 Baths
$206,000

25 Shepard Road
5 Bedrooms, 3.5 Baths
$327,300

3 Hunter's Ridge
4 Bedrooms, 3.5 Baths
$535,000

GREATER NEW HAVEN COMMUNITIES
City of New Haven

Population 100 years ago: 86,045 *Settled April 1638, Names August 1640, Incorporated 1784*

VITAL STATISTICS

Population	123,470
Per Capita Income	$12,968
Median Household Income	$25,811
Cost of Education Per Pupil	$8,102
Teacher:Pupil Ratio	1:18

MAJOR EMPLOYERS

Yale University	8,670
Yale-New Haven Hospital	6,000
SNET	3,820
Hospital of St. Raphael	3,570
Southern Connecticut State University	815
United Illuminating	780
Sargent & Company	735
Knights of Columbus	625
Metro North	565
U.S. Repeating Ams Co.	560
New Haven Register	440
Community Health Care	370
New Haven Ambulance	335
Regional Water Authority	310
Starter Sportswear	305
Robby Len Fashions	300
Ives, Division of Leigh Products	300
Jewish Home for the Aged	290
New Haven Savings Bank	270
Wiggin & Dana	260
Simkins Industries	250
Pirelli-Armstrong Tire	230

INDEX TO ORGANIZATIONS
(with beginning page number reference)

Albertus Magnus College	226
Chamber of Commerce	8
Gateway Comm. Tech. College	223
Hospital of St. Raphael	268
Knights of Columbus	280
New Haven Police Department	162
New Haven Public Schools	158
New Haven Ravens	24
Science Park	282
Southern CT State University	224
Theatre, Dance, Music, Other Arts Groups	65
Visitors and Convention Bureau	9
Yale-New Haven Hospital	266
Yale University	232

John DeStefano, Jr.
Mayor, City of New Haven

OFFICE OF THE MAYOR
CITY OF NEW HAVEN · CONNECTICUT 06510

JOHN DESTEFANO, JR.
MAYOR

Dear Visitor or Resident:

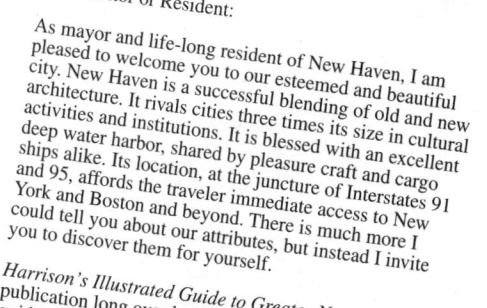

As mayor and life-long resident of New Haven, I am pleased to welcome you to our esteemed and beautiful city. New Haven is a successful blending of old and new architecture. It rivals cities three times its size in cultural activities and institutions. It is blessed with an excellent deep water harbor, shared by pleasure craft and cargo ships alike. Its location, at the juncture of Interstates 91 and 95, affords the traveler immediate access to New York and Boston and beyond. There is much more I could tell you about our attributes, but instead I invite you to discover them for yourself.

Harrison's Illustrated Guide to Greater New Haven is a publication long overdue. I offer special thanks to the guide's author-producer, Henry S. Harrison, and to the publisher, the Real Estate Educational Foundation.

Sincerely,

John DeStefano Jr.
Mayor

* This creative impression is the work of Lindsay Chacon, a 3rd grader at the Woodward Avenue School.

Magnet High Schools & Programs

Career High School
21 Wooster Place
Charles J. Williams, Principal

Enrollment: 400+ students
Selection: Parent and student interview
Recommendations

The Career High School focuses on exposing its students to careers in health, business or computers. Yale-New Haven Hospital provides opportunities for volunteering, a Career Exploration program and a Mentorship Program. Apple Computer is another of the school's business partners, assisting the staff and students with computer projects. Students study anatomy alongside medical students at Yale Medical School. Students may also receive college credits through the school's partnership with Gateway Community College.

Cooperative Arts & Humanities High School
444 Orange Street
Edward Linehan, Principal

Enrollment: 420 students
Selection: Recommendation, interview
Evaluation of student's artistic ability

Cooperative Arts & Humanities High School is a regional magnet school for students with a high level of interest in the performing and creative arts. Known as the CO-OP, the school strives to offer a quality arts-focused program within the context of a comprehensive college preparatory education. Located one block from the heart of New Haven's arts community on Audubon Street, the school has established a close working relationship with the Arts Council and other arts organizations.

Educational Center for the Arts
55 Audubon Street
Robert Parker, Director

Enrollment: 165 Students
Selection: By application, with demonstrated artistic ability

The Educational Center for the Arts (ECA), located in the vibrant Audubon Street arts complex, provides arts education to talented students as the second half of their regular school day. Students from throughout the South Central CT area are served. ECA has five departments: dance, music, theater, visual arts and poetry/prose. Its educational goals include:

- development of individual artistic "voice"
- exposure to the art world
- placing art in historical context
- exploration within each art form
- collaboration between disciplines
- and cooperation among students and faculty.

High School in the Community
45 Nash Street
Patricia Lucas Morgillo, Facilitator

Enrollment: 240 students
Selection: Lottery

Established in 1970, High School in the Community (HSC) has been designated as an "exemplary education institution" by the U.S. Department of Education. The school will become a regional magnet school during the 1995-1996 school year. HSC offers a full academic program and strong college preparation, encouraging students to develop problem-solving skills, participate actively in classes and learn individual responsibility. The non-traditional schedule, with extended class periods, provides opportunities for varied approaches to learning.

The Hyde Leadership School
306 Circular Avenue, Hamden
Larry Conaway, Principal

Enrollment: 125 Students
Selection: Parent and student interview
Recommendations; essay application

The Hyde Leadership School is designed to develop each student's character: courage, integrity, concern for others, curiosity and leadership. Based on a concept developed at the Hyde School in Bath, Maine, the school differs significantly from traditional schools in three fundamental ways. (1) The school enrolls families rather than just students. Mandatory monthly parent meetings, retreats and family weekends help bridge the gap between home and school. (2) The *Discovery Program* offers an innovative approach to discipline. (3) Each student participates in a five-part curriculum, including college prep academics, community service, performing arts, leadership training, and athletics.

New Haven-Yale Saturday Seminar
at James Hillhouse High School
480 Sherman Avenue
Dr. Burton Saxon, Facilitator

Enrollment: 150 students
Selection: By application through individual school

A collaboration between the New Haven Public schools and Yale University, this program currently serves students from 18 area high schools. Seminars are taught on such topics as Chinese, Japanese, West African history, language and culture.

The Sound School
60 South Water Street
George Foote, Principal

Enrollment: 260 students
Selection: Lottery

Located on Long Island Sound at New Haven Harbor, the school offers students an opportunity to acquire high school diplomas while exploring a marine curriculum. The school provides career education in marine and fresh water resources, and the maritime trades. The water program includes sailing the 16 foot "sharpies" and classes aboard the 90-foot schooner, *Quinnipiack*.

CITY OF NEW HAVEN
New Haven Public Schools

There are approximately 19,000 children and over 1,700 teachers in New Haven's public school system, headed by the Superintendent of Schools, Dr. Reginald R. Mayo. There are 42 schools, which include five magnet high schools and seven other magnet schools and special programs.

New Haven has implemented several nationally-recognized reform efforts to upgrade its schools.

The **Public Schools' Partnership Program** matches businesses, colleges and non-profits with individual schools. These partnerships enrich the schools in a variety of ways, including providing mentors for students, teaching specialized classes, tutoring, staff training and development, and providing internships and scholarships. Local businesses in the Partnership Program include Fusco Corporation, the Hospital of Saint Raphael, IBM, *The New Haven Register*, People's Bank, SNET, Starter Sportswear, Inc., United Illuminating, and the Xerox Corporation.

The Yale Child Study Center **School Development Program,** developed by Dr. James Comer, is used in all 42 schools.

The **Social Development Project** is a system-wide intervention program funded by federal, state and foundation grants.

Superintendent of Schools **Dr. Reginald R. Mayo** *has been involved with the New Haven School system since his graduation from Virginia Union University in 1966. Dr. Mayo received his M.S. from Southern Connecticut State University in 1971, his Ed.D from Nova University in 1975, and his Ph.D. from the University of Connecticut in 1988. The Executive Director of School Operations for 8 years, Dr. Mayo was appointed Superintendent of Schools in 1988.*

Elementary & Middle Magnet Schools

Betsy Ross Arts Magnet School
185 Barnes Avenue
Brenda Holland, Principal

At Betsy Ross, 550 students in grades 5-8 study visual arts, theatre, dance, music, creative writing and photography, in addition to regular academic subjects. The school's philosophy is that the creative and expressive skills of the artist are the same skills required for success in the academic world. The school has been singled out by the U.S. Department of Education as one of the country's finest schools. Students are selected by lottery.

Troup Magnet Academy of Science
259 Edgewood Avenue
Richard Kaliszewski, Principal

The Academy, which enrolls 650 students in grades 5-8, focuses on science, mathematics and communications, using technology to assist and complement classroom instruction. The emphasis is on interdisciplinary approaches and direct, hands-on learning. Neighborhood students are selected first; remainder by lottery.

West Hills Magnet School
311 Valley Street (K-4); 103 Hallock Avenue (5-8)
Janice K. Romo, Principal

A racially and academically integrated school of 700 students, its innovative programs feature parental involvement and the Bank Street College Model of Education. Selection is by lottery, with consideration to ethnicity and income.

Jepson Non-Graded Magnet School
375 Quinnipiac Avenue
John Vigliotti, Principal

The Jepson Magnet School provides flexible grouping that allow its 160 students to work at their own pace. Cooperation, creativity and self-confidence are fostered in this special, multi-cultural elementary school environment.

The Language Academy at Clinton Ave. School
293 Clinton Avenue
Patricia DeRenzo, Principal

The 485 students in grades K-4 at the Academy study either English or Spanish as a second language, in addition to their regular academic program.

new haven parks

Wherever you live, work, or visit in New Haven, you're never very far from a patch of green. The city has an extraordinary network of parkland, totalling nearly one-fifth of its total land area.

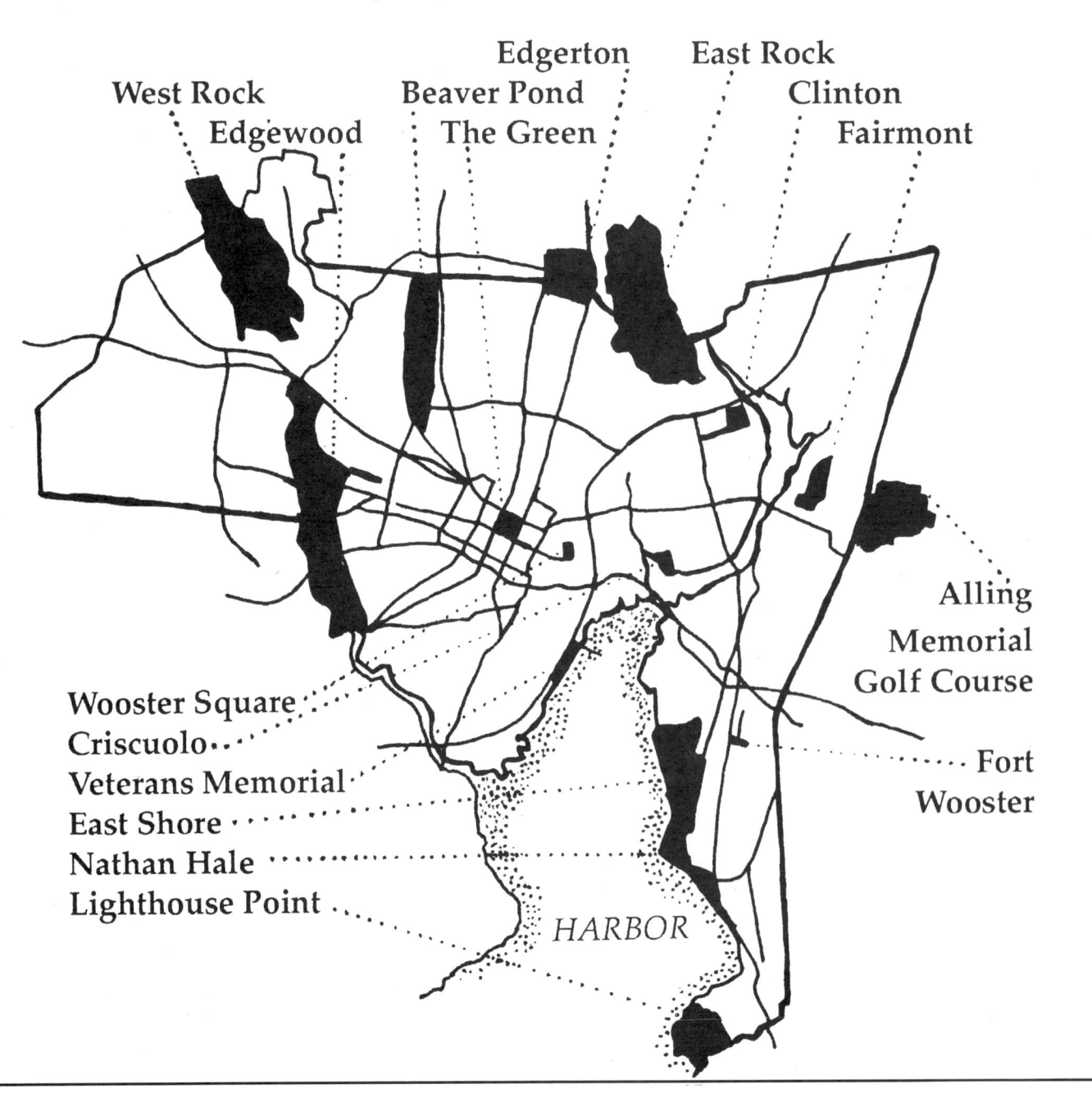

West Rock
Edgewood
Edgerton
Beaver Pond
The Green
East Rock
Clinton
Fairmont

Wooster Square
Criscuolo
Veterans Memorial
East Shore
Nathan Hale
Lighthouse Point

Alling Memorial Golf Course

Fort Wooster

HARBOR

CITY OF NEW HAVEN
Parks & Recreation

New Haven has over 130 parks and playgrounds covering 2,300 acres or 17% of the city's total land area. Most of the parks are open year-round. The following information on some of the larger parks was taken from publications of *Park Friends* and the New Haven Department of Parks, Recreation & Trees. For more information on any New Haven park, call 946-8019.

Alling Memorial Golf Course

This 146-acre park is located on the New Haven-East Haven line (take I-91 to Rte. 80 to Eastern Street) and includes an 18-hole par 71 golf course, a clubhouse with a pro shop and restaurant, and a practice green. The course is open March 1 to December 31, and has off-season rates in January and February. For information, call 946-8014.

Beaver Pond Park

A 101-acre park adjacent to Southern Connecticut State University, between Sherman Parkway and Crescent Street, Beaver Pond includes baseball, softball, and soccer fields, as well as tennis courts.

Center Green

In the heart of downtown New Haven, the Green comprises 16 acres bordered by College, Chapel, Church and Elm Streets. The Green is a popular spot for walking, sunning, picnicking, games and concerts.

Clinton Park

Located near the Quinnnipiac River in Fair Haven (Clinton Avenue and Bailey Street), this 22-acre park provides picnic spots and playground facilities.

East Rock Park

This beautiful 400-acre park which straddles the New Haven-Hamden line is a great place for walking, hiking and a variety of sports. (East Rock Road between State Street and Whitney Avenue.) The view from the summit offers a fantastic panorama of New Haven. Below the cliffs, at Orange and Cold Spring Streets, is College Woods, with basketball courts and a playground. On Mitchell Drive there are tennis and basketball courts, and a jogging track. Blake Field (Willow Street south of Foster) has more athletic fields. All of these facilities are open to the public. Call 946-6086 for more information.

East Shore Park

One of the newer city waterfront parks, on 131 acres with a slender beach (I-95 to Exit 50, right on Woodward Avenue), it is equipped with tennis courts, handball walls, soccer and baseball fields (three lighted), basketball courts, handicap-accessible exercise track, restrooms and an outdoor skating rink with warming house. For information call 787-8790.

Edgerton Park

Built in the English garden tradition, this 22-acre walled park (Whitney Avenue at Cliff Street) was donated to the City in 1964. Edgerton is a great place for quiet walks or relaxation, with a restored fountain court and a large community garden.

Edgewood Park

A meandering 123-acre park bordered by Yale, Whalley and Derby Avenues and the Boulevard, Edgewood is a nice place to walk, ride bikes or picnic. The upper park includes tennis and basketball courts. The lower park has playgrounds, ball fields and a duck pond. Edgewood is the site of the Spanish American War Memorial, Holocaust Memorial, and the Department of Parks headquarters. Coogan Skating Rink is to be renovated. Call 946-8028.

Fort Hale Park

On the water south of East Shore Park, this 54-acre park offers a beautiful harbor view, picnic areas, boat launching and a playground. Hours are seasonal. Call 946-8790.

Lighthouse Point Park

This 84-acre park on Long Island Sound is New Haven's most popular public beach. Facilities include a bathhouse, picnic areas, playing fields, a beautifully restored carousel, an historic 1840s lighthouse, and a bird sanctuary. In summer, there is an entrance fee for cars.

Vietnam Veterans Memorial Park

Formerly Long Wharf Park, this 17-acre park encompasses the west shore of New Haven harbor. (Exit 46 on I-95). The park holds the Vietnam Veterans Memorial and offers a pleasant harbor view and picnic facilities. The New Haven Information Center is inside the park.

West River Memorial Park

Near the West Haven border (Boulevard between Rte.1 and Rte.34) lies this 181-acre park with basketball courts, playing fields, hiking trails, and a wildlife sanctuary.

West Rock Park

A network of trails, the historic Judges' Cave, playing fields, and a spectacular view are among the attractions to this 625-acre state park (off Wintergreen Avenue in Westville). Across the street is the West Rock Nature Center, a 40-acre park with a mini-zoo, trails and picnic areas.

Deptartment Parks, Recreation & Trees	**946-8019**
Frank A. Williams, Director	

An important part of the progress made in crime-prevention in the City since Chief Pastore's appointment has been the implementation of community-based policing. The Department has moved away from operating centrally out of its main location on Union Avenue, and instead emphasizes its substations throughout the city, such as the **26 Charles Street Community Substation**. *A neighborhood substation serves as a place where citizens and the police work together to forge links and prevent crime in their community.*

A welcome addition to NHPD's outreach efforts in the community is the **Mounted Patrol Unit**. *Not only do the horses offer better police control of crowded events such as the Summertime Street Festival and the Special Olympics World Games, but they also make officers more approachable, offering another way to establish rapport with citizens.*

The New Haven Police Department is committed to maintaining and enhancing a strong neighborhood police presence and on-going collaboration with the communities. Mutual respect based on understanding between citizens and the police allows for the formation of effective partnerships to prevent crime, and means a safer city for us all.

PRIDE & PROGRESS

RESPECT · PARTNERSHIPS · NEIGHBORHOOD

CITY OF NEW HAVEN
Police Department

New Haven's Department of Police Service (NHPD), headed by Chief Nicholas Pastore, has received national recognition for its innovative and successful methods of fighting crime. The NHPD has over 450 officers and detectives, 100 civilian personnel and an annual budget of over $23 million.

The NHPD has embraced a philosophy of community-based policing, which places police services into nine "substations" scattered throughout the City, to create a partnership between New Haven's diverse racial and cultural communities and the police department. The NHPD recognizes that shared responsibility makes the City a better place to live.

Pastore's department has achieved tangible results: New Haven's crime rate has been dropping over the past few years, most notably in the number of murders, which has declined. Despite an unfortunate reputation to the contrary, New Haven continues to become a safer place to live. New Haven, like many post-industrial cities, struggles with the effects of crime and poverty.

> *"When you arrest somebody, it should be done with dignity and respect, not meanness. And arrest should be the last resort."*
>
> **Nick Pastore**
> **Chief of Police**

Nonetheless, there is room for optimism. Chief Pastore's attack on crime has focused on a "get-smart" strategy, rather than a more traditional "lock 'em up," militaristic approach. There is a new emphasis on foot patrols, drug treatment rather than imprisonment, and education/prevention programs, all designed to rebuild connections between the police and the communities. A federal, state and city task force recently arrested a large number of leaders of New Haven's major drug-dealing gangs, using information gathered in great part by community policing techniques. Attorney General Janet Reno recognized the remarkable accomplishments of this task force, and cited it as a model for similar violence prevention programs now being implemented nationwide.

*Chief of Police **Nicholas Pastore** is a native of New Haven who has served on the Police Department for more than 30 years. He was appointed Chief in 1990. Pastore earned his B.S. in Criminal Justice from the University of New Haven in 1979, and has become nationally-known for his non-traditional approaches to crime fighting. Under his leadership, the Department has implemented community-based policing, which has reduced the crime rate and has helped increase communication between the police and the communities.*

Unique to the NHPD is its close alliance with the Yale Child Study Center, part of Yale Medical School. The Yale Child Development Community Policing Program trains police officers in child and adolescent psychology, to help them understand children who are victims of and witnesses to violence. In addition, Yale faculty and specially-trained sergeants provide around-the-clock consultation services to officers responding to crisis calls. This program is part of an overall commitment to non-violent problem-solving techniques in neighborhood conflicts to help prevent serious crimes.

New Haven Police Department	
Non-Emergency Calls	946-6316
Public Information Officer	946-6271
Emergencies	911

City Wards and 1995 Polling Places

Ward #	Poll	Street Address
1.	Dwight Hall	67 High Street
2.	Firehouse	Goffe & Webster Streets
3.	Jewish Home For The Aged	169 Davenport Avenue
4.	Truman School	114 Truman Street
5.	Firehouse	Howard Avenue & Putnam Street
6.	West Hills Middle School	107 Hallock Avenue
7.	Hall Of Records - Hearing Room	200 Orange Street
8.	Conte Senior Center	21 Wooster Place
9.	East Rock School	133 Nash Street, Courtyard Entrance
10.	Wilbur Cross High School	181 Mitchell Drive
11A.	Bella Vista	343 Eastern Street
11B.	Bishop Woods School	1481 Quinnipiac Ave.
12.	Betsy Ross School	189 Barnes Avenue
13.	Firehouse	120 East Grand Avenue & Lenox Street
14.	Atwater Senior Center	26 Atwater Street
15.	Firehouse	Lombard & Poplar Streets
16.	Fair Haven Elderly	25 Saltonstall Avenue
17.	Firehouse	824 Woodward Avenue
18.	Firehouse	Lighthouse Road & Townsend Avenue
19.	Celentano School	400 Canner Street
20	Lincoln Bassett School	130 Bassett Street
21.	Martin Luther King School	580 Dixwell Avenue
22.	Isadore Wexler School	209 Dixwell Avenue
23A.	Dwight School	100 Edgewood Avenue
23B.	Berger Apartments	135 Derby Avenue
24.	Firehouse	120 Ellsworth Avenue
25.	Edgewood School	737 Edgewood Avenue
26A.	Davis Street School	35 Davis Street
26B.	Barnard School	Derby Avenue & Ella T. Grasso Blvd.
27A.	Mitchell Library	37 Harrison Street
27B.	Firehouse	105 Fountain Street
28.	Hillhouse High School	480 Sherman Parkway
29.	S.C.S.U. Field House Lobby	101 Wintergreen Avenue
30A.	Katherine Brennan School	200 Wilmot Road
30B.	West Hills School	311 Valley Street - Gymnasium

CITY OF NEW HAVEN
City Services & Phone Numbers

The following is a partial list of the many City Services and Frequently Used Phone Numbers, taken from 1995 City Services Guide published by the Mayor's Office of the City of New Haven.

CITY SERVICES

AIDS	946-6453
Counseling & Screening (Anon.)	1 (800) 342-2437
Alcohol Abuse	1 (800) 444-9999
Ambulance	911
Alcoholics Anonymous	624-6063
Arson Report Line (Confidential)	946-4455
Chemical Spills	1 (800) 242-8802
Child Abuse/Emergency	1 (800) 842-2288
Children (Missing)	1 (800) 843-5678
Cocaine	1 (800) 262-2463
Coast Guard/Search & Rescue	468-4400
Dumping, Illegal	946-6316
Domestic Violence	787-8104
Energy Assistance	1 (800) 842-1132
Fire Emergency	911
Gas Leaks	777-7311
INFOLINE	867-4150
Medical Emergency	911
Narcotics Anonymous	1 (800) 627-3543
Narcotics Enforcement	946-6929
Poison Control	1 (800) 343-2722
Police Emergency	911
Pothole Reports	946-5808
Power Outage Emergency	1 (800) 722-5584
Public Housing Maintenance	946-2960
Public Works Emergency	946-8334
Sexual Assault/Rape Crisis	624-2273
Sewer Back-up/Catch Basin	946-8155
Storm Emergencies	946-8210
Street Light Problems	931-6325
Traffic Signal Problems	946-8075
Water Co. Emergency Shut-off	562-4020
Venereal Disease Line	1 (800) 227-8922

FREQUENTLY USED PHONE NUMBERS

Airport (Tweed-New Haven)	946-7897
Airplanes (US Air & United)	946-8283
Amtrak - Metroliner (only)	1 (800) 523-8720
All Other trains	1 (800) 872-7245
Comcast Cablevision	865-0096
CT Transit - Bus Service	624-0151
Convention & Visitors Bureau	1 (800) 332-STAY
Consumer Protection	1 (800) 842-2649
Current Events & Activities	498-5050 (x1315)
Disabled Transportation	288-6282
Energy Assistance Hot Line	1 (800) 842-1132
Food Stamps (Social Services)	789-1997
Gas Leaks	777-7311
Health Department	946-7234
Housing Authority	946-2894
INFOLINE	867-4150
Legal Assistance (New Haven)	777-4811
Library, Main	946-8699
Mayor's Office	946-7683
Metro North Railroad	1 (800) 638-7646
Park Department	946-8024/8047
Parking Authority	946-8929
Public School Registration	946-8501
Regional Water Authority	624-6671
Social Services Administration	773-2160
Social Service of CT.	789-7555
Special Olympics (New Haven)	946-7847
Taxes (U.S. Internal Revenue)	1 (800) 829-1040
Telephone Repair (SNET)	611
Telephone Service & Equipment	811
United Illuminating (UI)	1 (800) 722-5584
Welfare Department	946-7269
Zoning Director	946-8237

City kids enjoy concrete pleasures, playing a typical city game of hopscotch.

These kids get the point across as part of a local initiative for early childhood immunization.

Mounting confidence in our award-winning community-based police enhances life in New Haven.

Of all the startling discoveries that emanate from Yale University, the biggest surprise revealed this May didn't come from a test tube or a research study. It came from the private decisions of 125 human beings – Yale professors, maintenance workers, office workers – to buy homes in the city in the past year.

All sorts of people it turns out, *want* to live in New Haven.

You heard that right. Despite all we hear about people fleeing cities - and that image has its share of truth throughout urban America – a separate phenomenon is transforming New Haven. A wide range of people are discovering they prefer city life to suburbia or exurbia. Especially New Haven life. And they're playing a part in making that life more exciting, more stable, more interconnected.

Take the 125 homebuyers discovered at Yale. A year earlier, in the interest of stabilizing the city around its campus, Yale started offering employees $2,000 a year over 10 years if they buy homes right in New Haven. The idea was to have homeowners living on-site, to have a stake in neighborhoods. The money helped offset the extra cost of taxes on city homes.

No one expected so many people to take advantage of the offer. Now Yale plans to extend its offer beyond this year to more employees. Two other major employers, the Hospital of St. Raphael and city government, have come forward with similar programs for their employees.

In May, the new homeowners gathered at Yale President Richard Levin's house to mark the program's success. They took turns with colored markers to write down the reasons they chose to buy in New Haven: The Peabody Museum. The cherry blossoms in Wooster Square. The lively mix of people of all backgrounds living and working and playing alongside each other in diverse neighborhoods. The brick-oven "apizza" invented and served uniquely here. Neighborhoods with distinctive shops and live music and neat schools within walking distance. The restored Lighthouse Park carousel. The grandeur of the renovated train station lobby or of the Victorian mansions on residential streets.

"You can bike to work," wrote one.

"Almost everything I want to do," wrote another, "is in New Haven."

Some have lived here since birth. Others of us came for college or a job. We may have talked about leaving, but some indescribable pull anchors us here. So we try to figure it out.

New York City's close enough, but not too close. The country's close, but the excitement of a city remains outside our doorstep. The York Square has interesting, out-of-the-way movies. The big musicals come to the Shubert, the social dramas to Long Wharf, the cutting-edge premieres to Yale Rep, while a host of smaller community troupes offer more experimental shows. There's a music scene, an art scene.

NEW HAVEN WANNABES
We Already Live Here...
by Paul Bass, Journalist

Yes, a big city has more. For most of us, this is more than we can get to, anyway. And it's a whole lot more than you find in cities quite larger than New Haven.

But that's the brochure stuff. It's all true, but something else, something intangible, makes New Haven the most desirable Connecticut city for people who have a choice of where to live. I believe it has to do with dreams. For a variety of reasons, New Haven is a place where dreams fly.

In addition to cultural experimentation, more experimentation on addressing social challenges has taken place here in the past half-century than in any other comparable city. Because we're small, that means anyone with an idea can try it out. From the successful neighborhood health clinics, to our model community policing efforts, from day-care co-ops to funky printing presses, evidence abounds that dreams can make a difference. Especially these days.

Take Chris Ozyck's dream. A young architectural planner and avid hiker and biker, Ozyck looked one day it the abandoned parking lots, trashed highway underpasses, and closed-off dank paths separating much of New Haven from its waterfront.

He imagined a hiking-biking trail with nature preserves, landscaping, public art, pocket parks. That trail became a reality in time for this summer's Special Olympics. That's just one example of how people have focused on how to transform a problem or bad news into new opportunities these days.

The collapse of the real-estate market has enabled working families to buy homes for the first time, and for city government and private employers to promote more stable neighborhoods.

The bucks have come in statewide for a new replica of the slave ship *Amistad* as a tourist attraction and educational tool. African captives hundreds of years ago mutinied on that boat. They were held in New Haven until a broad civil rights coalition did the unthinkable, and helped them win their freedom and return to Africa. There's that sense of history and community and dreaming again. It resonates today.

Professionals working with the *Vision Project* have sketched out a detailed plan for light-rail trolleys to connect people to New Haven's trains, buses, and airport.

Other committed thinkers are scrutinizing what kind of new small manufacturers can thrive in a city rather than a suburb or down South. There's talk about forming a not-for-profit holding company that would keep those manufacturers here once they succeed.

What it comes down to, most of all, is that something always seems to be happening in New Haven. And you don't get crushed in it.

Of course, there are setbacks. Of course New Haven, like any American city, is fighting some tough political trends. But its soul is intact. And the body around it is coming back.

Clowning around on Chapel Street —Andy Charney, popular New Haven mime, entertains an appreciative audience of city children.

NEW HAVEN NEIGHBORHOODS
Introduction

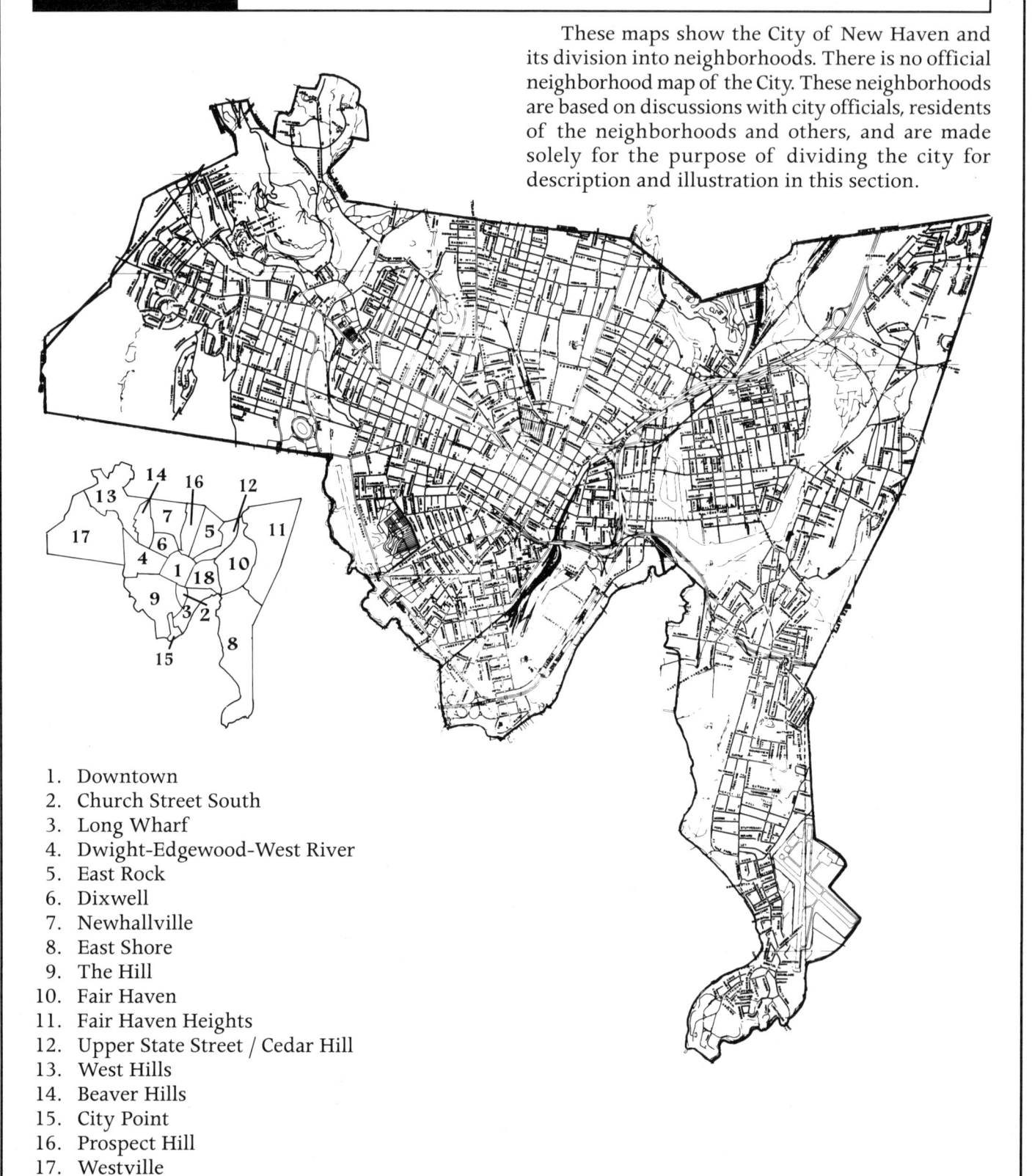

These maps show the City of New Haven and its division into neighborhoods. There is no official neighborhood map of the City. These neighborhoods are based on discussions with city officials, residents of the neighborhoods and others, and are made solely for the purpose of dividing the city for description and illustration in this section.

1. Downtown
2. Church Street South
3. Long Wharf
4. Dwight-Edgewood-West River
5. East Rock
6. Dixwell
7. Newhallville
8. East Shore
9. The Hill
10. Fair Haven
11. Fair Haven Heights
12. Upper State Street / Cedar Hill
13. West Hills
14. Beaver Hills
15. City Point
16. Prospect Hill
17. Westville
18. Wooster Square

NEW HAVEN ~ DOWNTOWN
Downtown Neighborhoods

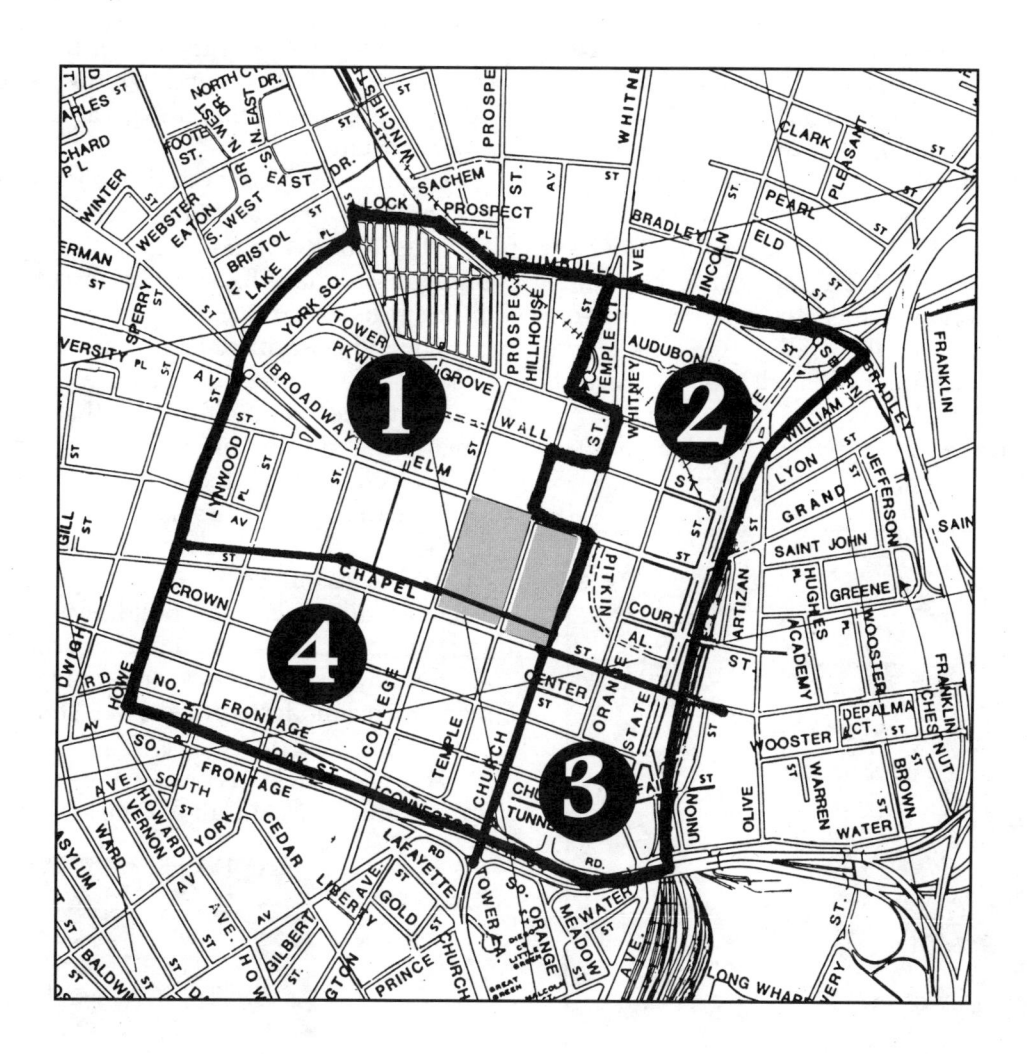

Sections of Downtown

1. **Yale**
2. **Government~Offices~Courts~Arts Area**
3. **Ninth Square**
4. **College & Chapel**

Downtown has been divided arbitrarily into four sections for purposes of illustration in this section. Section One, Yale, is covered on pages 232-264. The other sections are described on the following four pages.

NEW HAVEN ~ DOWNTOWN
Government~Offices~Arts

The northeastern section of downtown New Haven is packed tight with office buildings, the New Haven City Hall and Hall of Records, The Federal Office Building, three courts, SNET Headquarters and several operating buildings, two new condominium developments and the Audubon Arts Center.

The New City Hall stands facing the Green on Church Street. The new design preserves the handsome Clock Tower which is part of a 135-year-old Henry Austin facade. The Hall of Records at 200 Orange Street continues to hold all property records and vital statistics.

Also facing the Green is New Haven's new "Class A" Connecticut Financial Center tower.

The new One Century Tower building is on the corner of Grove Street and Whitney Avenue. Granite Square and State Street Plaza are a short distance away on State Street.

Channel 8 TV has its studios and headquarters at the corner of State and Elm Streets.

The Robert Giamo Federal Office building on Orange Street has a full-service post office and many different federal offices.

The old post office is now a Federal Court. The Greek Temple style Court House facing the Green on Elm Street is a State Court that handles traffic violations and other minor offenses. The new court building on Church Street at the corner of Wall Street contains the rest of the state courts.

On the opposite corner of Church & Wall is the handsome Art Deco SNET headquarters building. There are six other SNET buildings in this area.

Whitney Grove Square at the corner of Whitney Avenue and Grove Street is a new mixed-use development with a modern office tower, stores and condominiums.

At the corner of Whitney Avenue and Audubon Street is the new Audubon Court Office Building.

Audubon Street between Whitney Avenue and Orange Street is the exciting New Haven Arts District which includes condominiums, stores and restaurants. In the district are the headquarters of the Community Foundation for Greater New Haven and the Arts Council. Some of the arts facilities include the Neighborhood Music School, Creative Arts Workshop, Media Arts Center, Educational Center for the Arts, two theaters and Artspace.

NEW HAVEN ~ DOWNTOWN
Ninth Square

The section of downtown now called Ninth Square is one of the nine squares that made up the original nine-square layout of New Haven. The area is bounded on the North by Chapel Street, on the East by State Street, on the South by Crown Street, and on the West by Church Street.

A new neighborhood is emerging in the old Ninth Square Historic District, which is listed in the National Register of Historic Places. The redevelopment of this area is a joint venture of McCormack Baron and Associates of St. Louis, and The Related Companies Limited Partnership, headquartered in New York. These two companies are experts in the redevelopment of urban areas, including the restoration of historic properties.

This area of downtown New Haven was active prior to World War II, but after the War, it suffered a decline. Businesses moved away and the buildings deteriorated.

Phase I of Ninth Square, which is now fully-funded and almost complete, consists of 335 rental units, 50,000 square feet of ground-level retail and commercial space, two parking decks, various parking lots, landscaped courtyards and walkways.

The cost of this phase is $87 million dollars. Of the 335 apartments, 123 are in historically significant structures and the remainder are in newly constructed brick buildings.

Phase II includes 135 residential units and 27,000 square feet of additonal retail and commercial space.

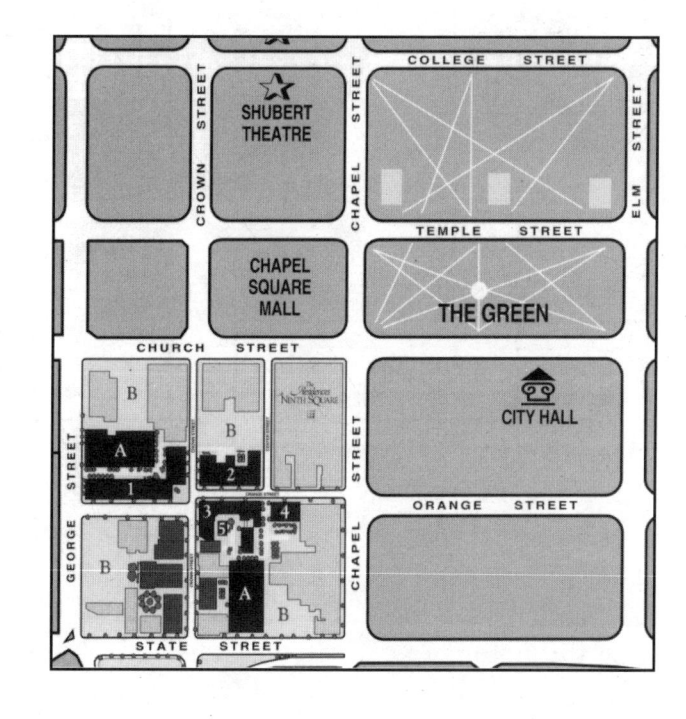

New Haven's Newest Neighborhood
Luxury 1- and 2-Bedroom Apartments at Attractive Prices

1. Stonehill House
2. The Chamberlain
3. Franklin Mews
4. Preston Mews
5. Carriage House

A. Garage
B. Surface Parking

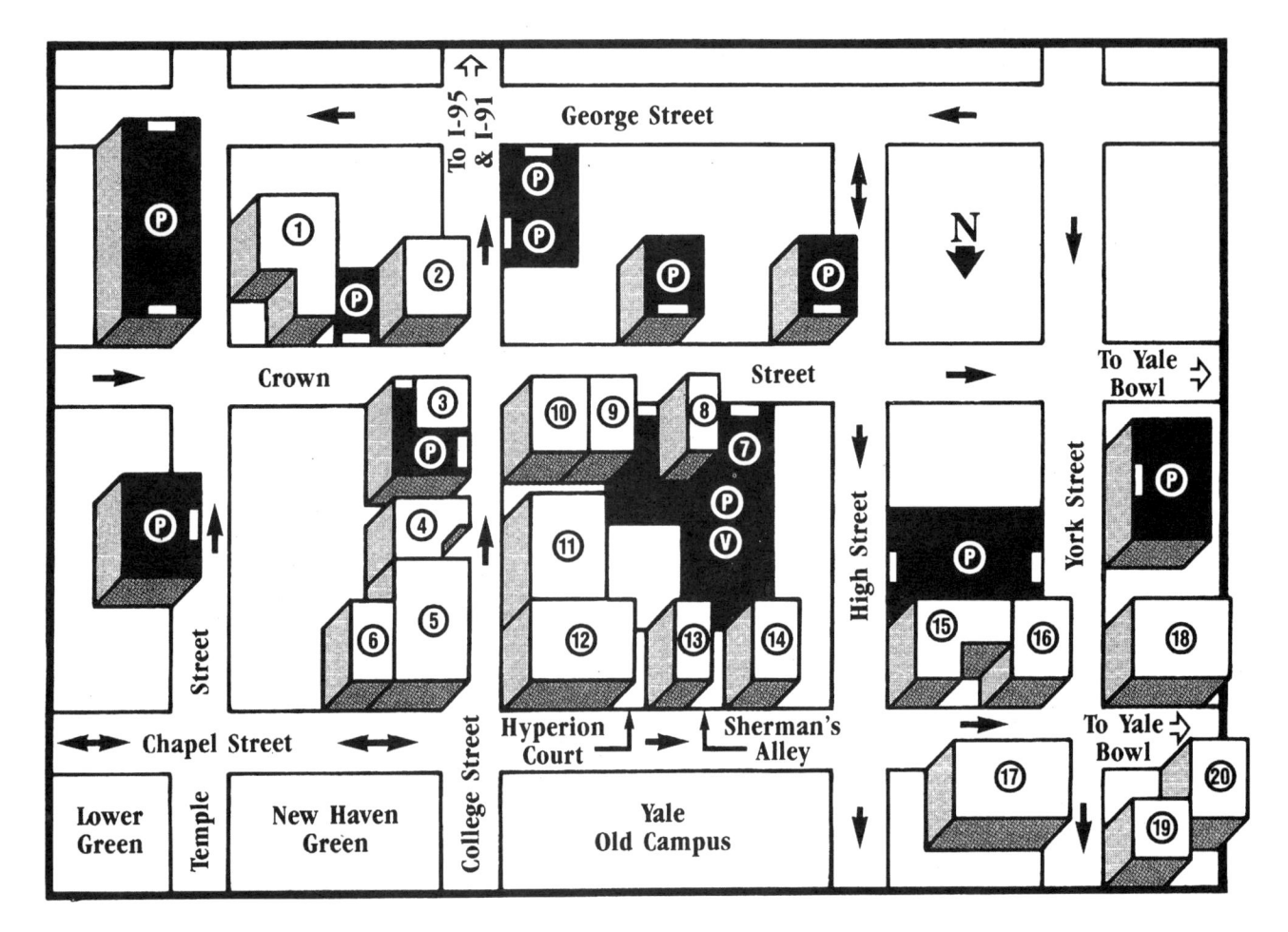

A Walking Guide to the Neighborhood

1. Kelly's Cobbler
2. Challenges Ultimate Sports Pub
   Spanky's
3. Boppers
4. Shubert Theatre
5. The Great Gatsby
   Wave Gallery
   The GAP
   Richter's Cafe
   Barker Animation
6. Sam Goody
7. Kirk's Service Parking
   National Car Rental
8. Louis' Lunch
9. China Hut
10. Bruxelles Brasserie & Bar
    Panache
    Samurai
    Caffé Adulis
11. Greg's Tailor Shop
    Pomegranate
    The Palace Theatre
    Star Shoe Repair
    Laura Ashley
    The Owl Shop
    The Anchor
12. Claire's Corner Copia

Willoughby's Coffee & Tea
Copper Kitchen
Endleman Gallery
Ascot Formal Shop
Raggs Fashion for Men
Bottega Giuliana
Rainbow Gardens
Sakia
Seychelles
Filmfest Video
Accentrix
13. Schiavone Mgt Co.
14. Urban Objects
    Spector Eye Care

Sugar Magnolia
Endleman Two
15. Yale Center for British Art
    Atticus Bookstore Cafe
    Scoozzi Trattoria & Wine Bar
16. Yale Repertory Theatre
17. Yale Art Gallery
18. Bangkok Gardens
    Photo Snap
    Dakota J's
19. Gentree Building
20. Copies Now
    Jong's Produce

NEW HAVEN ~ DOWNTOWN
Chapel & College

Outdoor events including sidewalk sales, face painting and just strolling around are part of life in the center city in the summer.

Every August, downtown New Haven's Summertime Street Festival features the city's only outdoor fashion show (below) on the main stage at Chapel and High Streets. The community's finest volunteers model the "hottest" fashions from boutiques in the College/Chapel Street district. The event is produced by Kathryn Garre Inc., Public Relations.

Andy Pippa

NEW HAVEN NEIGHBORHOODS
College & Chapel / Whitney-Grove-Elm

173

NEW HAVEN NEIGHBORHOODS
Church Street South

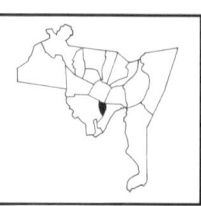

The Oak Street Connector, also known as Route 34, was finished in the middle 1950s. It obliterated the neighborhood called Oak Street, which had deteriorated into one of New Haven worst slums. Historically, Oak Street was the first home of the families of many of New Haven's prominent Jewish and Italian citizens.

The broad new highway, first four lanes and then widened to eight, is crossed only by overpasses. It separates the new Church Street South neighborhood from Downtown. At the same time, the area north of the Connector was also razed. It was rebuilt with the Coliseum, Knights of Columbus Headquarters, Macy's and Malley's department stores (both now vacant), Medical Professional Building and Hotel, high rise apartments and a massive Southern New England Telephone building.

Some people today feel that this area is also part of Church Street South and it is so named in some City documents. However, in this book the area north of the Oak Street Connector is included as part of the Downtown neighborhood.

New construction in Church Street South, which was formerly part of the Hill neighborhood, started in the late 1960s. *Tower One*, a facility for housing well elderly sponsored by the Jewish community, was completed in 1969. Its success soon led to the building of the adjoining *Tower East*.

The Church Street South Housing project was also completed in 1969. This well-planned, well-designed project ran into problems soon after it was completed and occupied, because of the lack of funds to keep it running as originally planned. It still provides suitable housing for many families and its financial problems seem to be more under control.

Union Station originally opened in 1918. After World War II, its condition began to deteriorate rapidly. After much delay, a new adjoining garage was constructed and Union Station was completely restored to its original magnificent appearance. Today, this handsome complex is the railroad and bus gateway to New Haven.

The massive Department of Police Services building was completed in 1973. Behind it, the old railroad headquarters has been renovated and is now used as the headquarters for the Board of Education and other city agencies.

Almost everything in the Church Street South neighborhood is new or modernized. This small neighborhood plays an important role in the functioning of the City.

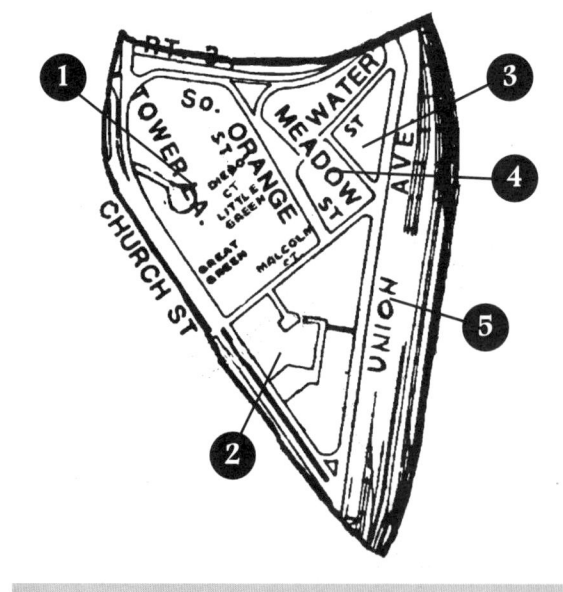

1. Tower I and Tower East
2. Church Street South Housing
3. New Haven Police Headquarters
4. Board of Education Building
5. Union Station & Parking Garage

NEW HAVEN NEIGHBORHOODS
Long Wharf

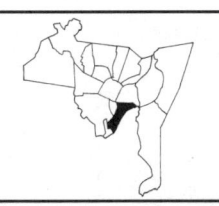

Long Wharf commercial activity began in the late 1800s, but problems with the mud in the harbor and the British take-over of 1779 delayed growth of the wharf area until the end of the century.

For forty years after the Revolutionary War, maritime activity blossomed along the Long Wharf. With new wharves, and the refurbishing of old facilities, this district between City Point and the estuary of the Mill and Quinnipiac Rivers became the center of New Haven's international trade, a place from which merchants exported meat, grain, cattle, lumber, and other products.

The fate of Long Wharf became unavoidably entangled in international conflicts when Thomas Jefferson passed the Embargo Act of 1807, which ended the export of goods to any foreign markets. Long Wharf entered a long period of decline.

In later years, other factors, including a serious fire in 1812, the construction of the Farmington Canal in 1835, and the rise of the railroad industry, contributed to its problems.

However, by the end of the 1940s, the city had initiated a plan which included dredging the harbor (to enable its use by large ships) and completely rebuilt Long Wharf. Landfill from the dredging of the Harbor was used as the foundation for the new Long Wharf and the Connecticut Turnpike. The Sargent Company and the tenants of the New Haven Food Terminal have been the backbone of revitalization in this district.

Long Wharf Today

A number of industries are now located along I-95 and Sargent Drive, including the Pirelli Company, CHCP, *The New Haven Register*, Sargent, and the Food Terminal. There are also two hotels and a large Maritime office complex and garage. TeleTrack has been converted into a sports center, the old Seamless plant at 1 Long Wharf has been renovated into an office building which contains the Hispanic clinic, the *Advocate* and the Visitors and Convention Bureau. Since 1965, Long Wharf Theatre has provided the highest quality of performance arts. The Rusty Scupper restaurant is located nearby on the harbor.

Along the waterfront, the rebuilt pier is the home of New Haven's fire boat and the *Liberty Belle* tour boat. A new park contains the Vietnam War Memorial.

New development in this area over the past four decades, brings Long Wharf into the 1990s with the renewed vitality it once enjoyed at the turn of the 19th century.

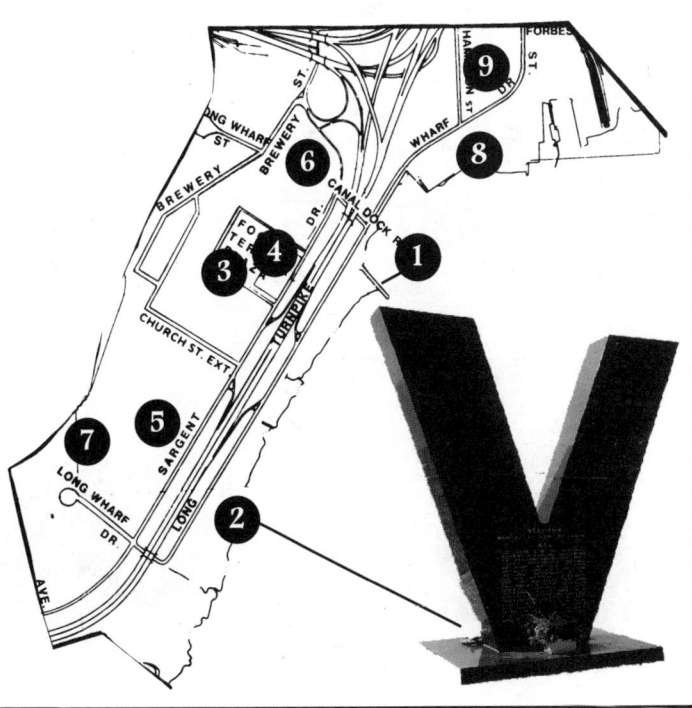

1. Long Wharf Pier
2. Vietnam War Memorial
3. Long Wharf Theater
4. Long Wharf Food Terminal
5. Gateway College
6. Pirelli Company
7. #1 Long Wharf
8. Maritime Office Center & Garage
9. Sports Haven

24 Benton Street
2 Bedrooms, 1 Baths
$65,900 / $62,400

190 Weybosset Street
3 Bedrooms, 1 Baths
$78,900 / $70,000

127 Greenhill Terrace
3 Bedrooms, 1 Baths
$79,500 / $79,500

17 Compton Street
7 Bedrooms, 3 Baths
$79,900 / $55,000

166 Mitchell Drive
3 Bedrooms, 2 Baths
$79,900 / $78,000

15 Stone Street
3 Bedrooms, 2 Baths
$84,900 / $74,000

89 Brooklawn Circle
3 Bedrooms, 1.5 Baths
$84,900 / $79,900

616 Smith Avenue
2/3 Bedrooms, 2 Baths
$89,900 / $79,000

1370 Ella Grasso Blvd
4/5 Bedrooms, 2.5 Baths
$99,000 / $92,500

31 Perkins Street
4 Bedrooms, 1.5 Baths
$99,000 / $85,000

90 Mountain Top Lane
2 Bedrooms, 1.5 Baths
$103,500 / $95,000

13 a.k.a. 31 First Avenue
3 Bedrooms, 2 Baths
$114,500 / $90,000

85 Pearl Street *(townhouse)*
3 Bedrooms, 2.5 Baths
$129,000 / $105,000

54 Raynham Road
2 Bedrooms, 1 Baths
$132,900 / $125,000

97 Dyer Street
4+ Bedrooms, 2 Baths
$139,000 / $124,000

NEW HAVEN NEIGHBORHOODS
Typical Property Sales

Shown on these two pages are recent typical house sales in the City of New Haven.
The first price is the listing price; the second is the sale price.

700 Townsend Avenue
4 Bedrooms, 3 Baths
$148,500 / $140,000

467 Ellsworth Avenue
5 Bedrooms, 2.5 Baths
$149,500 / $148,500

228 Colony Road
3 Bedrooms, 1.5 Baths
$154,900 / $142,000

279 Willow Street
4 Bedrooms, 2 Baths
$157,500 / $151,500

198 McKinley Avenue
6 Bedrooms, 2.5 Baths
$169,400 / $169,400

370 Stevenson Road
4 Bedrooms, 2.5 Baths
$173,500 / $169,000

171 Townsend Avenue
3+ Bedrooms, 2.5+ Baths
$224,900 / $170,000

233 McKinley Avenue
4/5 Bedrooms, 2.5 Baths
$229,000 / $204,000

656 Whitney Avenue
7 Bedrooms, 3.5 Baths
$289,000 / $250,000

701 Prospect Street
6+ Bedrooms, 3.5 Baths
$399,000 / $375,000

409 Humphrey Street
6 Bedrooms, 3.5 Baths
$535,000 / $535,000

1031 Forest Road
5+ Bedrooms, 4 Full Baths, 2 Half Baths
$535,000 / $431,000

NEW HAVEN NEIGHBORHOODS
Dwight~Edgewood~W. River

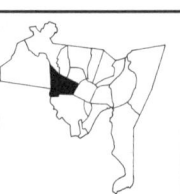

These three small neighborhoods still have some separate identification and separate neighborhood organizations, and it is not clear today whether they will go their separate ways or somehow join.

Until the middle 1800s, the southwestward development of the city skipped this area. Development stopped at Ellsworth, except for the Alms house, built in 1852, and an orphan asylum. Some large private homes were also built, several of which were owned by the Hubinger brothers. The Hubinger estate was developed into garden apartments. The commercial area of the Edgewood neighborhood along Whalley Avenue developed in the early 1900s.

Like many other neighborhoods, this area began to deteriorate after World War II. Some parts have recovered better than others.

The expansion of the Hospital of St. Raphael has helped the immediately surrounding area by locating physicians offices and other supporting services there. Four large nursing homes provide many job opportunities for neighborhood residents. The Berger Elderly Housing Development has a stabilizing effect on the neighborhood, as does the headquarters of the Greater New Haven Association of Realtors.

The proximity to synagogues and Jewish schools has attracted Orthodox Jewish families to the neighborhood, as they like to be within walking distance to their places of worship so they do not need to ride on the Sabbath.

Edgewood park is a 121-acre oasis in the heart of the city. The West River runs through the park. It contains an attractive playground area, a skating rink and many hiking trails. The road through the park is usually blocked off to traffic, making it a good place to bike and walk.

The Hospital of St. Raphael has taken steps to help provide stability to the Dwight/Edgewood/West River neighborhood.

An Upper Chapel Street Association actively promotes business along that portion of Chapel Street in the Dwight and Edgewood neighborhoods.

West River residents have formed a neighborhood association and, together with area merchants, are taking steps to improve the emerging neighborhood.

The Edgewood neighborhood association has recently been active in an attempt to reduce crime in and around Edgewood Park.

1. Greater New Haven Assoc. of Realtors HQ
2. Hospital of St. Raphael
3. Berger Housing for the Elderly
4. Coogan Skating Rink
5. Holocaust Memorial

NEW HAVEN NEIGHBORHOODS
East Rock

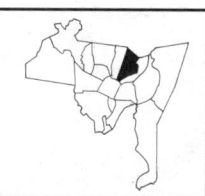

The East Rock neighborhood looks very similar to the way it did 65 years ago. More Yale graduate students, faculty and staff live here than anywhere else.

Much of the land which comprises this neighborhood was owned by three families: the Samuel Bishop family, the Eli Whitney family and the Reed family. Prior to 1835, there was practically no development in this section of New Haven. Orange Street was the first paved street in the city.

The Trumbull Street area between Whitney and Orange was essentially an expansion of the original settlement of the Nine Squares. The enormous John Anderson House on Orange Street was built in 1882 and was, until recently, a convent and part of the old St. Mary's School.

Residences in the rest of the neighborhood range from some very large ones on Whitney Avenue, Everit Street and Livingston Street across from the park, to modest multi-family houses in the Foster and Nicoll Street area.

The other significant new construction in the past 65 years is the Buckingham apartments, on a block bounded by Whitney Avenue, Cottage, Livingston and Linden Streets. All residences on this block are apartment buildings, except for three houses.

In 1956, Wilbur Cross High School was built at the base of East Rock on park land.

East Rock Park is technically part of this neighborhood, though it is really a regional resource. The East Rock Neighborhood Association demonstrated its strength when it was able to stop the construction of an I-95 connector from Willow Street to Whitney Avenue, which would have slashed through the neighborhood.

The Church of Christ Scientist on Whitney Avenue was built on the site of a mansion last owned by a Dr. Cushing, and built by a descendant of Eli Whitney. (President Franklin Roosevelt stayed there in 1938.)

The elegant New Haven Lawn Club, built in 1890, has new pristine tennis courts and a large swimming pool. Its membership is made up of the *Who's Who* of Yale and New Haven.

Shopping on Orange Street is an old world experience. The Hall Benedict Drug Store (1870) has looked the same for the last 65 years, except for the removal of the marble soda fountain after World War II. Across Linden Street is Romeo & Giuseppe's (called "Romeo and Joe's"), which has everything Italian, including attractive fruits, vegetables and homemade pastas at reasonable prices. The Prime Market, a full-line mini-supermarket, bills itself as a "social center." They still carry your bags to the car and deliver telephone orders. DeRosa's moved from State Street to the venerable Orange Market building soon after its owner's son won the lottery and they retired. DeRosa's fruits, vegetables, breads and cheeses are gourmet, and are priced accordingly.

Whitney Avenue's east side starts at Trumbull Street with a few stores. There are mostly offices north to Willow Street, and the rest of the area has residences and churches. Many old homes between Trumbull and Willow Streets have been converted into handsome professional offices.

The East Rock neighborhood has managed to avoid many of the problems that have plagued other neighborhoods, primarily because of its wide appeal to the Yale community.

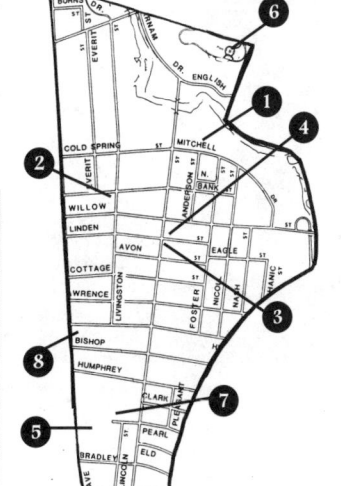

1. Wilbur Cross High School
2. Worthington Hooker School
3. Hall Benedict Drug Store (1870)
4. Romeo and Joe's
5. Yale Computer Center and Human Resources
6. Soldiers and Sailors Monument *(see p. 118)*
7. New Haven Lawn Club
8. 315 Whitney Avenue (1909); Author's office

Church of Christ Scientist

NEW HAVEN NEIGHBORHOODS
Dixwell

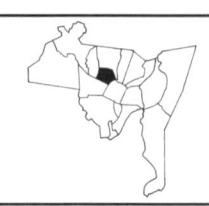

Today, Dixwell is one of New Haven's most developed and most densely populated neighborhoods. However, in the early years of the nineteenth century, only a small number of buildings stood near the current junction of Whalley Avenue, Goffe Street, and Broadway. As difficult as it may be to imagine, farmland dominated the Dixwell neighborhood throughout much of the 1800s, while Dixwell Avenue itself was built early in the following century.

During the mid-1800s, development in Dixwell continued at a steady but gradual rate, primarily around the Whalley-Goffe-Broadway junction. From this early phase in Dixwell's history, a significant African-American population resided in the area.

A number of institutions were founded during this time to serve Dixwell's growing community. The most prominent of these were undoubtedly the churches, among them the Varick Memorial African Methodist Episcopal Church, established around 1920, which was the first Black Methodist Church in the City. The Bethel African Methodist Episcopal Church (1842) and St. Luke's Episcopal Church (the third oldest Black Church in the United States) have also played an important role in the neighborhood.

Dixwell Avenue Congregational Church, which moved from Park Street to Dixwell Avenue in 1829, has taken the role as a leader in this district and has a strong activist tradition. This Church sided with the defense for the *Amistad* captors while also acting as a stop-over for the Underground Railway. Distinguished African-Americans such as abolitionist Amos Beman and Secretary of State Francis Cardoza both served as pastors of this church. The congregation has continued to take an active leadership role in the community, fighting against segregation and discrimination while assisting in the establishment of the Dixwell Community House (1920).

Between 1870 and 1920, dramatic residential and industrial expansion occurred in Dixwell. The Great Depression had an overwhelming impact. In blatant displays of discrimination, local industries laid off Black workers first, often in order to provide jobs for white laborers.

The city chose Dixwell as the site for one of the area's first housing projects when Elm Haven was built in 1937. Later redevelopment programs also focused on Dixwell in an attempt to rid New Haven of slums. A number of buildings were constructed in efforts to alter the condition of the neighborhood. However, this area is still plagued by drugs and crime. The Q House and many of the churches are now playing an important role in improving the neighborhood. The Dixwell Plaza is again reopened on Dixwell Avenue.

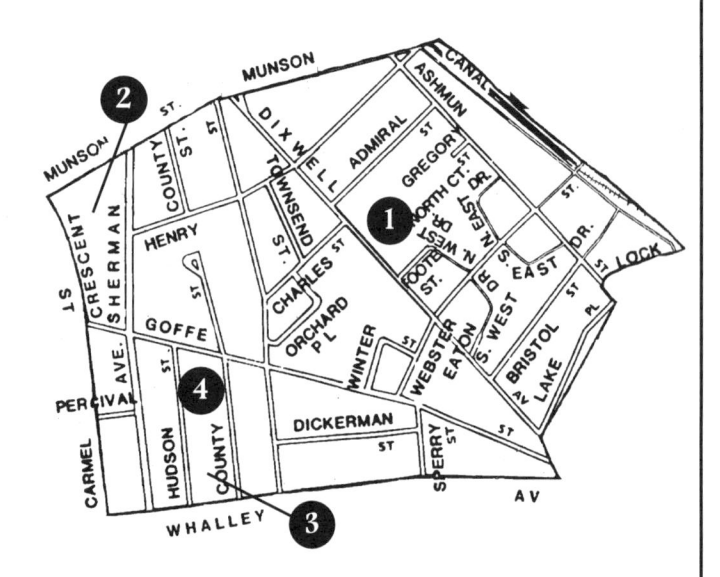

1. Dixwell Community House ("Q House")
2. Hillhouse High School
3. Connecticut Detention Center
4. National Guard Armory

NEW HAVEN NEIGHBORHOODS
Newhallville

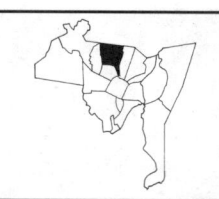

The history of the Newhallville neighborhood has been closely entwined with the fate of local industry since the early nineteenth century. While some Irish and German immigrants came to the area to work on the construction of the Farmington Canal (1823-1835), the establishment of a carriage factory in the southern sector of the neighborhood fueled the growth of Newhallville. In fact, the neighborhood's namesake, George Newhall, owned the Carriage Emporium Factory.

Most of Newhallville's land remained undeveloped until at least the 1850s. While development continued and population increased around Newhall's factory, another manufacturer, the Winchester Repeating Arms Company, moved into the neighborhood. Like the Carriage Emporium, the Winchester Company had an enormous impact on the district. The presence of these successful companies brought about residential expansion.

The majority of Newhallville's working class population was of German or Irish descent until the early 1900s, when Italian immigrants and African-Americans began to move to the neighborhood. Most people lived in the southern section until the implementation of the streetcar system opened up the northern sector to residential construction.

In 1930, the Olin Company purchased the Winchester Repeating Arms Company and began producing recreational and sports equipment. During World War II, they switched production to war materials. However, after the War, Olin failed to return to its previous peacetime success because of labor problems and the nature of the peacetime economy. As had been the case in so many of New Haven's more urbanized areas, this period of commercial economic decline caused the neighborhood's more affluent and mobile residents to move away to outlying suburbs. Newhallville became one of the city's poorest areas.

Newhallville Today

Plagued by crime, poverty, and the decline in the appearance of buildings in the area, Newhallville was one of the target areas for the city's Urban Redevelopment Plan of the 1960s and 1970s. Even today, it remains one of New Haven's poorest and most troubled neighborhoods. Almost 30% of this neighborhood's residents live below the poverty level.

More dramatic actions need to be taken to correct the problems which abound in this section of the city. One of the most significant changes for the good in Newhallville is the establishment and subsequent growth of Science Park. With a base of funding from the Olin Company, Yale, the City and the State, Science Park was developed as a high-technology park for start-up companies. Today, Science Park is home to over 100 small companies and three larger ones: Olin, Southern New England Communications and Kodak. The expansion of Albertus Magnus college has also had a favorable impact on the neighborhood.

1. Science Park
2. Albertus Magnus College
3. Lincoln-Bassett Community School
4. Hazel Street Community Substation

NEW HAVEN NEIGHBORHOODS
East Shore

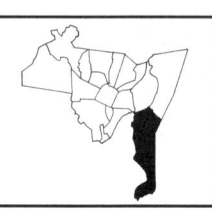

What is now being called the East Shore is bounded on the north by Ferry Street and the old railroad, east by East Haven and Tweed-New Haven Airport, south by Long Island Sound and west by the New Haven Harbor and the Quinnipiac River. It includes some of the land that in 1881 was transferred from East Haven back to New Haven. This land was annexed to New Haven, hence the nickname *Annex*. It had special tax status until 1918, when residents voted for full fledged status as a part of the City of New Haven.

It was here on July 5, 1779 that the British landed and then marched to New Haven for their one-day occupation of the city. The small contingent of soldiers at Black Rock Fort offered only token resistance to the overwhelming British landing party.

On the shore of New Haven Harbor is the land which was given to the Quinnipiac Indians in the 1630s as part of their payment for selling their land for the original New Haven colony.

Eleasar Morris settled here early in the 18th century. In 1779, Amos Morris had his house burned down by the British. The Pardee-Morris House at 325 Lighthouse Road was built in 1680. It survived the British invasion and still stands today. It is now owned by the New Haven Colonial Historical Society. Morris Cove, named after the Morris family, was a popular summer resort area in the late 1880s and early 1890s. Now most of the houses have been winterized and are occupied year round.

The Townsend family has lived in the same place since 1789. *Raynham*, their home, was built in 1804 and remodeled in 1865. It looks almost exactly as it did then, with the exception of the addition of bathrooms and electricity.

Henry Townsend and his wife Deborah are seventh generation Townsends living in *Raynham*. They carry on the long Townsend tradition of community service. Henry Townsend unsuccessfully ran for Mayor in the early 1960s. Deborah Townsend has written several historical publications. She is responsible for the planting of the beautiful cherry trees around Wooster Square.

The majority of East Shore residents have their roots in the Hill and in Wooster Square. It is a homogeneous neighborhood. About 75% of its people are Italian Roman Catholics and most of the rest are Irish Roman Catholics. A large number of residents attend Saint Bernadette's Church on Townsend Avenue.

Tweed-New Haven Airport is on the east side of the neighborhood, half in New Haven and half in East Haven. All of it is owned by New Haven.

The southern-most end is Lighthouse Park, with its landmark lighthouse, built in 1840, and its beautifully restored carousel. Lighthouse Park contains a large public beach and picnic area.

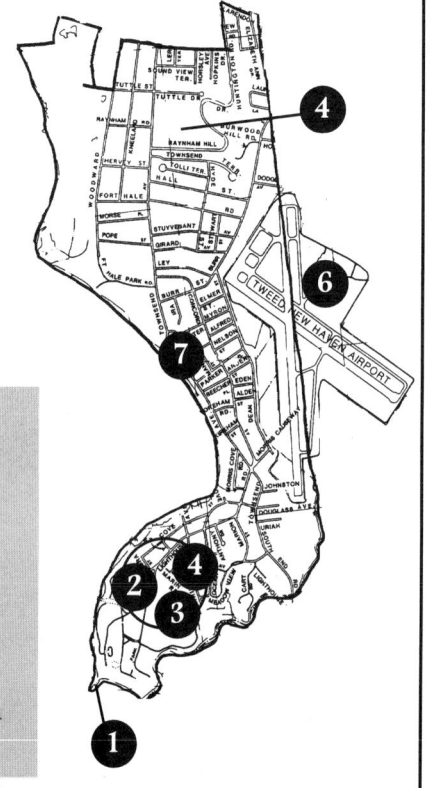

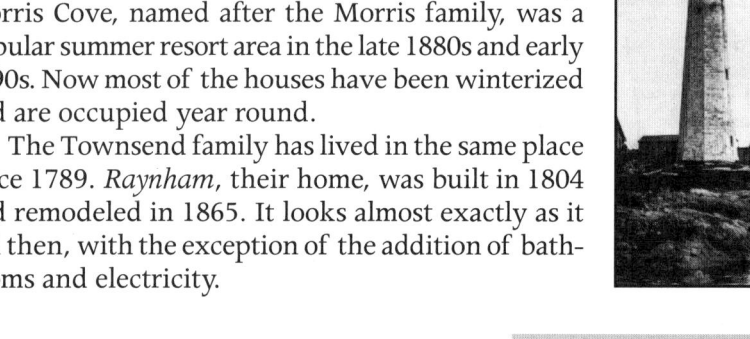

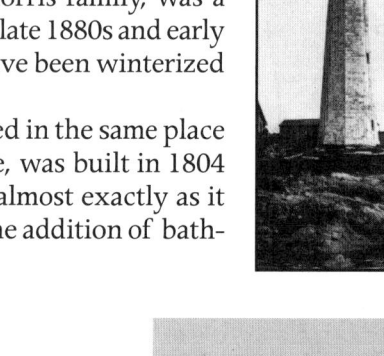

1. Lighthouse Park
2. Black Rock Fort
3. Fort Nathan Hale
4. Raynham House
5. Pardee-Morris House
6. Tweed-New Haven Airport
7. St. Bernadette's Roman Catholic Church

NEW HAVEN NEIGHBORHOODS
The Hill

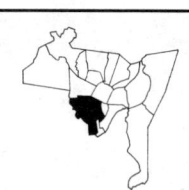

Before the late 1800s, the area now known as the Hill had seen only scattered settlement since the Puritans' arrival in 1638. However, by the turn of the 18th century, poor whites and poor [free] Blacks began to inhabit small dwellings just south of the Nine Squares. This area became known as Sodom Hill, which was eventually shortened to the neighborhood's current name.

Today, Yale-New Haven's Medical Complex sits on the outskirts of the Hill neighborhood, on the site of the first state hospital. Although some residential development had already taken place, architect Ithiel Town's hospital stood as the most significant building in the neighborhood until the middle of the century.

The majority of the Hill's residents were poor or working class. During the Civil War, members of the upper-middle class began to move to the elegant Queen Anne style homes which were being built along Howard Avenue.

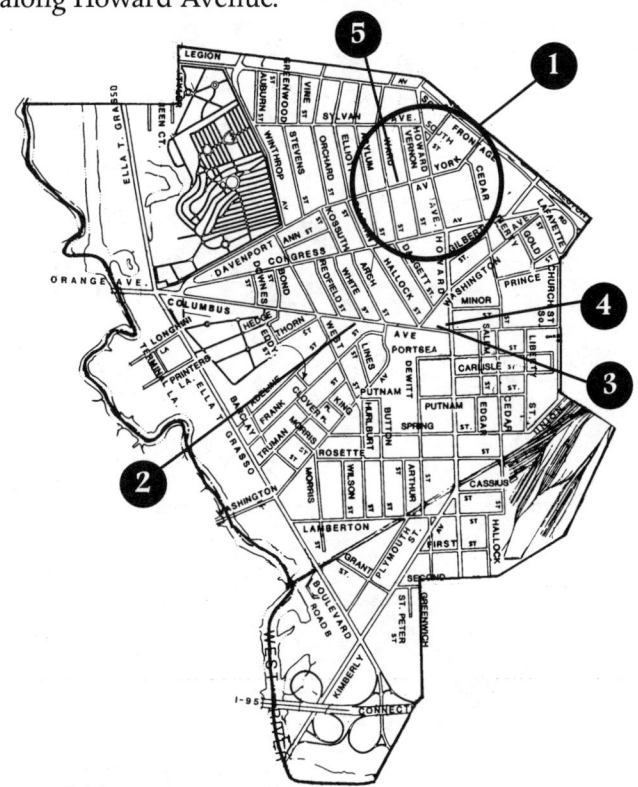

The founding of the Horse Railway had a significant impact on the Hill. Railway service allowed for an increase of residential and commercial development in the area. In addition, the construction of a facility for repairing trains from the New York and New Haven Railroad created a number of jobs. As a result, the Hill's working-class population continued to grow.

While immigrants from Europe came to live in this district and other areas immediately adjacent to downtown, the elegant homes along Howard Avenue continued to attract upper-middle class residents to the Hill. Its population increased dramatically during the last decade of the 19th century. To accommodate increasing demand for affordable housing, multi-family dwellings and duplexes became the most popular type of homes.

The Twentieth Century

From the 1890s well into this century, New Haven was deeply affected by a second wave of immigration from eastern Europe and Italy, and by the migration of African Americans from the South. The Hill became even more densely populated because of this influx of people, and emerged as an even more ethnically and racially diverse neighborhood. Beginning in the 1950s, the Hill entered a period of rapid decline. It was cut off from the downtown area by the newly built Oak Street Connector. In 1970, violent riots broke out in the Hill fueled by racial tensions.

Today, crime, violence, poverty, hunger, homelessness, and drugs still plague the Hill area. The expansion of the Yale-New Haven Medical complex and active redevelopment programs are making significant progress in solving the neighborhood's problems. There is no doubt that the Hill's problems must be confronted by the entire community, as they represent some of New Haven's greatest challenges.

1. Yale-New Haven Medical Complex
2. Hill Health Center
3. Roberto Clemente School
4. Davenport Public Library
5. Jewish Home for the Aged

NEW HAVEN NEIGHBORHOODS
Fair Haven

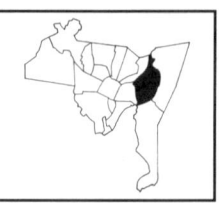

Fair Haven once covered a much larger land area on both sides of the Quinnipiac River, including today's Fair Haven Heights and East Shore. The early history of this neighborhood is closely tied to oystering *(see page 105)*.

Wooster Square ran out of room in the middle 1800s, and with a railway running from Fair Haven to downtown, it was natural that developers found the neighborhood suitable for the industrial and residential developments.

In 1866, Samuel L. Blatchley developed a huge tract of land between Chapel Street and Grand Avenue. On both sides of the wide Blatchley Avenue, he constructed moderately-priced housing for the industrial workers. At one time, the National Folding Box Company located in the neighborhood was the largest such company in the world.

A.C. Gilbert graduated from Yale 1908 and started a company to produce magic kits. At its peak, the A. C. Gilbert Company made erector sets, trains, chemical sets, magic kits and small appliances. It employed over 2,000 workers. Unfortunately, Gilbert and his son died during the post World War II decline, and the business closed in the 1960s.

The redevelopment along the Quinnipiac River started in the 1960s has been very successful. Some successful projects are the elderly housing apartment sponsored by the New Haven Savings Bank and the old brewery that was converted into attractive housing units. A local historic district was created in 1978.

New Haven's only beer brewery is located in Fair Haven. Its success has forced it to expand its facilities several times and to have some of its beer brewed out of state temporarily.

Today, areas of Fair Haven are still blighted and contain many boarded-up buildings and others that are in substandard condition. Although crime and drugs remain serious problems, there has been a significant return of middle class families to the area, especially along the Quinnipiac River.

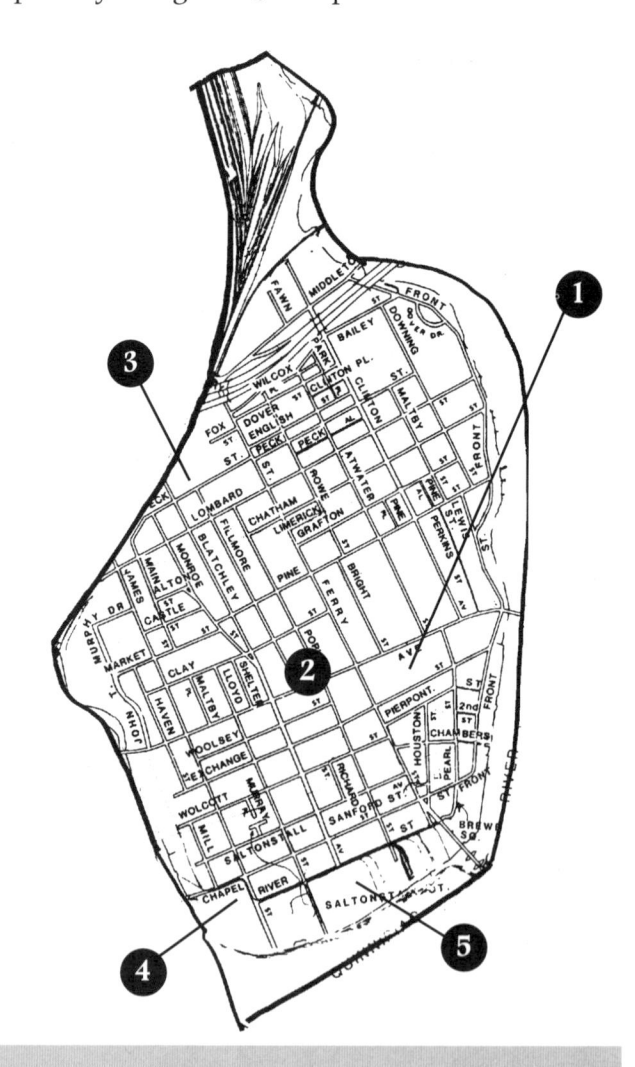

1. Fair Haven Junior High School
2. New Haven Savings Bank Housing for the Elderly
3. Former A.C. Gilbert site, now Erector Square
4. New Haven Brewing Company
5. Riverside Park

NEW HAVEN NEIGHBORHOODS
Fair Haven Heights

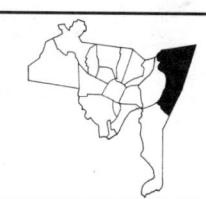

In the northern portion of New Haven's Annex, just east of the Quinnipiac River, is the Fair Haven Heights neighborhood. Its history is closely tied to that of Fair Haven, and until recently, they were considered to be the same neighborhood despite the fact that they were separated by the Quinnipiac River. Fair Haven Heights' scenic location overlooks the Quinnipiac River.

What is now called Fair Haven Heights used to be called Dragon. One explanation for this name is that there was a Dragon Tavern on the east bank of the River. The other is that the seals sleeping on the shores of the river looked like sleeping dragons. Although much of the area remained undeveloped for over a century, the Pardee Ferry, established in 1650, helped spur the growth of a small settlement by providing transportation across the Quinnipiac.

For the most part, Dragon's small population remained isolated from surrounding areas until late in the 18th century. However, the construction of the Dragon Bridge (1790-1792), allowed for an easier commute between East Haven and Fair Haven, while also opening up the area to increased development.

The early history of this area is mostly about oystering and ship building. The fate of the Fair Haven Heights economy during the 1800s depended upon that of the oyster industry. Because of this dependence, the initiation of oyster exporting in the 1830s led to a boom in residential development along the east shore of the Quinnipiac River.

Unlike Fair Haven, the Heights did not develop as an industrialized area. However, there was commercial and industrial development south along the shoreline, near the Tomlinson Bridge. In the 1960s, the Jet Line pipeline was constructed to carry oil from the tankers unloading in New Haven throughout New England. There is still a steady stream of trucks which pick up oil from the storage tanks along the river and carry it throughout Connecticut and Western Massachusetts.

The northern-most portion of Fair Haven Heights was the last area in this district to undergo significant development. Dominated by farmland, this area around Middletown Avenue remained sparsely populated and underdeveloped until well into this century. Today, it is home to a number of commercial and retail establishments as well as the Cine 1-2-3-4, one of the city's two remaining movie theaters.

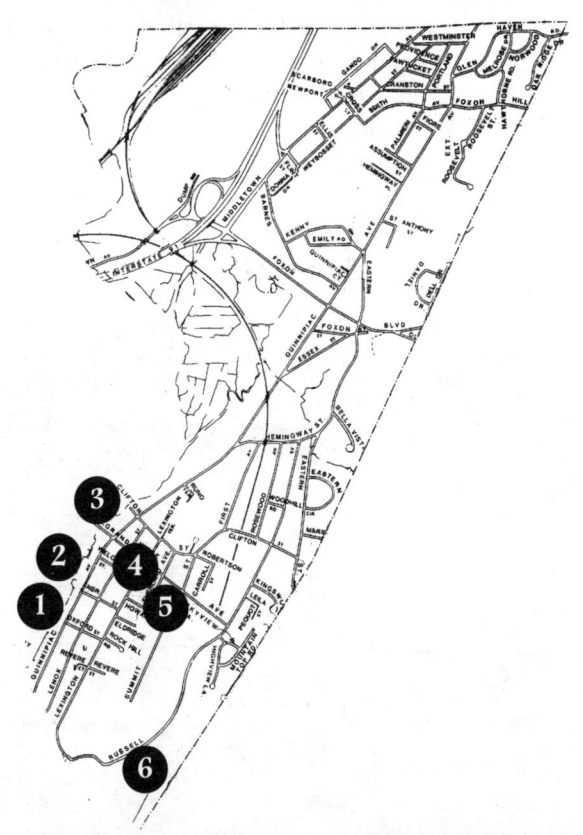

1. Oil Tank Farms
2. Restored oyster houses and docks on east bank of Quinnipiac River
3. Restored Dragon Bridge, now the Red Bridge
4. Pilgrim Church (1851)
5. St. James Episcopal Church (1844)
6. Municipal golf course

Over the past fifteen years, Upper State Street has emerged as a thriving neighborhood comprised of retail shops, restaurants, professional offices and a significant residential population. While stores like Standard Food Market, Quality Fish Market and PJ's Deli cater to a local clientele, people from the greater New Haven community have rediscovered the Upper State Street district because of specialty stores such as Another Dimension, Bohemia, the Alley Cat and Solemate.

Patrons from around the city also visit this area to dine at one of the neighborhood's wide variety of restaurants which include: Gennaro's Ristorante d'Amalfi; Christopher Martins; Thai Orchard; Azteca; and Haya's Japanese restaurant. The district has many pizza places, the best-known of which is Modern Pizza, with its authentic brick oven similar to the famous Wooster Street restaurants. For the connoisseur of French pastry, the neighborhood offers Marjolaine. For evening entertainment, you can go to an Malone's (an Irish bar), or to Dempsey's or Arthur's.

In addition to its many fine shops and restaurants, the neighborhood is also home to a top-notch animal hospital. The New Haven Central Hospital for Veterinary Medicine, at 843 State Street, is always open, and includes among its affiliate doctors some of the area's best-known veterinarians.

Originally known as "Neck Lane," State Street is one of the oldest roads which linked New Haven to areas north of the city, and until the 19th century, it also served as the only route which led across the Mill River to Fair Haven. Throughout much of the 19th century, most of the development in this area focused upon the construction of residences. By the 1870s, however, commercial and industrial growth took place along Upper State Street. Small manufacturers, such as The Elm City Dye Works and Laundry, established factories. A number of retail business also opened along this well-traveled road.

Until 1900, middle working class "Yankees" and Irish-Americans comprised the majority of the Upper State Street population. However, by the turn of the century, a number of Italian and Polish immigrants had come to the area to live and work. As the community became larger and more diverse, institutions such as St. Stanislaus Church and a Polish American Club were founded.

There was a surge in both residential and commercial development along Upper State Street during the first half of the 20th century. However, as was the case for many of New Haven's neighborhood's, the post-war era brought a period of economic decline. In 1965, I-91 was constructed to facilitate travel to New Haven's suburbs and to alleviate traffic tie-ups along city streets. However, because merchants had depended upon steady traffic along the street, the construction of I-91 actually fueled the decline of this neighborhood.

The highway also divided Upper State Street from the Jocelyn Square area to the east, which had previously been a part of the neighborhood. As a result, I-91 not only cut off commercial areas from other patrons, but also alienated former residents from their own community.

The division between Upper State Street and Cedar Hill has disappeared, and most people now consider them to be one neighborhood. However, there is not universal agreement about this, so we have maintained the two names.

In 1968, the City of New Haven targeted Upper State Street as an area for urban renewal, but its efforts met with little success. However, in 1979, a number of residents and business owners formed the Upper State Street Association. By joining forces with city officials, the Association brought about dramatic changes which attracted new businesses to Upper State Street and enabled current businesses to renovate their buildings. This alliance between residents, merchants, and city officials brought about the return of a commercially-successful Upper State Street.

NEW HAVEN NEIGHBORHOODS
Upper State Street

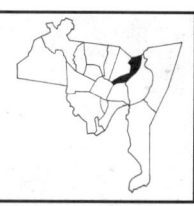

Nephra "Neffie" Lambert-Harrison, a feisty, uncompromising Maine Coon cat, lived to age 20 under the expert and loving care of the New Haven Central Hospital for Veterinary Medicine.

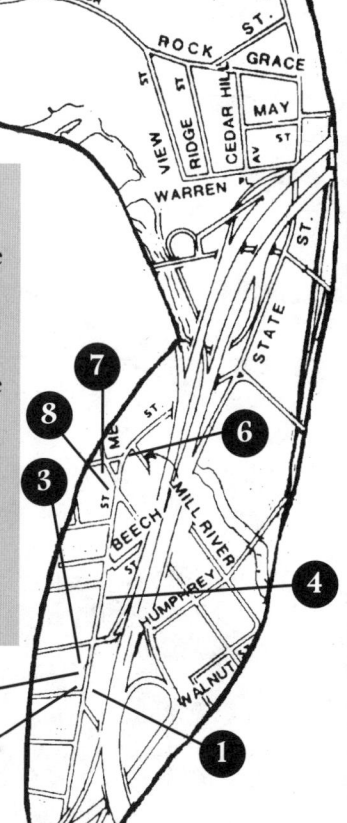

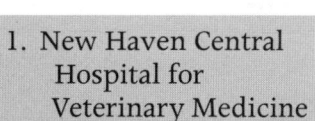

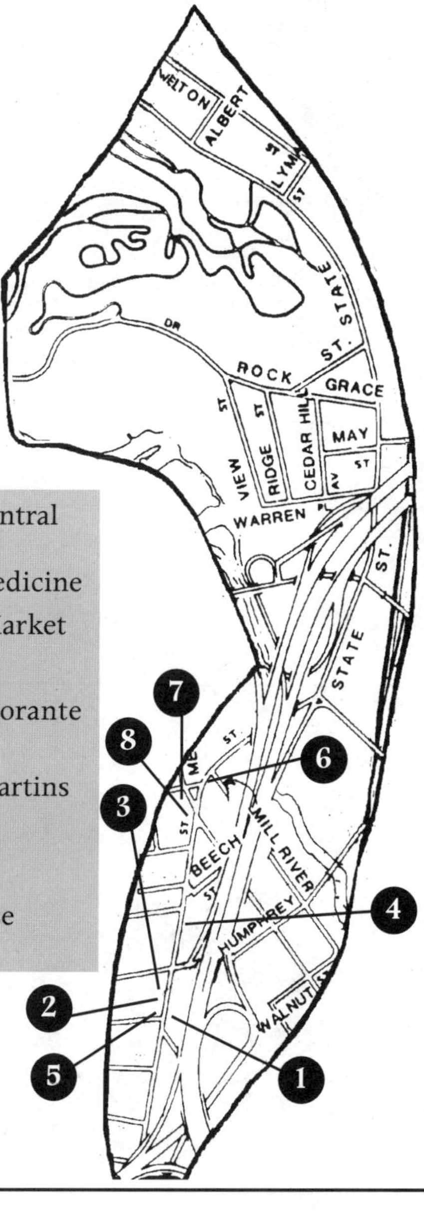

1. New Haven Central Hospital for Veterinary Medicine
2. Quality Fish Market
3. Modern Pizza
4. Genarro's Ristorante d'Amalfi
5. Christopher Martins
6. Thai Orchid
7. Azteca
8. Haya's Japanese Restaurant

NEW HAVEN NEIGHBORHOODS
West Hills

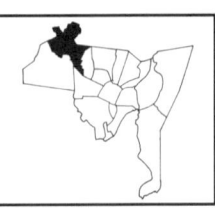

The West Hills neighborhood is in the northwest corner of New Haven. Much of it is taken up by West Rock State Park, a 625-acre park with beautiful views of the city. From the top of West Rock, you can see most of New Haven and on a clear day, across Long Island Sound over to Long Island, more than 30 miles south.

West Rock is best remembered historically as the place where the Regicides, accused of killing the King of England, hid while they were being hunted. The Three Judges Cave is on the road to the summit of West Rock. At the base of the park is the West Rock Nature Center, with its excellent collection of native animals and birds.

Some parts of Southern Connecticut State University are in the West Hills neighborhood, including the Moore Field House and Jess Dow Field.

One of the City's largest cemeteries, Beaverdale Memorial Park, is located off Fitch Street. On the Hamden-New Haven town line is the old Pine Rock Quarry. A small part of the neighborhood extends to Whalley Avenue, and includes the Mishkan Israel Synagogue, Westville, and City cemeteries, and a half dozen other small cemeteries facing Jewel Street.

PURSUING THE REGICIDES
The pursuers of Goffe and Whalley, the Judges of Charles I, passed over a bridge near NewHaven, Con. while the Judges were concealed underneath

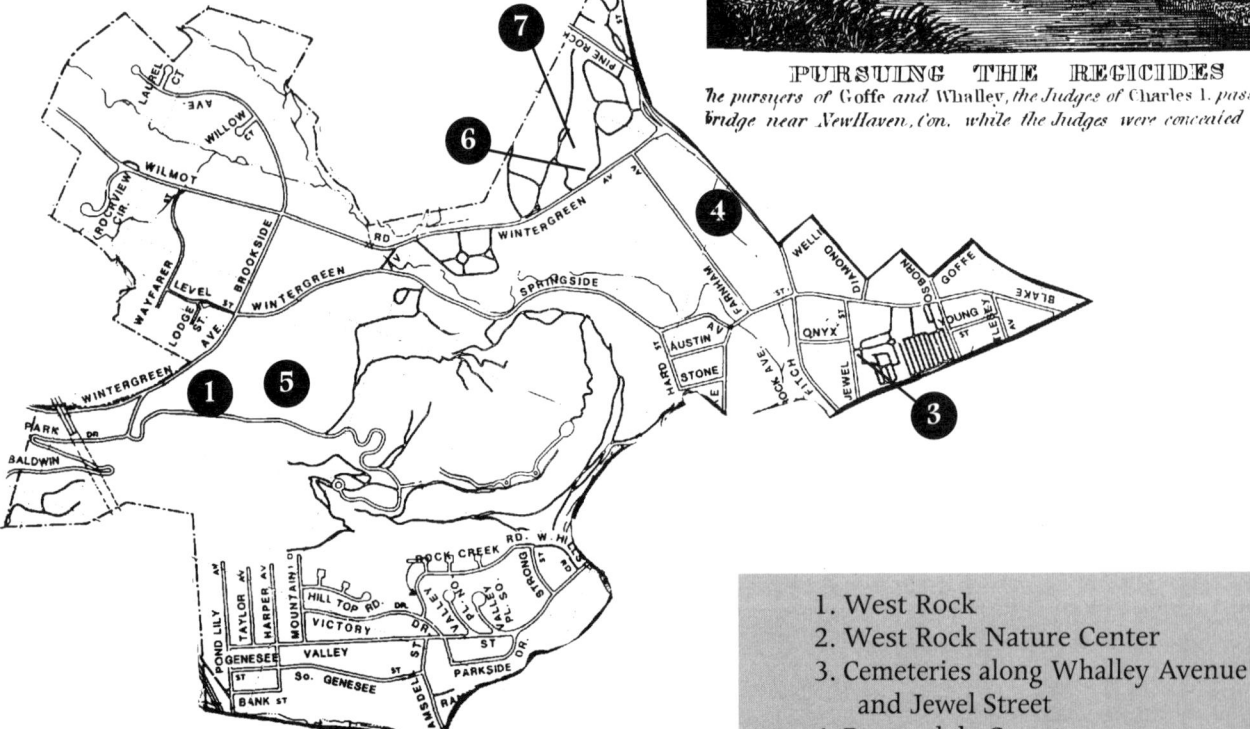

1. West Rock
2. West Rock Nature Center
3. Cemeteries along Whalley Avenue and Jewel Street
4. Beaverdale Cemetery
5. Judges' Cave
6. Moore Field House
7. Jess Dow Field

NEW HAVEN NEIGHBORHOODS
Beaver Hills

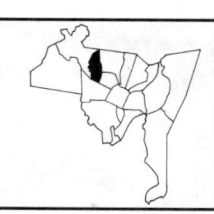

The belief in the importance of simple design, high quality and function played a central role in the development of one of New Haven's youngest neighborhoods, Beaver Hills. Until late in the 19th century, the area bounded by the neighborhoods of West Hills, Dwight, and Dixwell remained primarily farm land, swamp, and forest. In 1908, the formation of the Beaver Hills Company marked the birth of the Beaver Hills neighborhood.

Early History

Selden Osborn owned land near the Beaver Ponds during the early 1800s, and was the first person known to have settled in this area of the city. In 1850, Osborn sold his 100-plus acres to former Yale student George Mead. During his time at Yale, Mead had frequented the woodlands near Osborn's home and had become fond of the area. Although he left the land undeveloped during his lifetime, his heirs founded the Beaver Hills Company and formed a planned community for middle income residents.

Those in charge of the Beaver Hills Company set up very strict guidelines in order to maintain aesthetic and physical control of the developing community. The Beaver Hills Company placed restrictions on what types of homes could be built. The Company planted trees along the new streets and sidewalks in Beaver Hills and reserved the right to veto any architectural plans. The construction of Bungalow, Colonial Revival, and Tudor Revival style homes, and the careful design/lay-out of the streets contributed to the success of this uniform and attractive section of the city.

In many ways, the growth of Beaver Hills resembles the planned neighborhoods which sprung up throughout the country after World War II. In fact, the successful development of this neighborhood was one of New Haven's first planned communities. Like many of the suburbs of later years, the success of Beaver Hills was closely linked to the popularity of the automobile. The area came to be known as one of New Haven's "auto suburbs."

Since its inception, the Beaver Hills neighborhood has remained an area inhabited primarily by middle- and upper-middle class residents, including a number of employees and students from Southern Connecticut State University, which moved its campus to Beaver Hills in 1953. Beaver Hills has been a racially integrated area since the middle of the century, and at present time is home to approximately equal numbers of African-Americans, Jews, Protestants and Catholics.

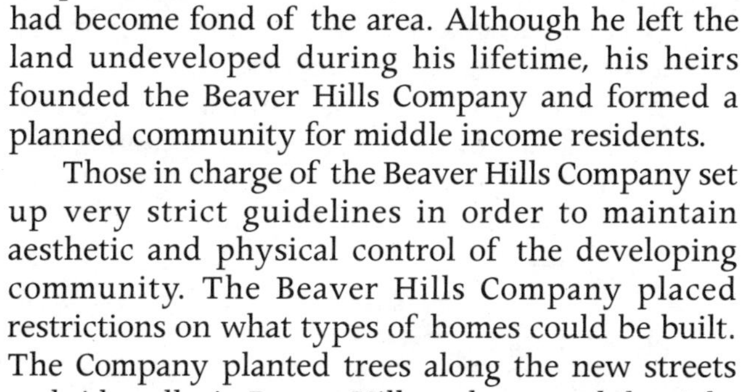

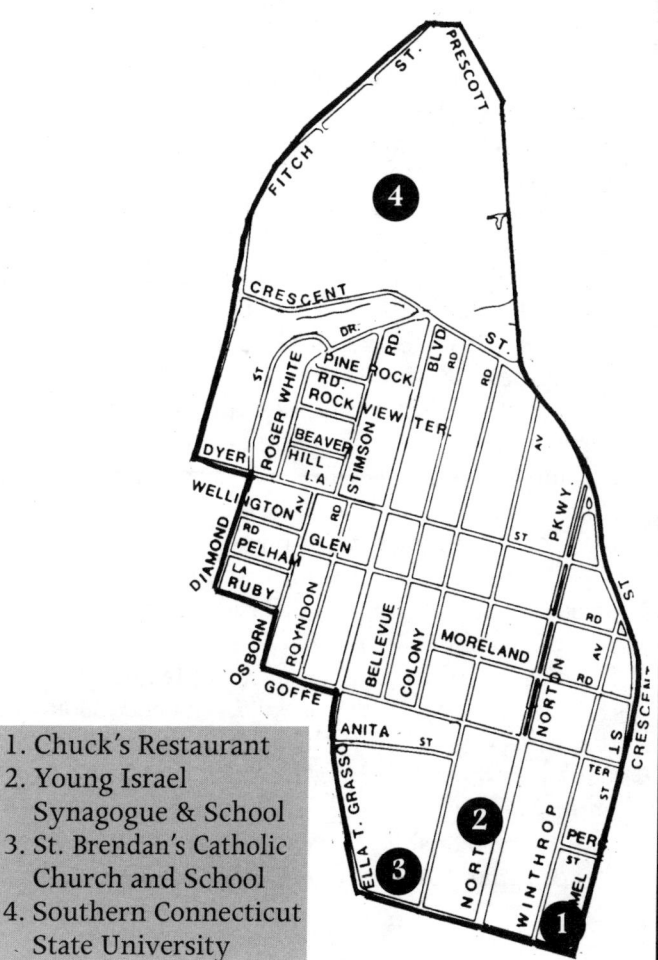

1. Chuck's Restaurant
2. Young Israel Synagogue & School
3. St. Brendan's Catholic Church and School
4. Southern Connecticut State University

NEW HAVEN NEIGHBORHOODS
City Point

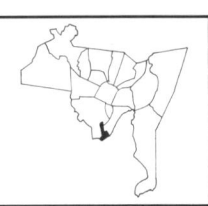

When the oyster industry was flourishing in the early 1800s, many of the Fair Haven oyster companies had facilities at what was then called Oyster Point. There were once ten oyster processing plants in the area.

The south end of Howard Avenue saw the development of many large homes in the 1880s, and was one of the most fashionable neighborhoods in New Haven. The end of Howard Avenue has maintained the characteristics of a fishing village for over 100 years.

The construction of I-95 cut off the tip of Howard Avenue from the Hill neighborhood. Many residents of this isolated area claim that the City Point neighborhood starts south of I-95; that part north of the interstate has become part of the Hill neighborhood. However, people living and working north of I-95 claim that City Point extends north to the rear of the properties facing Lamberton Street, and that is how it is described in this book

As part of the interstate construction and harbor-dredging programs, land along the water on the west side of the harbor was drained and filled. In 1984, a large condominium project called Harbor Landing was started with 300 units planned, to be developed in several stages, complete with a club house and marina. Over 100 units have been completed.

In 1973, the area was designated an Urban Renewal area. Some larger houses were renovated with the help of federal urban homesteading grants.

At the end of one of the few remaining docks is the attractive Chart House Restaurant. Its large glass windows and open deck provide an opportunity to eat and drink while observing the boats in New Haven Harbor. City Point Marina has a full complement of boats which call it home.

The Sound School is located at 60 South Water Street. It offers a unique educational opportunity at the high school level. It occupies a multi-story building and has its own docking facilities where the 90-foot Schooner *Quinnipiak* is docked. Some of the subjects available to the students who attend the school are boat-building, fisheries gear technology, natural resource management, environmental appreciation, seamanship, aquaculture production, nautical drafting and vessel handling and safely.

Schooner, Inc. is a private community-based organization founded in the 1970. It provides students with a variety of programs, ranging from a few hours to weeks, that teach about the many aspects of life on Long Island Sound.

The residents of City Point, especially those south of I-95, are intent on preserving the flavor and character of this small, unique New Haven neighborhood.

1. 164 Howard Avenue Queen Ann style house (1885)
2. 111 South Water Street, oysterman's home (1849)
3. Bay View Park
4. Harbor Landing Condominiums
5. Chart House Restaurant
6. City Point Marina
7. Sound School

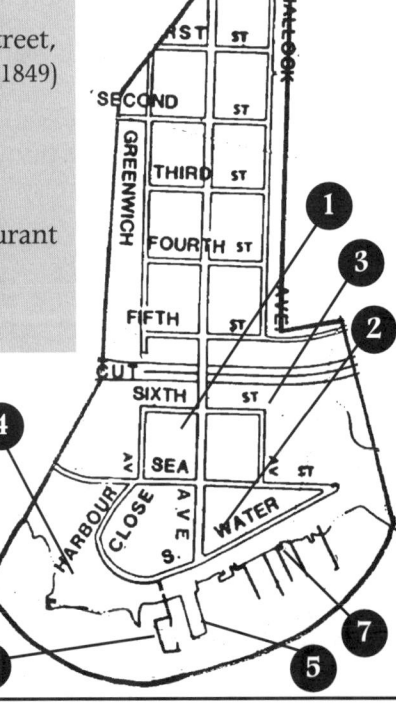

NEW HAVEN NEIGHBORHOODS
Prospect Hill

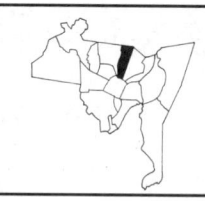

The Prospect Hill neighborhood is the most elegant and exclusive neighborhood in New Haven. This is reflected by the presence of the Yale Divinity School, Yale Science Complex, and Albertus Magnus College here. The history of this district between Whitney Avenue and Newhallville has been closely intertwined with educational institutions for well over a century.

The southern part of the neighborhood includes Hillhouse Avenue between Trumbull and Sachem Streets. This beautiful street is covered in the Walking Tour of Hillhouse Avenue, beginning on page 133. The block bounded by Sachem Street, Whitney Avenue, Edwards Street and Prospect Street is all owned by Yale and is now called Science Hill. It too is covered in the separate Yale section of this book on page 261.

New Haven lawyer and legislator James Hillhouse engineered the original development of this neighborhood. Development occured at a very slow pace in the early 1800s after Hillhouse bought the land. By the mid-1800s, a number of homes had been built along Hillhouse Avenue. The only home north of Sachem Street was Hillhouse's estate.

During the mid-1800s, the neighborhood became interconnected with local educational institutions, as the result of efforts made by Benjamin Silliman, Sr. The Scientific School was founded in 1847 as a center where "practical and scientific education" would take place.

The Connecticut Agricultural Experiment Station between Huntington Street and East Rock Road is over a hundred years old.

When Frederick T. Brewster willed that his mansion be torn down, his estate *Edgerton* was given to the city and is today's Edgerton Park.

The neighborhood's connection to institutions of higher learning continued when Albertus Magnus was established in 1925.

From the turn of the 20th century through the 1930s, there was a period of rapid and impressive residential development in the northern section of this area, on and around Prospect and St. Ronan Streets. This development along new and old streets alike was characterized by large Tudor Revival and Colonial Revival homes.

After World War II, the Foote School moved to Loomis Place and has continued to expand since then. The Yale Divinity School occupies a large tract of land between St. Ronan and Prospect Streets.

Most of the post-World War II garden apartments along Prospect Street are now occupied by people connected to Yale. Albertus Magnus continues to expand, both by building and by acquiring some of the mansions along Prospect Street.

There has been a significant decline in the value of some of the large houses, caused both by the general decline in the real estate market and by their very high taxes. This has made them accessible to families who in the past could not afford them. The desirability of the neighborhood continues to be the highest in New Haven.

1. Hillhouse Avenue
2. Science Hill
3. Peabody Museum
4. Author's house
5. Foote School
6. Yale Divinity School
7. St. Ronan Street
8. CT Agricultural Experiment Station
9. Edgerton Park

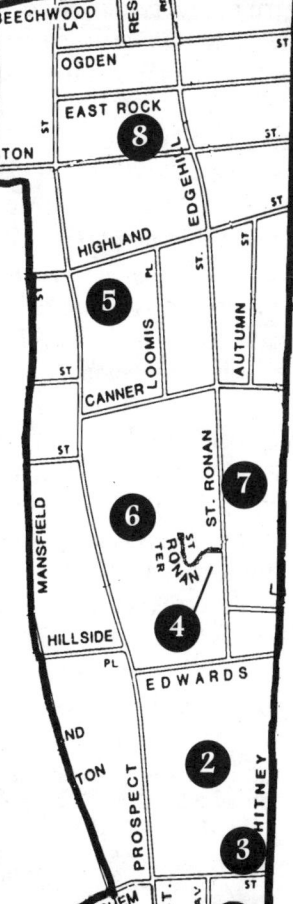

A few of the New Haven settlers had located in Westville in 1640, but the land lying to the west of the West River remained remarkably undeveloped until well into the 1800s. Prior to the 1850s, its economy was based primarily on subsistence farming. The emergence of Westville Village as the core of the community had begun very slowly as early as the 1750s with the establishment of mills and factories in the area. These relatively successful industries produced matches, paper, and hardware.

In the late 1800s, Westville Village underwent a period of rapid expansion in the wake of industrialization and technological advances. Roads and bridges were constructed to facilitate travel between the town of Westville and New Haven. The building of these roadways and the rise of industry in the area sparked the growth of its population. By 1900, Westville Village alone had 700 residents.

Its expansion and the strengthened ties between the town and the city of New Haven fueled a struggle over the annexation of Westville in 1870. While Westville residents succeeded in holding off the takeover of their town for a short while, by 1897 Westville had become a special ward of New Haven, and in 1923, it became a part of New Haven.

Growth of residential areas occurred after the turn of the twentieth century. The 360-plus acres of land named *Edgewood* by former owner Donald Grant Mitchell was divided into lots which were sold individually. Now known as Old Westville, wide streets and elegant homes characterize the area which lies between Forest Road and Yale Avenue and between Fountain Street and Derby Avenue. Since its establishment, Old Westville has remained one of New Haven's best residential neighborhoods and now serves as home to former Mayor Richard C. Lee, State Representative Patricia Dillon, U.S. Senator Joseph Lieberman.

Beverly Hills was developed as a section of Westville in the years immediately following World War II. Unlike Old Westville, Beverly Hills is composed primarily of one-family ranch style homes which were designed to attract middle-income families to the suburbs. In addition to the large homes in Old Westville and the more modest houses in Beverly Hills, there are also a few high- and low-rise apartment buildings and a few condominium complexes along Fountain Street.

Edgewood Park offers everyone in the city a patch of green where they can feed ducks, shoot hoops, or explore tree-lined paths. The park is the site of New Haven's Spanish American War and Holocaust Memorials.

Westville Today

During the late 1960s and early 1970s, Westville experienced a period of economic distress. However, the past decade has seen the rebirth of Westville Village with its renewed popularity as a residential neighborhood, comprised of approximately 6,700 people. Today, almost half of Westville's working-age residents are either professionals or they work in management positions.

Hopkins is located on a large tract of land high on a hill off Forest Road. The Yale Sports Complex is on the South side off Derby Avenue. It now includes the new Connecticut Tennis Center.

Westville's economy no longer depends primarily upon industry, but instead relies on retail businesses. With the renovation of the Village in the early 1980s, a number of upscale and antique stores have joined long-time Village residents such as Hallock's Appliances, Jackson Marvin Hardware, The Cape Codder, 500 Blake Street, and D'Andreas Pharmacy. Despite the resurgence of Westville Village and Whalley Avenue as retail centers, Westville remains one of the most popular residential neighborhoods in New Haven.

NEW HAVEN NEIGHBORHOODS
Westville

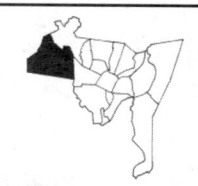

Westville is home to the Yale Athletic complex, which includes the Yale Bowl, the Connecticut Tennis Center, and Yale Field (nearby in West Haven), where the New Haven Raven's play.

Experimental plastic house on Laurel Road, designed by Valerie Batorewicz

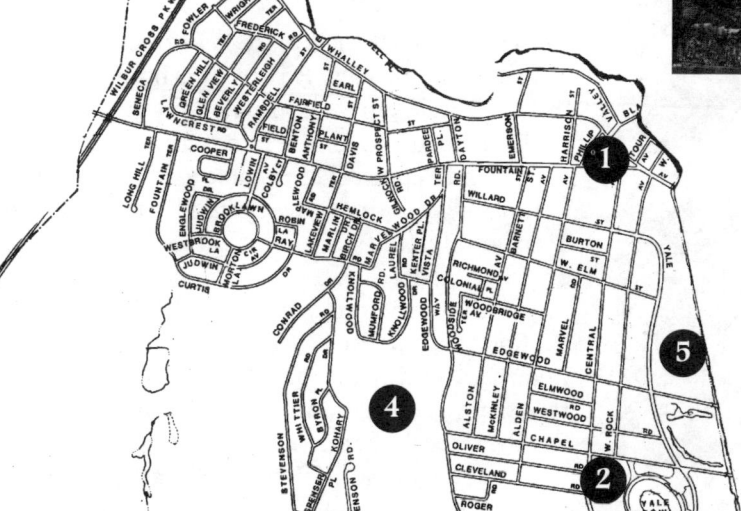

1. Westville Center
2. Yale Bowl
3. Connecticut Tennis Center
4. Hopkins
5. Edgewood Park

As in many other sections of New Haven, very little development occurred in the Wooster Square neighborhood until after the first quarter of the nineteenth century. Wooster Square Park was built east of the original Nine Squares, and named in honor of New Haven's Revolutionary War hero, David Wooster. The establishment of the Square marked the birth of the neighborhood. Prominent residents of New Haven constructed homes on the Square. These elegant homes set the standard according to which adjacent houses would be built over the next fifty years.

While residential growth took place around the Square, the eastern portion of this district became New Haven's industrial center. An influx of Irish immigrants during the middle of the century fueled the rise of carriage, clock, and other manufacturing in this area. In the years following the Civil War, Wooster Square's industrial growth continued at sites near the Harbor. Because of this emphasis on industrial expansion, a number of middle-class homes were destroyed to make room for more factories. The increasing population and the destruction of homes in Wooster Square created overcrowded living conditions in the tenement houses inhabited by the neighborhood's working-class residents.

During the last two decades of the 1800s, a second wave of immigration occurred, this time bringing people from Italy and eastern Europe. Initially, the arrival of Italians into Wooster Square created tensions between the new immigrants and the dominant Irish-American population in the neighborhood, but after the turn of the century, Wooster Square was transformed into the center of New Haven's Italian-American community.

The Twentieth Century

Unlike most of the city's working class neighborhoods, Wooster Square experienced a period of dramatic decline in the years leading up to the Second World War. The rising popularity of the automobile and the destructive impact of the Depression on the overall economy caused many companies to fold, including Wooster Square's successful carriage manufacturers. With this industrial decline came the deterioration of Wooster Square's homes and commercial buildings.

The city government set out to redevelop Wooster Square beginning with Redevelopment Plans of 1953. The I-91 and I-95 Interstates were constructed during this time to lighten the burden of traffic on local roadways. One of the consequences of their construction was that they cut off most of Wooster Square from the Harbor, and I-91 bisected the neighborhood, essentially creating a natural barrier between the less affluent and industrial sectors from the central Square area.

Wooster Square Today

Today, Wooster Square is known to most as the "Little Italy" of New Haven. It is home to two of the finest pizzeria's in the country, Sally's and Pepe's, who both claim to be the originators of pizza. Besides Sally's and Pepe's other notable establishments in this neighborhood include Consiglio's, DelMonaco's, Tony and Lucille's, Maresca's, and Lucibello's Bakery on Olive Street.

Wooster Square became New Haven's first Historic District in 1970, and most of the beautiful homes around the Square have been refurbished to represent the harmonious charm that characterized the Park area when it was first constructed.

In the summer, Wooster Square is alive with a seasonal and religious festivals enjoyed by people from all parts of the city.

Christopher Columbus, hero of the neighborhood's Italian-American community, welcomes visitors to Wooster Square Park in the heart of New Haven's "Little Italy."

NEW HAVEN NEIGHBORHOODS
Wooster Square

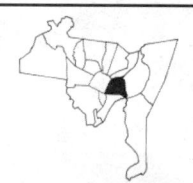

Etching of 91 Olive Street by Joseph Jaqua

1. Wooster Square
2. Columbus Statue
3. St. Michael's Catholic Church
4. Conte School
5. Strouse Adler Company
6. St. Paul's Episcopal Church
7. St. Casimir's Church on Green Street
8. New Haven Fire Headquarters
9. Pepe's Apizza
10. The Spot Apizza
11. Sally's Apizza

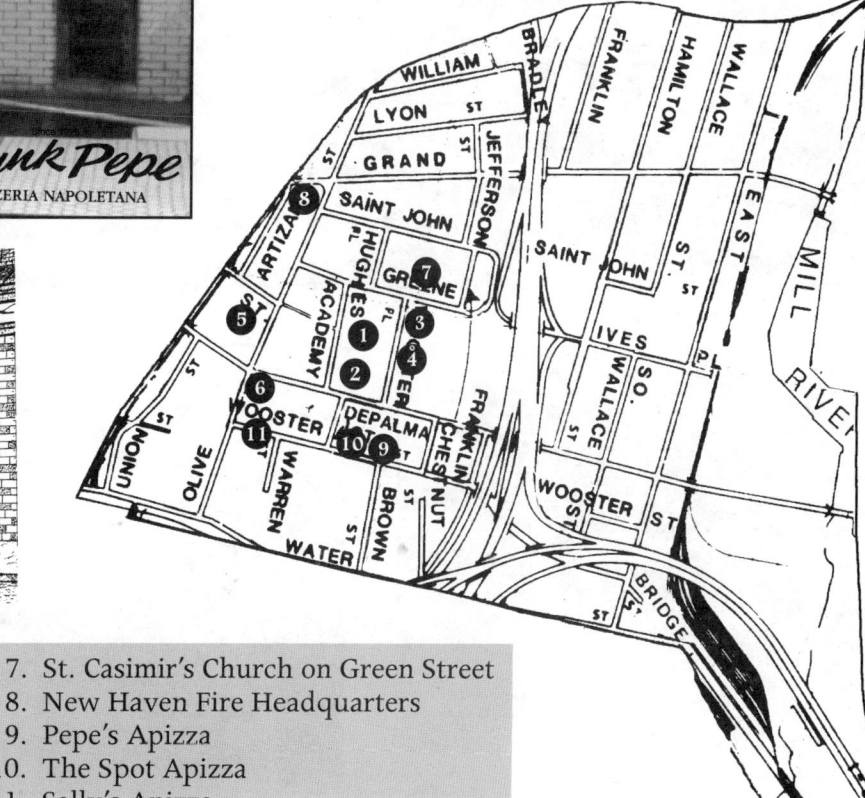

GREATER NEW HAVEN
Problems

Greater New Haven suffers from the problems of poverty, crime and drugs at a level which is typical for an area of its size and population. Various steps being taken to solve these problems are covered elsewhere in this book. The six problems illustrated below are relatively small, but their impact on our psyche and our image is very negative. One of the most important things we learned in preparing to host the Special Olympics World Games is that we can solve problems when we want to. These are the problems that can and should be solved next.

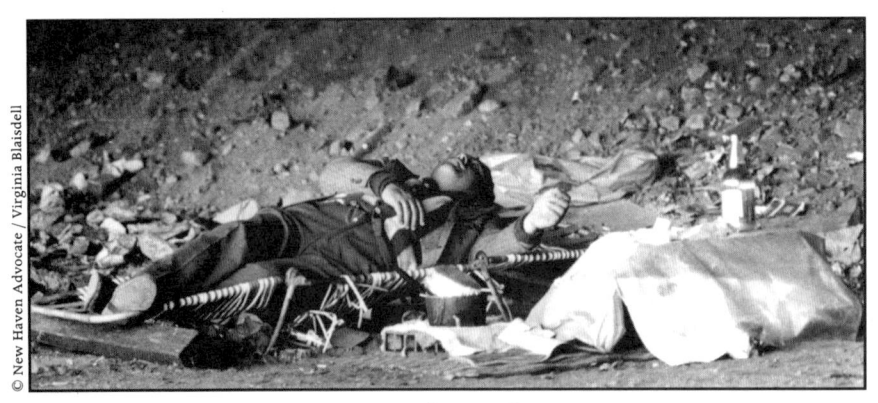

Homeless people

Boarded-up houses

Ugly outdoor advertising signs

Panhandlers

Rubbish everywhere

Vendors at Long Wharf

SHOWPLACE OF MODERN ARCHITECTURE
Introduction

It is not by accident that New Haven has become nationally known as a showcase of contemporary architecture. Rather, it is a direct result of efforts by Vincent Scully, the eminent Yale Professor of Art History; Whitney Griswold, Yale's President in the 1950s; and New Haven's popular eight-term Mayor Richard C. Lee.

Yale enjoyed a period of magnificent building during the 1920s and 1930s, led by James Gamble Rogers. His buildings, designed for Yale's undergraduate residential colleges, were mostly Gothic and Georgian in style. They are some of the best examples of these styles in the country.

In the late 1940s, Yale planned a new art gallery for the corner of Chapel and High Streets. Scully persuaded those in charge to depart from the traditional Gothic and Georgian styles and commission Louis Kahn to design the building. The success of the Yale Art Gallery led to many further commissions for Kahn, and marked the beginning of New Haven's plunge into modern architecture. Kahn died 30 years later while working on his last building, the Yale Center for British Art.

Gothic & Georgian Era

Yale commissioned several significant modern buildings during the 1950s. Douglas Orr designed the Accelerator Laboratories (1993); Community Services Building (1965) [soon to be the Knights of Columbus Museum]; Laboratory for Clinical Investigation (1965); Police Services Headquarters; Creative Arts Workshop on Audubon; and the Air Rights Garage over Route 34.

The Josiah Willard Gibbs Laboratory (1955) was designed by Paul Schweikle. Next, the Yale Art and Architecture building was designed by Paul Rudolph, then Chairman of the Architecture Department. Its unique design included thirty interior levels, and a revolutionary construction technique of poured molded concrete. It stunned the architectural world and received worldwide publicity. Rudolph used similar techniques for the 1,280 car Temple Street Parking Garage in 1961.

The Contemporary Era

Eero Saarinen's design of the Ingalls Hockey Rink (1957) caught Yale President Griswold's imagination. The rink, made of poured concrete with an aluminum roof, has no supporting interior columns. Saarinen was later to become world-renowned for his gullwinged TWA Terminal at Kennedy Airport, and the St. Louis Arch.

Gordon Bunshaft of Skidmore, Owings & Merrill designed the stunning Beinecke Rare Book and Manuscript Library in 1961. Its walls of translucent marble allow a glow of diffused light to enter the space in an ever changing array of colors, without endangering the rare manuscripts in the library's permanent collection.

Saarinen built Morse and Stiles Colleges at Broadway and Tower Parkway, and the matching Yale Co-Op store. These buildings were made of poured aggregate, and fit in beautifully with their Gothic neighbors. Saarinen died in 1961, when he was moving his firm to Hamden. His associates, Kevin Roche and John Dinkeloo, took over the building of the New Haven Coliseum with a 2,700 car overhead garage, completed in 1969, and the world-class Knights of Columbus Headquarters, completed in 1967.

Philip Johnson, famous for his glass house in New Canaan, took over the building of Pierson-Sage Square at the head of Hillhouse Avenue between Whitney and Prospect. The Kline Biology Tower and the Kline Geology Laboratory were completed in 1966.

Internationally-known Bauhaus architect Marcel Breuer worked simultaneously on the Pirelli Armstrong Rubber Company headquarters at Long Wharf, and the Becton Engineering and Applied Science Center on Prospect Street. Both structures were completed in 1966. He also designed the East Rock School, completed in 1972

By the mid 1960s, New Haven was becoming the model redevelopment city in the country. New buildings were springing up everywhere. Mayor Richard Lee caught the modern architecture fever, and convinced other city leaders of the importance and uniqueness of New Haven's architectural legacy. The exceptional buildings that followed were also designed by:

- Vincent C. Amore
- Edward Larrabee Barnes
- Crang & Boack
- Frank Chapman
- Allan Dehar Associates/Alexander Purves
- Ellerbe, Inc.
- Frank O. Gehry Associates
- John Johansen
- Gerald M. Kagan
- Kallmann, McKinnell & Wood
- Peter Millard
- Charles Moore
- Herbert S. Newman Associates
- Cesar Pelli
- William F. Pederson
- Roth and Moore
- Shepley, Bulfinch, Richardson & Abbott
- Skidmore, Owings & Merrill
- Robert Venturi
- Robert Wendler/Paul Pizzo
- King Lui Wu

The buildings in the 11 pages that follow are grouped by location, each with an accompanying map.

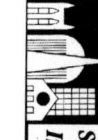

1. Dept. of Police Services Headquarters (1973)
1 Union Avenue • Douglas Orr, de Cossy, Winder, New Haven

2. Community Services Building (1965)
1 State Street • Douglas Orr, de Cossy, Winder, New Haven
Future home of the Knights of Columbus Museum.

3. Richard C. Lee High School (1964)
100 Church St. South • Kevin Roche, John Dinkeloo and Associates, Hamden.
Renovated into an office building (1992), Herbert S. Newman Associates.

4. Church Street South Housing (1969)
Church St. South • Charles Moore Associates
with Moore, Lindol/Turnbull Whittaker, New Haven

5. Tower One & Tower East (1969/1970)
18 Tower Lane • Charles Moore Associates, with Moore, Grover and Harper, New Haven

6. Union Railroad Station Renovation and Parking Garage (1990)
50 Union Avenue, New Haven
Herbert S. Newman Associates, New Haven

7. Knights of Columbus Headquarters (1967)
1 Columbus Plaza • Kevin Roche, John Dinkeloo and Associates, Hamden

8. New Haven Veterans Memorial Coliseum (1969)
269 South Orange St • Kevin Roche, John Dinkeloo & Associates, Hamden

SHOWPLACE OF MODERN ARCHITECTURE
Church St, N. & S. of Rt #34

Temple Street Parking Garage (1962)
Temple Street between North Frontage Road and Crown Street
Paul Rudolph, New Haven

Temple Medical Hotel (1991)
229 George Street • Robert Wendler/Paul Pizzo, New Haven

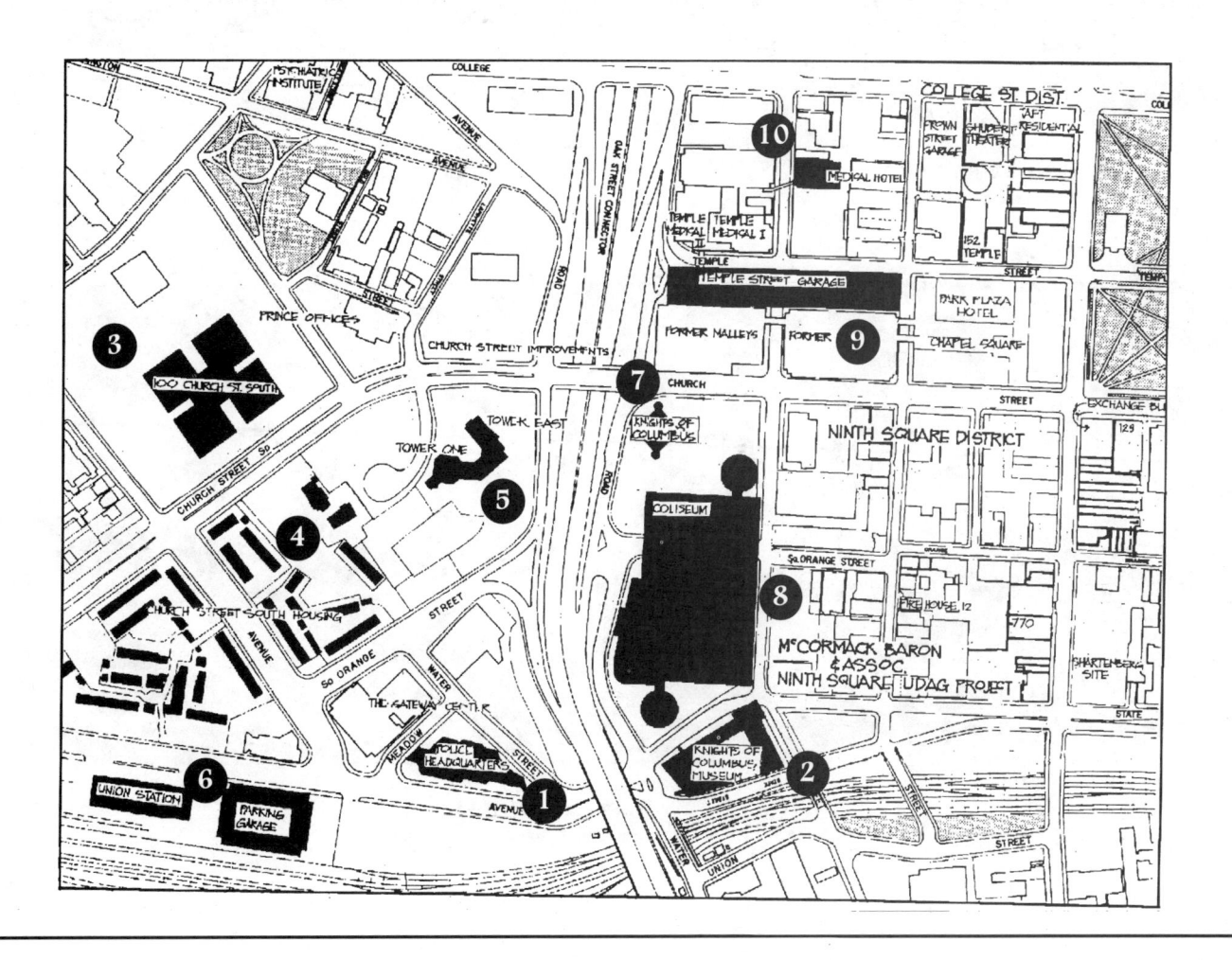

Yale Psychiatric Institute (1990)
*184 Liberty Street • Frank O. Gehry Associates, Santa Monica, CA
and Allen Dehar Associates, New Haven*

Doctor's Office Building (1976)
860 Howard Avenue • King Lui Wu, New Haven

Yale Physicians Building (1988)
800 Howard Avenue • Ellerbe, Inc., Washington, D.C.

Yale Boyer Center for Molecular Medicine (1994)
295 Congress Avenue • Cesar Pelli & Associates, New Haven

Children's Hospital (1994)
Howard Avenue • Shepley, Bulfinch, Richardson & Abbott, Boston, MA
Note: Image is a composite of two photographs.

SHOWPLACE OF MODERN ARCHITECTURE
Yale Medical Complex

Laboratory of Epidemiology and Public Health (1965)
60 College Street • Philip Johnson, New York, NY/Douglas Orr, New Haven

Crawford Manor Housing for the Elderly (1965)
9 Park Street • Paul Rudolph, New Haven

Air Rights Garage (1976~80)
66 York St. • Douglas Orr, de Cossy, Winder, New Haven

Yale Laboratory of Clinical Investigation (1965)
*60 Davenport Avenue
Douglas Orr, de Cossy, Winder, New Haven*

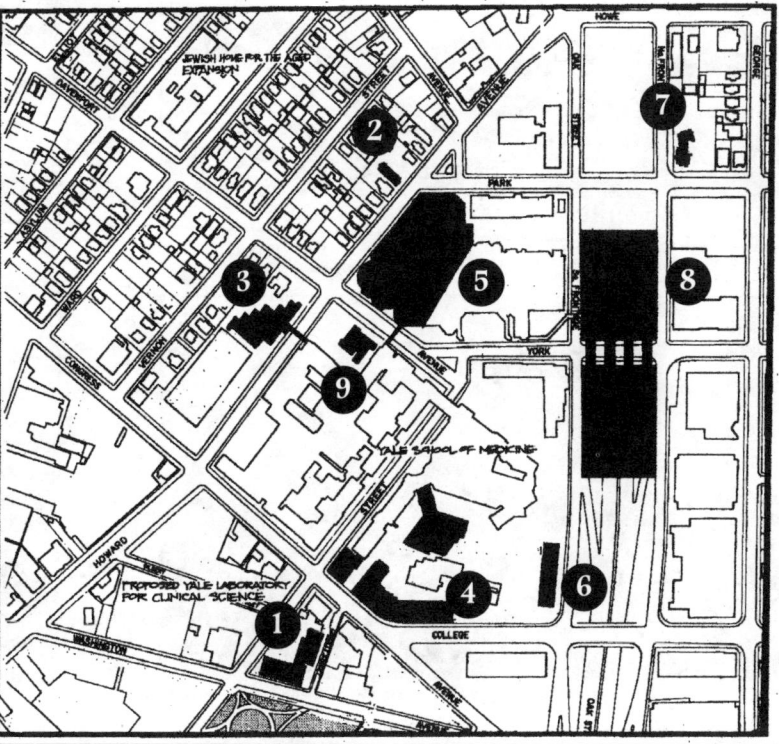

① Becton Engineering and Applied Center (1968)
15 Prospect Street • Marcel Breuer, New York, N.Y.

② Manuscript Senior Society (1963)
344 Elm Street • King Lui Wu, New Haven

③ Art and Architecture Building (1963)
180 York Street • Paul Rudolph, New Haven

④ Yale University Art Gallery (1953)
1111 Chapel Street
Louis Kahn, Philadelphia, PA/Douglas Orr, New Haven

⑤ Samuel Morse & Ezra Stiles Colleges (1960)
Yale University, 302 York Street
Eero Saarinen and Associates, Bloomfield Hills, MI

⑥ Yale Co~op Store (1961)
77 Broadway • Eero Saarinen and Associates, Bloomfield Hills, MI

SHOWPLACE OF MODERN ARCHITECTURE
Yale ~ Main Campus

Yale University Center for British Art (1973)
1080 Chapel Street
Louis Kahn, Philadelphia, PA/Douglas Orr, New Haven

Beinecke Rare Book & Manuscript Library (1961)
Wall and High Streets • Gordon Bunshaft, Skidmore, Owings & Merrill, New York, NY ; Outdoor court Isamu Noguchi

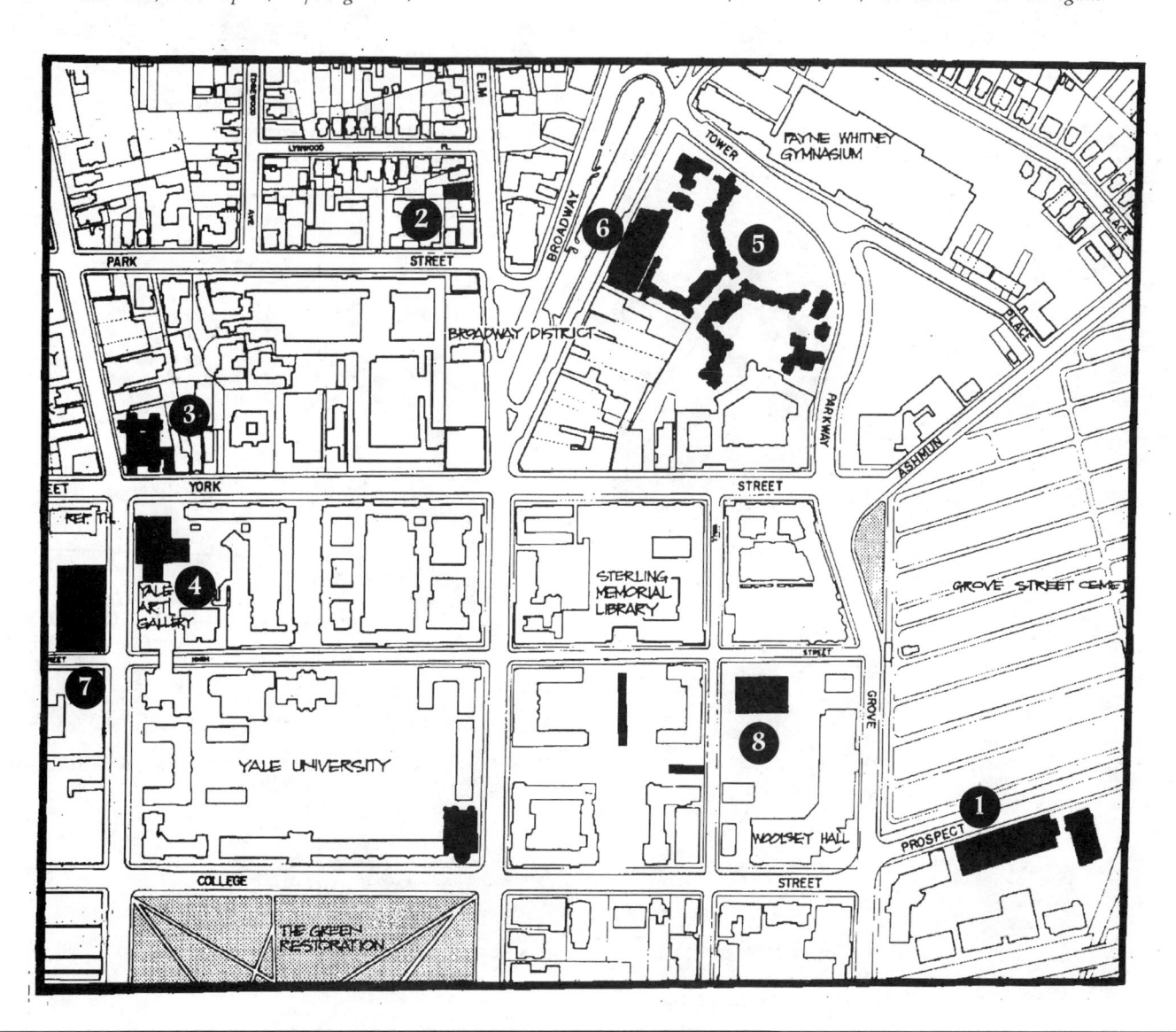

One Century Tower (1990)
Church Street • Cesar Pelli & Associates, New Haven

State Plaza Office Building (1987)
State and Olive Streets • Herbert S. Newman Associates, New Haven

Audubon Court Housing and Stores (1988)
Audubon Street • Herbert S. Newman Associates, New Haven

New Haven Foundation Building (1990)
70 Audubon Street • Vincent C. Amore, West Haven

City Hall Renovations and Additions (1994)
165 Church Street • Herbert S. Newman Associates, New Haven

Whitney Grove Square (1987)
1 Whitney Avenue (above)
Herbert S. Newman Associates, New Haven

County Court House (1971)
235 Church Street (left)
William F. Pederson, New Haven

Not Pictured:

A. Ives Memorial Free Public Library, Renovations and Additions (1990)
133 Elm Street • Hardy Holzman Pieffer Associates, New York, NY

B. Central Fire Headquarters (1961)
952 Grand Avenue • Peter Millard, Carlin, Pozzi and Millard, New Haven

C. Creative Arts Workshop (1972)
Audubon Street • Douglas Orr, de Cossy, Winder, New Haven

D. 59 Elm Street, Office Building Renovations (1984)
59 Elm Street • Roth & Moore, New Haven

E. McQueeney Towers, Elderly Housing (1973)
358 Orange Street • Frank Chapman, New Haven

SHOWPLACE OF MODERN ARCHITECTURE
Whitney/Audubon/State

Granite Square (1990)
700 State Street • Gerald M. Kagan, New Haven

Audubon Court Office Building (1988)
55 Whitney Avenue • Roth & Moore, New Haven

New Haven Savings Bank (1972)
195 Church Street • William F. Pederson, New Haven

Connecticut Financial Center (1990)
157 Church Street
Crang & Boack, Toronto, Canada

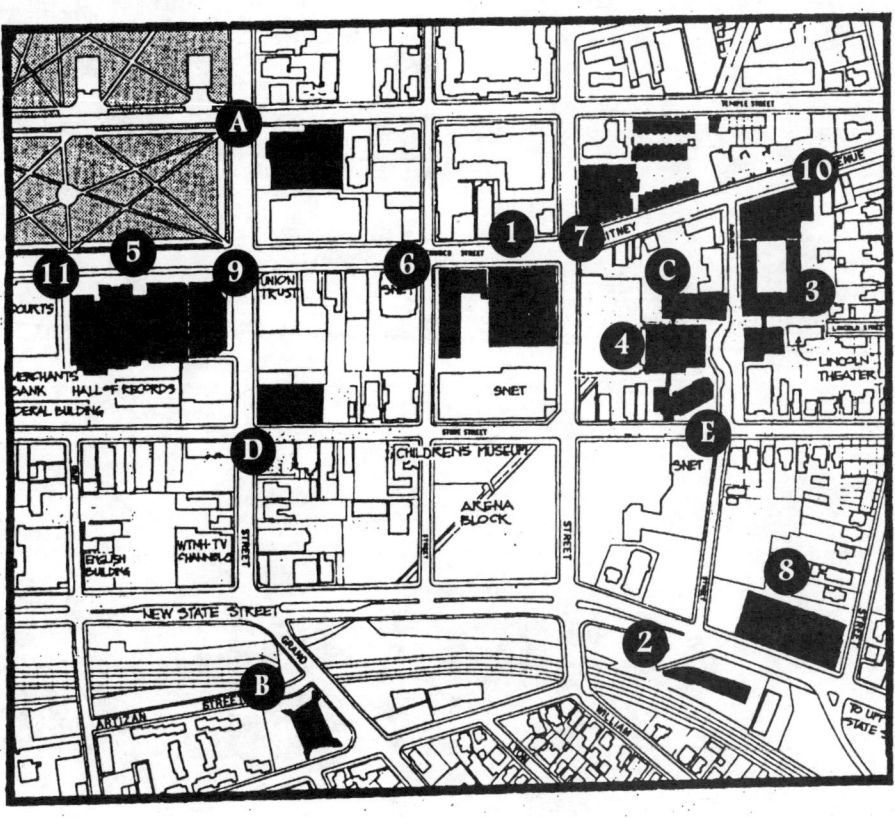

1

East Rock Community School (1972)
Willow and Nash Streets
Marcel Breuer, New York, NY

2

First Presbyterian Church (1966)
704 Whitney Avenue • John Dinkeloo, Hamden

3

United Church of Christ (1968)
217 Dixwell Avenue • John Johnson, New York, NY

4

Dixwell Community House (1970)
197 Dixwell Avenue
Herbert Newman Assoc., New Haven
with Edward Cherry

5

Nuclear Structure Laboratory (1963)
260 Whitney Avenue
Douglas Orr, de Cossy, Winder, New Haven

SHOWPLACE OF MODERN ARCHITECTURE
Dixwell/Pierson Sq./East Rock

Ingalls Hockey Rink (1957)
73 Sachem Street

Eero Saarinen and Associates, Bloomfield Hills, MI

First Church of Christ Scientist (1950)
691 Whitney Avenue • Douglas Orr, New Haven

Pictured Elsewhere

A. Bass Center for Structural & Molecular Biology (1994) p. 261
266 Whitney Avenue • Kallmann, McKinnell & Wood Architects, Boston

B. Kline Biology Tower (1966) p. 261
219 Prospect Street • Philip Johnson, NY, NY

C. Kline Geology Laboratory (1966) p. 261
210 Whitney Avenue • Philip Johnson, NY, NY

D. Luce Center for International Studies (1995) p. 136
34 Hillhouse Avenue • Ed Barnes, New Haven

E. Seely G. Mudd Library (1984) p. 251
38 Mansfield Street • Roth & Moore, New Haven

Not Pictured

F. Goffe Street Fire House (1973)
Goffe and Webster Streets
Robert Venturi, Venturi and Rauch, Philadelphia, PA

G. Greely Memorial Forestry Labratory (1959)
370 Prospect Street • Paul Rudolph, New Haven

H. Married Graduate Student Housing (1960)
291-311 Mansfield Street • Paul Rudolph, New Haven

I. School of Management
(1961, as Yale Computer Center)
60 Sachem Street • Gordon Bunshaft, Skidmore, Owings & Merrill, NY, NY
Renovations and Additions (1977-1978)
Edward Larrabee Barnes, NY, NY

J. Arthur K. Watson Hall
Renovations and Additions (1986)
51 Prospect Street • Roth & Moore, New Haven
location not indicated on map

K. Whitney Avenue Firestation (1962)
362 Whitney Avenue
Peter Millard, Carlin, Pozzi and Millard, New Haven

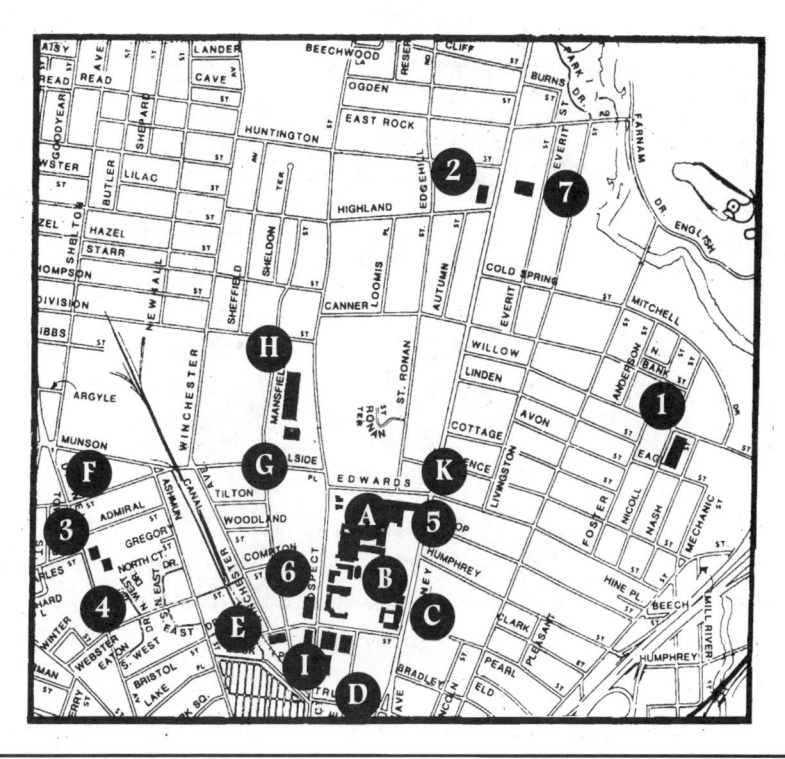

207

Maritime Center & Garage (1988)
555 Long Wharf Drive • Robert Wendler, New Haven

Pirelli Armstrong Rubber Company (1968)
500 Sargent Drive • Marcel Breuer, New York, NY w/ Robert Gatje

Teletrack *(now Sports Haven)*
600 Long Wharf Drive • Herbert S. Newman Associates, New Haven

Conte School (1960)
21 Wooster Place • Skidmore, Owings & Merrill, New York, NY

Tennis Center of Connectiut (1991)
*Derby Avenue • Edward Larrabee Barnes, New York, NY
with Browning Day Mullins Dierdorf, Inc.*

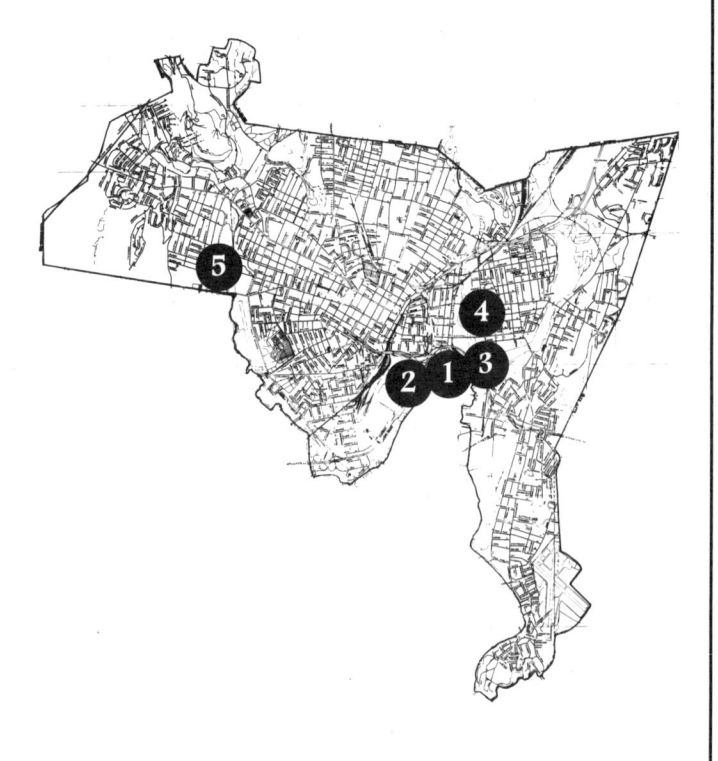

HISTORIC NEW HAVEN BUILDINGS
Walking Tour Guide

THE MAP OF HISTORIC NEW HAVEN

0 — N — 1/4 mile

The following six pages are a guide to a Walking Tour of buildings selected as New Haven Landmarks by the New Haven Preservation Trust. The map above shows the location of each building, primarily on the Green, on the Yale campus, or in the Wooster Square neighborhood. The New Haven Preservation Trust selects buildings of architectural and historic merit and designates them as New Haven Landmarks. Some are public buildings with regular business hours; however, many of these buildings are still private homes or businesses which are not normally open to the public. (Occasionally, special arrangements may be made for private viewings.) The drawings and most of the text which follow are by William Hersey and John Kyrk, first published in a pamphlet based on a design by Edward G.A. Kubler for the New Haven Preservation Trust. For more information about the Trust, call 562-5919.

209

1. CITY HALL (1861)
On Church Street facing the Green. City Hall is one of the country's earliest and finest designs in the High Victorian style. It is a work of Henry Austin, and contains an elaborate iron staircase. The polychrome facade in various sandstone and limestone shades was restored in 1976. The historic facade was incorporated into the new City Hall in 1993-94.

2. POST OFFICE/FEDERAL DISTRICT COURT (1913)
On Church Street. Designed by James Gamble Rogers of New York, the building is a monumental Greek Revival structure. Its proposed demolition in 1967 was successfully opposed by the Preservation Trust.

3. TRINITY EPISCOPAL CHURCH (1813-14)
On the Green. The church was built by Ithiel Town as one of the first Gothic style structures in America. In the interim there have been considerable modifications made both inside and out.

4. FIRST CONGREGATIONAL CHURCH (1812-15)
Also called Center Church, it was built on the Green by Ithiel Town, based on plans of Asher Benjamin, Boston architect and publisher. Today's exterior is essentially the original. The interior was first remodeled in 1842 by Henry Austin. Remains of the old Colonial burying ground rest in the church crypt.

5. UNITED CONGREGATIONAL CHURCH (1812-15)
Also called North Church, it was built by David Hoadley. Renovations have restored the Federal interior style, although the shallow dome, ceiling ornament and chandelier are original. The design was derived from James Gibbs' St. Martin's-in-the-Fields in London.

6. NEW HAVEN FREE PUBLIC LIBRARY (1908)
Elm and Temple Streets. The library was designed by New York architect Cass Gilbert to harmonize with the churches on the Green. The interior has been extensively renovated in recent years, while preserving the handsome facade.

7. TRINITY LUTHERAN CHURCH (1870)
292 Orange Street. This High Victorian Gothic structure was designed by David R. Brown. The steeple has been modified somewhat since construction.

8. WILLIAM PINTO HOUSE (c. 1810)
275 Orange Street. The house has been modified for commercial use. The front bay window is recent, though other details, including the Palladian window, are part of the original design. Inventor Eli Whitney is thought to have lived there at the end of his life.

9. JOHN COOK HOUSE (1807)
35 Elm Street. The city's oldest stucco building, a late Colonial structure with an attic ballroom added after 1814, is used today for offices.

10. TIMOTHY BISHOP HOUSE
36 Elm Street. This is the city's best surviving example of a Federal town mansion; its spacious center hall and woodwork remain largely intact. Its design is attributed to David Hoadley.

11. CONNECTICUT SAVINGS BANK (1906)
47 Church Street. Now occupied by Centerbank, the Greek Revival design was by New York architects Gordon, Tracy and Swartwout. The fine interior is a recent restoration.

12. LOUIS' LUNCH (c. 1895)
263 Crown Street. Louis' is a small restaurant owned by three generations of the Lassen family and said to be the place where the hamburger originated. Built at 202 George Street, the structure was relocated to its present site in 1975.

13. RALPH INGERSOLL HOUSE (1829)
143 Elm Street. The building, currently used as the offices of Yale's School of Music, is an early Greek Revival design of Ithiel Town and Alexander J. Davis, built by Nahum Hayward. Certain interior restorations have been made.

14. JOHN PIERPONT HOUSE (1767)
149 Elm Street. Now home to the Yale Visitor's Center, the house has served as the previous home of both Yale's Faculty Club and its Undergraduate Admissions Office. The house has a center-chimney plan typical of the Georgian style.

15. JONATHAN MIX HOUSE (1799)
155 Elm Street. Now the Graduate Club, the building exemplifies the Federal style of architecture. Its interior has been greatly modified over the years, but still features a large stone hearth in the "Great Hall."

16. NICHOLAS CALLAHAN HOUSE (1762-6)
175 Elm Street. Now Elihu, a Yale Senior Society, the building has been much altered through the years. Originally it was used by Callahan as a tavern which became a favorite with the Tories.

17. CONNECTICUT HALL (1705)
Located on the Old Campus, it is Yale University's oldest remaining structure. It was built by Francis Letort and Thomas Bills according to the design of Harvard University's Massachusetts Hall. A designated National Historic Landmark.

18. THE OLD LIBRARY (1842)
Now Dwight Hall, it is Yale's second oldest building and the first of many done in the Gothic Revival style. It is also architect Henry Austin's first major work.

19. SKULL AND BONES (1856)
64 High Street. It is the oldest of Yale's Senior Societies. The building, a Greek Revival design, was enlarged in 1883 and again in 1903.

20. WOLF'S HEAD (1924)
210 York Street. A Yale Senior Society, it was designed as part of "Fraternity Row" in the early 20th century by New Yorker Bertram Goodhue.

21. Mory's (c. 1800)
306 York Street. Yale's famed private club, and a favorite haunt of the Whiffenpoofs singing group, has occupied this Federal style house since 1912.

22. Grove Street Cemetery Gate (1845)
High and Grove Streets. It is considered the finest of several such Egyptian Revival gates built in Northeastern cities; this one is by Henry Austin.

23. Book and Snake (1900)
214 Grove Street. The structure was built by R. H. Robertson of New York in the manner of a Greek temple for this Senior Society.

24. Scroll and Key (1869)
490 College Street. Home to this Senior Society, the building is New Haven's only remaining building by Richard Morris Hunt in his unusual, unique style.

25. Elizabethan Club (c.1810)
459 College Street. Also known as the Leveerett Griswold House, the building contains a Palladian window in its front gable dating from its construction in the Federal era.

26. Peletiah Perit House (1860)
55 Hillhouse Avenue. The building is an Italian Renaissance revival design by Sidney Mason Stone; a large library wing was added at the rear after 1888.

27. John P. Norton House (1848–9)
52 Hillhouse Avenue. Now part of Yale University, it is a towered Italian Villa designed by Henry Austin. Its appearance has been altered somewhat since its construction.

28. Aaron Skinner House (1832)
46 Hillhouse Avenue. A distinguished Greek revival dwelling built as a boys' school by Alexander J. Davis. Additions have been made several times, including one in the 1850s usually considered to be the work of Henry Austin.

29. Mary Prichard House (1836)
35 Hillhouse Avenue. It is a Greek revival design of Corinthian order by Alexander J. Davis, built by Nelson Hotchkiss and Ira Atwater.

30. Abigail Whelpley House (c. 1800 *or* 1827)
31 Hillhouse Avenue. It may possibly have been built elsewhere. Henry Austin modified its original Federalist character with the addition of a mansard roof in the 1860s.

31. Old Wolf's Head (1884)
77 Prospect Street. Now Yale University offices, this building is the design of McKim, Mead and White of New York, their only building in New Haven.

32. James Dwight Dana House (1849)
24 Hillhouse Avenue. Now Yale offices, the building was designed by Henry Austin, and clearly shows his interest in Hindu architecture. This National Historic Landmark adjoins the route of the Farmington Canal.

33. Berzelius (1910)
76 Trumbull Street. A Yale Senior Society, the tomb-like structure was built of Indiana limestone by New York architect Donn Barber.

34. William Kingsley House (c.1845)
31 Whitney Avenue. Also known as Kingsley-Havemeyer, it is a simple Greek Revival house slightly altered in 1934. It was moved from 105 Grove Street to its present location in 1976.

35. Temple Mishkan Israel (1896)
55 Audubon Street. Now home to the Educational Center for the Arts (ECA), it was the first major construction undertaken by New Haven's Jewish community. The Spanish Renaissance edifice is the work of the New York firm of Brunner and Tryon.

36. Chaplin~Apthorp House (1806)
58 Trumbull Street. Originally built by James Chaplin on Whitney Avenue, where it was briefly occupied by inventor-painter Samuel F. B. Morse, the house was relocated twice, first on Hillhouse Avenue, and in 1838, to its present site.

37. John C. Anderson House (1882)
444 Orange Street. This is an extravagant and expensive example of late Victorian Second Empire style. It has now been converted into offices, having previously housed St. Mary's convent.

38. Nehemiah Sperry House (1857)
466 Orange Street. Distinguished by a double-bow front, the building no longer has its original shutters and roof balustrade.

39. Everard Benjamin House (1838)
232 Bradley Street. A graceful Greek Revival house, it had a broad lawn at its original Orange Street site, before Lincoln Street cut through from Trumbull, and shows the influence of Ithiel Town and Henry Austin.

40. Wayland Cottage (c. 1855)
135 Whitney Avenue. This small Gothic Revival farmhouse stood at the gate of Judge Wayland's estate. The addition at the rear is recent.

41. Row Houses (1871)
552-562 Chapel Street. Designed by architect David Brown, these houses are unified into one structure by mansard roofs and decorative details from the French Second Empire style. They face Wooster Square Park.

42. Willis Bristol House (1845)
584 Chapel Street. Designed by architect Henry Austin, the house is now divided into apartments. Indian and Islamic architectural details give the house an exotic air.

43. James English House (1845)
592 Chapel Street. The structure was designed by Henry Austin for a Connecticut governor. A third floor was added in 1876.

44. Henchman Soule House (1844)
600 Chapel Street. The Greek revival building is now occupied by the St. Paul's Church Home. Formerly the house had a roof parapet.

45. Oliver B. North House (1852)
604 Chapel Street. Now apartments, the building was designed by Henry Austin in the Italian villa style. Its first owner was not North but a Cincinnati merchant named King. The tower has been restored by the Trust.

46. Nelson Hotchkiss I House (1850)
621 Chapel Street. Now apartments, the building is generally attributed to Henry Austin. It has a late Greek revival porch, although other details seem to echo the Italian Renaissance.

47. William Lewis House (1850)
613 Chapel Street. Now apartments, the building is in the Italian villa style, probably by Henry Austin.

48. Nelson Hotchkiss II House (1850)
607 Chapel Street. The building is a stuccoed brick house, divided now into apartments, with a double-bow front. A balustrade originally ran around the edge of the roof. The design suggests the influence of Henry Austin.

49. John Robertson House (c. 1835)
37–39 Wooster Place. This building is a double house in which both units are contained within the outline of one dwelling. Many alterations have been made to the exterior.

50. Theron Towner House (c. 1836 *or* 1844)
11 Wooster Place. Now a funeral home, this is the only example in Wooster Square of a Greek revival porch with a full row of columns. At one time there was an ornamental railing around the roof.

51. Russell Hotchkiss House (1844)
7 Wooster Place. The cast-iron balconies were probably added to this apartment building in the 1850s. The third floor with its ornamental cornice was added in 1873.

52. Matthew Elliot House (1832)
541 Chapel Street. Now a funeral home, this is an unusual example of the Greek revival style. A carved white parapet once surrounded the roof.

The following buildings, although they are beyond the range of the walking tours, are nevertheless of historic interest.

53. Goffe Street Special School (1864)
106 Goffe Street. It was built in the Federal style by Henry Austin as the first school for black children in New Haven.

54. Othniel Marsh House (1878)
360 Prospect Street. Now Marsh Hall, the building was designed by J. Cleveland Cady of New York. It was built in massive brownstone for the paleontologist and founder of the Peabody Museum, who bequeathed it to Yale in 1899. It became the first building of the Forestry School and a National Historic Landmark.

55. Elizabeth Hooker House (1914)
123 Edgehill Road. By Delano and Aldrich of New York, this is a handsome, red brick French manor house with a walled court, and extensive gardens with a stream.

56. Charles Atwater House (1890)
321 Whitney Avenue. Designed by New York architects Babb, Cook and Willard, this is one of the city's last remaining examples of the Shingle style. Recent remodeling for offices has preserved the fine interiors of the building.

57. Boathouse (1909)
74 Forbes Avenue, East Haven. Designed by Peabody and Stearns of Boston, this structure was built for Yale as the Adee Boathouse, and was remodeled for commercial use in 1969.

58. Raynham (1804)
709 Townsend Avenue. Started as a Federalist country estate surrounded by spacious meadows overlooking the harbor, this building was transformed into a Victorian Gothic Villa in 1856. It is still preserved both inside and out.

59. Pardee~Morris House (1860 and later)
325 Lighthouse Road. A property of the New Haven Colony Historical Society, this extensive structure was initially built in stages over nearly a century. It was then burned by British troops in 1779; what timbers, stone walls and chimneys survived were used again in its reconstruction.

60. Lighthouse (1840)
In East Haven's Lighthouse Point Park. Marking the east entrance to New Haven Harbor, it is the second lighthouse on the site, replacing an earlier wooden one.

Choate Rosemary Hall

Choate Rosemary Hall is an independent, secondary boarding school in Wallingford, 15 miles north of New Haven. The school originated as Rosemary Hall, founded in 1890, and The Choate School, founded in 1896. The schools merged in 1974 to form the not-for-profit Choate Rosemary Hall Foundation, Inc. The present school enrolls 974 students in grades 9-12 from the United States and 35 foreign countries. Close to a third of the student body receives financial aid, which totalled $3 million in 1994-95.

The 400-acre campus consists of 116 houses, dormitories, and classroom buildings in a residential setting. Students live in houses or dormitories, together with resident faculty and their families. Nationally renowned artists, dance and theater companies, as well as students, perform and display their work at the Paul Mellon Arts Center's two theaters, art gallery, recital hall, and studios.

The Science Center includes 22 classrooms and laboratories, a 150-seat auditorium, a conservatory, and a rooftop celestial observation platform. The Language Learning Center contains a 34-station language laboratory.

The Andrew Mellon Library holds 49,000 books, periodicals, English and foreign language newspapers, archives, and audiovisual materials.

Over 120 networked computers are used for computer instruction and as tools in writing and research. Students have direct access to the Internet and its international electronic mail capabilities, as well as to the World-Wide WEB.

Academic Summer Program includes the Writing Project, the John F. Kennedy Institute of Government, and Connect, a math and science program for girls entering 7th and 8th grades. Choate's Connecticut Scholars program is a collaboration between public and private schools coordinated with the Connecticut Association of Urban Superintendents. Students from urban school systems participate in an enrichment program in mathematics, science, or American government, and receive college counseling. Connecticut Scholars receive a grant toward the cost of the program based on financial need.

The school's Statement of Purpose says, "Choate Rosemary Hall is an independent school where talented students and teachers from diverse backgrounds live and learn together imaginatively. As we build community spirit from the richness of difference, we better prepare for an increasingly interdependent world." Academic programs include computer education, English, arts (including music and theater), foreign languages (French, German, Greek, Italian, Japanese, Latin, Russian, Spanish), history and social sciences, mathematics, psychology, philosophy, religion, sciences, independent interdisciplinary study, travel and study abroad, intercultural exchanges, and physical education.

Current issues at the school include making community service a requirement for all members of the Choate Rosemary Hall community and enhancing the intercultural exchange program. Five Russian students recently completed an exchange at the Choate, and five Choate students will study in Russia in September 1995.

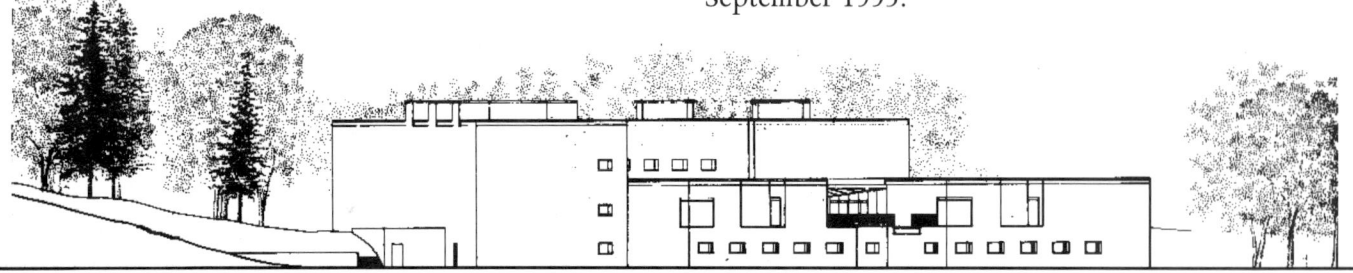

Edward Shanahan
Headmaster

Choate Rosemary Hall   697~2000
333 Christian Street, Wallingford

EDUCATION
Preparatory Schools

Cheshire Academy

Cheshire Academy is a coed college preparatory school, founded in 1794. The Academy offers its day and boarding students multiple opportunities to discover and realize their potential for growth. The curriculum is designed to develop the academic skills needed for successful college study. The Lower School, which offers an extended day option, will be adding a grade level each year, so that by the year 2000, Cheshire Academy will offer a full program, K - 12, with an optional post graduate year. At every level, Cheshire Academy strives to enhance students' self-esteem and social, physical and moral strengths.

The beautiful 100 acre campus is located in a rural setting, 15 miles northwest of New Haven. English, foreign languages, mathematics, history and science courses are offered at each level, including advanced placement and honors, and are supplemented with fine arts and computer courses. The Reading Department teaches basic to advanced skills for middle schoolers, and also offers an invaluable course in study skills for post-graduates.

The Learning Center offers remediation in the language arts and math skills for qualified students. With the aid of a college counseling team, 99% of the graduates enroll in colleges and universities such as Dartmouth, Boston College, Bowdoin College, and Mt. Holyoke.

Cheshire Academy students are given a full and well-rounded education while attending small classes (10:1 student/teacher ratio) and receiving individual attention. The diverse student population (17 countries and 14 states are represented) allows each student to be exposed to a wealth of experiences and insights through friendships with peers from different cultures and backgrounds.

Each of the 50 faculty members contributes his or her own special talents toward the goals of caring for each student, and encouraging that student to grow as part of the school community, while being respectful of the uniqueness of the individual.

The Cheshire Academy experience leaves students with a solid foundation for success in college and later life, and allows them to develop friendships they will have forever.

John Hyslop, Headmaster

Cheshire Academy 272~5306
10 Main Street, Cheshire

Hopkins

In 1660, Edward Hopkins, a seven-time governor of the Connecticut Colony, bequeathed his estate to the American colonies to establish schools "for the breeding up of hopeful youths for the public service of the country."

With that bequest, 335 years ago, Hopkins Grammar School was founded in a one-room schoolhouse on the New Haven Green. In 1925, the all-boys school moved to its present location on Forest Road, in the Westville section of New Haven.

The union of Day Prospect Hill and Hopkins Grammar in 1972 created Hopkins, a co-ed preparatory day school serving 600 students in grades seven through twelve. While Hopkins has seen many changes over the years, its mission remains faithful to Edward Hopkins vision so many years ago.

Hopkins provides a well-rounded and challenging program for talented, highly motivated students of diverse backgrounds.

The academically rigorous, demanding environment prepares grads for enrollment at top-ranked colleges and universities across the country. Nearly one quarter of the Hopkins senior class is recognized each year by the National Merit Scholarship Program, typically the highest percentage in the State of Connecticut.

Thomas "Tim" Rodd, Jr. Headmaster

Hopkins is fortunate in its hilltop site which provides a breathtaking view overlooking the City of New Haven. The 70 year-old campus includes 104 acres of fields, facilities and woodlands. A modern athletic facility containing three gyms, training and weight rooms, and a competitive swimming pool which was built in 1985. All of the major academic buildings—Baldwin Hall, Hopkins House, Lovell Hall, the Reigeluth gymnasium, and the Day Prospect Hill building—were constructed after 1925 when the Hopkins Grammar School moved to its current site. In 1994, the Adam Kreiger Challenge Course, one of the most comprehensive outdoor challenge facilities in New England, was constructed in the newly acquired Hopkins woods.

Summerbridge/New Haven is an enrichment program at Hopkins which is highly successful in preparing inner-city 5th and 6th graders for a rigorous academic high school experience. Hopkins stresses commitment, personal responsibility and service in its curriculum and encourages all students to participate in its community service program.

Hopkins   397-1001
986 Forest Road

Additions have been made to Baldwin Hall since this early photo was taken. Today, the building houses the school's science facilities.

EDUCATION
Preparatory Schools

Hamden Hall Country Day School

Hamden Hall Country Day School, founded in 1912, is a coeducational college-preparatory day school educating students in pre-kindergarten to grade 12. It is dedicated to the pursuit of academic excellence and to developing the social and emotional maturity of its students. It emphasizes individuality, independence, and innovation built on a solid intellectual foundation.

The 8-acre campus is located on a tree-shaded knoll overlooking Lake Whitney. Situated in a residential area of Hamden, the campus is just north of Yale University, and within easy reach of several other colleges and universities. The school's 12-acre athletics complex is located two miles north of the main campus.

The Lower School offers a balanced program of academics, physical education, the arts, and cultural enrichment. The curriculum challenges youngsters with a stimulating skills- and concept-based program that fosters curiosity, independence, and the ability to think clearly. A caring and nurturing environment helps children explore their talents and develop the skills and self-discipline needed to succeed in a demanding, competitive world.

The Middle School curriculum, based on a solid foundation of fundamental skills maintains rigorous standards. Students take courses in English, foreign languages, mathematics, fine arts, science, and history. There are honor sections for students who can benefit from accelerated programs. Departments coordinate curricula, and topics are often team-taught so that assignments reinforce one another.

The Upper School curriculum combines traditional college-preparatory courses with a variety of semester and full-year electives. In most subjects, students are grouped in classes according to their ability and background in the subject area, enabling them to progress at their own rate.

Hamden Hall offers a wide variety of extra-curricular activities to enrich student life. The school encourages active participation by all students in the hope that they will discover hidden interests and talents.

Hamden Hall seeks academically able and involved students who will make a significant contribution to the school community and who will benefit from the fine and varied programs offered.

Headmaster James Maggart meets with a group of students on the Whitney Avenue campus.

Hamden Hall   865-6158
1108 Whitney Avenue, Hamden

The Country School

The Country School is an independent day school located in Madison and offering classes from pre-kindergarten through 8th grade. Small classes and a faculty/student ratio of 1 to 9 allow students to receive individual attention. The Country School offers a nurturing environment and a strong sense of community characterized by close relationships among students and teachers.

The curriculum includes strong academics, balanced by a rich program of visual arts, music, and physical education. Traditional courses are enriched by a computer education program and foreign language instruction, including French beginning in Kindergarten, and Latin and Spanish in the 7th grade. Environmental education is featured on the 14-acre campus which offers a country setting with wooded areas. Students in the Upper School (Grades 5-8) enjoy special opportunities, including a full interscholastic sports program, community service, an outdoor education program, leadership opportunities and electives ranging from music theater to computer graphics. Fifth and sixth grade students have a Life Skills program, and seventh and eighth grade students meet in small groups with faculty advisors who help them develop decision-making skills and a strong sense of values. Optional programs include: an after school program until 6 pm; traditional and Suzuki music instruction in piano, violin, cello, and guitar; and a summer program.

The Country School   421~3113
341 Opening Hill Road, Madison

The Foote School

The Foote School in New Haven was founded in 1916 by Martha Babcock Foote. Since its inception, Foote has had as its goal excellence in education. Called "progressive," as it reflected the move away from the formal disciplines and the strictures on the mind and spirit, Mrs. Foote's school held that creativity was important and that learning should be joyous. The curriculum leads children to experiment and determine their own directions at the same time that it sets high standards, fosters a sense of responsibility, and teaches respect for craftsmanship and pride in a job well done.

The Foote School occupies ten modern brick buildings containing classrooms, a library, science laboratories, a theatre, two computer labs, a gymnasium and offices on a nine acre wooded site close to Yale University. Approximately 460 boys and girls from a wide range of backgrounds take part in Foote's kindergarten through grade nine curriculum. The school has approximately eighty faculty and staff members.

Foote was a child-centered school long before the concept became widely accepted. The well-being and happiness of each child are paramount. Foote School classsrooms are exciting and informal places. Although the school day is a busy one, the pace is varied and ample opportunity for quiet reflection is available. Limited class size, small group instruction and individualization help each student achieve. Close relationships between students and teachers often develop, continuing as the child progresses through the grades.

Central to Foote's strong academic program is its commitment to a multicultural curriculum designed to provide students with an appreciation of human differences, to celebrate diversity and to eliminate prejudice. Concern for aesthetic as well as intellectual development has led to a sequential program in Art, Music, and Drama. It teaches not only the fundamentals of these disciplines, but encourages creativity and originality as well.

The tradition of excellence at the Foote School fosters high academic standards, the encouragement and development of each child, and the provision of a rich experience beyond the traditional curriculum to create a unique program.

Jean G. Lamont
Head of School

The Foote School   777~3464
50 Loomis Place

EDUCATION
Preparatory Schools

Lauralton Hall

Lauralton Hall in Milford, founded in 1905 by the Sisters of Mercy, is the oldest Catholic college preparatory school for girls in Connecticut. The 440 girls in grades 9-12 commute from 32 towns in New Haven and Fairfield Counties. The student body is enriched by girls from many cultural, social and religious backgrounds.

The student-teacher ratio is 13 to 1, and the school excels in college preparation, with many honors and advanced placement courses. Lauralton Hall stresses mastery of analytical and critical thinking skills, problem solving, and the ability to communicate ideas. Guidance seminars and individual conferences are an integral part of student's schedule for four years, with ongoing evaluations facilitating each student's success.

Lauralton Hall has an outstanding record in academic achievement, with 100% of each graduating class entering more than 50 different colleges and universities.

Some of the other activities offered on campus are music, art, drama, flute choir, concert chorus, academic teams, interest clubs, social activities, community service, and cultural trips. The school has 12 varsity sports and CIAC and CCIAC membership. Sports include: cross-country, soccer, swimming and diving, volleyball, indoor track, basketball, softball, track and field, tennis and golf, and cheerleading for Lauralton Hall and Fairfield Prep.

The spacious 30-acre campus is housed in a park-like setting in Milford, with a large Victorian Mansion as its focal point.

Lauralton Hall 877-2786
200 High Street, Milford

Milford Academy

Founded in 1916 and presently located in the town of Milford, Milford Academy has been a leader in education for almost 80 years. Classes are small, enabling each teacher to devote more time to the individual student. Teachers can diagnose the weaknesses of each student at an early stage and correct them, and can recommend a student to the tutoring staff for additional help when needed.

The small classes also provide ample opportunity for group discussions and questions. Individual activities and projects allow the student to accelerate according to ability and achieve their full potential. In addition to the 12 grades of classes, the Milford Academy is also well-known for its outstanding post-graduate program, a transition year for some students who want to strengthen skills before applying to college. With the assistance of the guidance director, students make college selections after considering future career plans. The Academy has a college placement rate of 90%.

On-campus facilities include a gymnasium, a soccer and football field, a baseball diamond, a six-lane Olympic-size swimming pool and outdoor basketball and tennis courts for leisure-time activities. Milford Academy's sports programs have attracted national attention with many football, basketball, and baseball players eventually drafted by major league teams.

The Academy's intellectual expectations are high. However, it recognizes that each student is unique and may not excel in every subject. Teachers work with each individual to recognize personal talents and strengthen them, while overcoming areas of relative weakness. The library is conducive to quiet study and research. A resource section houses encyclopedias and other research materials needed for term papers.

Milford Academy 878-5921
150 Gulf Street, Milford

Saint Thomas's Day School

Saint Thomas's, in New Haven, is a small, coeducational day school serving approximately 158 children in Junior Kindergarten through Grade 6. Saint Thomas's has always welcomed children from all backgrounds, believing that children who learn and grow together develop openness and respect for others. Tolerance and appreciation of individual gifts and backgrounds are fundamental, as is a secure environment which enables children to learn in an atmosphere of trust and encouragement.

Saint Thomas's Day School is a diverse community of children, teachers, parents and parishioners working together to foster learning in the context of faith and personal commitment. As a mission of Saint Thomas's Episcopal Church, the school strives to educate children broadly, by cultivating intelligence while engaging heart and spirit. The School seeks to motivate children of diverse races, creeds and backgrounds to become independent thinkers who appreciate, understand and serve others. Generous financial aid sustains our commitment to a broad-based student body.

Saint Thomas's is a lively place, where children are actively engaged in learning. They may be found practicing a skit in a foreign language, discovering "mystery powders" in science, preparing a medieval feast, painting a mural, excitedly solving a math puzzle, singing in Chapel or taking a trip to Ellis Island in New York City. Our diversified, sequential curriculum is based on the developmental stages of childhood, and balances conceptual learning with basic skills. Through small group instruction, teachers extend personal guidance and individualized teaching. Subjects include reading, language arts, mathematics and social studies under the direction of the head teacher. Special teachers in art, science, music, computers, Spanish, French, library, religious education and physical education complete the core program.

The spirit of Saint Thomas's is embodied in its quality of care and concern for each child and every family. Our Extended Day Program offers experienced, caring teachers and supervised activities until 5:30 pm. Saint Thomas's Day School also has a Summer Program for Young Children, ages 4-11, from late June through early August. Morning, afternoon, and full-day sessions are offered and participants need not be affiliated with Saint Thomas's. There are three two-week interdisciplinary morning sessions centering on the themes of water and boats, air and flight, and land and wheels. The afternoon program is recreational, with swimming, outdoor activities, excursions to local parks and the shore.

St. Thomas's Day School   776-2123
830 Whitney Avenue

Wightwood School

Wightwood School is a progressive day school located in Branford, serving 90 boys and girls in Pre-K to Grade 8. The School combines "academic challenge and direct experience in a warm, supportive atmosphere." Individual attention and a low student-teacher ratio are emphasized. The program focuses on math, reading, creative writing, and environmental science. A recognizable progression of themes runs through the curriculum, increasing in complexity as the children grow older. Each level uses one or more themes designed to reinforce development. Spanish, art, and music are taught in all grades. Vacation and summer programs are available. Wightwood provides tuition assistance on the basis of financial need and availability of funds. These grants are awarded annually, by application.

Transportation for Branford residents is available through the town of Branford. Bus service is provided from New Haven for an additional fee. The student body reflects the socioeconomic and racial diversity found in New Haven and its surrounding communities. Parental involvement and volunteerism is encouraged throughout the school. Wightwood is situated in a contemporary building set on 3.5 acres of land with open space, playground facilities, a basketball court, and two ponds connected by a meandering stream. The school year begins in early September and traditionally ends in mid-June.

Wightwood School   481-0363
56 Stony Creek Road, Branford

EDUCATION ~ COLLEGES
Gateway Community College

Gateway Community Technical College began on November 16, 1992, when the state legislature approved the new name for the institution created by the merger of South Central Community College and Greater New Haven State Technical College. Gateway is licensed and accredited by the Board of Governors for Higher Education in Connecticut and is accredited by the New England Association of Schools and Colleges.

The Long Wharf campus in New Haven offers associate degrees and certificates in academic and career programs. The North Haven campus offers associate degrees and certificates in high-tech engineering and technology programs. Additionally, courses are offered at satellite centers throughout greater New Haven.

As the fastest growing community technical college in Connecticut, Gateway now serves over 5,000 students with 57 full-time and over 150 part-time faculty.

The college offers approximately 60 programs including business, social sciences, liberal arts, allied health, hospitality management, office administration, science, mathematics, and engineering technologies. Gateway's programs are designed to meet local employment needs, as well as the needs of its students.

Gateway provides a supportive environment through its many student services. The faculty and staff are committed to assisting students in achieving their goals. The Career Development Center on each campus assists students in making career decisions and in finding employment opportunities. Academic counseling is available to all students.

The Center for Education Services provides academic support to all students who wish to make use of this facility, providing a wide range of self-paced graded curriculum materials, tutorial assistance and related services. Video and computer-assisted tutorials are available for review and practice of basic skills, math, English and the sciences. Placement testing, learning disabled academic support and tutoring workshops are offered.

Many women in transition have children, jobs or other responsibilities which present difficulties in their returning to the classroom. A special program, *Women In Transition,* offers support and direction to help these women succeed. While course content, academic achievement and credit requirements for participants are identical to those of the general curriculum, a unique set of courses form the core of *Women in Transition's* academic program.

Gateway conducts a wide variety of social, cultural and special activities which enrich both the college and community. More than 40 organizations are sponsored by the Student Government, including a newspaper, yearbook and literary magazine.

Gateway Community-Technical College is also proud to be a member of the National Junior College Athletic Association.

Technical Schools

Baran Institute of Technology
15 Kimberly Ave, West Haven
934-7289

Connecticut Institute of Technology
2 Elizabeth St, West Haven
397-4940

Connecticut School of Electronics
286 Ella T. Grasso Blvd, New Haven
624-2121

Data Institute
109 Church St, New Haven 787-1990
40 Commerce Park, Milford 877-9889

Stone Academy
1315 Dixwell Ave, Hamden
288-7474

Technical Careers Institute
11 Kimberly Ave, West Haven
932-2282

Eli Whitney Regional Vocational Technical School
71 Jones Rd, Hamden 397-4045

Platt Regional Vocational Technical School
600 Orange Ave, Milford 877-2771

Paier College of Art
20 Gorham Ave, Hamden
287-3030

Buildings
1. Davis Hall
2. Pelz Gymnasium
3. Multicultural Center
4. Power Plant
5. Jennings Hall
6. Morrill Hall
7. Seabury Hall (Admissions)
8. Student Center
9. Engleman Hall
10. RB Bldgs. 7, 8, 9, 10
11. Buley Library (see #29 Wintergreen Bldg.)
12. Lyman Center
13. Earl Hall
14. Plant Maintenance
15. Connecticut Hall (Food Service)
16. Schwartz Hall (Residence Hall & Housing Office)
17. Lang Social Work House
18. Orlando Public Health Bldg.
19. Brownell Hall (Residence Hall)
20. Farnham Hall (Residence Hall)
21. Wilkinson Hall (Residence Hall)
22. Chase Hall (Residence Hall)
23. Hickerson Hall (Residence Hall)
24. Neff Hall (Residence Hall)
25. Temporary Bldg. TE
26. University Police and Granoff Student Health Center
27. Moore Fieldhouse
28. Jess Dow Field
29. Wintergreen Bldg. (Temporary Library)
30. North Campus Residence Complex

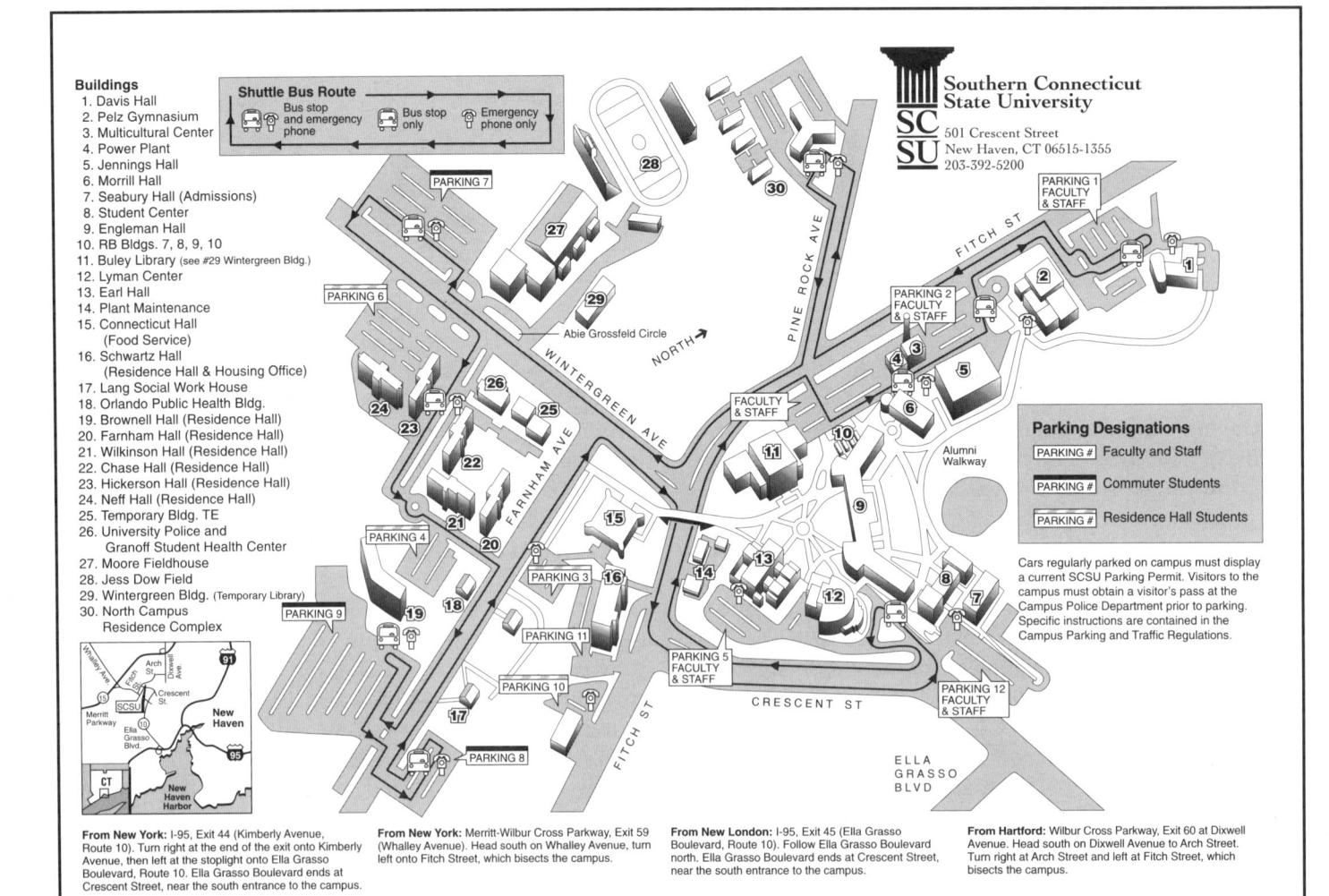

Shuttle Bus Route
- Bus stop and emergency phone
- Bus stop only
- Emergency phone only

Southern Connecticut State University
501 Crescent Street
New Haven, CT 06515-1355
203-392-5200

Parking Designations
- PARKING # — Faculty and Staff
- PARKING # — Commuter Students
- PARKING # — Residence Hall Students

Cars regularly parked on campus must display a current SCSU Parking Permit. Visitors to the campus must obtain a visitor's pass at the Campus Police Department prior to parking. Specific instructions are contained in the Campus Parking and Traffic Regulations.

From New York: I-95, Exit 44 (Kimberly Avenue, Route 10). Turn right at the end of the exit onto Kimberly Avenue, then left at the stoplight onto Ella Grasso Boulevard, Route 10. Ella Grasso Boulevard ends at Crescent Street, near the south entrance to the campus.

From New York: Merritt-Wilbur Cross Parkway, Exit 59 (Whalley Avenue). Head south on Whalley Avenue, turn left onto Fitch Street, which bisects the campus.

From New London: I-95, Exit 45 (Ella Grasso Boulevard, Route 10). Follow Ella Grasso Boulevard north. Ella Grasso Boulevard ends at Crescent Street, near the south entrance to the campus.

From Hartford: Wilbur Cross Parkway, Exit 60 at Dixwell Avenue. Head south on Dixwell Avenue to Arch Street. Turn right at Arch Street and left at Fitch Street, which bisects the campus.

Southern Connecticut State University
501 Crescent Street
New Haven, CT 06515-1355
203-392-5200

EDUCATION ~ COLLEGES
Southern Connecticut State

Southern Connecticut State University, a fully accredited institution of higher education, offers courses and programs leading to bachelor's and master's degrees in the arts and sciences, and in various professional fields. Southern also offers a sixth-year diploma in several special areas. Governed by the Board of Trustees for the Connecticut State University, Southern receives its principal support from legislative appropriations.

Founded in 1893 as the New Haven State Normal School, Southern became a four-year college in 1937. Ten years later, the School joined with Yale's Department of Education to offer a graduate program leading to a master of arts degree. In 1954, with Southern changing and growing to meet the needs of its students, Southern (then the New Haven State Teachers College) assumed complete responsibility for this graduate program. As a result, Southern made its name during the 1950s and 1960s preparing teachers in virtually every major scholastic area. Today, it is difficult to enter any elementary or secondary school in Connecticut without finding at least one Southern alumnus on its faculty.

Southern has continued its growth as a modern, diversified center of higher learning, opening up entirely new fields of study and research. In March 1983, Southern became a university, completing its evolution. It is now organized into six schools: Arts and Sciences, Business, Education, Library Science and Instructional Technology, Professional Studies, Graduate Studies, and Continuing Education.

Southern provides educational and cultural opportunities for everyone in the community. Its Continuing Education program offers courses, day or evening, for personal enrichment or professional advancement. Its clinics provide diagnosis and treatment of speech, hearing, reading problems and learning disabilities. Southern also plays host to conferences, institutes, workshops, exhibitions, and performances that both instruct and delight.

The University's greatest strength is its faculty, educated in recognized universities around the world. Faculty members are selected on the basis of their scholarly competence in a specialized field. Books, articles in professional journals, and other scholarly publications by Southern faculty are in colleges and libraries throughout the country.

Michael J. Adanti *is President of Southern Connecticut State University. Mr. Adanti is a former Mayor of the City of Ansonia.*

Southern's 168-acre campus consists of a variety of recreational and learning centers. The John Lyman Center for the Performing Arts features an open-thrust stage as the focal point for its 1,568-seat theater. The center's Robert Kendall Drama Lab houses the Theatre Department's instructional program, and offers an excellent space for experimental plays. Moore Fieldhouse contains an unusually large gymnasium surrounded by a 220-yard track. Irma Pelz Gym's two gymnasiums house a specially equipped gym for gymnastics, and a six-lane swimming pool. Southern's newest multi-purpose athletic facility, Dow Field, a lighted outdoor complex, seats 6,000 and accommodates football, soccer, field hockey and track, physical education classes and intramurals.

To perform its role effectively and responsibly, Southern Connecticut State University accepts students without regard to race, color, sex, age, disability, creed, national origin, or sexual preference.

Southern Connecticut State   392-5200
501 Crescent Street, New Haven

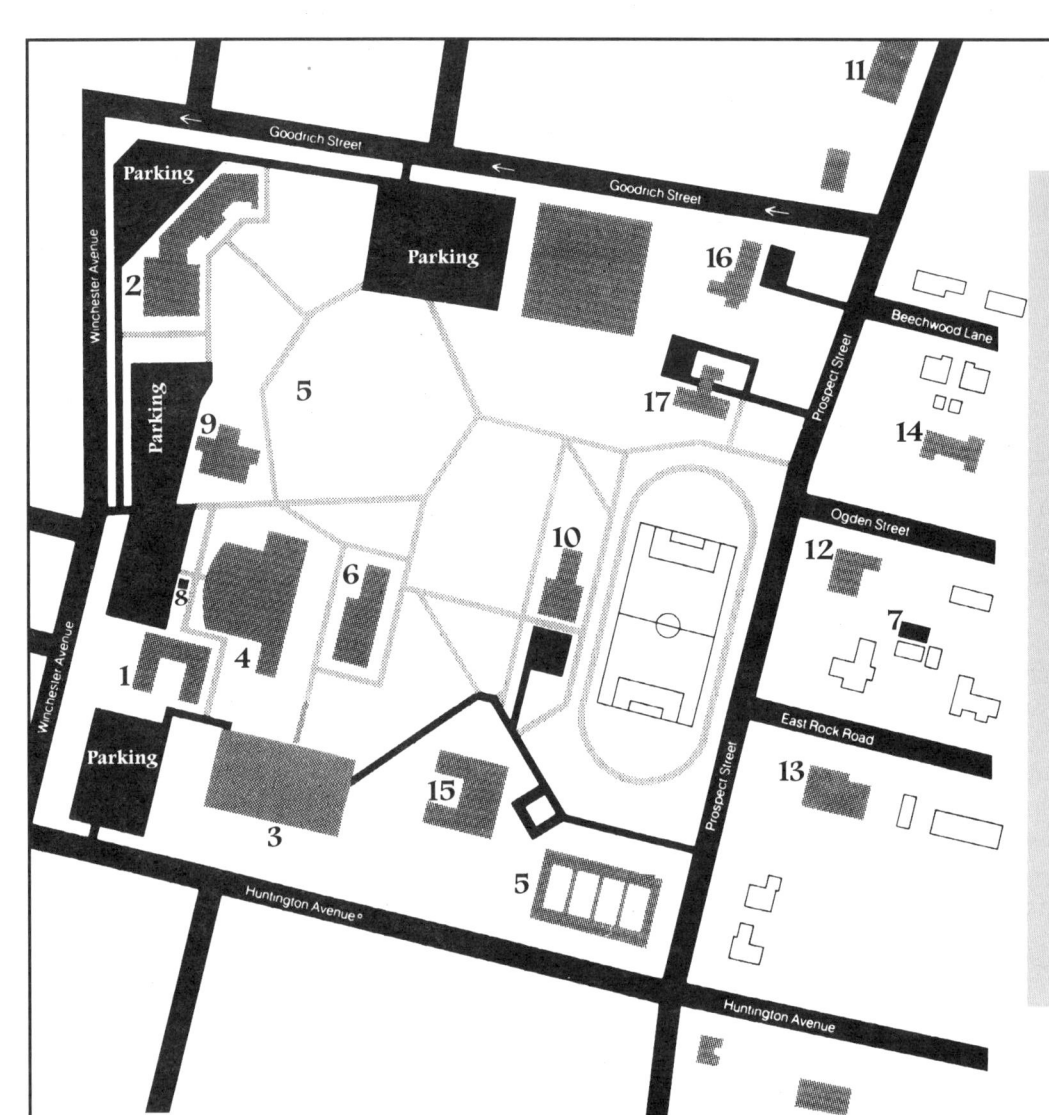

1. ACT 2 Theater
2. Aquinas Hall
3. Cosgrove, Marcus & Messer Sports Center
4. Campus Center
5. Celentano Playing Fields & Tennis Courts
6. Dominican Hall
7. Grace Chapel
8. Weldon Hall, ELS Language Center
9. Walsh Hall
10. McAuliffe Hall
11. McKeon Hall
12. Mohun Hall
13. Nilan Hall
14. Reynolds Hall
15. Rosary Hall
16. Sansbury Hall
17. Siena Hall

Rosary Hall, which today houses the College library, was constructed at 700 Prospect Street in 1905, based on designs by the Boston firm of Peabody and Stearns. The 50,000-square-foot Colonial Revival structure was originally a wedding gift to Rebecca and Louis Stoddard from her parents. Built on a large U-shaped plan around a rear terraced courtyard, Rosary Hall has had few major alterations in the shift from private estate to college library. Over 50 original rooms have been preserved. Except for the Frederick Brewster estate Edgerton (1910), which was demolished to make Edgerton Park a few blocks away, the house is probably the largest residence ever built in New Haven.

EDUCATION ~ COLLEGES
Albertus Magnus College

Albertus Magnus College was founded in 1925 by the Dominican Sisters of St. Mary of the Springs, in Columbus, Ohio. Albertus was the first Catholic residential liberal arts college for women in New England. Founded on the Dominican ideals of scholarship and the search for truth, the College was named for the medieval scholar, St. Albert the Great.

Albertus Magnus sits atop Prospect Hill, on the New Haven-Hamden border, in a residential neighborhood of stately homes. At its founding, the College was housed in Rosary Hall at 700 Prospect Street, which today serves as the library. Completed in 1905, this Palladian mansion was originally known as *Ten Acres* when it was the home of Louis and Rebecca Stoddard. Designed by the noted Boston firm of Peabody and Stearns, *Ten Acres* was generally regarded as the finest house in New Haven. Louis Stoddard was a prominent financier and international sportsman who headed the United States Polo Association; he stabled his horses in what is now the College's Act 2 Theater. The Dominican Sisters acquired the property in 1924 for a women's college. In 1983, after sixty years, Albertus Magnus became coed.

Over the years, the College expanded by acquiring neighboring mansions. Today, the campus comprises fifty acres and twenty buildings. The graceful older buildings serve as administrative offices and student housing, while newer buildings provide space for academic and social activities. The Celentano Track, Courts, and Playing Fields (1988), and the Cosgrove, Marcus, & Messer Athletic Center (1989), provide excellent athletic facilities. In 1990, Albertus Magnus joined the NCAA Division III, and now fields varsity teams in several sports for both women and for men.

Since its founding, Albertus Magnus has stressed the humane values and habits of mind acquired from studies in the liberal arts. The emphasis is on undergraduate teaching, with small classes and individual attention given to students. An extensive internship program gives students the opportunity to gain work experience and establish professional contacts.

Albertus Magnus continues to meet the needs of students with innovative programs of study. The Accelerated Degree Program, established in the Continuing Education Division in 1986, enables adult learners to pursue a degree in a timely fashion. The College established its first graduate program in 1991, with the Master of Arts in Liberal Studies Program.

The Tri-Session Plan, introduced in 1993, has placed Albertus Magnus in the forefront of higher education reform. By attending three sessions per academic year, instead of two, students can obtain a degree in three years, saving considerable time and money. Leading educators have cited the Albertus Magnus Tri-Session Plan as a model in the effort to control the soaring cost of a college education.

Albertus is an independent institution of higher education, chartered by the State of Connecticut, and accredited by the New England Association of Schools and Colleges. Albertus Magnus admits men and women of all races, beliefs and cultures.

Julia M. McNamara *is President of Albertus Magnus College. She is also the first woman to Chair the Board of Trustees of Yale-New Haven Hospital.*

Albertus Magnus College   773~8550
700 Prospect Street, New Haven

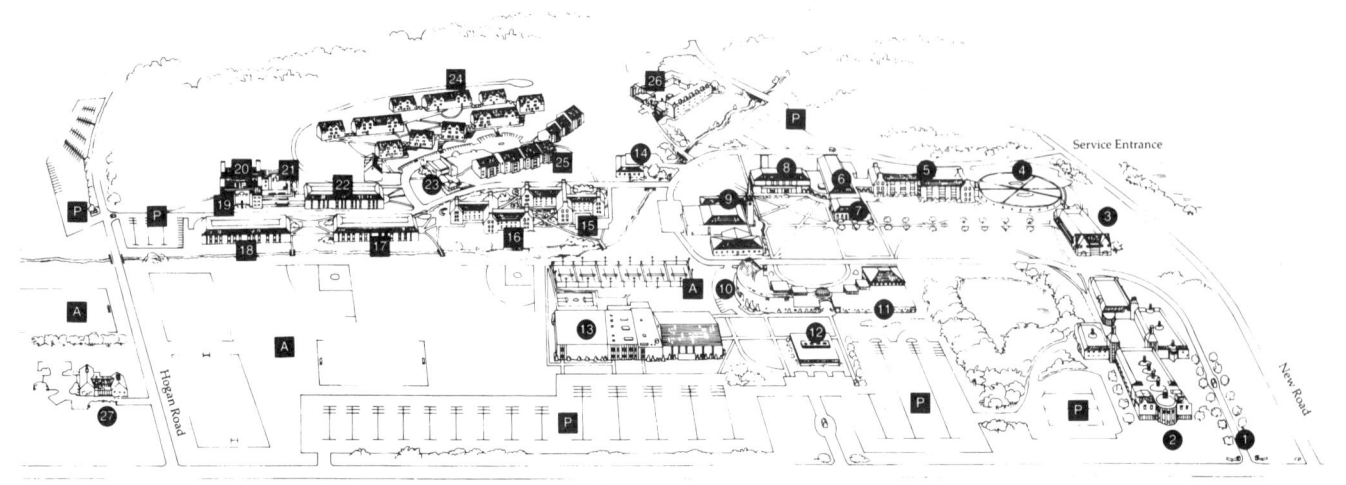

① Main Entrance	⑥ Carl Hansen Student Center *Visitor's Information Campus Store*	⑪ School of Business & Communications Center	⑯ Dana English Hall *Residential Life Office*	㉓ Student Affairs Center *Rathskeller (Snack Bar)*
② School of Law Center *(Open, September 1995)*		⑫ Faculty Office Building	⑰ Larson College Hall	㉔ The Village
③ Echlin Health Sciences Center	⑦ Alumni Hall	⑬ Gymnasium-Recreation Center	⑱ Philip Troup Hall	㉕ The Hill
	⑧ Dining Hall		⑲ Sahlin Hall	㉖ New Residence Hall
④ Clarice L. Buckman Center & Theater	⑨ Library Building *Admissions*	⑭ Facilities Building	⑳ Founders Hall	㉗ Alumni House
		⑮ Irmagarde Tator Hall *Health Center Security Office*	㉑ Bakke Hall	Ⓟ Parking Lots
⑤ Tator Hall	⑩ Admissions Parking		㉒ Perlroth Hall	Ⓐ Athletic Fields

Quinnipiac College, the school formed by the merger of Larson College and the Junior College of Commerce, was originally located on Whitney Avenue, across from Lake Whitney. In 1966, the School moved onto 100 acres of land on Mt. Carmel Avenue. Appropriately, the library was one of the first buildings finished on the new campus. The **Quinnipiac College Library Tower** *is the centerpiece of the College's Campus at the foot of Sleeping Giant Mountain in Hamden. The tower's carillon is dedicated to Nils G. Sahlin, the third president of the College, who served from 1956-1968.*

QUINNIPIAC COLLEGE

Courtesy Quinnipiac College

EDUCATION ~ COLLEGES
Quinnipiac College

An independent, coeducational institution founded in 1929, Quinnipiac College is located on a scenic 180-acre campus in Hamden, adjacent to Sleeping Giant Mountain and State Park. Its faculty is dedicated to excellence in teaching and to the maintenance of a superior learning environment, conducive to the intellectual and social development of its 5,000 students. Rigorous and innovative academic programs prepare students for undergraduate and graduate degrees in business, health science, liberal arts, and law. Outstanding internships and clinical experiences offer students the opportunity to apply what they learn in the classroom to the world around them, and help them understand the demands of a career.

During the last decade, Quinnipiac College has experienced unprecedented growth, and has become one of the most successful colleges in the Northeast. Full-time undergraduate enrollment has increased by 48 percent in eight years. Innovative programs have been strengthened by the recent completion of the state-of-the-art Lender School of Business and the Ed McMahon Mass Communications center. The School of Law Center will open in the fall of 1995.

Quinnipiac is a close-knit community with a college-wide student/faculty ratio of 15/1 and an average class size of 25. Undergraduates in the Business or Health Sciences Schools take 40 percent of their courses in the humanities, the arts, and the social sciences as part of the College Curriculum. These courses provide a solid foundation, helping students develop critical and creative thinking skills, communicate effectively, write clearly, and make informed judgments.

The Study Abroad Program places students in structured learning environments in other countries. The College has established agreements with colleges and universities in 12 foreign countries, opening the door to foreign study for eligible students. Quinnipiac is also a member of several collegiate consortia which enable students to pursue their studies in virtually any part of the world. In almost all instances, credits earned at a foreign institution are transferable.

Quinnipiac offers a variety of living arrangements. Quadruples, triples, suites, townhouses, and apartments are available for the 2,100 students who live on campus. Living in a residential "theme house" that focuses on wellness and a quiet study atmosphere is also an option. Meals are served in the *Cafe Q* an the Student Center, and the *Rathskeller* serves pizza and snacks during evening hours.

Quinnipiac College's location near Sleeping Giant State Park offers trails ideal for jogging, walking, or bicycling. A 24,000-square-foot modern fitness center includes: studios for aerobics, dance, yoga, and the martial arts; a large free-weight room and exercise machine center; and basketball, volleyball and tennis courts. The main gymnasium seats 1,500 and includes two basketball courts, a press box, locker rooms, training rooms, a steam room, and staff offices.

The College attracts renowned speakers, widely-respected for their achievements. Recent visitors to Quinnipiac have included Archbishop Tutu of South Africa, Nobel Laureate Betty Williams, former hostage Terry Anderson, author Tom Wolfe, and research scientist Jane Goodall.

John Lahey *is President of Quinnipiac College. He is currently chairman of the Executive Committee of the Connecticut Conference of Independent Colleges.*

Quinnipiac College 288~5251
275 Mount Carmel Avenue, Hamden

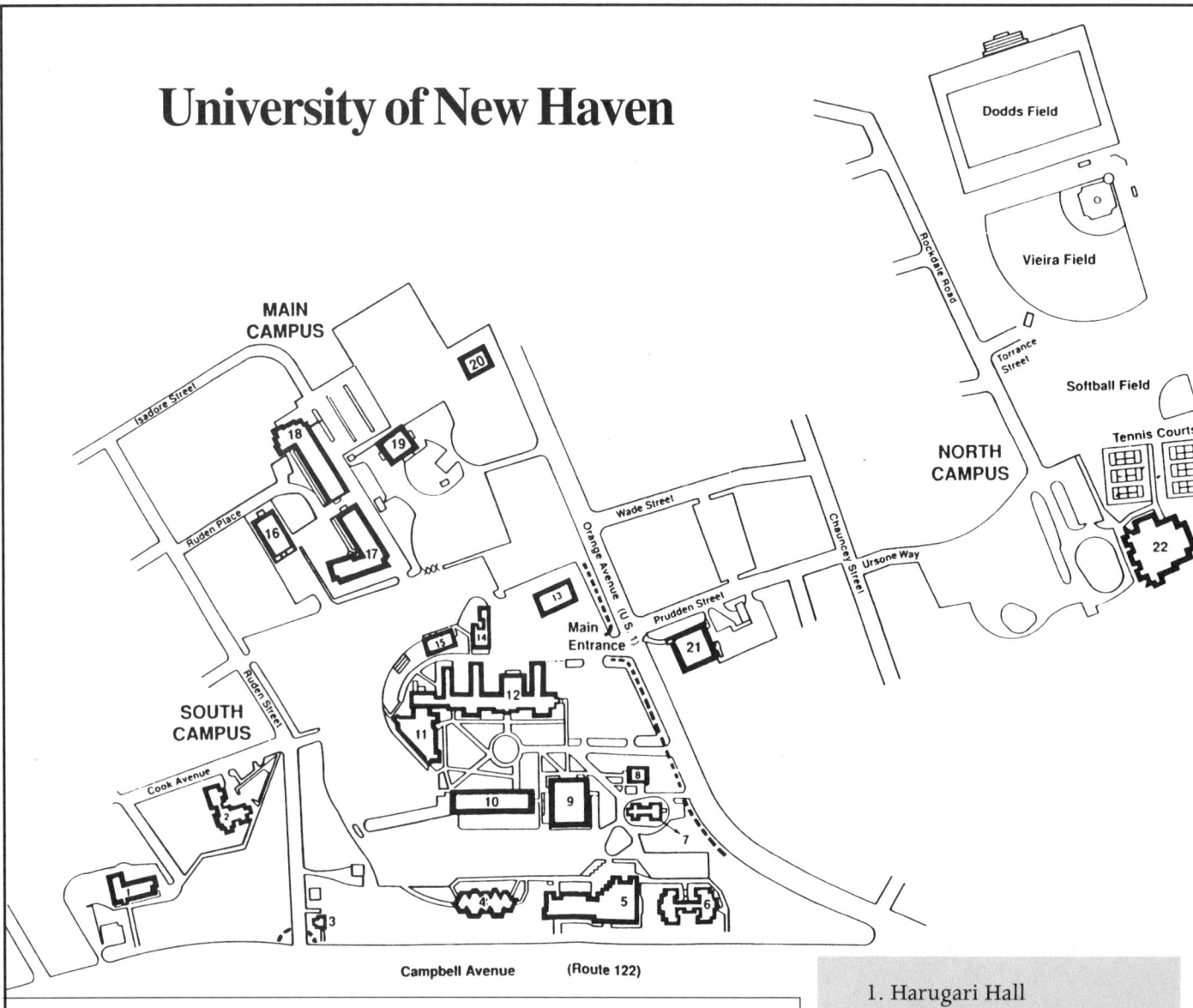

University of New Haven

1. Harugari Hall
2. Student Services Building
3. 1124 Campbell Avenue
4. Graduate School
5. Dodds Hall
6. Freshman Residence Hall
7. Gate House
8. Campus Store/Security
9. Student Center
10. Buckman Hall
11. M.K. Peterson Library
12. Maxcy Hall
13. Admissions & Financial Aid
14. Maintenance Shop
15. Psychology Building
16. Helen Ann Hall
17. Parc Vendome Hall
18. Olympic Heights Hall
19. Arbeiter Maenner Chor
20. 446 Orange Avenue
21. Echlin Hall
22. Gymnasium

EDUCATION ~ COLLEGES
University of New Haven

The University of New Haven combines outstanding degree programs relevant to today's career market with faculty chosen for their interest in teaching, their concern for students, and their considerable academic accomplishments. Students enjoy a flexible, well-balanced program which prepares each individual for a productive future.

Founded in 1920, UNH is an independent, coed university offering approximately 85 undergraduate and 29 graduate degree programs in accounting, arson investigation, biology, business administration, computer science, communications, criminal justice, dental hygiene, English, engineering, environmental science, forensic science, history, hotel management, mathematics, marketing, music and sound recording, and tourism and travel.

Located in West Haven on a 76-acre hilltop overlooking Long Island Sound, the university is large enough to provide diversity and depth, yet small enough to offer individualized programs in a friendly atmosphere conducive to learning.

At UNH, undergraduate students complete a core curriculum of liberal, humanistic courses as well as specialized majors designed to prepare them for productive careers. Classroom preparation may be supplemented by cooperative education assignments, internships and field study, to provide students with hands-on experience.

UNH is proud of its distinguished full-time faculty; more than 90 percent of instructors hold the highest degree in their field. They are joined by adjunct professors who, in addition to academic degrees, bring professional expertise to the classroom.

There are 23 major facilities on campus. A large modern library, computer services center, contemporary classrooms and offices, a fully-equipped gymnasium, and four residence halls serve the needs of the students.

The Counseling Center, the Center for Learning Resources, and the Health Services Center are staffed by professionals available to students on a regular basis. The Career Development Office boasts an excellent placement record.

Lawrence "Larry" DeNardis *is President of the University of New Haven. He is a former State Senator and a former U.S. Congressman for Connecticut's 3rd District.*

Day, evening and graduate student governments coordinate social activities at UNH. Campus media includes WNHU-FM Radio, a student newspaper and the yearbook.

UNH is an NCAA Division II member. The Charger football team won the Northeast Region title in 1992, and the UNH varsity baseball team has participated in the College World Series eleven times. Sports programs for women at UNH are a vital part of the university's athletic program. The volleyball team has participated in eleven NCAA championships, reaching the quarterfinals twice.

The university's mission is quality education at an affordable price. To that end, financial aid counselors work hard to assist everyone who desires a UNH education, carefully reviewing each student's needs when determining aid awards.

University of New Haven   932~7000
300 Orange Avenue, West Haven

All photos Michael Marsland/Yale OPA

YALE UNIVERSITY
History

Yale's historical roots trace back to the 1640s, when the Reverend John Davenport led an effort to establish a college in the colony of New Haven, using the English and European tradition of instruction in the liberal arts to prepare leaders for the commonwealth. It was not until 1701, however, that his vision was realized.

As legend has it, ten Connecticut Congregational ministers met at the Reverend Samuel Russell's parsonage in the town of Branford, each with a gift of books for the "founding of a College in this colony." Their leader was James Pierpont, the young minister of the church in New Haven, who had inherited some volumes collected by John Davenport for the new college. As a result of this meeting, Yale began in accordance with the principle that the true university is a collection of books.

The charter granted by the Colony of Connecticut in 1701 stated the founders' purpose: "To create a Collegiate School, wherein youth could be instructed in the Arts and Sciences and fitted up for publick employment both in Church and Civil State." The original seat of the college was at Killingworth, in the residence of the Reverend Abraham Pierson, the first President (then called Master or Rector). Upon Pierson's death in 1707, the college moved to Saybrook. In 1716, it took its final migration to New Haven, whose citizens pledged sums of money toward the construction of a suitable building. Unfortunately, these funds were insufficient, and construction came to a standstill.

However, in 1718, London businessman Elihu Yale, a retired East India merchant and philanthropist born in New England, and step-grandson of one of John Davenport's original New Haven colonists, gained immortality. Whether moved by the idea of a college in New Haven, or by a desire to bolster his own reputation, Yale donated three bales of East India goods, some books, and a portrait of George I, which together brought at sale £562, a substantial sum in those days, and the largest private contribution made to the college for over a century. The Trustees, stirred by a lively sense of gratitude, voted to name the new building Yale College.

Connecticut Hall

Connecticut Hall, on the Old Campus, across from the Green on College Street, is the oldest building still in existence on the Yale campus, as well as in New Haven. It is the single remaining Georgian college building built between 1750 and 1753 by masons Francis Letott and Thomas Bills.

In 1797, a fourth story was added. The building was thoroughly renovated in 1882, and remodeled in 1905 by architect Grosvenor Atterbury. It was restored again in 1954 with a gift from 1929 graduate Paul Mellon's Old Dominion Foundation. A *National Historic Landmark*, it also carries the *Landmark Plaque* of the New Haven Preservation Trust.

Original Mission

The founding clergymen believed strongly in the value of the liberal arts and in the College's mission to prepare its students for lives of public service. The original course of study followed old, established texts. Preparation for public service meant educating the ablest youth in the languages of learning and in the Protestant faith. This education enabled students to assume responsible leadership in the colony government or to undertake further training for the Congregational ministry.

A Changing World

As the 1700s continued, the new college began to grow. Donations of books on science, philosophy, literature, and theology made Yale's library the most advanced in the colonies. The first endowed professorship, the Livingston Professorship of Divinity, was established in 1756. In 1780, a chapter of the then-secret society, Phi Beta Kappa, was founded.

A rapidly expanding American population brought a larger and more diverse student body to Yale, with a decreasing proportion headed for the ministry. All around the College, the simple life of the early colonies was giving way to the complex political and social realities of a nation getting ready for revolution. During the dawn of July 5, 1779, Yale's President Reverend Ezra Stiles went up to the steeple of the college with a telescope and sketched what he saw as he watched the landing of the British expedition that was to occupy New Haven the next day. Yale students joined New Haven residents in an unsuccessful effort to stop the British from occupying the city.

By the end of the century, American society had changed, and Yale's curriculum had become broader and more flexible. The College began to shed its Congregational Church affiliation; what remained constant were Yale's ties to its earliest traditions of liberal arts education and public service. In 1795, Timothy Dwight became president of Yale and, during his 22 years as president, started the transition from college to university.

Sheffield-Sterling-Strathcona Hall (SSS) houses, among other things, the offices of the Dean and Registrar of Yale College. The Sheffield section, to the left of the tower contains office space used by Yale's Psychology Department. The Sterling Tower contains faculty offices and psychology labs. The Strathcona section contains a major lecture hall, which is used by a campus film society for viewings, and more offices, including those of the Yale Teacher Preparation Program.

YALE UNIVERSITY
History

Yale Becomes a University

In the 1800s, Yale established, one by one, the graduate schools that would make it a true university. The Yale Medical School was chartered in 1810, followed by the Divinity School in 1822 and the Law School in 1824. The Graduate School of Arts and Sciences, which followed in 1847, awarded the first Ph.D. earned in the United States, in 1861. Next came the schools of Art (1865), Music (1894), and Forestry and Environmental Studies (1900). More recently, Yale has added the schools of Nursing (1923), Drama (1955), Architecture (1972), and Management (1974).

In the early 1840s, the first rowing barges in the country appeared at Yale, and in 1852, Yale raced against Harvard in what may have been the first intercollegiate contest of any kind in the United States. Intramural football games took place on the Green in the 1840s. When Walter Camp formalized the game now known as American football, it became a Yale passion that spread throughout the United States. In 1865, the Civil War game of baseball started with a game against Wesleyan, and in the 1870s, track meets began.

The first college art gallery was founded in 1832, when Yale acquired the John Trumbull paintings of the American Revolution and set aside a building for their display. The present Gothic Style art gallery on Chapel Street was built in 1928. In 1953, a modern addition by Louis Kahn was added. The British Art Museum, donated by Paul Mellon to house his collection of British Art and illustrated books opened in 1977.

Women were first admitted to Yale as undergraduates in 1969.

This marker, on the side of Bingham Hall, and today's decorative fence inside the Old Campus, both on the College Street side, are all that remain to commemorate **The Old Yale Fence**. *This fence, part of which stood across College Street from the Green, marked the division between Town and Gown.*

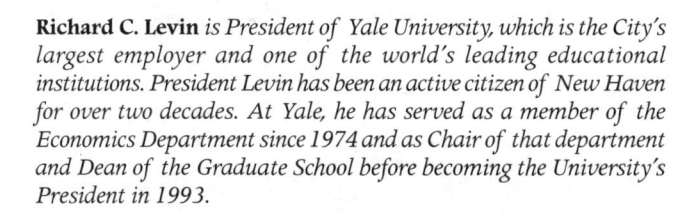

Richard C. Levin *is President of Yale University, which is the City's largest employer and one of the world's leading educational institutions. President Levin has been an active citizen of New Haven for over two decades. At Yale, he has served as a member of the Economics Department since 1974 and as Chair of that department and Dean of the Graduate School before becoming the University's President in 1993.*

Yale Today

From an original graduating class of one student, a faculty consisting of the Rector and one tutor, and a single wooden building, Yale has matured into one of the world's great universities, with over 10,000 students in the undergraduate College and ten graduate and professional schools, studying for 27 different degrees. The School's endowment is estimated to be over $3 billion dollars.

Yale has deep roots in the City of New Haven. Its buildings include contributions from distinguished architects of every period in the University's history, with styles that range from New England Colonial to contemporary architecture, in locations from the golf course woods in the Westville section, to prime downtown property.

Altogether, Yale has approximately 225 buildings containing almost 11 million square feet of space. Assuming an average value of $100 per square foot, these properties are worth over a billion dollars.

The growing financial partnership between Yale and New Haven is symbolized by the Yale-New Haven Agreement of October 1990, in which Yale agreed to make voluntary payments to the City for fire service and golf course taxes, an annual figure of $1.5 million dollars. Other notable financial contributions of Yale to New Haven are the $50 million dollars of endowment money targeted for economic development. Yale's active role in securing financing for the 9th Square development project incorporates $12.5 million dollars from the Yale endowment. Other contributions include development of the Volvo Tennis Sports Complex and participation in Science Park and rebuilding the Broadway area of New Haven.

Yale's new President Richard C. Levin has reaffirmed the School's commitment to a deepening partnership with New Haven. Under his leadership, the University has begun its "Buy in New Haven" program, which aims to increase the amount of goods and services Yale buys from local businesses, in an effort to improve the local economy. The University is also making investments in the revitalization of city neighborhoods through its Yale Homebuyer Program, which provides a cash benefit of $2000 per year for 10 years to any full-time employee who buys and lives in a home in the city before the end of 1995.

Alison F. Richard *is a world-renowned anthropologist who is serving as Provost, the University's chief academic officer after the President. Ms. Richard coordinates and oversees the educational policies of all sectors of Yale, including the undergraduate college, the graduate and professional schools and the various centers for research and scholarship.*

As Secretary of Yale University, **Linda Koch Lorimer** *serves as one of the principal advisors to President Richard C. Levin and is one of the six Officers of the University. Among her many responsibilities are planning and overseeing Yale's external relations in New Haven. She is a former college president and a former trustee of Yale.*

All photos from author's collection

Yale University
Yale Today

237

Berkeley College is named in honor of Bishop George Berkeley, in recognition of his gifts to Yale in 1732-33.

❶

Branford College is named for the town of Branford, CT, where the group of ministers met in 1701 to establish in the Colony the Collegiate School, which later became Yale University. Harkness Tower, with its carillion, is part of Branford College.

❷

Calhoun College is named to honor statesman John Caldwell Calhoun, B.A. 1804, LL.D. 1822. He served as vice-president of the United States in the 19th-22nd Congresses and became a U.S. Senator in 1832.

❸

Davenport College commemorates Reverend John Davenport, one of the founders of the New Haven Colony. To the left of the arch at the college entrance are the arms and motto of Coventry, England, where Davenport was born; to the right are the arms and motto of New Haven.

❹

Timothy Dwight College is named in honor of Reverend Timothy Dwight, B.A. 1769, eighth president of Yale (1795-1817), and his grandson of the same name, B.A. 1849, 12th president of Yale (1886-99), and the last minister president.

❺

Jonathan Edwards College is named for the Reverend Jonathan Edwards, B.A. 1720, theologian and philosopher. He also served as President of Princeton for a short time before his death in 1758.

❻

Morse College is named in honor of Samuel F. B. Morse, B.A. 1810, M.A. 1816, LL.D. 1846, artist and inventor of the telegraph.

❼

Pierson College is named to honor the first Rector (President) of Yale, the Reverend Abraham Pierson. He was a 1668 graduate of Harvard, and was elected in 1701 as Rector of the Collegiate School, serving until his death in 1707.

❽

Saybrook College was named for the town of Saybrook, CT, seat of the Collegiate College until its move to New Haven in October 1716, and site of the the school's first Commencement Exercises.

❾

Silliman College is named for Benjamin Silliman, B.A. 1796, Professor of Chemistry, Mineralogy and Geology from 1802-1853. The house of lexicographer Noah Webster, B.A. 1778, once stood on the southwest corner of the site of Silliman College.

❿

Ezra Stiles College is named for the seventh President of Yale, Reverend Ezra Stiles, Class of 1746. Stiles served as Professor and President from 1778 to 1795.

⓫

Trumbull College is named to honor Jonathan Tumbull, LL.D. 1779. Trumbull was the Governor of Connecticut during the American Revolutionary War.

⓬

Arms courtesy Yale University Printing Service/Office of the Secretary

YALE UNIVERSITY
Residential Colleges

In the early 1930s, Edward S. Harkness (Class of 1897) provided funds to establish the residential colleges of Yale. English universities, primarily Oxford and Cambridge, provided the model for the residential college system. Each college surrounds a courtyard and has its own dormitory rooms, dining room, and library. A resident Master oversees activities in each college.

This distinctive system divides the undergraduate population into separate communities, and enables Yale to offer both the vast resources of a major university and the intimacy of a small college environment. Branford, Calhoun, Davenport, Jonathan Edwards, Pierson, Saybrook and Trumbull were built in 1933, Berkeley in 1934, Timothy Dwight in 1935, and Silliman in 1940. Ezra Stiles and Morse were finished in the early 1960s.

The residential colleges range in style from Saybrook's Gothic Wrexham Tower to Davenport's Georgian cupola to the angular walls of Morse and Ezra Stiles, architect Eero Saarinen's vision of a futuristic Tuscan village.

The Master lives in the college, and works closely with students and Fellows. One tradition is the Master's Tea, where students meet scholars, artists, journalists and political celebrities. The Dean of each college, who also lives within the College, supervises students' academic progress, and serves as a personal counselor.

As Dean of Yale's undergraduate school, Yale College, **Richard H. Brodhead** *guides what many consider to be the best undergraduate school in the nation. Prior to assuming the deanship in 1993, Dean Brodhead was an active member of the Yale English faculty and a sought-after lecturer among undergraduates.*

Yale's 12 Residential Colleges, located in the heart of downtown New Haven, are: (1) Berkeley, (2) Branford, (3) Calhoun, (4) Davenport, (5) Timothy Dwight, (6) Jonathan Edwards, (7) Morse, (8) Pierson, (9) Saybrook, (10) Silliman, (11) Ezra Stiles, and (12) Trumbull.

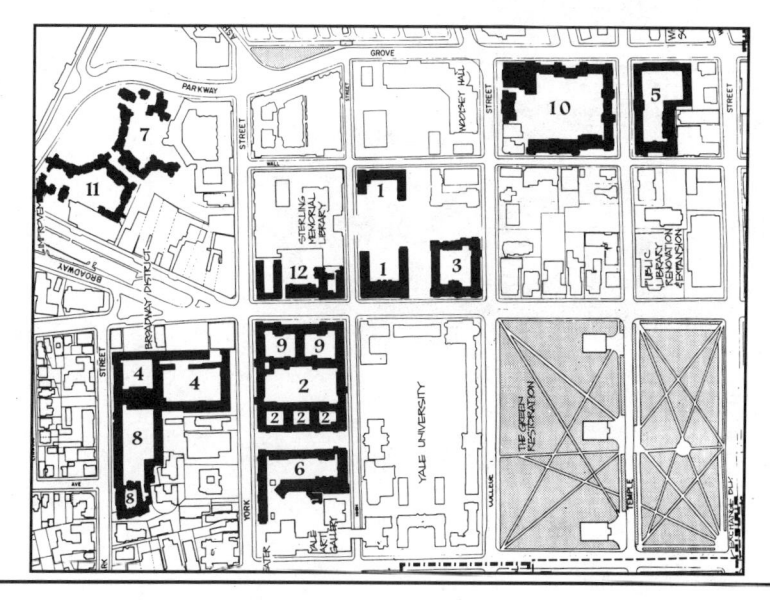

Graduate School of Arts & Sciences

The Yale Graduate School of Arts and Sciences awards the degrees of Doctor of Philosophy, Master of Philosophy, Master of Arts, and Master of Science. The work of the Graduate School is carried on in the divisions of the humanities, social sciences, and biological and physical sciences, which encompass 63 departments and programs.

Yale began to offer graduate education in 1847, and in 1861, it conferred the first Ph.D. degree awarded in North America. In 1876, Yale became the first American university to award a Ph.D. to an African-American.

With the appointment of a Dean in 1892, the Graduate School was formally established. In the same year, women were first admitted as candidates for the doctorate. Since the turn of the century, the Graduate School community has grown vigorously and now includes postdoctoral students, fellows, and research scholars in addition to a faculty of 750 and a student body of 2,500. Each year, approximately 5,000 students apply for admission to the Graduate School of Arts and Sciences.

Thomas Appelquist, *the Eugene Higgins Professor of Physics at Yale, became Dean of the Yale Graduate School of Arts and Sciences in 1993. A leading researcher in the area of elementary particle physics, Professor Appelquist has made important contributions to quantum field theory.*

Divinity School

Yale Divinity School is interdenominational and completely nonsectarian. The students represent fifty religious denominations and groups. Instruction is provided in the history, doctrines, and polity of all the major church bodies. The Divinity School offers programs of study leading to the degrees of Master of Divinity (M.Div), Master of Arts in Religion (M.A.R.), and Master of Sacred Theology (S.T.M.). In 1973, the Institute of Sacred Music, linked to the School of Music and the Divinity School, was founded.

Training for the Christian ministry was a main purpose in the founding of Yale College in 1701. An enlarged recognition of the needs of the ministry led, however, in 1746, to the establishment of a Professorship of Divinity, through the efforts of President Thomas Clap. This, in turn, developed, in 1822, into a separate department, later known as the Yale Divinity School.

The Divinity School is housed principally in the Sterling Divinity Quadrangle, built in 1931-32, by a gift from the trustees of the estate of John W. Sterling, B.A. 1864. The Quadrangle includes Marquand chapel, a classroom building, an administration building, library buildings, a refectory, a common room, the Institute of Sacred Music building and eight dormitories.

Yale Divinity School Dean, **Thomas W. Ogletree**, *is a graduate of Birmingham-Southern College, Garrett Theological Seminary, and Vanderbilt University. Rev. Ogletree joined the Yale faculty in 1990 as Dean and Professor of Theological Ethics at the Divinity School.*

YALE UNIVERSITY
Graduate & Professional Schools

School of Law

The primary purpose of the Yale Law School is to train lawyers as leaders in the public and private sectors. The School has sought to train lawyers for public service and teaching as well as for private practice, and has taken a broad view of the role of law and lawyers in society. This professional orientation is designed to produce lawyers who are creative, sensitive, and open to new ideas.

In 1777, Yale President-designate Ezra Stiles looked into "establishing and endowing Professorships of Law in the American universities." Actual instruction in law began in 1801, with the appointment of Professor Elizur Goodrich, who lectured to undergraduates on municipal and international law. The Law School was founded in 1824, although the first LL.B. degree was not conferred until 1843.

After the Civil War, the modern law library was organized, the first law school building constructed and the *Yale Law Journal* begun. Led by Simeon E. Baldwin, the faculty of the Law School played a significant part in founding the American Bar Association and the Association of American Law Schools. The School was noted for pioneering graduate programs in law, and the degree of Master of Laws was first offered in 1876.

By 1902, the LL.B. curriculum had been extended from two to three years and in 1911, the School required a B.A. of all incoming students. In 1903, under the influence of Professor Arthur L. Corbin, the School moved away from lectures and recitations to the "case method" of instruction, which was developed by Langdell at Harvard and formally adopted by the Yale faculty in 1912.

By the time Thomas Swan was appointed Dean in 1916, the Yale Law School was emerging as an important intellectual center for legal studies, with a distinctive viewpoint and curricular policy. The addition to the faculty of William Howard Taft, who had been a U.S. President and was a future Chief Justice of the Supreme Court, added a new note of political distinction to the scholarly faculty.

Deans Robert Hutchins (1927-29) and Charles Clark (1929-39) made the next contributions. With their guidance, the faculty and Corporation decided that Yale should remain a small school, with an excellent faculty-student ratio. They made the decision to admit only 100 students each year. Links to social sciences were forged, and faculty members were drawn into public service by the New Deal administration in Washington, after the stock market crash in 1929, and the beginning of the Great Depression. Yale at this time became a center of the realist movement.

Anthony T. Kronman *was named dean of the Yale Law School in 1994, becoming the first dean in the nation to hold both a philosophy and a law degree from Yale.*

The post-realist period at Yale has been marked by efforts to fashion better approaches to the theoretical and practical study of law. Progress has been made in integrating law with the humanities and the social sciences. Economists, historians, political scientists, psychologists, psychoanalysts, philosophers, and sociologists have been members of the faculty since the early 1930s and have contributed to the development of a better understanding of law.

The Sterling law buildings were completed in 1931 with funds provided by the trustees of the estate of John W. Sterling (Yale, 1864). These Gothic buildings of brick and limestone were designed by architect James Gamble Rogers to recall the English Inns of Court, and are embellished with symbolic sculptures and stained glass medallions.

Yale Law School is on the approved list of the American Bar Association and is a charter member of the Association of American Law Schools.

As the 21st century nears, the Yale School of Medicine strives to make humane and science-based medicine responsive to the needs of individuals and society. The School of Medicine faculty, research and training staff includes 4,015 people, with an annual budget totaling over $403 million. The School's missions encompass education, research, patient care and community service.

The Medical Institution of Yale College was chartered by the Connecticut General Assembly in 1810. Three years later, the Institution formally opened with 37 students, and the following year, conferred its first degrees.

The student thesis, hallmark of the Yale system of medical education, began in 1839. The thesis develops students' critical judgment and application of the scientific method to medicine, and gives them the opportunity to work closely with the School's distinguished faculty.

The first African-American student graduated in 1857, and in 1916, the first female students were admitted. The Department of Epidemiology and a nationally-accredited School of Public Health were established in 1918.

Medical students learn to formulate critical clinical decision-making skills, and to work as part of multi-disciplinary healthcare teams to meet local, regional, national and global needs. Each year, 100 students enroll in the school's four-year program. Their medical education occurs at a time when diverse social, economic, and political forces are reshaping the configuration of the healthcare system. The clinical medicine that they will practice will, in part, result from the transfer of basic science from the bench to the bedside at Yale, one of the world's greatest research-intensive medical schools.

Dean Gerard N. Burrow, M.D., *is an endocrinologist and a 1958 graduate of the School of Medicine.*

Students interested in research and teaching careers in the biological and biomedical sciences may pursue graduate programs leading to the Ph.D. degree. Interdisciplinary graduate programs ensure that students have a broad and flexible choice of research opportunities with Yale faculty in a variety of disciplines.

Programs are housed within ten departments, linked by common research interests, academic courses and faculty members with joint appointments. Most programs are based at the School of Medicine. They include: cell biology, cellular and molecular physiology, genetics, immunobiology, molecular biophysics and biochemistry, neurobiology, neuroscience and pharmacology.

A limited number of highly-qualified students are enrolled in the seven-year M.D./Ph.D. Program, offered by the School of Medicine and Yale's Graduate School of Arts and Sciences.

The Department of Epidemiology and Public Health prepares students of diverse ages, nationalities and professional backgrounds for careers in public health practice, research and teaching. Students usually affiliate with one of seven divisions: biostatistics, chronic disease epidemiology, environmental health sciences, health policy and resources, infectious disease epidemiology, international health or microbiology.

Established in 1971, the Yale Physician Associate Program, a two-year certificate program, educates physician associates in the medical model. Graduates are distinguished from other advanced healthcare practitioners by the extent of their decision-making authority in patient care, diagnosis and treatment. Their people-oriented healthcare complements the clinical work of physicians.

Biomedical research has never been more exciting, with advances in molecular and cellular biology, genetics and the neurosciences translating into major clinical breakthroughs. Yale is especially

YALE UNIVERSITY
School of Medicine

well-suited to bring together the molecular pathophysiology of the individual with the health of the general public, continuing YSM's tradition of excellence in the biomedical sciences, clinical medicine, and public health, and responding to the social challenges posed by the health problems which afflict society.

The scope of biomedical research at Yale is diverse, with many programs taking a multi-disciplinary approach to solve health problems and develop new treatments. Much research is supported by the federal government, which has designated Yale for a number of awards, including the Cancer Prevention Research Unit, Cancer Center, both Children's and General Clinical Research Centers and the Claude D. Pepper Older Americans Independence Center.

Yale scientists identified Lyme disease in 1975, and have continued to conduct leading research on it. Significant research is being conducted on memory and learning, Parkinson's disease, stroke and the care of elderly people. New techniques have been developed in using magnetic resonance imaging techniques and in helping infertile couples. New knowledge is being developed on children's health and emotional issues, ranging from diabetes and cancer to Tourette's Syndrome and autism.

Faculty physicians at the medical school provide specialized care and services to a wide variety of individuals. Yale physicians treat inpatients at the Yale-New Haven Hospital, the Children's Hospital at Yale-New Haven, the Department of Veteran's Affairs Medical Center, the Connecticut Mental Health Center and the Yale Psychiatric Institute (YPI). Yale physicians also provide comprehensive specialty outpatient care.

The Office of Referral Assistance (Tel: 785-4851) provides information about all of the School's clinical programs. The office staff assists physicians and patients seeking the professional services of Yale faculty physicians. The School's many specialized clinical programs include: AIDS Clinic; Cancer Center; Cerebrovascular Center; diagnosis and treatment of inherited disorders; general counseling; endolaparoscopic surgery; learning disorders; Lyme disease; adult and pediatric organ transplant; spine disorders and scoliosis; sports medicine; and Vascular Center.

Many staff, students, and faculty volunteer, with approximately 50 community outreach and service programs. Volunteer opportunities range from an effort to enhance the delivery of services to those children affected by violence to a mobile van program to provide medical care to people at city soup kitchens.

In recent years, student volunteerism has increased to address the pressing social problems facing New Haven. Students provide medical care to the homeless, and teach human anatomy to New Haven high school students in Yale medical labs. They also conduct their Adolescent Substance Abuse Program in city schools, and pair with children with chronic illnesses or extended hospital stays to give them the additional support they need.

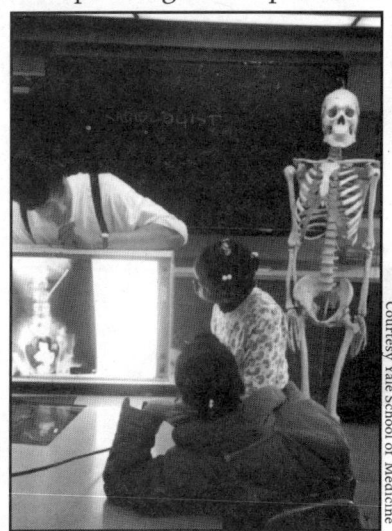

By educating health professionals, fostering quality healthcare and conducting diverse biomedical research, the Yale University School of Medicine continues its role as a national leader in health and medicine, and as an important resource for the City of New Haven and the entire Northeast region.

School of Architecture

*Dean **Fred Koetter**, an architect and urban planner, has won recognition from the American Institute of Architects, the Boston Society of Architects, the magazine* Progressive Architecture *and the National Endowment for the Arts.*

The task of architecture is the creation of human environments. Architectural design, as a comprehensive creative process, is the focus of the School. A three-year program leads to a Master of Architecture as does a two-year post-professional program. A two-year program for advanced, independent research leads to a degree of Master of Environmental Design in a joint-degree program with the School of Management.

Architecture as an art was taught at the Yale School of Fine Arts in the late 1800s. The stage was set for this pioneering step in art education in 1832, with the opening of the Trumbull Art Gallery, the first university-connected gallery in the country. In 1869, the Yale School of Fine Arts began, under the direction of John Ferguson Weir.

The first full-time professor of architecture was appointed in 1905, and in 1916, the Department was founded, with Everett Victor Meeks at its head. The first Bachelor of Architecture degree was conferred in 1942 and the first Master's in 1947. Studies in City Planning were introduced in 1941, leading to a Master of City Planning degree. In 1961, a Department of City Planning was established and, in 1963, a Master of Urban Studies was begun.

In 1963, the School moved to the Art and Architecture building at the corner of York and Chapel Streets, which was designed by Paul Rudolph. The Master of Environmental Design degree was inaugurated in 1966.

In 1972, the School of Art and Architecture split to become two autonomous schools. Though working in close association under one roof, they are administered separately. Yale's excellent program of study in Architecture is recognized throughout the world.

School of Art

*Since 1983, painter and art professor **David Pease** has been Dean of the School of Art. Dean Pease's paintings have been included in over 275 group exhibitions since 1953, and are in many permanent collections, including the Whitney Museum of American Art in Manhattan.*

The study of the visual arts at Yale began in 1832, with the opening of the Trumbull Gallery, founded by patriot-artist, Colonel John Trumbull, former aide-de-camp to General Washington.

A highly successful art exhibition held in 1858 led to the establishment of an Art School in 1864, through the generosity of Augustus Russell Street. The new educational program was placed in the hands of an Arts Council, one of whose members was the painter-inventor, Samuel F. B. Morse.

When it opened in 1869, it was the first art school connected with an institution of higher learning. Classes in drawing, painting, sculpture, and art history were introduced.

The art collections in the old Trumbull Gallery were moved into Street Hall, another building endowed by Street. These were augmented by the acquisition of the Jarves Collection of early Italian paintings in 1871.

The School of Art grants the degree of Master of Fine Arts and offers professional instruction in the interrelated areas of graphic design, painting and printmaking, photography and sculpture. The Art and Architecture Gallery provides exhibition space for the work of students.

YALE UNIVERSITY
Graduate & Professional Schools

School of Drama

The Department of Drama was founded in the School of Fine Arts in 1924. The school is centered in University Theater, built in 1925 through the generosity of Edward S. Harkness, a 1897 Yale graduate. In 1925, George Pierce Baker brought to Yale his playwriting course and workshop. The first Master of Fine Arts in Drama was conferred in 1931.

In 1955, the Department was reorganized as a separate professional school granting Master of Fine Arts and Doctor of Fine Arts in Drama degrees. The Yale Repertory Theatre was founded by the School of Drama in 1967 to create a closer relationship between academic training and the practicing professional theater.

The goal of Yale School of Drama is to prepare its students for careers in professional theater, most particularly in repertory and ensemble productions with permanent theater companies.

The Yale School of Drama, together with the Yale Repertory Theatre, offers a unique program of theatrical training. Degree programs encompass acting, directing, design, playwriting, dramaturgy and dramatic criticism, technical design, production and stage management.

The school also grants special certificates to those students who complete the three year program without having the usual prerequisite bachelor's degree.

Dean of the School of Drama & Artistic Director of Yale Repertory Theatre **Stan Wojewodski, Jr.** *has taught in many of the nation's most distinguished theater training programs. He was artistic director of Center Stage in Baltimore before joining the Yale faculty in 1990.*

School of Music

In 1854, the sum of $5,000 was presented to Yale College by Joseph Battell "for the support of a teacher of the science of music to such students as may avail themselves of the opportunity."

In 1885, the Yale Corporation approved the appointment of Gustave Jacob Stoeckel. Stoeckel waged an active campaign to establish a department of music at Yale. He was appointed Battell Professor of Music in 1890, the year in which Yale's first music courses for credit were offered.

The first Bachelor of Music degrees were awarded in 1894. When Professor Stoeckel retired, Samuel Simons Sanford, Professor of Applied Music, and Horatio Parker, Battell Professor of the Theory of Music, succeeded him. Sanford's efforts led to the establishment, in 1894, of the Yale School of Music, and in 1904, Professor Parker was made the Dean.

Albert Arnold Sprague Memorial Hall was constructed in 1917 through the generosity of Mrs. Sprague and her daughter. The graduate division of the School was established, and the Master of Music degree first conferred, in 1932.

The School of Music became exclusively a graduate school in 1958, requiring an undergraduate degree for admission, and conferring only the Master of Music degree. Other degree programs leading to the Master and Doctor of Musical Arts were introduced in 1968. The Institute of Sacred Music is a graduate center within Yale University for the interdisciplinary study of worship, music, and related arts. It was established in 1973 with a generous gift from the Irwin Sweeney Miller Foundation.

Distinguished American composer **Ezra Laderman** *assumed the position of Dean of the School of Music in July 1989. Mr. Laderman's music has been performed by many orchestras of international stature, and his work has premiered on major urban center stages.*

School of Management

Stanley J. Garstka, *Acting Dean of the School of Management, is a trustee of the MBA Enterprise Corps, and an expert in the bankruptcy process and ways to reform it. His current research focuses on the practice of active investing and modern financial theory.*

The Yale School of Management prepares students for leadership in business, government, and non-profit organizations through a Master's program in Public and Private Management (MPPM).

The School's emphasis on management, as opposed to policy creation, distinguishes its program from those of public policy schools. On the other hand, the Yale approach recognizes that effective business leaders must understand the interactions of business and government, and the political contexts in which they occur, which distinguishes the MPPM from traditional MBA program.

The program focuses on developing practical management skills rather than functional expertise. The program stresses the importance of interpersonal skills and the need for team-based, goal-oriented methods of working to solve problems. The School strives to balance individual initiative with an ethic of cooperation and group work.

The School has long focused on training leaders, a philosophy many business schools have only recently embraced. Old-style managers were taught that management consisted of planning, staffing, directing, and controlling. Leaders, on the other hand, begin with a clear concept of goals. They then involve others in making their vision a reality, by inviting participation and empowering colleagues in the pursuit of shared objectives.

School of Nursing

Yale's School of Nursing began in 1923. Under the direction of its first Dean, Annie W. Goodrich, it established a new pattern for nursing education, with student instruction and experience based upon an educational plan, rather than an apprenticeship.

After 1934, the School of Nursing admitted only college graduates. Fifteen years later, an advanced program in mental health nursing was established.

In 1952, the Yale Corporation decided that the University could contribute most effectively to the advancement of nursing if its efforts were concentrated on a graduate degree program for nurses. Programs in public health nursing and psychiatric nursing were also added.

A revised curriculum was implemented in 1959-1960, and further expanded in 1969 to include pediatric nursing. In 1974, a medical-surgical program in nursing was added to the curriculum.

In 1970, a three-year program for non-nursing college graduates was begun, adding a basic professional nursing component to the graduate specialization programs. In September 1992, a program was added in nursing systems and policy, now nursing management and policy.

The Yale Corporation approved a plan to develop a Doctorate of Nursing Science program in 1992, and the first class was formed in 1994.

Judith B. Krauss, *dean and professor of the Yale School of Nursing, has shaped and promoted the goals of advanced practice in her ten years with the School. Dean Krauss is a noted authority on the care of people with serious and persistent mental disorders.*

YALE UNIVERSITY
Graduate & Professional Schools

School of Forestry and Environmental Studies

The mission of the School of Forestry and Environmental Studies is to provide leadership through education and research in the management of natural resource systems and environmental problems. The School develops leaders for major institutions that shape the earth's environment. Through its research activities, the School fosters study in areas of importance for resource and environmental management and conservation.

The School's faculty lend their expertise to state and federal environmental commissions; serve on the boards of environmental groups; act as consultants; and publish their research. To maintain a flow of information on a global scale, the School encourages communication, research and exchange with colleagues worldwide.

Yale University has played a leading role in the development of American conservation and natural resource management since the 1800s, when Yale graduates such as William Henry Brewer, Othniel C. Marsh, Clarence King, and George Bird Grinnell were deeply involved with the exploration of the West, and with the proper use of Western resources.

In 1900, that tradition was strengthened when the University established the Yale Forestry School. Nine of the 14 Chiefs of the U.S. Forest Service have been graduates of the School, which is the oldest such organization in the country.

The School was founded with a gift from the Pinchot family. Gifford Pinchot (Yale, 1887), was the first American to receive professional forestry training in Europe. He became one of the leading figures in President Theodore Roosevelt's administration, and created and served as first Chief of the U.S. Forest Service. Originator of the phrase "conservation of natural resources," he defined conservation as "the wise use of the earth for the good of present and future generations." It has been the School's mission to turn Pinchot's vision of conservation into educational and professional reality. Leading that quest until 1940 was the School's first dean, Henry S. Graves (Yale, 1892).

Since 1900, the most important contribution of the School to the well-being of the nation and the world has been its 3,400 graduates. They have departed to every continent with a mission: to maintain a healthy global environment and to use modern scientific and environmental management techniques to solve real problems.

Each decade has presented its challenges and the School has responded to the leading problems of the day. In 1972, its name was changed to the School of Forestry and Environmental Studies, since in its broadest sense, its mission is the scientific long-term management of world ecosystems.

Jared Leigh Cohon, *Dean of the School of Forestry and Environmental Studies, specializes in planning for ecosystem management and analysis.*

Special Programs and Centers

- Center for Coastal and Watershed Systems
- Center for Environmental Law and Policy
- Hubbard Brook, New Hampshire ecosystem study
- Industrial Environmental Management
- Institute of Forestry in Napal
- Museology
- Solid Waste Policy
- Tropical Resources Institute
- Urban Resources Initiative
- Weyerhaeuser Center for Forest Resource Management and Policy

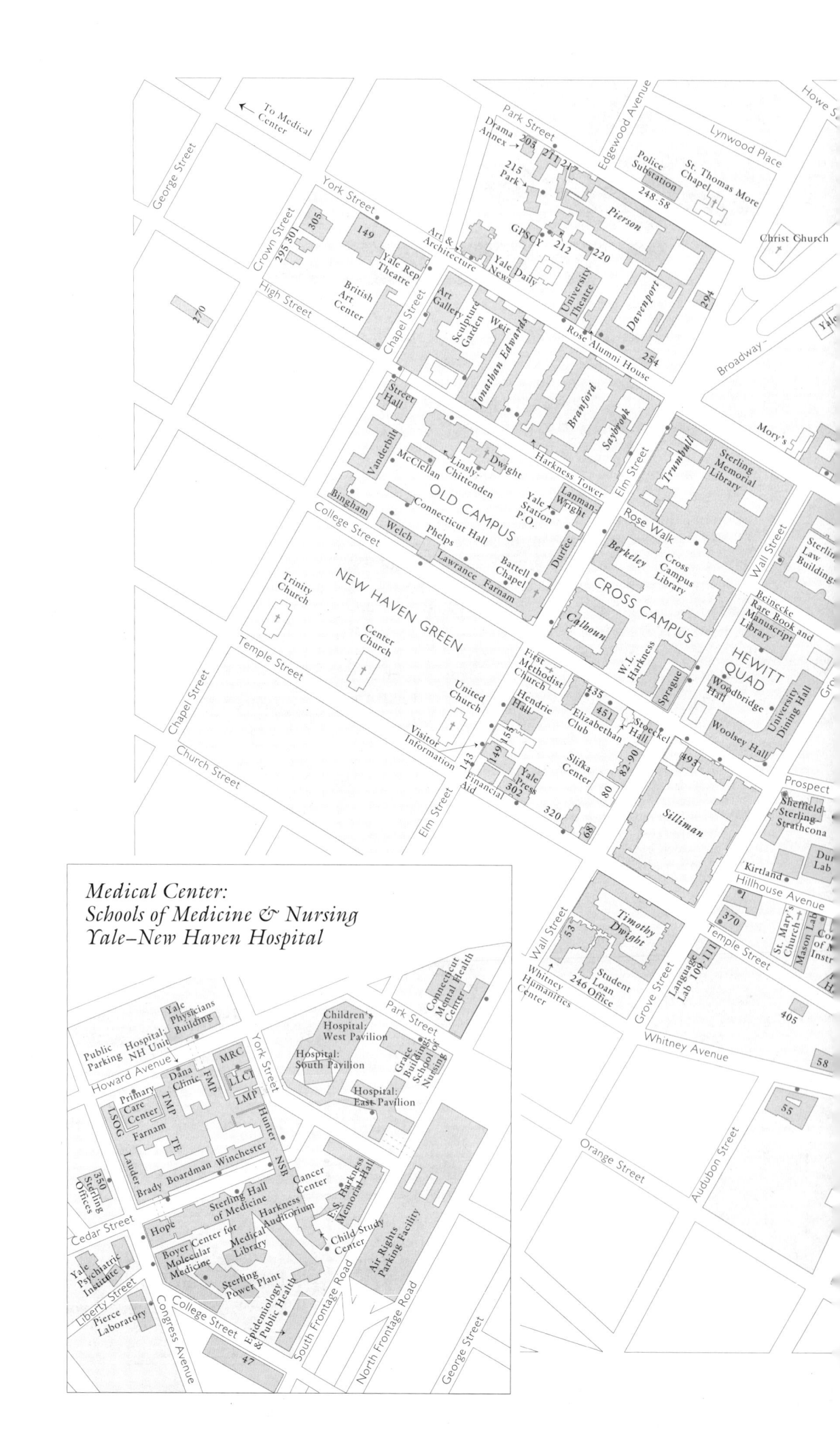

Medical Center:
Schools of Medicine & Nursing
Yale–New Haven Hospital

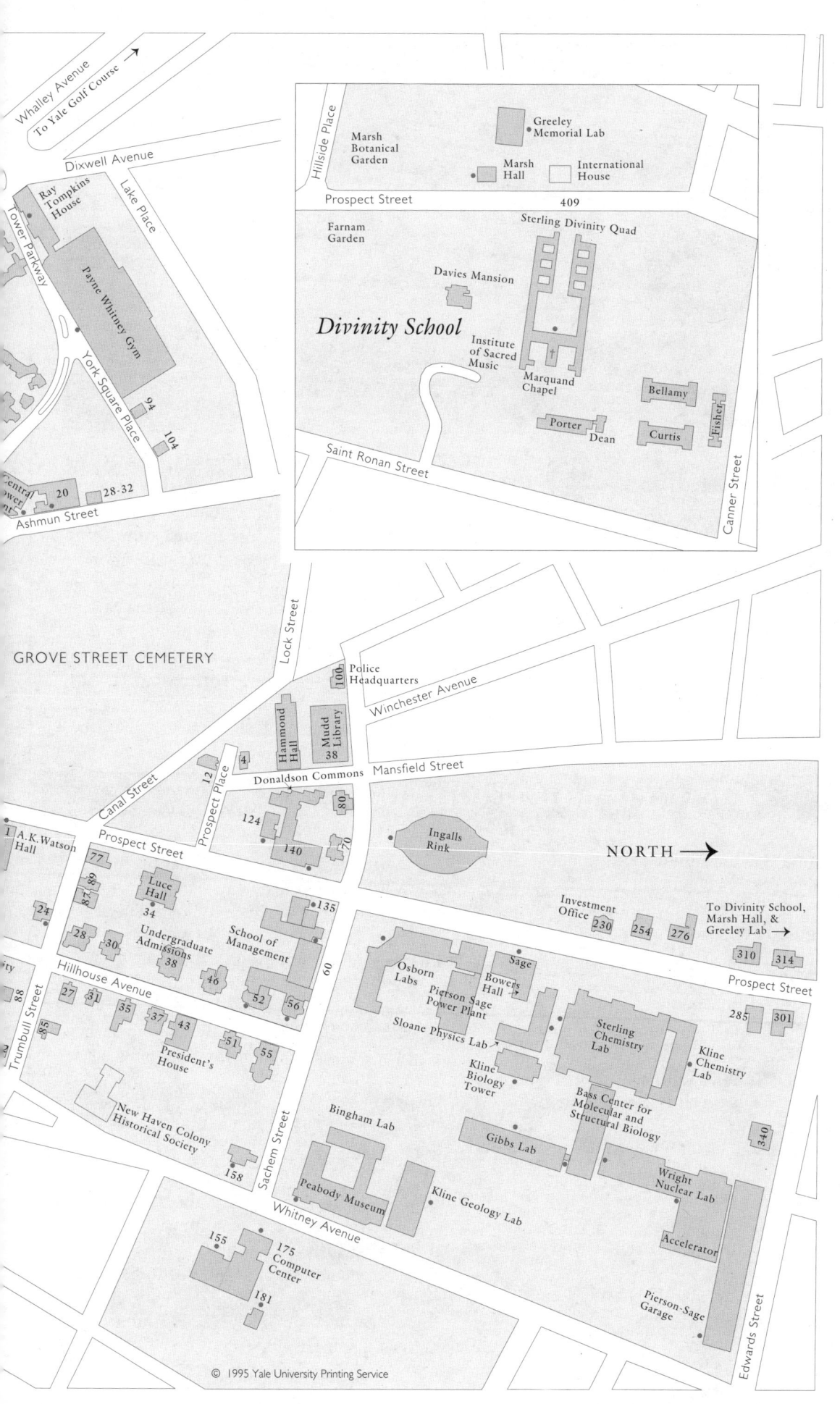

YALE UNIVERSITY

Beinecke Rare Book & Manuscript Library

The Beinecke Rare Book and Manuscript Library, 123 Wall Street, was designed by Gordon Bunshaft of Skidmore, Owings and Merrill, and completed in 1963. Beinecke is constructed of translucent, gray Vermont Woodbury granite and looks like a marble box floating above a granite plaza. Its Courtyard is made of white Imperial Danby marble, framed in granite. It was designed by Isamu Noguchi and contains massive symbolic sculptures of a sun, representing energy, a pyramid, representing the geometry of the earth or the past, and a cube, representing chance.

The Beinecke Rare Book and Manuscript Library holds 515,912 volumes, including an original Gutenberg Bible dating back to the 1400s, in a temperature and humidity controlled atmosphere.

Departmental Libraries

- **Anthropology Library**, Kline Biology Tower
  219 Prospect Street; 20,489 volumes
- **Art & Architecture (A&A) Library**, A&A Building
  180 York Street; 101,053 volumes
- **Astronomy Library**, 217 Gibbs Research Labs
  260 Whitney Avenue; 17,114 volumes
- **Chemistry Library**, Sterling Chemical Lab
  225 Prospect Street; 13,160 volumes
- **Classics Library**, Phelps Hall
  344 College Street; 23,200 volumes
- **Cowles Foundation for Research in Economics**
  30 Hillhouse Avenue; 13,334
- **Divinity School Library**
  409 Prospect Street; 392,575 volumes
- **Drama Library**
  222 York Street; 28,436 volumes
- **Engineering Library**, Becton Center
  15 Prospect Street; 44,367 volumes
- **Epidemiology and Public Health Library**
  60 College Street; 16,686 volumes
- **Forestry Library**, Sage Hall
  205 Prospect Street; 96,510 volumes
- **Geology Library**, Kline Geology Laboratory
  210 Whitney Avenue; 110,049 volumes
- **Kline Science Library**, Kline Biology Tower
  219 Prospect Street; 346,611 volumes
- **Law Library**, Sterling Law Building
  127 Wall Street; 744,968 volumes
- **Lewis Walpole Library**
  154 Main St., Farmington, CT; 29,343 volumes
- **Mathematics Library**, Leet Oliver Memorial Hall
  12 Hillhouse Avenue; 25,112 volumes
- **Medical Library**, Sterling Hall of Medicine
  333 Cedar Street; 387,956 volumes
- **Music Library**, Sprague Memorial Hall
  987 Wall Street; 139,606 volumes
- **Ornithology Library**, 305 Bingam Laboratory
  21 Sachem Street; 7,776 volumes
- **Social Science Library**
  140 Prospect Street; 82,760 volumes
- **Statistics Library**
  24 Hillhouse Avenue; 4,536 volumes
- **Yale Center for British Art**
  1080 Chapel Street; 42,576 volumes

YALE UNIVERSITY
University Libraries

Many consider the Yale Libraries to be the best in the world. Together, they contain over ten million volumes, including books, a huge collection of maps, records, manuscripts, coins, and other objects.

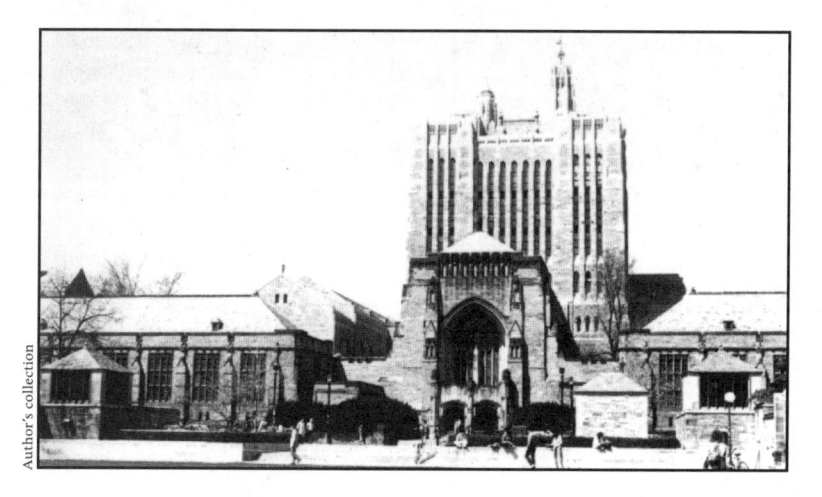

Sterling Memorial Library

Sterling Memorial Library, located on High Street, is the the largest library on campus. The building features a great 16-story Gothic granite tower and houses 4,357,191 volumes. The Library, designed by James Gamble Rogers, was completed in 1930.

Cross Campus Library

Cross Campus Library is a two-story library with 202,224 volumes. It is connected to the Sterling Memorial Library, and is located underground between High and College streets. Designed by Edward Larabee Barnes, it was completed in 1971.

Seeley G. Mudd Library

The Seeley G. Mudd Library, at 38 Mansfield Street, contains 1,016,907 volumes, plus many U.S. and foreign government publications. It is the most recent addition to the Yale library system. The building was designed by Roth and Moore.

*The name **Carmen Cozza** has become synonymous with Yale football. Since he took the helm in 1965, there have been 174 wins, ten Ivy League Championships, 18 winning seasons, six Ivy League MVP recipients, seven NCAA Post-Graduate Scholarship winners, seven First-Team Academic All-Americans, five National Football Foundation Hall of Fame Scholar-Athletes and five Rhodes Scholars. Cozza's accolades include: a Gold Key from the Connecticut Sports Writers Alliance; a Gold Medal from the Walter Camp Football Foundation; seven time Kodak District I Coach of the Year, four time UPI New England Coach of the Year, Eastern Coach of the Year, and national Coach of the Week recognitions.*

*The **Yale Bowl**, 251 Derby Avenue, West Haven, first used for the Harvard-Yale football game on November 21, 1914, was erected from gifts totaling $507,000. When it was built, the structure was the largest arena erected since the Roman Coliseum. It has a seating capacity of 70,874 and represents the spectacular use of reinforced poured concrete. It covers about 25 acres of Yale Field. Charles A. Ferry was the designer and engineer in charge of construction. In front stands the brick and concrete Walter Camp Gate.*

***Walter Camp**, a Yale player and coach from 1876-1910, revolutionized what had been a crude combination of rugby and soccer, and is known as the father of modern football. His inventions included the forward pass, the series of downs, the scrimmage line, the quarterback position, and the All-American team. The Walter Camp Gate honors his memory.*

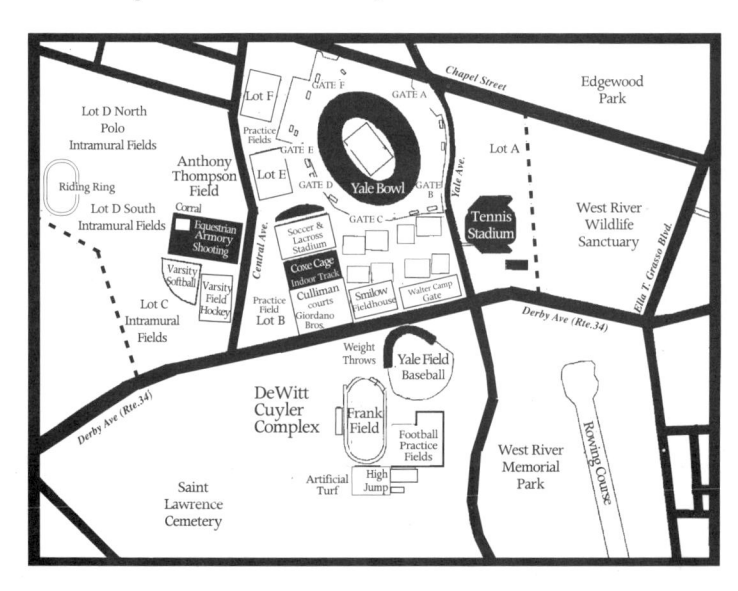

Yale Athletic Facilities

Yale has many sports facilities which are used for both its Varsity and Intramural programs. Among these facilities are:

Armory
Bob Cook Boat House
Coxe Cage
Cullman Courts
DeWitt Cuyler Field
Yale Golf Course
David S. Ingalls Rink
Intramural Boat House
Lapham Field House
Phipps Polo Field
Ray Tompkins House
Payne Whitney Gymnasium

The map at right shows the fields, stadiums, and other facilities, including the Yale Bowl, at the Yale sports complex off Derby Avenue in New Haven and West Haven.

YALE UNIVERSITY Athletics

Payne Whitney Gymnasium, at 70 Tower Parkway, was built in 1932 as a memorial to Payne Whitney, B.A. 1898. Designed by John Russell Pope, it is the largest gym in the Western hemisphere. The building is Gothic style, constructed of Briar Hill sandstone, and contains rowing tanks, a practice pool, locker rooms, basketball courts, rooms for boxing, wrestling, and fencing. The northern wing has squash courts, a running track, and a basketball amphitheater. The southern wing has a large exhibition pool and several handball courts.

Tom Beckett became Yale's Director of Athletics in April 1994. As head of the Yale Sports Programs, Beckett oversees 33 varsity teams as well as a wide variety of club and intramural sports. He came to Yale from Stanford University, where he served as Associate Director of Athletics since 1983.

Yale's Varsity Teams

Sport	W/M	Phone
Baseball	M	432-1467
Basketball	W	432-1487
Basketball	M	432-1483
Crew	W	432-1412
Crew, heavyweight	M	432-1413
Crew, lightweight	M	432-1409
Cross Country	W	432-1405
Cross Country	M	432-1406
Fencing	W/M	432-2137
Field Hockey	W	432-1497
Golf	W/M	432-0895
Gymnastics	W	432-2138
Hockey	W	432-1482
Hockey	M	432-1478
Lacrosse	W	432-1486
Lacrosse	M	432-1494
Soccer	W	432-1492
Soccer	M	432-1495
Softball	W	432-1407
Squash	W	432-1489
Squash	M	432-2483
Swimming	W/M	432-2447
Tennis	W	432-1493
Tennis	M	432-1495
Track	W	432-1405
Track	M	432-1406
Volleyball	W	432-1408
Water Polo	M	432-2447
Wrestling	M	432-2136

There are at least eight senior secret societies at Yale according to *Buildings and Grounds of Yale University*, published in 1979 by the Yale University Printing Service. Elizabeth Mills Brown's *New Haven: A Guide to Architecture and Urban Design* also locates and describes their buildings. These societies are unique to Yale. Membership benefits mostly occur after graduation, when these elite members continue to network and establish a strong web of power.

Knowledgeable people agree that each society takes in only 15 juniors each year as members. In **Skull and Bones**, during their first year, they are called Knights; thereafter, they are called Patriarchs.

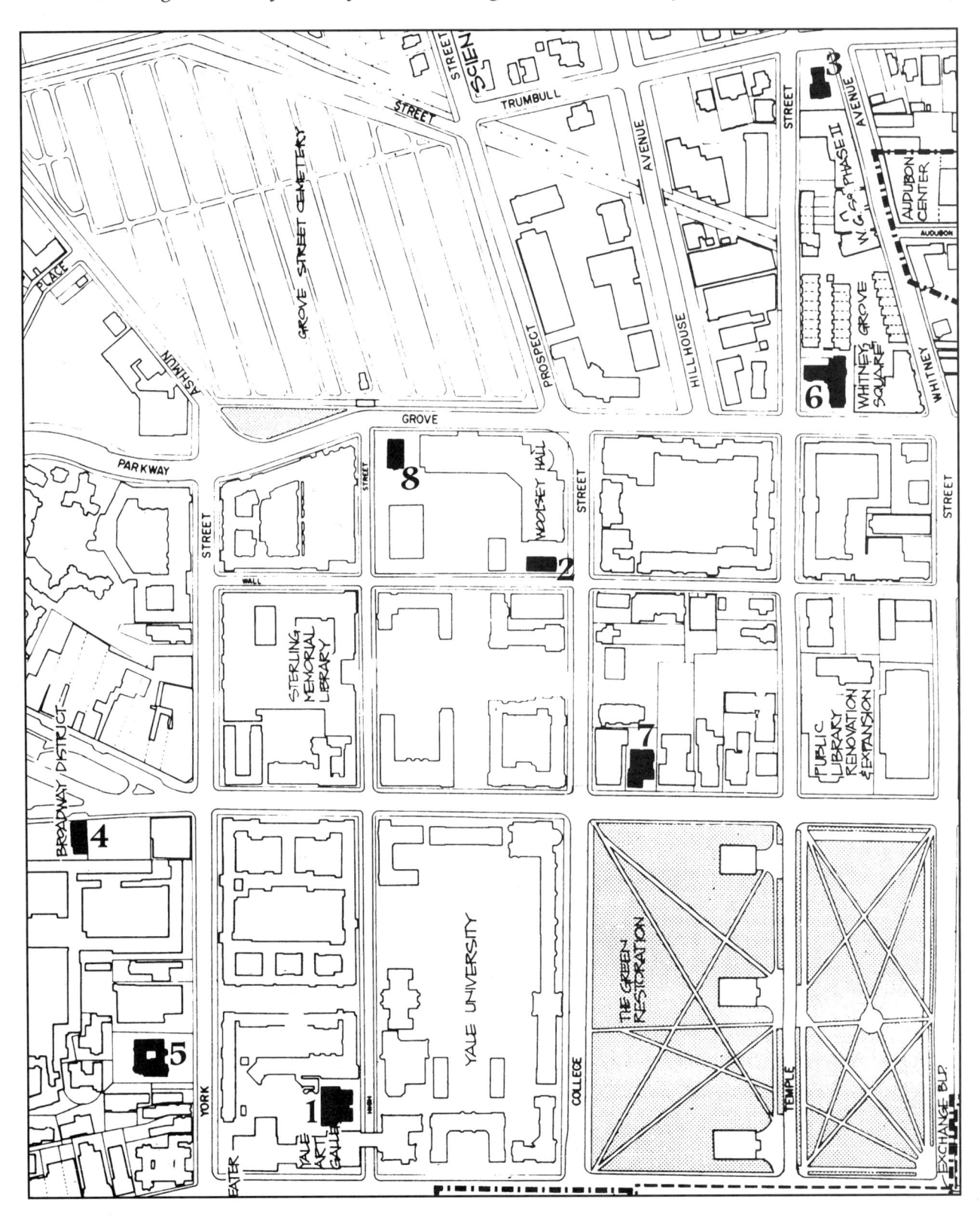

YALE UNIVERSITY
Senior "Secret" Societies

Skull and Bones
Skull and Bones (left) was founded in 1832. The founders built their hall in 1856. It was enlarged in 1883 and 1903, and a garden was added in 1918. Bones' "tomb" is a New Haven Preservation Trust Landmark. The recorded owner and location of the structure is Russell Trust Associates, 64 High Street.

Scroll and Key
Scroll and Key (right) was founded in 1841. Richard M. Hunt was the architect for the present building, which was built in 1869. The structure is a New Haven Preservation Trust Landmark. The recorded owner and location is Kingsley Trust Associates, 848 College Street.

Berzelius
Berzelius (left) was founded in 1848. The tomb was built in 1910 by New York architect Don Barber. Originally a Sheffield Scientific School fraternity, the building was converted to a senior secret society in 1933. The building is a New Haven Preservation Trust Landmark. The recorded owner and location is Berzelius Trust Association, 76 Trumbull Street.

Manuscript

Manuscript (left) was founded in 1952, and has been in the present location since 1962. King Lui Wu was the architect for the house, completed in 1962. The recorded owner and location is Wrexham Trust Association, 344 Elm Street.

Wolf's Head

Wolf's Head (right) was founded in 1883. In 1924, the present building was built from Bertram G. Goodhue's design. Its original home, at 77 Prospect Street, was sold to Yale. Both structures are New Haven Preservation Trust Landmarks. The recorded owner and location is The Phelps Association, 210 York Street.

Saint Elmo

Saint Elmo (left) was founded as Delta Phi in 1889 in the Sheffield Scientific School. The first clubhouse was built in 1895 near the present building, erected in 1912, and sold to Yale when Saint Elmo became a senior society in 1962. A portion of the building is used by the society. The recorded owner and location is the Reinlander Trust Association, 109 Grove Street.

Elihu

Elihu (right) was founded in 1903. In 1911, the club purchased an 18th century building which flourished as a Tory Tavern until it was confiscated in 1781. Everit V. Meeks was the architect for the large addition and alterations. The property is a New Haven Preservation Trust Landmark. The recorded owner and location is the Elihu Club, Inc., 175 Elm Street.

YALE UNIVERSITY
Senior "Secret" Societies

Book and Snake

Book and Snake was founded 1863. The tomb was built in 1901 by architect Louis R. Metcalfe. The building was converted to a senior society in 1933. The structure is a New Haven Preservation Trust Landmark. The recorded owner and location is Stone Trust Corporation, 214 Grove Street.

Just for the fun of it, here are some of the best rumors available about how these secret senior societies operate. Some sources are New Haven children who have managed to sneak into the buildings, newspaper articles and the book, *The Secret Cult of THE ORDER* by Anthony C. Sutton (Research Publications, Phoenix, AR 1984). The children assure me that there are secret tunnel entrances from other nearby buildings, which explains why you rarely see anyone going in or out of the buildings. There is also no visible explanation of the persistently reported excessively high water bills.

Until 1953, all Yale Juniors were herded into a square on "Tap Night," and those selected for membership were tapped on the shoulder by current members and asked if they would accept a membership invitation. It was a very traumatic night for both those who were accepted and the majority of students who were not. A persistent rumor for over 100 years is that the initiation ceremony requires the initiate to lie naked, sometimes in a sarcophagus, tell the secrets of their sex life to the other initiates, and then wrestle nude in mud piles.

The October 16, 1989 *New Haven Advocate* ran a front page story reporting that the bones of Indian chief Geronimo had been stolen from his grave by George Bush's father, and now reside in the Skull and Bones tomb on York Street.

When Skull and Bones admitted some women in 1991, their alumni did not approve and information about their lawsuit appeared in the local newspapers. The record revealed that former President George Bush, Associate Supreme Court Justice Potter Stewart, Time, Inc. founder Henry R. Luce, publisher and commentator William F. Buckley, Massachusetts Senator John Kerry and Rhode Island Senator John Chafee were all parties to the suit. All the societies now admit females as well as non-white members.

It is obvious that Yale, which banned most fraternities years ago, still condones these secret senior societies.

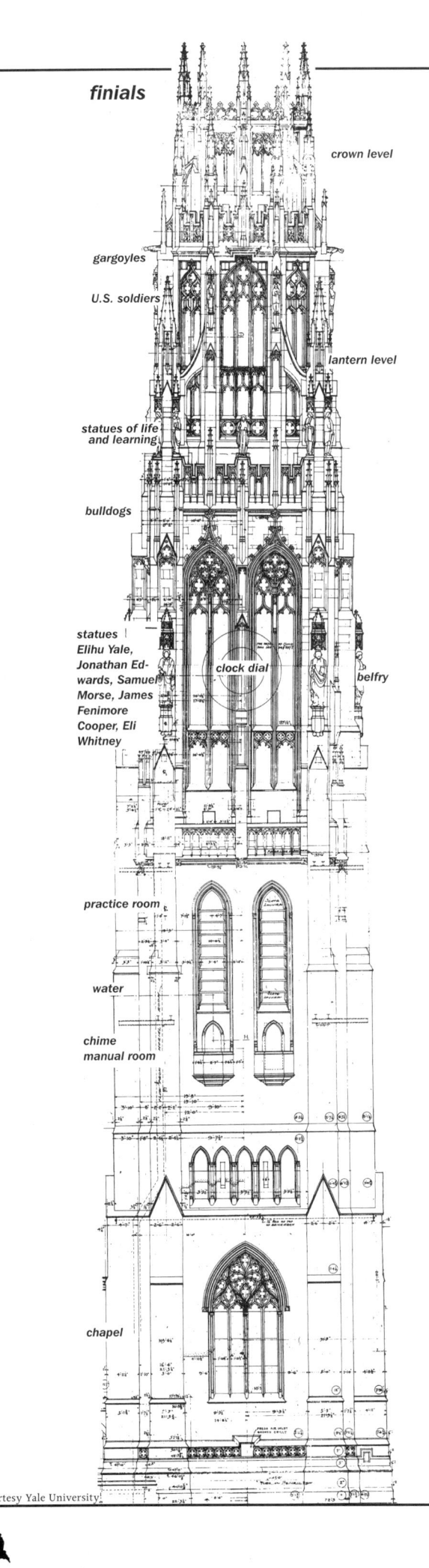

Harkness Tower often appears on lists of America's ten finest buildings because it is a magnificent example of Gothic style architecture. In 1981, Yale completely restored the 60-year-old, 216-foot-tall building to its original grandeur.

The tower's construction was funded by the family of Stephen V. Harkness, Class of 1889, who had made his fortune with the Rockefellers in Standard Oil. The tower is dedicated to Charles Harkness, who died in 1916. Construction began in 1917, but was interrupted by World War I. It was completed in 1921.

Inside the tower is an elegant two-story chapel. Immediately above it is room holding the console that controls the huge ten chime bells cast by John Taylor & Co., of England. Each has cast into it the motto "For God, For Country, For Yale - 1921." Forty-four additional bells were added to the carillon in 1966, completing four full octaves & enabling full concerts to be played on the bells. Over the console room is a large water tank originally used for fire protection.

On the outside, about half way up, the tower is ringed with statutes of Eli Yale, Jonathan Edwards, Samuel Morse, James Fenimore Cooper and Eli Whitney. With a good set of field glasses, you can see the bulldogs on the next level. These bulldogs are topped by statutes of life and learning.

Continuing up the tower, the lantern level comes next, followed by statutes of soldiers in uniforms of various wars. A Gothic tower wouldn't be Gothic without its gargoyles, which stick out just below the crown level, topped with beautiful detailed finials.

YALE UNIVERSITY
Religion

Yale Religious Ministry

Yale Religious Ministry is an on-campus association of clergy and non-ordained representatives of various religious faiths. It is available for counseling, both formal and informal sessions regarding academic, personal and social concerns. The University Chaplain and Associate Chaplain are appointed to serve the entire Yale community. The Reverend Elmore McKee was the first University Chaplain, followed by Sidney Lovett, William Sloan Coffin, John Vannorsdall, and Harry B. Adams. Now, Reverend Jerry Streets serves as Chaplain, with Associate Chaplain Reverend Cynthia Terry.

Campus Chapels

Marquand Chapel

Marquand Chapel is located at 409 Prospect Street, in the Sterling Divinity Quadrangle. Designed by Delano and Aldrich, the chapel, constructed from handmade waterstruck brick in the Georgian Colonial style, perpetuates the tradition of 18th century New England.

Rev. Frederick J. "Jerry" Streets *oversees the spiritual life of the Yale community, fostering concern for ethical issues on the campus and working with members of all religious denominations.*

Battell Chapel

Battell Chapel, located at the corner of College and Elm Streets, dates back to New Haven's Puritan past when Thomas Clap, then Yale's President, decided that Yale students should have a congregation. Built in 1874-76 and named in honor of Joseph Battell, B.A. 1923, who donated funds in 1863, this high Victorian building of brown sandstone was designed by Russell Stergis, Jr.

Dwight Memorial Chapel/Dwight Hall

Located in Dwight Hall *(see photo, next page)*, also home of the Chaplain's Office, on the Old Campus, the building, designed by Henry Austin, was erected of Portland sandstone in Early Victorian Gothic in 1842-46. Built to house the college library, the building was remodeled in 1931 to contain Dwight Memorial Chapel.

Campus Chaplaincies

- The Church of Christ in Yale, Battell Chapel
- Episcopal Church at Yale
- Lutheran Campus Ministry
- Baptist Campus Ministry
- St Thomas More Chapel and Center
- Roman Catholic Chaplaincy
- B'nai Brith Hillel Foundation
- Church of Jesus Christ of Latter-Day Saints
- Islamic Students Association
- Korean American Campus Ministry
- New Haven Zen Center

YALE UNIVERSITY
Dwight Hall at Yale

Founded in 1886 as the Yale University Christian Association, Dwight Hall was incorporated 12 years later as an independent, non-profit, educational and religious organization. Although the Hall often works in close cooperation with Yale, its budget and officers are chosen by undergraduates and alumni rather than by the University.

The Hall is a place where students can respond to their own needs while helping others. Projects include educational and mentoring programs for area youngsters, programs serving the elderly, and initiatives addressing health care, housing, literacy, homelessness and hunger.

Yale Hunger and Homelessness Action Project provides volunteers for area soup kitchens and the Drop in Center. Christmas In April is a one-day project in which Yale students work with members of the community to provide home repair services to low income, elderly, and disabled homeowners.

Many programs develop a community base and a life of their own. The International Student Center was begun by students in 1949. Marrakech, a program for mildly retarded young adults is another long-sustained program. The New Haven Halfway House, founded in 1967, maintains the distinction of being the oldest traditional living facility of its kind in Connecticut.

In 1968, the Hall developed the Summer Intern Project, a creative effort that enables 10-20 students to spend the summer months working full-time in the community on a project of their own design. FOCUS, a young program by Dwight Hall standards, is a week-long orientation to New Haven through community service for sophomores.

During the past decade, the Hall has expanded its programs to include 2,000 volunteers, over 60 student-coordinated volunteer projects, and a diverse network of student involvement in more than 100 area agencies.

*A New Haven native and Yale alumna, **Susan I. Fowler** is the General Secretary of Dwight Hall at Yale, the center all of the varied volunteer service activities that Yale students undertake each year.*

Dwight Hall *is home not only to the organization by the same name, but also to Dwight Memorial Chapel and the Yale Chaplain's Office. The building was built to house Yale's library, and did so from 1889 to 1930, when Sterling Memorial Library opened. Constructed of Portland sandstone in the Early Victorian Gothic style between 1842 and 1846, it was architect Henry Austin's first major work. After the library moved, the building was remodeled from designs by Charles Z. Klaunder to contain the Dwight Memorial Chapel.*

YALE UNIVERSITY
Science Hill

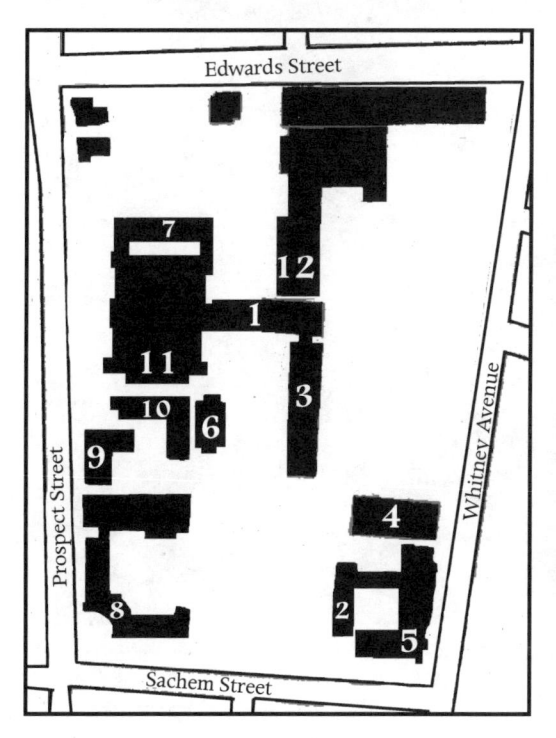

Facilities on Yale's Science Hill

(1) Bass Center for Molecular & Structural Biology
(2) Bingham Lab*
(3) Gibbs Lab
(4) Kline Geology Lab
(5) Peabody Museum**
(6) Kline Biology Tower
(7) Kline Chemistry Lab*
(8) Osborn Lab*
(9) Sage Hall*
(10) Sloane Physics Lab*
(11) Sterling Chemistry Lab
(12) Wright Nuclear Lab*

*not pictured   ** see page 262

All photos this page from author's collection

The **Peabody Museum of Natural History** was founded in 1866, inspired by the geological interests of Benjamin Silliman, and enriched by the fossil collections of its first Director, Othniel C. Marsh. It contains one of the greatest scientific collections of fossils, especially dinosaurs, in North America, including the largest intact brontosaurus in the world. In addition to its Great Dinosaur Hall, with Rudolph Zallinger's Pulitzer Prize winning mural, The Age of Reptiles, the exhibition areas feature mineralogical and ornithological collections, the animal kingdom, and the history of the cultures of the Americas. Workshops and laboratories in paleontology, anthropology, zoology, and evolutionary biology make the Peabody a working museum.

The **Yale University Art Gallery**, located at 1111 Chapel Street, was founded in 1832 when the University acquired John Trumbull's paintings of the American Revolution and set aside a building for their display. The gallery occupies two connecting buildings. The first, built in 1928, follows the design of an Italian Gothic palace. The second, built in 1953, was designed by architect Louis Kahn. The gallery has extensive collections in ancient, medieval, and Renaissance art, with works by European and American masters from virtually every period, plus a rich collection of modern art. It also has archeological artifacts and art from Yale's excavations of Pre-Columbian, African, Near Eastern and Far Eastern art.

Yale Repertory Theatre, at 120 Chapel Street, was the former home of the Calvary Baptist Church, built in 1871 and designed by Rufus G. Russell. The building was acquired by the University in 1966, upon relocation of the church. The theatre, a part of the School of Drama, opened in 1969. A major renovation was completed in 1975 to accomplish the transition from church to theatre, under the direction of architect Patricia V. Tetrault.

The **Yale Center for British Art**, 1080 Chapel Street, which opened in 1977, holds the largest collection of British art and illustrated books outside of the United Kingdom. The works date from Elizabethan times to the present. Paul Mellon, B.A. 1929, gave the basic collection to Yale, along funds for the construction of the Center. The last design of architect Louis Kahn, facing his first major commission, the Yale Art Gallery across Chapel Street, the Center building reflects its dual role as a public museum and a major research institute. The Center also offers a wide variety of public programs.

YALE UNIVERSITY
Art & Performance Spaces

Albert Arnold Sprague Memorial Hall, at 470 College Street, was completed in 1917 and named in honor of Colonel Sprague, B.A. 1859, in whose memory the gift was made by his family. This Georgian brick building by Coolidge & Shattuck contains classrooms, practice rooms, a recording studio, and an auditorium for chamber music recitals, concerts. The first floor was renovated in 1955, based on a design by architect J. Russell Bailey, to create the John Herrick Jackson Music Library at 98 Wall Street, a gift made in honor of Jackson, B.A. 1934, by his family.

Woolsey Hall, at College & Grove Streets, is one of the Bicentennial Buildings, erected in 1901-02 with funds donated by alumni to commemorate Yale's 200th anniversary. The buildings were designed by Carrere & Hastings, of Indiana limestone. The auditorium, with 2,700 seats, contains the massive John Stoughton Newberry Memorial Organ, given by his family. Another wing is the University Freshman Dining Hall, seating 1,200. The circular Memorial Hall and domed rotunda is the central unit and main entrance. Memorial plaques commemorating Yale men who died in wars hang on the walls. The 2nd floor Presidents' Room is used for official functions.

The **University Theatre**, at 222 York Street, designed by Blackall, Clapp & Whittemore and erected in 1925-26, was the gift of Edward S. Harkness, BA. 1897. This is a Collegiate Gothic building of limestone, seam-faced granite ashlar, and brick. The main auditorium and balcony seats 674 people. The building also holds an experimental theatre, offices, lecture and exhibition rooms, workshops, and rehearsal rooms for the School of Drama. The facade was redesigned in 1931 by James Gamble Rogers, and a third-story addition was built in 1957, from designs by Henry F. Miller. The Drama School Library is housed there.

YALE UNIVERSITY
The Yale Co-Op

An architecturally distinguished college store with a fine book department, the Yale Cooperative Corporation (Yale Co-Op), has evolved over the years into an unusual emporium, with a tempo all its own. In 1885, a group of students and instructors formed the association to reduce the cost of living in the Yale community by sharing the profits from the store's business among its members. The Co-Op is a separate corporation, not a part of the University, and is operated strictly for its members' benefit. There are no stockholders to receive dividends, nor bondholders to receive interest.

The original store was housed in a laboratory on the Old Campus, and then moved to Connecticut Hall. In 1930, the store moved to 300 York Street, now Toad's Place. Between 1957 and 1959, it expanded to include a store facing Broadway where the book department was located. This building was linked up back-to-back with the York Street building, in the commercial area just off the campus. Both were leased from Yale University.

Membership was later opened to alumni, who could shop in person or by mail. Increased enrollment brought many new member services and much broader merchandise selections for both members and non-members.

The Co-Op's continued growth led to negotiations in 1960 with the University for construction of the Co-Op's present building. The 50,000 square foot building was designed by architect Eero Saarinen, designer of neighboring Morse and Stiles colleges.

Although the primary function of the Co-Op is to serve its members, it does a large business with non-members from the New Haven community, because of the store's distinctive merchandise, ambiance, service, and prices.

The Yale Co-Op describes itself as "a community educational store specializing in merchandise for college-oriented families." In 1965, sales of non-required books exceeded those of required course books for the first time. Today, the Co-Op is Connecticut's largest bookstore with over 76,000 titles in three separate locations.

The Yale Co-Op is the first college store in the country to introduce an "Estate Sale" book department. Purchases of prominent academic libraries, as well as duplicates from university libraries, make this unique service available.

The Corporation is guided by a Board of Directors of not less than fifteen members, elected for two year terms and representing students, faculty, alumni and members of the Yale administration. The General Manager, serves as President and CEO, and is a voting member of the Board. Harry W. Berkowitz, President since 1991, is the first non-Yalie President in the Co-Op's 110-year history.

In 1987, a separate medical branch was opened adjacent to the Yale Medical School and Yale New Haven Hospital. The Co-Op's clever toll-free number, 1(800) ELI-YALE, has increased sales. Membership dues are $5 for one year, $15 for four years, and $25 for a gold life card membership.

Sketch courtesy Yale Co-Op

Medical Services

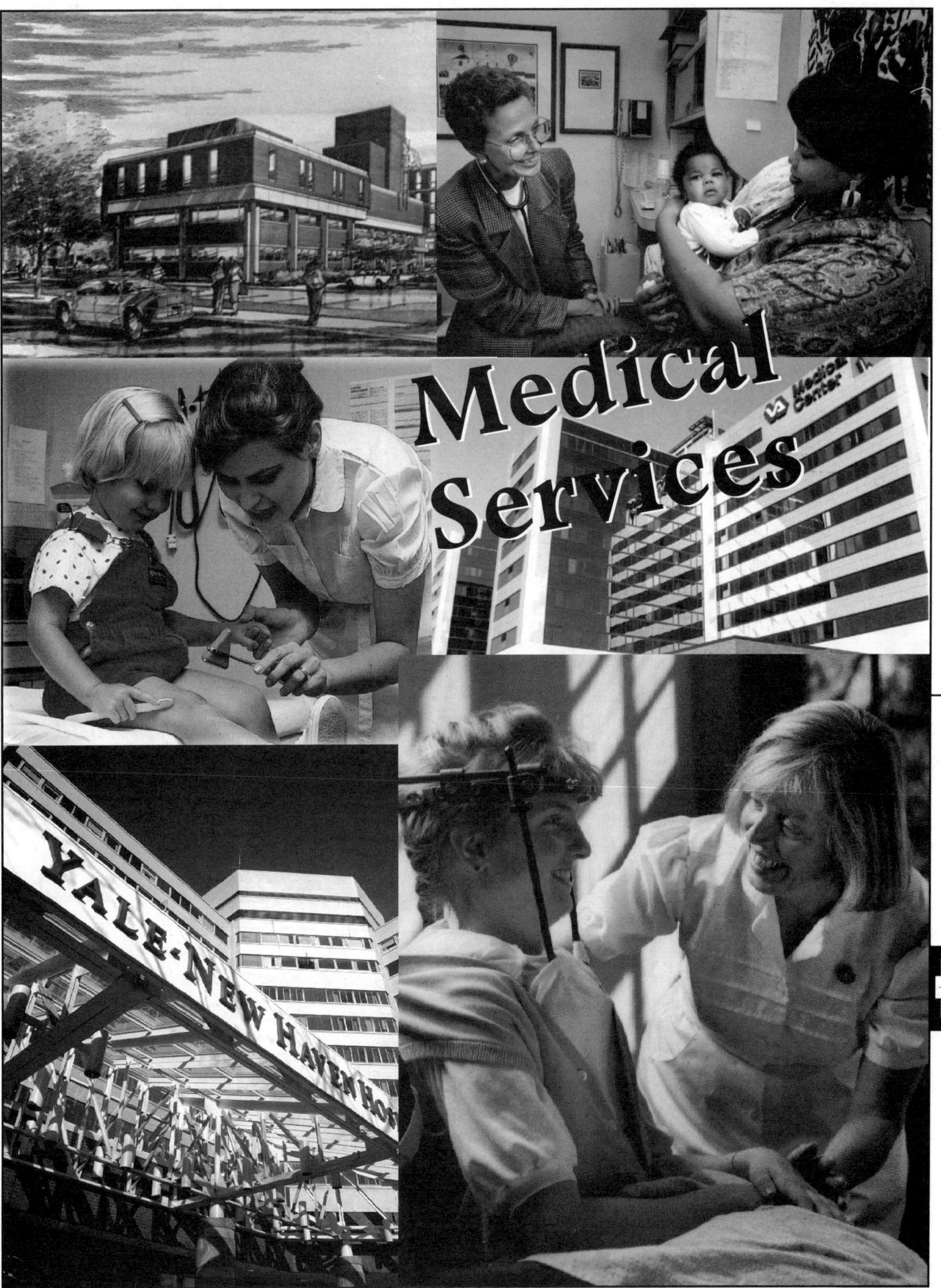

Above and above-left, circa 1900

For more than 160 years, Yale~New Haven Hospital has cared for the people of southern Connecticut... and the world!

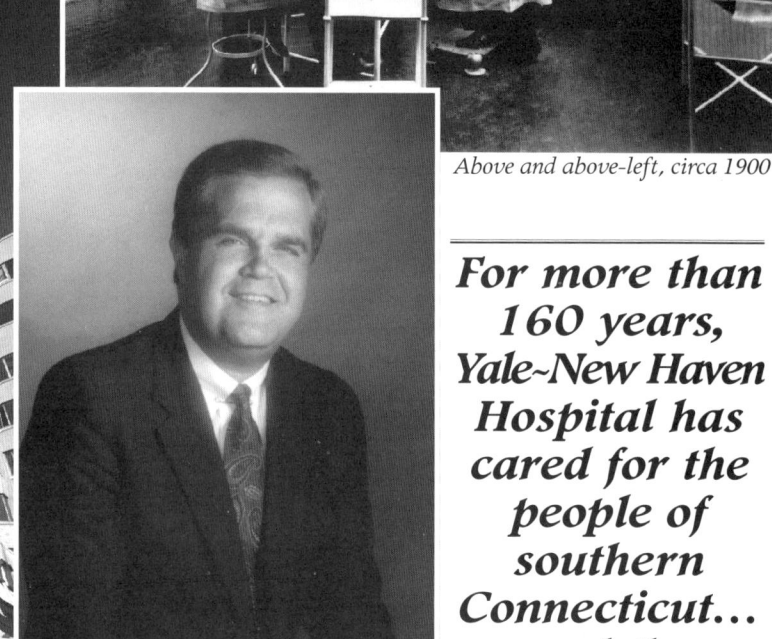

Joseph A. Zaccagnino
President & CEO
Yale-New Haven Hospital

Photos courtesy Yale-New Haven Hospital

A Pioneer in Medical Science

1942	first successful clinical use of penicillin
†1942	first use of chemotherapy as cancer treatment
1944	first to allow healthy newborns to stay in rooms with mothers
†1949	first artificial heart pump (now at the Smithsonian)
†1956	first open heart surgery in Connecticut
1957	fetal heart monitored for the first time
1960	first intensive care unit for newborns
†1966	developed the phrenic nerve pacemaker
†1975	identified and named Lyme disease
†1978	developed insulin infusion pump for diabetics
†1983	first *in vitro* birth in New England
†1984	New England's first skin bank
1985	world's first Fetal Cardiovascular Center
†1991	first in Connecticut to use ECM0, a sophisticated life support system
1993	first in Connecticut to use stereotactic biopsy to diagnose breast cancer
1994	first in Connecticut to use epidural endoscopy to diagnose elusive back pain

Transplants (firsts in Connecticut):
cornea (1952), kidney (1967), liver (1983), heart (1984), bone marrow (1988), heart-lung (1988), pancreas (1989), single lung (1990), heart from unmatched donor (1992)

†Indicates a joint-project of Yale-New Haven Hospital and the Yale School of Medicine

MEDICAL SERVICES
Yale~New Haven Hospital

Founded in 1826 as Connecticut's first hospital and the nation's fifth, Yale-New Hospital (YNHH) is a 900-bed private, nonprofit facility that ranks among the premier medical centers in the world. The hospital's history is filled with medical achievements of national significance and its broad spectrum of services is conveniently close for Connecticut's three million residents.

YNHH provides a wide range of services, including trauma and emergency care, cardiac services, organ transplantation, adult and child psychiatry, the Yale Cancer Center and Connecticut's most comprehensive pediatric services located in the new Children's Hospital at Yale-New Haven. From the highly complicated to the routine, Yale-New Haven is ideally qualified in diagnosis and treatment.

In addition to acting as the primary teaching hospital for the Yale School of Medicine, Yale-New Haven is the largest acute care provider in southern Connecticut and one of the Northeast's major referral centers. Investment in the best equipment is coupled with a commitment to a specialized staff of 5,000 of the region's most highly qualified healthcare professionals.

The *Children's Hospital at Yale-New Haven* is Connecticut's largest and first comprehensive children's hospital and reflects a unique collaboration between obstetric and pediatric specialists. YNHH has a long-standing tradition of caring for mothers and babies together. In the 1940s, YNHH introduced "rooming in," bringing babies into the rooms with their mothers. Today, pregnant women can turn to Yale-New Haven for childbirth and fitness classes, expertise in finding and treating medical problems before birth, help in finding a doctor for their child, comfort during delivery, personal care for both mother and baby, support after leaving the hospital and specialized services for the treatment of all childhood diseases and problems.

The *Yale Cancer Center*—the only one in southern New England designated as a comprehensive cancer center by the National Cancer Institute—is at the forefront of the nation's efforts to prevent, treat and cure cancer. It includes the Yale Breast Care Center and a mobile mammography van.

Other specialty services include: a Level I Trauma Center; a comprehensive transplant program (offering heart/lung, heart, kidney, liver, pancreas, bone marrow, bone and cornea transplants), neurology (including stroke, epilepsy surgery, multiple sclerosis and Parkinson's Disease); dermatological expertise (including skin cancer and photopheresis); a burn center with skin transplant expertise; endocrinology services, including a diabetes center and kidney stone lithotripsy; and advanced laparoscopy services.

From 24-hour emergency services on the ground floor to a life-saving helipad on the roof, Yale-New Haven is uniquely prepared to care for everything from broken arms to heart transplants with the competence and sensitivity expected of a world class institution.

Yale~New Haven is uniquely prepared to care for everything from broken arms to heart transplants with the competence and sensitivity expected of a world class institution.

Despite a reputation which draws patients from around the world, the bulk of the hospital's patients—almost 70 percent—are from the New Haven area, and almost half of those are from Elm City itself. The hospital stays focused on its neighborhood and city. Yale-New Haven's commitment to the community goes back to its roots in 1826, when the hospital was founded as a charitable institution to care for the city's poor. Today that commitment is evident in programs such as Connecticut's largest AIDS Care Program, partnerships with the city's schools, community health screenings, assistance for staff home purchases or renovations in the Hill neighborhood, minority nursing scholarships, and more.

Last year, the hospital provided $25 million in free or under-compensated care for the poor and the elderly. In addition, YNHH serves its community with health services, health promotion, and education, as well as primary care for local residents. The hospital works to improve access to care and is a leader in dealing with such pressing issues such as infant mortality, lead poisoning, infectious diseases, and substance abuse.

Yale~New Haven Hospital	**785~4242**
20 York Street, New Haven	
Physician Referral Service	**785~2000**

*Sister Anne Virginie, President
Saint Raphael Healthcare System
James J. Cullen, President, Hospital of Saint Raphael*

The Saint Raphael Healthcare System is dedicated to the better health of each individual and to providing an integrated network of comprehensive care services for Greater New Haven.

In 1994 alone, St. Raphael's provided almost $28 million in cash and in-kind services to the community.

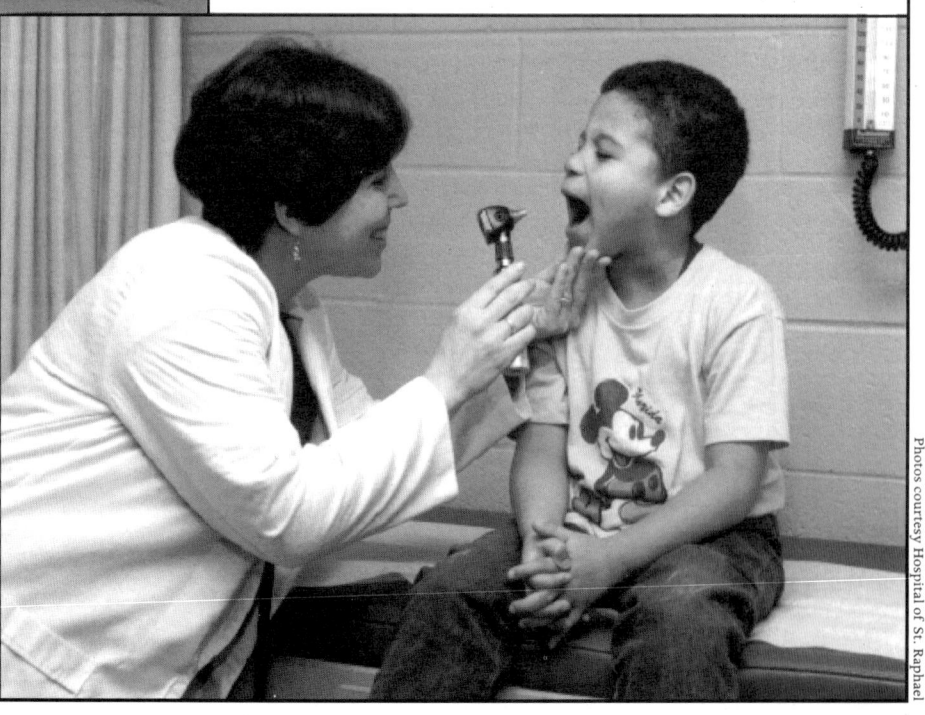

Photos courtesy Hospital of St. Raphael

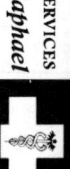

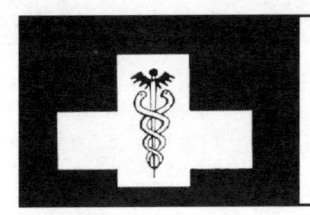

MEDICAL SERVICES
Hospital of St. Raphael

The Saint Raphael Healthcare System—which includes the Hospital of Saint Raphael, Saint Regis Health Center, the Saint Raphael Foundation, DePaul Health Services, Xavier Services Corporation, and Seton Real Estate—is focused on the better health of the Greater New Haven community. The System is committed to efficiently providing a continuum of quality services from health and wellness programs, to primary care and ambulatory services, in- and out-patient acute care, rehabilitation, and long-term care.

The Hospital of Saint Raphael, founded in 1907 by the Sisters of Charity of Saint Elizabeth, is the oldest member of the Saint Raphael Healthcare System. A 491-bed acute care community teaching hospital affiliated with Yale University School of Medicine, the Hospital of Saint Raphael provides sophisticated, compassionate care in an environment which respects the dignity of each person.

The Hospital of Saint Raphael lists many "firsts" among its accomplishments. It was the first community hospital in Connecticut to open a coronary care unit and today has the state's largest dedicated cardiothoracic intensive care unit. The Hospital was one of the first in New England to perform open-heart surgery and the first in New England with a radiation center. In 1994, Saint Raphael's became the first hospital in New England to use a robotic arm in the operating room to assist surgeons with laparoscopic surgery.

The Hospital of Saint Raphael, in collaboration with its medical staff, has led the way in innovative outreach programs, including the nationally-acclaimed Project MotherCare, a mobile prenatal and primary care clinic for women and children; award-winning Project ElderCare, a partnership with the City of New Haven to provide community-based health care to senior citizens; CareCard, a health and fitness program for adults 55 and older; and *Better Health* magazine, providing health and wellness information to more than 145,000 households throughout Greater New Haven.

The Hospital of Saint Raphael is a regional dialysis center and a federally-designated regional trauma facility. It also has developed innovative adolescent and adult psychiatric programs, and treats thousands of patients each year at the Father Michael J. McGivney Center for Cancer Care, one of the most unique and progressive outpatient cancer treatment facilities in the country today.

Saint Raphael's Occupational Health Plus is the state's most comprehensive occupational health program, providing prevention, injury treatment, and rehabilitation services for hundreds of businesses throughout Greater New Haven. With facilities in Branford, New Haven and Wallingford, its services include acute injury management, employment physicals, rehabilitative services, occupational health nursing, wellness programs and health screenings, drug screenings and programs to help companies meet Occupational Safety and Health Association standards.

Saint Regis Health Center, the Saint Raphael Healthcare System's 125-bed skilled nursing facility, provides high-quality, long-term care for older adults. Saint Regis also offers a restorative care program for people who need short-term skilled nursing care and/or rehabilitation services following hospitalization and before they return home, or move to a less specialized facility. The only Catholic nursing home in Greater New Haven, Saint Regis offers residents the expertise of a wide range of physicians and medical professionals in a variety of specialties, along with all of the resources at the Hospital of Saint Raphael.

The Saint Raphael Healthcare System has a long history of community commitment. In 1994 alone, the System provided almost $28 million in cash and in-kind services to the community. This included charity care; donations of medical supplies and equipment; non-reimbursable clinical services; employee volunteer time in health promotion and community service; scholarships; employee contributions to local agencies; and education and training.

The Saint Raphael Healthcare System is also working to stabilize and improve our neighborhood with programs to help employees purchase nearby homes, and, through Seton Real Estate, selectively acquires abandoned and dilapidated buildings. The System also provides scholarships to neighborhood residents pursuing healthcare careers; and funds and operates several school-based clinics and a nationally recognized neighborhood reading room at the local police substation. The Saint Raphael Foundation, in partnership with its volunteers and donors, has generated more than $32 million over its 20-year history to support and develop Saint Raphael's facilities, programs and services.

Hospital of St. Raphael   **789-3000**
1450 Chapel Street, New Haven

Need-A-Physician?   **789-4304**
Physician Referral Program

VA Medical Center

The Department of Veterans Affairs Medical Center in West Haven is a 590-bed facility which includes a 90-bed nursing care unit. It is a clinical campus of Yale University School of Medicine—all the medical center's physicians are Yale faculty members.

The medical center offers a full array of acute, secondary and long-term inpatient and outpatient care to veterans. It houses Connecticut's only Positron Emmision Tomography (PET) center and is also the home of specialized national VA- programs in epilepsy, stroke, blindness rehabilitation, post traumatic stress disorder (PTSD), alcoholism and schizophrenia. One hundred eighty-eight of its beds are for psychiatric patients, making West Haven VAMC the largest *acute care* psychiatric hospital in the state. Other beds are used for treatment of medical and surgical conditions, for intermediate care and for rehabilitation. It is also home to the VA's Eastern Blind Rehabilitation Center, which provides services to visually impaired veterans from throughout the Northeast.

Ninety-seven percent of patients treated at the center come from Connecticut, about 85 percent from New Haven and Fairfield counties. The medical center also has a primary care clinic at the Coast Guard Academy in New London, providing services to southeast Connecticut. With over 180,000 visits annually and an average inpatient census of 463, the medical center is ranked among the top four VA medical centers for research funding. Its research program directly benefits patient care.

Care at VA medical centers is free to eligible veterans of America's armed forces. At West Haven's center, eligible veterans include those with service-connected disabilities and veterans whose annual income is below approximately $20,000. Some 90,000 of Connecticut's 350,000 veterans are eligible for free care at West Haven under current guidelines.

VA Medical Center   932~5711
950 Campbell Avenue, West Haven

Gaylord Hospital

Gaylord Hospital is a 121-bed rehabilitation hospital located on 500 acres in Wallingford, CT. Patients come to Gaylord because they have experienced an acute accident or illness that in all probability will leave them with some kind of disability.

Gaylord Hospital is nationally known for its rehabilitation programs for traumatic brain injury, spinal cord injuries, stroke, pulmonary diseases and chemical dependency. Its staff provides rehabilitation nursing; physical, occupational, respiratory, speech and resocialization therapy; and social services. Gaylord's goals are to return patients to independent living and to help them live a full life. About 80% of the patients return home after discharge.

In addition to its in-patient facility, Gaylord offers outpatient rehabilitation services at three area sites and has expanded its Industrial Rehabilitation Program to the Gaylord/Long Wharf Rehabilitation Center in New Haven. These programs offer a continuum of care and are designed to help an injured worker return to the job in the least amount of time with the maximum medical improvement. The program also provides educational services to employers on injury prevention and Americans with Disabilities Act compliance.

Prior to rehabilitation, many patients and families believe their ability to make choices has been taken away. It is Gaylord's goal to help restore those choices.

In a work simulation, a client in Gaylord's Industrial Rehabilitation Program performs an overhead assembly to determine endurance.

Gaylord Hospital   284~2800
Gaylord Farm Road, Wallingford
Industrial Rehabilitation Program   284~2784

MEDICAL SERVICES
Regional Hospitals

Masonic Home and Hospital

The Masonic Home and Hospital, a 548-bed, multi-licensed nursing facility which combines the advanced medical services of a hospital with all the services and amenities found in the best skilled nursing facilities, is located in Wallingford, 10 miles north of New Haven.

Built on the site of the original 18-bed home, which opened in 1895, the facility today provides ambulatory care services, geriatric assessment, a rehabilitation unit, a geriatric medical psychiatric unit and an acute care geriatric hospital.

The non-profit facility, open to the public, is owned and operated by The Masonic Charity Foundation of Connecticut, founded in 1889. The Foundation also operates *Ashlar Village,* one of the relatively few accredited continuing care retirement communities in Connecticut, and *Ashlar* of Newtown, a 158-bed skilled nursing facility in upper Fairfield County. The Village is located on Mt. Tom, on the Wallingford campus, overlooking the Quinnipiac River Valley.

Tours of the hospital and grounds are available every Sunday, or daily through the volunteer office (phone 284-3980). The grounds feature a statue of George Washington in his Masonic regalia, the only one of its kind in New England.

Masonic Home & Hospital   284-3900
22 Masonic Avenue, Wallingford

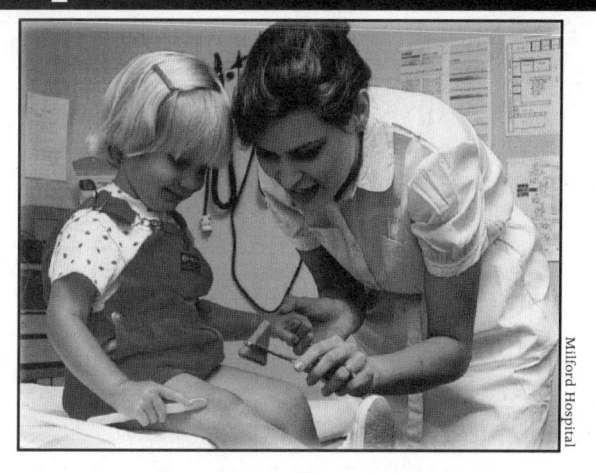

Milford Hospital

Milford Hospital is a full-service medical center. Founded in 1920, Milford Hospital combines state-of-the-art technology with compassionate, considerate care. The hospital offers the very latest medical procedures and tests in a quiet suburban environment.

At Milford Hospital, quality care means dedicated doctors and nurses, skilled therapists and technicians, advanced technology, efficient and reliable diagnostic testing and laboratory analysis. The hospital takes pride in its superior emergency room services, outpatient surgery facility, health education programs and home care services.

A new building program is currently in progress. The new facility will expand the hospital's outpatient and acute care services.

Milford Hospital   876-4000
2047 Bridgeport Avenue, Milford

Hill Health Center

In 1993, Hill Health Center celebrated 25 years of service to the New Haven community. The primary mission of making comprehensive health care available and accessible to low income individuals and families is as challenging today as it was during the formative years of the Center.

Services were initially limited to children and youth residing in the Hill community. There has been tremendous growth and expansion of services, new sites have been acquired and the main clinic has undergone major renovations and expansion. Today, with a staff of over 300, the Center serves residents of all ages in the greater New Haven area and has offices in West Haven and Milford as well.

Over the years, in addition to providing comprehensive primary care, responding to the unique needs of the population was and is a top priority of the Center.

Hill Health Center   773-1134
400 Columbus Avenue, New Haven

The Center offers: Early Stimulation Program, teenage Infant and Child Care Services, Comprehensive Perinatal Care Program, South Central Rehabilitation Center, Grant Street Partnership, Women's Corner, Northside Community Outreach Services, Community Programs for Clinical Research on AIDS, AIDS Case Management, school-based health services, Homeless Health Care, outreach services and others.

Fair Haven Community Health Clinic

The Fair Haven Community Health Center brings health care closer to those who need it most in the Wooster Square and Fair Haven neighborhoods. These New Haven neighborhoods are ethnically diverse. The central clinic is located on Grand Avenue, the main street of Fair Haven. A sliding fee scale is offered so that all people are welcomed for services.

The Center sprung from the idealism and reforms of the 1960s. Twenty-three years ago it was a small store-front clinic housed in a local elementary school. Last year, more than 42,000 visits were made for many types of care, including:

- Women, Infant and Children's Program, a state and federally funded nutrition and education program
- Pediatric care for 1200 children under the age of 6
- Comprehensive health care for adults
- On-site service at the Bella Vista Elderly Housing Complex
- School-based clinics for teenagers
- Social Services

Sandra Flatow, pediatric nurse, at well baby clinic with a patient.

Fair Haven Clinic   777-7411
374 Grand Avenue, New Haven

Like the rest of the nation, the Fair Haven Community Health Center has watched the health care reform debates. As the nation struggles with reform, the Center continues to provide high quality health care day-to-day, one person at a time.

MEDICAL SERVICES
Outpatient Services

Clifford W. Beers Guidance Clinic

The early mental hygiene movement in the U.S. was begun in New Haven by a young Yale graduate, Clifford Whittingham Beers. Supportive public response to his publication of his experiences as a psychiatric patient in his autobiography, *A Mind That Found Itself*, led him to organize an advocacy movement for the mentally ill. He worked to ameliorate the conditions within mental institutions, to make available outpatient treatment for all psychiatric patients and their families—regardless of their ability to pay—and to prevent mental illness through public education, based on his strong belief that mental illness was curable.

The Clifford W. Beers Guidance Clinic, established in 1913, is the oldest outpatient mental health clinic in Connecticut. A community based child mental health agency committed to the psychological and physical well being of children, adolescents and their families, Beers' mission is to detect, treat, prevent and reduce the incidence of psychiatric disorders.

The clinic not only provides direct services on both an outpatient and inpatient basis, but also engages in public awareness programs to help the community understand mental illness so as to help identify and resolve early issues before they become critical problems. Graduate level psychologists, social workers and nurse clinicians also train at Beers. A cornerstone of Beers' service delivery is collaboration with other social service agencies, schools and community-based organizations to ensure that the total needs of clients are met.

Today, the Clinic serves over 1,000 patients annually in more than 8,000 visits. Services include emergency inpatient evaluations, 24-hour telephone triage, and intensive short-term outpatient treatment. Clients at the Clinic reflect the socioeconomic, racial and ethnic diversity of New Haven.

The Clinic is an non-profit agency which receives support from the Connecticut Department of Children and Families, the United Way of Greater New Haven and Branford, the Community Fund of Guilford, the Town of Guilford and the City of New Haven. Clients' fees and income from grants and fundraising events help to cover the cost of service provision.

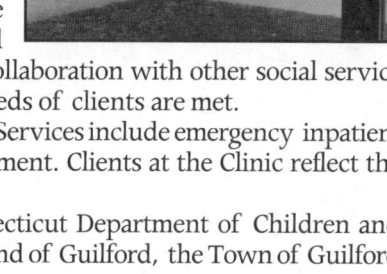

Clifford Beers Clinic   495~6816
93 Edwards Street, New Haven

Gesell Institute

For nearly 50 years, research at the Gesell Institute, a nonprofit organization, has provided fundamental knowledge about the behavior of children between birth and sixteen years. The belief that all children, young children especially, learn best in environments that respect their developmental level means it is very important for both parents and teachers to understand that children develop at different rates. Because all children do not do the same things at the same age, we must respect each child's growth and development as unique.

Children deserve to feel secure and successful both at school and at home. Security and self-esteem are fundamental to learning and normal development. Trust in a child's natural abilities and respect for the individual is the keystone towards this goal.

Services provided by the institute include: psychological evaluations for children 2-1/2 to 12 years of age; evaluations to determine a child's developmental readiness for a grade level; workshops for educators who want to learn how to administer Gesell's developmental evaluations and books for parents and teachers interested in knowing more about the typical behavior of children from birth to 16 years of age.

Gesell Institute   777~3481
310 Prospect Street, New Haven

Nursing Homes

Ansonia

Mariner Health Care of So. CT
126 Ford Street
Phone: 736-1100 CCNH: 90

Branford

Branford Hills Healthcare Ctr
189 Alps Road
Phone: 481-6221 CCNH/RHNS: 190

Cheshire

Cheshire Convalescent Ctr
745 Highland Avenue
Phone: 272-7285 CCNH/RHNS: 120

Elim Park Baptist Home, Inc.
140 Cook Hill Road
Phone: 272-3547 CCNH/RHNS: 90

Greenery Ext. Care Ctr
50 Hazel Drive
Phone: 272-7204 CCNH: 210

Marbridge Retirement Ctr
665 West Main Street
Phone: 272-2901 HA: 25

Derby

Derby Nursing Home
210 Chatfield Street
Phone: 735-7401 CCNH: 120

Marshall Lane Manor
101 Marshall Lane
Phone: 734-3393 RHNS: 120

East Haven

Laurel Woods
451 North High Street
Phone: 466-6850 CCNH: 120

Lombardi Rest Home
37 Clark Avenue
Phone: 469-6652 HA: 16

Stewart Rest Home
93 High Street
Phone: 467-1038 HA: 16

Talmadge Park
Talmadge Avenue
Phone: 469-2316 CCNH: 62

Teresa Rest Home, Inc.
57 Main Street
Phone: 467-0836 HA: 22

Yorkshire Manor
4 French Avenue
Phone: 467-1234 HA: 25

Guilford

Fowler Nursing Ctr, Inc.
10 Boston Post Road
Phone: 453-3725 CCNH: 90

Marotta Manor, Inc.
148 Whitfield Street
Phone: 453-9795 HA: 20

W. Lake Lodge Health Care Fac.
109 West Lake Avenue
Phone: 488-9142 CCNH: 60

Hamden

Arden House, Inc.
850 Mix Avenue
Phone: 281-3500 CCNH: 360

Garden View Manor
1840 State Street
Phone: 624-1558 HA: 20

Hamden Health Care Ctr
1270 Sherman Lane
Phone: 281-7555 CCNH: 120

Highvue Manor
2730 State Street
Phone: 248-3437 HA: 47

Whitney Ctr Medical Unit
200 Leeder Hill Drive
Phone: 281-6745 CCNH: 59

Whitney Manor Convalescent Ctr
2800 Whitney Avenue
Phone: 288-6230 CCNH: 150

Madison

Madison Health Care
34 Wildwood Avenue
Phone: 245-8008 CCNH: 90

Watrous Nursing Center
9 Neck Road
Phone: 245-9483 CCNH: 45

Four Corners Rest Home, Inc.
306 Naugatuck Avenue
Phone: 878-0177 HA: 19

Milford

Mediplex of Milford
245 Orange Avenue
Phone: 876-5123 CCNH: 120

Mediplex Rehab. & Skilled Nursing of Southern CT
2028 Bridgeport Avenue
Phone: 877-0371 CCNH: 120

Milford Health Care Ctr, Inc.
195 Platt Street
Phone: 878-5958 CCNH: 120

Pond Point Health Care Ctr
60 Platt Street
Phone: 878-5786 CCNH: 140

New Haven

Atrium Plaza Health Care Ctr
240 Winthrop Avenue
Phone: 789-0500 CCNH/RHNS: 240

Carewell Rest Home
260 Dwight Street
Phone: 562-8596 RHNS: 45

Clifton House Rehab Ctr
181 Clifton Street
Phone: 467-1666 CCNH: 195

Cove Manor Conv. Ctr, Inc.
36 Morris Cove Road
Phone: 467-6357 CCNH: 70

Hannah Gray Home
235 Dixwell Avenue
Phone: 562-3617 HA: 13

Haven Rest Home, Inc.
5 University Place
Phone: 624-6222 HA: 11

Jewish Home for the Aged, Inc.
169 Davenport Avenue
Phone: 789-1650 CCNH/RHNS: 218

Marionette Home for the Aged
289 Quinnipiac Avenue
Phone: 468-7727 HA: 10

Mary Wade Home
118 Clinton Avenue
Phone: 562-7222 CCNH/RHNS/HA: 103

Haven Nursing Ctr
50 Mead Street
Phone: 777-3491 CCNH: 91

Riverview Rest Home
92-94 Lexington Avenue
Phone: 468-7325 HA: 50

Saint Paul's Church Home
600 Chapel Street
Phone: 624-1450 HA: 11

St. Regis Health Ctr
1354 Chapel Street
Phone: 865-0505 CCNH: 125

West Rock Health Care Ctr
34 Level Street
Phone: 389-9744 RHNS: 90

Windsor Castle Health Care
915 Ella T. Grasso Boulevard
Phone: 865-5155 CCNH: 120

North Branford

Evergreen Woods
88 Notch Hill Road
Phone: 488-8000 CCNH: 40

North Haven

Clintonville Manor
201 Clintonville Road
Phone: 239-8017 RHNS: 120

Montowese Health Care Ctr
163 Quinnipiac Avenue
Phone: 624-3303 CCNH: 100

Orange

Lydian Corporation
324 Grassy Hill Road
Phone: 878-0613 RHNS: 27

Orange Health Care Ctr
225 Boston Post Road
Phone: 795-0835 RHNS: 60

Prospect

Country Manor Health Care Ctr
64 Summit Road
Phone: 758-4431 CCNH: 150

Eastview Manor, Inc.
170 Scott Road
Phone: 758-5491 HA: 30

Shelton

Flora & Mary Hewitt Mem Hosp
230 Coram Avenue
Phone: 924-4671 CCNH/RHNS: 206

Gardner Heights, Inc.
172 Roacky Rest Road
Phone: 929-1481 CCNH/RHNS: 179

Shelton Lakes Res. & Hlth Care Ctr
5 Lake Road
Phone: 924-2635 CCNH/HA: 109

Wicke Health Ctr, Inc.
584 Long Hill Avenue
Phone: 929-5321 CCNH: 120

Trumbull

Maefair Health Care Ctr
21 Maefair Court
Phone: 459-5153 CCNH: 120

Saint Joseph's Manor
6448 Main Street
Phone: 268-6204 CCNH/RHNS/HA: 297

Wallingford

Brook Hollow Health Care Ctr
55 Kondracki Lane
Phone: 265-6771 CCNH: 180

Masonic Home and Hospital
22 Masonic Avenue
Phone: 284-3900 CCNH/RHNS/HA: 468

Regency House of Wallingford
181 East Main Street
Phone: 265-1661 CCNH: 130

Skyview Health & Rehab Ctr
35 Marc Drive
Phone: 265-0981 CCNH: 97

West Haven

Arterburn Home, Inc.
267 Union Avenue
Phone: 934-5256 RHNS: 40

Bentley Gardens Hlth Care Ctr
310 Terrace Avenue
Phone: 932-2247 CCNH: 98

Forest Hills Guest Home
462 Derby Avenue
Phone: 387-4329 HA: 17

Harbor View Manor
308 Savin Avenue
Phone: 932-6411 CCNH/RHNS: 120

Seacrest Retirement Ctr
588 Ocean Avenue
Phone: 934-2676 HA: 45

Sound View Nursing Ctr, Inc.
Care Lane
Phone: 934-7955 CCNH: 102

West Wynde Nursing Ctr
555 Saw Mill Road
Phone: 934-8326 CCNH: 120

Woodbridge

Willows of Woodbridge
225 Amity Road
Phone: 387-0076 CCNH: 86

Key

CCNH Chronic & Convalescent Nursing Home
HA Home for the Aged
RHNS Rest Home with Nursing Supervision

Numbers that follow indicate total number of beds

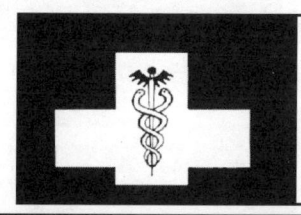

MEDICAL SERVICES
Nursing Services

Hospice

The Connecticut Hospice originated the U.S. Hospice movement 21 years ago. Today, the nation's first Hospice serves over 2,000 patients and families every year in a program directed to provide comfort and quality of life for terminal patients. No one is turned away for lack of ability to pay.

The Connecticut Hospice is located in Branford, in the first U.S. building expressly designed for hospice care. It provides 52 inpatient beds for management of pain and symptoms, psycho-social and spiritual support, and help for the patient's total family unit. Patients may, if they wish, come for a time of respite while discomfort is dealt with so that they may return home. Care for the family is continued through the bereavement period.

Home care is provided through offices located in Derby, Norwalk and Wallingford in addition to Branford. Most patients are able to remain in hospice home care throughout their hospice journey, though if inpatient care becomes appropriate, transfer from home to inpatient care can be readily arranged.

In both home and inpatient care, an interdisciplinary team meets patient/family needs. Physicians, nurses, social workers, pastors, pharmicists, artists and trained volunteers comprise the team.

The Connecticut Hospice was also the first teaching hospice. Today its John D. Thompson Hospice Institute for Education, Training and Research offers courses, lectures, technical assistance and publications to help train healthcare leaders from around the country in hospice principles and practices.

Connecticut Hospice   **481~6231**
61 Burban Drive, Branford

Visiting Nurse Associations

The Visiting Nursing Associations in Greater New Haven serve people of all ages, providing everything from prenatal to geriatric care. In the comfort and security of the patient's home, they care for people with all kinds of illnesses; people returning from the hospital; people with disabilities needing rehabilitation; people with terminal illnesses; and even people needing help with personal care and household chores. VNA care givers include registered nurses, private duty nurses, home health aides, companions, homemakers, physical and occupational therapists and social workers.

Branford VNA
40 Kirkham Street
Branford 06405
488-8357

Community Care Services
345 Highland Avenue
Cheshire 06410
272-2745

VNA Services of CT
300 Seymour Drive
Derby 06418
734-3340

VNA of Guilford
669 Boston Post Road
Guilford 06437
453-8051

VNA of Madison
560 Durham Road
Madison 06443
245-0436

Milford VNA
16 Dixon Street
Milford 06460
878-5967

VNA of South Central
   Connecticut, Inc.
One Long Wharf
New Haven 06511
777-5521

Regional VNA
1151 Hartford Turnpike
North Haven 06473
288-1623

Orange VNA
525 Orange Center Road
Orange 06477
891-2165

Wallingford VNA
701 Center Street
Wallingford 06492
269-1475

Connecticut Mental Health Center

Each year, the Connecticut Mental Health Center takes care of 5,500 people. Some have serious mental disorders. Some are experiencing a severe crisis in their lives. Others have symptoms which interfere with their day-to-day existence, such as feelings of overwhelming sadness or fear. Some need to deal with drug or alcohol addictions.

Once someone enters treatment at CMHC, a team of mental health professionals—psychiatrists, social workers, psychiatric nurses, and psychologists—plan and guide further care. Most individuals coming for treatment will receive outpatient care with a therapist assigned to them. Many can be helped with medication. Some need community services to help them manage their environment.

At all levels, CMHC offers some of the finest mental health care in the country. CMHC was founded in 1965 as an innovative cooperative partnership between the Yale University School of Medicine and the Department of Mental Health of the State of Connecticut. The hope was that by working together, they could make progress in the treatment of mental illness. Since then, CMHC has become a leader in clinical treatment, professional training and research in mental health care in the state and in the nation.

CMHC offers some of the finest mental health care in the country.

Among its many vanguard programs are its Substance Abuse Treatment Unit, which recently opened a $3.3 million building for research into the causes and treatment of addictions. CMHC's outreach efforts were greatly enhanced when it recently received $4 million to serve New Haven's homeless mentally ill.

To address specific problems and disorders, CMHC also has an Anxiety Clinic, an Obsessive-Compulsive Disorder Clinic, a Clinical Neuroscience Research Unit, and an Hispanic Clinic for the special needs of Spanish-speaking individuals.

At the Consultation Center, programs are aimed at helping many people in the community. These include individuals suffering from or at risk for mental disorders, families of the mentally ill, caregivers for a range of different problems, and those in need of self-help initiatives.

In recent years, CMHC has used its unique position and expertise to help solve problems. For example, the Center brought together representatives of several agencies to develop a task force to deal with specific problems facing high school students.

CMHC also organizes many conferences and workshops which are open to the public. Some are geared to special groups, such as caregivers. Others are designed to educate the public about mental illness. Other efforts, such as a recent conference on domestic violence, have convened diverse groups of professionals to examine special topics.

All services at the Connecticut Mental Health Center are available without regard to one's ability to pay. The Center is an Equal Opportunity Employer.

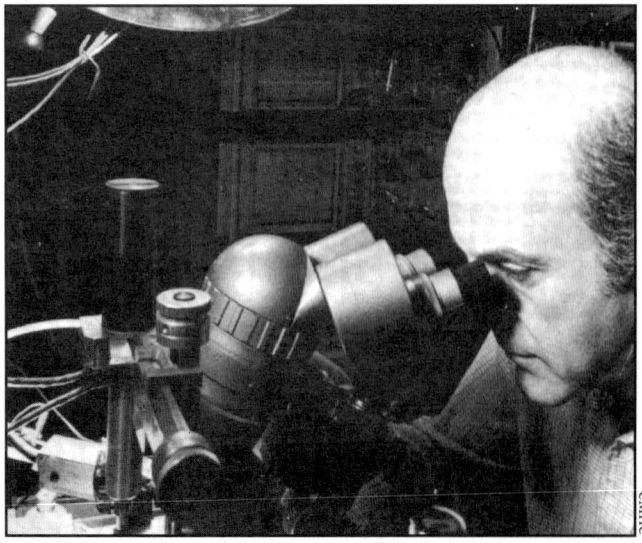

CT Mental Health Center   789-7300
34 Park Street

Research into mental health issues is an important part of CMHC's work to benefit patients in Connecticut and the rest of the nation.

MEDICAL SERVICES
Mental Health Services

Yale Psychiatric Institute

For 60 years, Yale Psychiatric Institute has held a national reputation as a facility specializing in hospital-based treatment of severe mental illness in adolescents and young adults. It is a major component of the Department of Psychiatry at the Yale University School of Medicine and all faculty and staff are appointed by Yale University.

The clinical focus of YPI is to provide evaluation and intensive treatment to patients with serious emotional problems. YPI offers inpatient and outpatient services designed to meet a wide range of patient needs. Services offered include those that treat patients with affective, psychotic and psychosocial disorders, as well as alcohol and drug abuse.

Staffing patterns reflect the needs of patients for secure, comprehensive, individualized treatment. The professional staff includes psychiatrists, psychologists, psychiatric social workers, nurses, recreational, creative arts and occupational therapists, and other mental health workers. Each patient's care is supervised by a senior psychiatrist who oversees the multi-disciplinary treatment team. Staffing for the Outpatient and Community Services Divisions includes medical and non-medical personnel specially trained to facilitate transition of patients from inpatient hospitalization back to community life.

As part of Yale School of Medicine, the Institute supports an active program of research on the causes and treatments of many severe psychiatric disorders, and serves as a major training site for psychiatry residents, psychology fellows and medical, nursing, and social work students. The clinical, academic and research programs of the Institute are integrated to reflect the highest standards of contemporary psychiatric practice in patient care.

YPI supports an active program of research on the causes and treatment of severe psychiatric disorders.

Yale Psychiatric Institute 785~7201
184 Liberty Street

Yale Psychiatric Institute is located in downtown New Haven near Yale-New Haven Hospital and Yale Medical School Complex.

Great Programs & Initiatives in Greater New Haven

The programs described below are a few of the many charitable undertakings in our communities. We have not listed the service organizations, and other charitable activities, such as the United Funds, Red Cross and the many health-related charities, as they are similar to those in other U.S. cities. These few were chosen to represent the wide range of programs which strive to meet the needs of the aged, homeless, young and poor in our area, providing everything from housing and emergency food, to mental health support and drug and alcohol education. A complete listing of such organizations is available from INFOLINE - a 24-hour service of the Southern New England Telephone Company, the United Way and the State of Connecticut. For referral to sources of help, call INFOLINE at 1(800) 203-1234. *(In case of life threatening emergencies, call 911.)*

Habitat for Humanity of New Haven   785-0794
649 Howard Ave., New Haven
José Lewis Bedolla, Executive Director

A nationally recognized house reclamation program, Habitat volunteers restore abandoned or dilapidated houses using donated materials. Prospective owners, who meet low-income parameters, provide their own "sweat equity" as well. The restored property is then purchased by them for less than market value.

FISH Emergency Food Line   481-5681

An emergency food bank and delivery service primarily for the home bound, elderly and disabled. They provide one emergency meal to a person in need every 60 days, and then transfer needy people to other programs, except in special circumstances.

Rachel's Table   387-2424 x325   9-4 Mon-Fri
Sue Rosen, Executive Director

An initiative of the Jewish Federation of Greater New Haven, this food savings program works with caterers, restaurants and food wholesalers throughout the area to salvage useful and nutritious food that would otherwise be wasted; it is redistributed to various soup kitchens and emergency food programs.

City of New Haven ~ Fighting Back   946-8445
165 Church Street, New Haven
Barbara Geller, Project Director

Funded by a major grant from the Princeton-based Robert Wood Johnson Foundation, *Fighting Back* is a community-based prevention program whose goal is "to reduce the demand for drugs and alcohol in the City of New Haven." Their successful grant proposal was one of only 14 chosen out of 300 applications. Block grants to units in community substations of the NH Police Department allow decisions about programming to be made based on local assessments of needs and resources. Self-esteem, cooperation and academic improvement programs are among those funded.

Institute for Learning in Retirement   795-4178
Nancy Sykes, POB 6182, Hamden, CT 06517-0128

The Institute was founded in 1989 to offer alternative learning experiences for older citizens. Most study groups run from 4 to 8 weekly sessions, and any of the 250 members can take courses and submit ideas for courses they wish to teach or coordinate. Albertus Magnus provide free classroom space and clerical support; Quinnipiac College provides mailing help.

Columbus House   773-9673
200 Columbus, New Haven
Skip Ferry, Executive Director

Columbus House is an emergency shelter for the homeless, which opens at 4:30 each afternoon and receives people on a first-come-first-served basis. When the shelter is full, 38 men and 14 women will have a warm supper, a shower, a clean bed for the night, and access to 4 case managers and a Drug and Alcohol counselor during their brief stay, free of charge. At 7:30 in the morning, everyone leaves. The house is staffed by three Residential Supervisors.

L.E.A.P.   773-0770
Leadership, Education & Athletics in Partnership
254 College Street, Suite 501, New Haven
Henry J. Fernandez, Executive Director

LEAP was founded in 1992 as a summer enrichment program for 200 children from poor neighborhoods in New Haven. Now it operates in five neighborhoods in New Haven, and in New London and Hartford, and accommodates 900 youngsters in all. The LEAP summer program provides mentoring counselors who work with small groups of children ages 7-14, and live in their neighborhoods, in unused apartments provided by the City. Each Counselor develops an eight week curriculum based on a model, and designed around weekly themes, with corresponding daily classroom activities, reading books and related field trips. Counselors are drawn from 5 colleges and area high schools, and work in teams, with a Senior and Junior counselor assigned to each group. LEAP participants have access to services of Yale Child Study Center, and continue in the academic enrichment program, now expanded to include an afterschool and weekend program as well.

Vision for a Greater New Haven   782-4310
Heather Calabrese, Project Manager

A unique cooperative brainstorming effort of over 2,000 citizens and volunteers from all walks of life, Vision developed a civic agenda for New Haven. Among the 37 goals articulated and adopted in a series of meetings were: creating an arts/cultural mecca for the region; providing a safe environment with responsive police protection; offering a family and child-friendly city with good resources and support services; enhancing regionalism with local accountability, regional allocation of resources and services, and an equitable tax structure. Citizens interested in Vision can join the action groups which have formed to work on these goals.

GREATER NEW HAVEN
Charitable Organizations

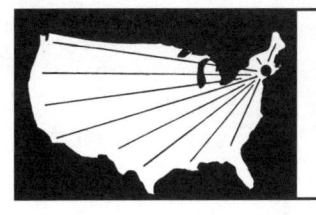

The Community Foundation for Greater New Haven

For 65 years, the Community Foundation for Greater New Haven has helped people to make charitable investments in our communities by contributing gifts and bequests to build permanent endowments. Each year this endowment supports the work of hundreds of people in carrying out important community initiatives and programs. The Foundation is one of the oldest of its kind in the country, and its endowment is probably the largest in relationship to the population of the area it serves.

The Foundation was established in 1928, and now has assets of over $119 million dollars. Since its founding, the Foundation has made grants in the Greater New Haven area totalling $80 million dollars. The endowment consists of over 300 named funds which honor donors and those people who are selected for honor by the donors.

In 1994, the Foundation awarded grants of over $5 million dollars. These ranged from support for small neighborhood projects through the Foundation's *Neighborhood Program*, and grants to particular initiatives such as L.E.A.P. and FISH, Inc. *(see page 278)*, to community-wide projects, like *Health Valley 2,000* in the Lower Naugatuck Valley, and the Visions Project's *Vision for a Greater New Haven*.

Community Foundation   **777-2386**
for Greater New Haven
Alan E. Green, Executive Director
70 Audubon Street, New Haven 06510

Dixwell Community House has served New Haven for over 70 years. "Q" House offers many programs, from educational and recreational activities for children 6-13 (such as homework assistance, one-to-one tutoring, biddy basketball and the Future Executives Club), to teen outreach services, like the *Youth Center*, *Youth Helping Youth* and drug education, plus family education and intervention programs, including *Lifeline Food Distribution*, *Tough Love* and *Workfare*. Membership is open; services are free or low cost. "Q" House accepts donations from members and friends in support of its programs.

Dixwell Community House   **772-2665**
Theodore F. Hogan, Jr., Executive Director
197 Dixwell Avenue, New Haven 06511

JCC's new $12 million dollar, 106,000 sq. ft. facility opened in 1993. People of all races and religions are welcome as members. JCC was established in 1912 in New Haven. The new 54-acre campus offers a multi-purpose recreational, social and fitness program for people of all ages, with handicap-accessible swimming (indoor and out), gyms, racquetball courts, and facilities from a modern fitness center to meeting spaces for 600. Programs range from daycare and afterschool care to basketball, dance, karate and summer camp for ages 2-15. Adult classes, concerts and exhibits are on-going. Membership is open; no one is denied participation due to inability to pay.

Jewish Community Center   **387-2522**
Howard Schultz, Executive Director
360 Amity Road, Woodbridge 06525

The "Y" is a great family facility, with swimming, fitness, childcare, youth sports, camping, and a Nautilus and Healthy Heart Center. Indoor/outdoor pools, tennis courts, and hiking trails make it a natural for people of all ages. Membership is open to all, and fees are based on ability to pay.

YMCA of Hamden/North Haven   **248-6361**
Suzanne Friedbacher, Executive Director
1605 Sherman Avenue, Hamden 06514

St. Peter's Basilica in Vatican City

The restoration of the facade of St. Peter's Basilica, one of Christendom's most important structures, was a Knights of Columbus project.

WORLD HEADQUARTERS
DAUGHTERS OF ISABELLA - FILLES D'ISABELLE

Founded in 1897 as the Knights of Columbus auxiliary, the first Circle of the Daughters of Isabella was formed in New Haven. The Daughters of Isabella has Circles throughout the U.S. and Canada. Present membership is 115,000. Their World Headquarters is located at 375 Whitney Ave. in New Haven. Sharon Carlo is the residential manager.

The thirteen International Board members meet here biennially to conduct their business. The purpose of the Daughters is to unite Catholic women, ages 16 and up, for spiritual benefits and to promote higher ideals within society. They offer a variety of spiritual and social programs to their members.

Daughters of Isabella World Headquarters
375 Whitney Avenue, New Haven
(203) 865-2570

Knights of Columbus Charitable Work

In 1994, members of the Knights of Columbus Orderwide volunteered more than 48.7 million hours of service and contributed $100 million dollars to a variety of charitable causes. Included in that figure is approximately $16.7 million donated by the Supreme Council from the New Haven office. Over the past 10 years, total charitable disbursements amounted to $867 million. Total hours of volunteer service during that same time period is 339,570,882.

For many in the New Haven area, the Special Olympics World Games is a good introduction to what Knights of Columbus volunteerism is all about. The Order has been involved in Special Olympics since its founding in 1968. When New Haven was chosen as the site for the 1995 Games, the Knights of Columbus signed on as one of its chief supporters and volunteer backers. First, the Knights made a $1 million dollar contribution to the Games in early 1994. The Order also pledged to provide upwards of 6,000 volunteers for Knights of Columbus Olympic Town. In addition, the Connecticut State Council of the Knights of Columbus has been the chief organizer of the first-ever Host Town Program, which gives athletes from countries around the world a close-up look at life in over 120 Connecticut cities and towns.

St. Mary's Church at 5 Hillhouse Avenue in New Haven was the site of the founding of the Knights of Columbus by Father McGivney in 1887.

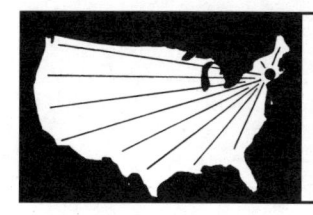

SUPREME COUNCIL HEADQUARTERS
Knights of Columbus

The Knights of Columbus was founded in New Haven in 1882 at St. Mary's Church on Hillhouse Avenue by Father Michael J. McGivney, a Catholic priest. Today, the Knights of Columbus is the world's largest Catholic family organization, with more than 1.5 million members in approximately 10,000 councils (lodges) throughout North America, Mexico, the Caribbean and the Philippines. The international headquarters or Supreme Council office has always been in New Haven.

Portrait of Father McGivney, 1990, by R.W. Whitney

Father McGivney, a native of Waterbury, founded the Knights to help Catholic men remain steadfast in their Catholic faith through mutual encouragement; to promote closer ties of fraternity among them; and to setup an elementary system of insurance so that widows and children of members would be protected.

The name *Knights of Columbus* was chosen to signify that, like knights of old, the group embodied the ideals of spirituality and service to the Catholic Church, their country and their fellowman. The name was also chosen to emphasize that Catholics had been involved in the discovery, exploration and colonization of the North American continent.

By 1905, the Knights of Columbus was deeply rooted in New England, extended along the Atlantic seaboard into Canada, branched west from Quebec to California, and extended south to Florida as well.

The Knights belong to several races and speak many different languages. They are diverse, and yet in their perspective and commitment, they are one. They have dedicated themselves to four ideals: Charity, Unity, Fraternity and Patriotism.

The Supreme Knight: A Modern Leader

After assuming leadership in 1977, Supreme Knight Virgil C. Dechant embarked on a series of projects designed to strengthen the Order, the Catholic Church, the family and the individual members. The visibility of the Knights of Columbus has grown in New Haven, in the Catholic Church and in society in general, as a result of his leadership.

In 1982, during the centennial celebration of the Knights of Columbus, the Order presented a check for $1.2 million to Vatican Secretary of State, Cardinal Agostino Casaroli. This check represented the annual earnings from the Knights of Columbus *Vicarius Christi Fund* established by the Order to help the Holy Father fund his personal charities. Since 1982, more than $20 million dollars have been given to the Pope from this fund, with the corpus of the fund remaining intact.

Support for the Holy Father and the Church Universal takes many forms. At the request of Pope John Paul II, the Knights of Columbus financed the restoration of the facade of St. Peter's Basilica in Vatican City, between 1985 and 1987.

The Order has been especially proud to support the evangelical efforts of the Holy Father, particularly in relation to financing the satellite costs for televising major events from the Vatican, such as the annual Christmas and Easter Masses.

Support for the Catholic Church is a hallmark of Knights of Columbus activity at all levels of the organization. That support takes many forms and ranges from financial support for the varied projects of the national bishops' conferences of the countries where the Order exists, to financial and volunteer support for thousands of local priests in parishes where Knights of Columbus and their families live.

Over the years, the Order has been honored to help Mother Teresa and her Missionaries of Charity. The Order has been similarly honored to promote vocations to the Catholic Church through funds to help recruit and train future priests, sisters and religous.

An important motto of the Knights of Columbus is "*For Brother Knights by Brother Knights*", which is used in reference to the Order's insurance program. Knights of Columbus life insurance and related products are exclusively sold to members of the Order and their families by professionally trained Knights of Columbus insurance agents. The Order's insurance program, with more than $27 billion in force, consistently receives top ratings from Standard & Poors and A.M. Best Company.

Major Employers: Greater New Haven
Below are most of the companies employing 300 or more employees.

Over 5,000 Employees
Yale University	New Haven
Yale-New Haven Hospital	New Haven

1,001 ~ 5,000 Employees
Allegheny Ludlum Steel	Wallingford
Bayer Pharmaceuticals	West Haven
Cytec Industries	Wallingford
So. New England Telephone	New Haven
Griffin Hospital	Derby
Hospital of St. Raphael	New Haven
U.S. Surgical Corporation	North Haven
Blue Cross Blue Shield of CT	North Haven
Pratt Whitney Aircraft	North Haven
United Illuminating Company	New Haven
U.S. Veterans Hospital	West Haven

501 ~ 1,000 Employees
Bic Corporation	Milford
Bristol Myers	Wallingford
Schick Divn. of Warner-Lambert	Milford
Milford Hospital	Milford
Subway Franchise World HQ	Milford
Southern CT State University	New Haven
Olin Corporation	Cheshire
Sargent and Company	New Haven
Knights of Columbus	New Haven
Metro North Railroad	New Haven
Stop & Shop Companies	North Haven
U.S. Repeating Arms Co.	New Haven

300 ~ 500 Employees
Ansonia Copper & Brass	Ansonia
Bank of Boston	New Haven
Fire-Lite Alarms	Northford
New Haven Savings Bank	New Haven
New Haven Register	New Haven
Circuit Wise	North Haven
Echlin, Inc.	Branford
Community Health Care	New Haven
Golf Digest	Trumbull
New Haven Ambulance	New Haven
North East Graphics	North Haven
Lenders Bagel Bakery	West Haven
Marlin Firearms Company	North Haven
Physicians Health Services	Trumbull
Pitney Bowes	Trumbull
Regional Water Authority	New Haven
Sikorsky Aircraft	Trumbull
St. Joseph's Manor	Trumbull
So. New England Telephone	Hamden
So. New England Telephone	North Haven
Starter Sportswear	New Haven
Quinnipiac College	Hamden
University of New Haven	West Haven
Uniroyal Chemical	Bethany
Robby Len Fashions	New Haven

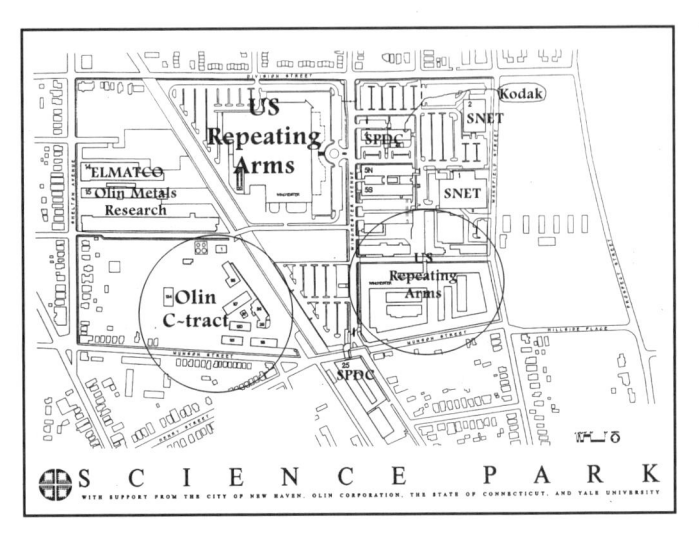

Located conveniently close to the Interstate 91 Trumbull Street interchange (Exit 3), Science Park is a modern building complex offering a unique business and technology community. Over $3 million dollars in new financial resources for customizing space inside the facility are available, to helping growing companies obtain exactly what they need.

U.S. Repeating Arms facility in Science Park opened in 1994. This 300,000 sq. ft. modern office and manufacturing complex, with 600 employees, is a $13 million dollar investment in the future. It incorporates the best ergonomic features and concepts gleaned from other world-class manufacturers and showcases a $25 million dollar investment in new equipment by the firm.

BUSINESS AND INDUSTRY
Science Park

Science Park was established in 1982 on the 80-acre site of the former Winchester Arms manufacturing complex in the Newhallville neighborhood of New Haven.

The key to the future success of Science Park was the donation of the land and old buildings by the Olin Corporation, and Yale University's agreement to provide financial and technical support, including opening Yale's library and computer resources to the proposed tenants.

Science Park was an early entrant into the new concept of "business incubators" which are places where small businesses and start-up companies can find flexible spaces and flexible leases to fit their limited budgets, and meet their future needs for room to expand. Today there are over 500 similar incubator parks around the country.

The park is managed by the Science Park Development Corporation, a non-profit partnership with the State of Connecticut, Yale University, the City of New Haven and its neighborhoods, to develop the former Olin Corporation's 80-acre industrial site into a high-technology park for new and start-up companies.

Today, Science Park has three large established facilities and about 100 small companies in their "incubator" stage. The established companies are U.S. Repeating Arms Corporation in a new 300,000 sq. ft. facility, the Southern New England Telephone Company's 100,000 sq. ft. Customer Support and Training Center, and a division of Kodak.

A dozen new or rehabilitated buildings offer almost a million square feet of laboratory, manufacturing and office space in the Park.

According to Yale President Richard C. Levin: "The University is committed to the success of Science Park, which promotes the economic vitality of the region. The University's contribution of technology as well as human and financial resources form an important part of Yale's on-going partnership with the State of Connecticut, the business community and our neighbors in New Haven. We are eager to pursue the possibilities for a new biomedical park near the Yale School of Medicine which can build upon, and supplement, the successes to date of Science Park."

Since President Levin's statement, the proposed Biomedical Park on the Route 34 Connector has come closer to reality.

For almost 5 years, William W. Ginsburg was the President and moving force behind Science Park's development. He is now Assistant Secretary of the U.S. Department of Commerce.

David C. Driver, new President and CEO of Science Park, sums up his first year as follows: "Among the important events marking this year has been the start of the development process for the Biomedical Park. Science Park is recognized nationally as an example of successful cooperation between the private, public and academic sectors.

David C. Driver, President of Science Park

Science Park Development Corporation
Five Science Park
New Haven, CT 06511   **(203) 786-5000**

MEDIA
Newspapers, Radio, Television

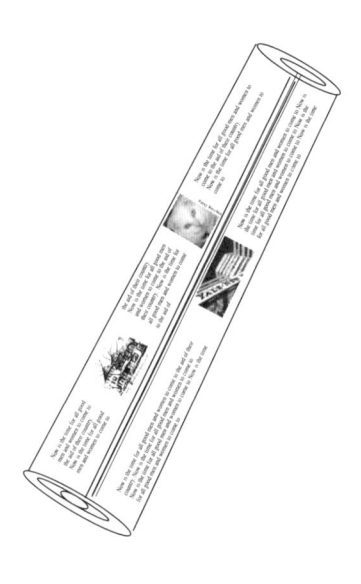

Daily Newspapers

Connecticut Post	410 State Street Bridgeport	(800) 423-8058
New Haven Register	40 Sargent Drive, New Haven	(203) 789-5200
Waterbury Republican American	389 Meadow Street, Waterbury	(203) 574-3636

Weekly & Monthly Newspapers

The Advisor	22 Broadway, North Haven	(203) 239-5404
Beth-wood News	378 Boston Post Road, Orange	(203) 795-0666
Branford Review	230 Main Street, Branford	(203) 488-2353
Connecticut Home and Leisure	284 Racebrook Road, Woodbridge	(203) 799-1658
Connecticut Life	5 Edwards Street, New Haven	(203) 498-5120
Inner City	50 Fitch Street, New Haven	(203) 387-0354
New Haven Advocate	1 Long Wharf, New Haven	(203) 789-0010
Our Town Newspaper	378 Boston Post Road, Orange	(203) 795-0666

Radio

WELI 960 AM	Radio Towers Park, Hamden	(203) 281-9600
WEZN 99.9 FM	10 Middle Street, Bridgeport	(203) 366-9321
WFIF 1500 AM	90 Kay Avenue, Milford	(203) 878-5915
WJMJ 88.9 FM; 107.1 FM	467 Bloomfield Avenue, Bloomfield	(203) 562-7889
WKCI 101.3 FM	Radio Towers Park, Hamden	(203) 248-8814
WNHC 1340 AM	112 Washington Avenue, North Haven	(203) 234-1340
WNHU 88.7 FM	300 Orange Avenue, West Haven	(203) 934-9296
WPLR 99.1 FM	1191 Dixwell Avenue, Hamden	(203) 287-9070
WWYZ 92.5 FM	1 Broadcast Lane, Waterbury	(203) 247-1102
WXCT 1220 AM	473 Denslow Hill Road, Hamden	(203) 288-8282
WYBC 94.3 FM	1191 Dixwell Avenue, Hamden	(203) 432-4118

Television

CT Public Television	20 Lincoln Way, New Haven	(203) 777-7506
Channel 3, WSFB	3 Constitution Plaza, Hartford	(203) 728-3333
Channel 8, WTHN	8 Elm Street, New Haven	(203) 784-8888
Channel 13, BFTV	886 Maple Avenue, Hartford	(203) 956-1303
Channel 18, NHTV	21 Broadway, North Haven	(203) 234-0025
Channel 20, WTXX	Peach Orchard Road, Waterbury	(203) 758-3900
Channel 26, WTWS	216 Broad Street, New London	(203) 444-2626
Channel 28, WNHW	24 Rockdale Road, West Haven	(203) 932-3500
Channel 30, WVIT	1422 New Britian Avenue, Hartford	(203) 789-0801
Chanel 59, WTVU	8 Elm Street, New Haven	(203) 784-8888

Courtesy Laurel Vlock

PEOPLE
Federal & State Judges

Federal Judges

Listed below are Federal judges who reside in Greater New Haven. The office address and telephone number is listed for each federal judge.

UNITED STATES COURT OF APPEALS FOR THE SECOND CIRCUIT

Ralph Winter	55 Whitney Avenue, New Haven 06510	(203) 773-2353
Daniel Mahoney	55 Red Bush Lane, Milford 06460	(203) 878-9370
Guido Calabresi	141 Church Street, New Haven 06510	(203) 773-2291
Jose A. Cabranes	141 Church Street, New Haven 06510	(203) 773-2147

UNITED STATES DISTRICT COURT DISTRICT OF CONNECTICUT

Chief Judge Peter C. Dorsey	141 Church Street, New Haven 06510	(203) 773-2427
Senior Judge Ellen B. Burns	141 Church Street, New Haven 06510	(203) 773-2105
Senior Judge Joan G. Margolis	141 Church Street, New Haven 06510	(203) 773-2350

State of Connecticut Judges

Listed below are State judges who reside in Greater New Haven. The name and community of residence is listed for each state judge.

Supreme Court Justice Robert J. Berdon, Branford
Supreme Court Justice Flemming L. Norcott, Jr., New Haven
Appellate Court Justice Paul M. Fote, Branford
Appellate Court Justice Barry R. Schaller, Madison
Chief Administrative Judge John T. Downey, New Haven
Administrative Judge Barbara A. Coppeto, Milford
Administrative Judge Joseph A. Licari, Jr., New Haven

SUPERIOR COURT JUDGES
Judges are listed by seniority.

Willaim Hadden, Jr., Hamden
JoAnne K. Kulawiz, Orange
Ronald J. Fracasse, Cheshire
George W. Ripley, Shelton
Barbara Coppeto, Milford
Leander C. Gary, New Haven
Joseph A. Licari Jr., North Haven
Joseph B. Clark, New Haven
John J. Ronan, Milford
George N. Thim, Trumbull
Socrates H. Milalakos, Cheshire
Joseph P. Flynn, Ansonia
Richard Damiani, North Haven
Karen Nash Sequino, New Haven
Thomas Corradino, Branford
Thomas V. O'Keefe, Jr., No. Branford

Joseph T. Gormley Jr., Trumbull
Michael Hartmere, Milford
Robert C. Flanagan, East Haven
Leonard M. Cocco, Trumbull
Beverly J. Hodgson, New Haven
Edward J. Leavitt, West Haven
Sidney Axelrod, Madison
Bruce W. Thompson, Branford
Elaine Gordon, Branford
Hadley W. Austin, Madison
Clarance J. Jones, Madison
Jon C. Blue, Hamden
Christine S. Vertefeuille, Cheshire
Ronald D. Fasano, North Haven
Patrick J. Clifford, Madison
Joseph H. Pellegrino, Hamden

John W. Moran, Milford
Jonathan E. Silbert, Guilford
Bruce L. Levin, Orange
Linda K. Lager, Woodbridge
Patty Jenkins Pittman, Hamden
Robert J. Devlin, Jr., Guilford
Jon M. Alander, Hamden
David W. Skolnick, Woodbridge

SUPERIOR COURT SENIOR JUDGES
Howard F. Zoarski, Branford
Martin L. McKeever, Orange
Jerrold H. Barnett, Bethany
Robert P. Burns, Branford

1994-1995 New Haven Board of Aldermen

26: Moakley   20: Smith
24: McCormack   3: Dawson   23: Brooker   7: Armmand
1: Civin   25: Ahern   15: E. Perez   16: Avila   13: Astarita   6: Krevit
19: Gallo   17: Naclerio   5: Perez   29: Goldfield   27: Voigt
4: Reyes   8: DeLauro   2: Martson   10: Schmalz   22: Rogers
18: Piscottano   14: Kroogman   28: Braffman
Not Pictured: 9: Pakutka   11: Lampo   12: Grasso   21: Rev. Marks   30: Moore

PEOPLE
1994~95 Aldermanic Board

The Aldermanic Board meets the first and third Monday of every month, except holidays, in the aldermanic chamber, 165 Church Street, second floor. During the summer, the Board meets the first Monday of the month.

Joshua I. Civin (1~D)
P.O. Box 200954, 06520-0954
436-2366

Olivia Martson (2~D)
228 Dwight St., 06511-4505
787-3638

Anthony Dawson (3~D)
24 Ann St., 06519-1202
787-0677

Tomás Reyes Jr. (4~D)
President
56 Redfield St., 06519-1208
776-8444

Jorge Perez (5~D)
391 Howard Ave., 06519-2407
562-4373

Rita Krevit (6~D)
18 Tower Ln., Apt. 754, 06519-1764
562-2246

Esther Armmand (7~D)
111 Park St., Apt. 7-R, 06511-5455
624-4587; 782-1106

Luisa DeLauro (8~D)
95 Olive St., 06510-4905
865-8052; 777-4880

John R. Pakutka (9~D)
460 Humphrey St., #6, 06511-3761
772-3303

Robert N. Schmalz (10~D)
110 Linden St., 06511-2425
562-7233; 772-7713

Gaetano J. Lampo (11~D)
120 Dell Dr., 06513-1706
468-8955

Frank Grasso Jr. (12~D)
1426 Quinnipiac Ave., 06513-1739
467-8304

Sandra Astarita (13~R)
140 Summit St., 06513-4103
467-5609

Robin I. Kroogman (14~D)
19 Perkins St., 06513-3210
773-3259

Eduardo Perez (15~D)
138 Monroe St., 06513-3036
782-1992

Raul Avila (16~D)
200 Blatchley Ave., 06513-3805
782-0751

Matt Naclerio (17~D)
508B Woodward Ave., 06512-1965
468-8404; 495-7555

Ann Piscottano (18~R)
21 Ira St., 06512-3919
466-0644

George D. Gallo (19~R)
500 Prospect St., #4F, 06511-2166
787-5511; 776-9222

Ron Smith (20~D)
45 Butler St., 06511-1836
773-9177

Rev. Scott Marks (21~D)
487 Dixwell Ave., 06511-1704
787-9372

Stanley Rogers (22~D)
201 Winchester Ave., 06511-3505
776-0645

Alvis D. Brooker (23~D)
31 Batter Terr., 06511-5205
776-9759

Elizabeth McCormack (24~D)
66 Pendleton St., 06511-4309
387-5495

Nancy V. Ahern (25~R)
295 West Rock Ave., 06515-2130
387-2977

David Moakley (26~D)
250 Kohary Dr., 06515-2419
397-1275

Philip Voigt (27~D)
28 Pelham Ln., 06511-2855
387-3421

Elaine A. Braffman (28~D)
222 Cotony Rd., 06511-1622
562-9494

Carl Goldfield (29~D)
25 Roydon Rd., 06511-2806
782-2064

Willie J. Moore (30~D)
21 Valley Pl. N., 06515-1224
389-0075

State Senate

Legislative Office Building, Hartford 06106-1591
Democrats 240-8600; (800) 842-1420; TDD 240-0164
Repulicans 240-8800; (800) 842-1421; TDD 240-0163

State House

Legislative Office Building, Hartford 06106-1591
Democrats 240-8500; (800) 842-1902; TDD 240-0160
Repulicans 240-8700; (800) 842-1423; TDD 240-0161

State Senators

District	Senator	Party	Mailing Address	Home Phone
10	Toni Nathaniel Harp	D	26 Lynwood Place, New Haven 06511	865-2232
11	Martin M. Looney	D	132 Fort Hale Road, New Haven 06512	468-8829
12	William A. Aniskovich	R	15 Grove Avenue, Branford 06405	483-9280
14	Win Smith, Jr.	R	334 Edgefield Avenue, Milford 06460	878-1486
15	Thomas F. Upson	R	827 Oronoke Road, #10-1, Waterbury 06708	753-1193
17	Joseph J. Crisco, Jr.	D	1205 Racebrook Road, Woodbidge 06525	389-8788
21	George L. Gunther	R	890 Judson Place, Stratford 06497	378-8572
22	Lee Scarpetti	R	319 Whitney Avenue, Trumbull 06611	268-9856
34	Brian McDermott	D	359 North Elm Street, Wallingford 06492	294-9198

State Representatives

District	Representative	Party	Mailing Address	Home Phone
83	James W. Abrams	D	91 Midland Drive, Meriden 06450	237-9646
85	Mary M. Mushinsky	D	188 South Cherry Street, Wallingford 06492	269-8378
86	Robert M. Ward	R	817 Totoket Road, Northford 06472	484-0339
87	Curtis D. Andrews, Jr.	R	5 Rainbow Court, Hamden 06514	281-1357
88	Nancy Beals	D	255 Ridgewood Avenue, Hamden 06517	248-3243
89	Vicki Orsini Nardello	D	8 Laurel Lane, Prospect 06712	758-5888
90	Mary G. Fritz	D	43 Grove Street, Wallingford 06492	269-1169
91	Peter F. Villano	D	133 Armory Street, Hamden 06517	562-5251
92	Patricia A. Dillon	D	68 West Rock Avenue, New Haven 06515	387-9798
93	Howard A. Scipio	D	30 Bellevue Road, New Haven 06511	562-9233
94	William R. Dyson	D	196 Mansfield Street, New Haven 06511	777-3460
95	John S. Martinez	D	40 Sea Street, New Haven 06519	624-9321
96	Cameron C. Staples	D	102 Nash Street, New Haven 06511	773-9123
97	Chris DePino	R	20 Ira Street, New Haven 06512	467-9306
98	Patricia Widitz	D	160 Deer Lane, Guilford 06437	453-9924
99	Michael P. Lawlor	D	3 Atwater Street, East Haven 06512	469-9725
101	Peter Metz	R	99 Bishop Lane, Madison 06443	245-2219
102	Dominic A. Buonocore	R	9 Brainerd Road, Branford 06405	488-8109
103	Lucien A. DiMeo	R	531 Wintergreen Avenue, Hamden 06514	248-6066
104	Vincent J. Tonucci	D	26 Fairview Terrace, Derby 06418	734-5206
105	John W. Betkoski	D	54 Munson Road, Beacon Falls 06403	729-5727
112	William J. Varese	R	21 Benedict Road, Monroe 06468	261-8598
113	Richard O. Belden	R	14 Keron Drive, Shelton 06484	924-1757
114	Ellen Scalettar	D	1265 Racebrook Road, Woodbridge 06525	387-2388
115	Stephen D. Dargan	D	215 Beach Street, #1-G, West Haven 06516	937-1985
116	Louis P. Esposito, Jr.	D	56 Lakeview Avenue, West Haven 06516	397-8588
117	Raymond V. Collins, Jr.	R	6 Morris Street, West Haven 06516	933-2428
118	James A. Amann	D	515 Popes Island Road, Milford 06460	783-1910
119	Richard Roy	D	43 Howe Street, Milford 06460	878-8030
120	J. Vincent Chase	R	Whippoorwill Lane, Stratford 06497	375-2063
121	Terrence E. Backer	D	125 Jefferson Street, Stratford 06497	378-8399
122	Lawrence G. Miller	R	60 Peace Arce Lane, Stratford 06497	377-1523
123	Dale W. Radcliffe	R	4 George Street, Trumbull 06611	452-0855
133	Paul Martin Tymniak	R	225 Whites Hill Lane, Fairfield 06430	259-9604
134	John E. Stone, Jr.	R	195 Carroll Road, Fairfield 06430	225-4661

GREATER NEW HAVEN
More People...who help make us "Great"

This section of the book presents more of the people who make a significant contribution to the overall quality of life in the greater New Haven area. Over 500 people in our area are listed in Marquis Who's Who in America. *This concentration of "notables", compared to our size, is probably greater than anywhere else in the country. Information about people who are included in any other part of the book is not repeated here. Page numbers refer the reader to further information or photos. Because of space limitations, most prominent Yale scientists and scholars are not included here. Yale's various deans and high officers are found in the separate Yale section of the book. This list could not include most clergy, doctors, dentists, lawyers, accountants and other professionals who practice in the Greater New Haven area. Those who are shown are included here because of their activities outside of their professions. Also omitted are hundreds of fine educators at our many schools, colleges and universities. The only government officials included are our Congresswoman, the Senator who lives in our area, and the Mayors in the Communities Section. Our Judges, State Senators, Representatives, and New Haven's Aldermanic Board are listed on separate pages. The Presidents and CEOs of major local industries were included, based on the size of their companies, in recognition of the many people who are employed by them. We tried to select a broad cross-section of men and women from all walks of life to represent the many hundreds of people who help enhance the quality of life in our communities and show the wide range of caring and involved citizens who live and work in greater New Haven. We know there are many worthy people who have been left out, who well deserve this public recognition. If you feel someone has been left out of this section who should be included in our next edition, please let us know by completing and returning the form at the end of this book. We hope you enjoy meeting some of the people who help make greater New Haven truly "A Great Place To Live, Work, Study and Visit."*

Francis "Fran" Adams, Jr.
Fran Adams is District Director at Merrill-Lynch, Past President of the New Haven Symphony Orchestra, and the force behind the founding of the Symphony's Steinert Society.

Michael Adanti
President of Southern Conn. State University. *(See page 225.)*

Josef & Cecle Adler
A stockbroker at Prudential Securities, Joe Adler and his wife Cecle are constantly active in Jewish Community affairs, and are major fundraisers for the JCC, ADL,& UJA.

Jean Adnopoz
Past Member of the Executive Committee of Yale-New Haven Hospital, Jean Adnopoz is also an Associate Clinical Professor at Yale Child Study Center, and founder and director (1977-1985) of the Coordinating Council for Children in Crisis. She is chairwoman of the Prevention Committee of *Fighting Back*, and on the National Crime Prevention Council. Jean is a child advocate and author on caring for AIDS children and their families.

Melinda Agsten
A partner at Wiggin and Dana, she is a founder of WOWPAC, a women's political action group.

Bryan Anderson
As Executive Director of the New Haven Housing Authority, Bryan Anderson controls one of the largest public budgets in the City. He is a former New Haven development administrator, and ran Hamden's Development Office as well.

Thomas Appelquist
Dean of the Yale Graduate School of Arts & Sciences. *(See p. 240.)*

Mary & Robert Arnstein
Mary Arnstein was the first woman on the Board of the Water Company, and the second on the Board of the Yale-New Haven Hospital. She was a special assistant to Kingman Brewster when he was Yale's President. Mary is a tireless and effective fundraiser, specializing on capital campaigns, and public relations. Her husband Robert is a Clinical Professor of Psychiatry at Yale.

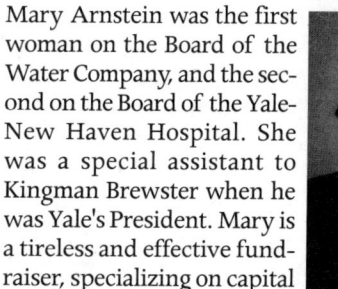

Judith Baldwin
Director of RCEE/ACES, a special ed program, and past President of the Arts Council, she is a former majority leader of the Board of Alderman, active with the Community Loan Fund, United Way and United Church on the Green.

Arthur Barbieri
Democratic Town Chairman, he has been involved in the New Haven political scene for over 35 years.

Nobel Barker
Artistic Director of the New Haven Ballet. *(See page 89.)*

Myrna Fenn Baskin
With 30 years experience in administration, fund-raising and counseling in music, education and community service, Myrna Baskin serves on many boards, including the Symphony, Shubert, Friends of Music (at Yale), and the New Haven Public Education Fund. She was active in the Arts Council, on the boards of Yale Art Gallery and the New Haven Chorale, served as Director of Development at Hopkins (1976-1984) and was Assistant Director of Family Relocation for New Haven's Redevelopment Agency. Myrna was a YWCA's *Women in Leadership* honoree.

Paul Bass
Award-winning political reporter for *The New Haven Advocate*, and editor of the former *Independent*, Paul Bass is known for his in-depth knowledge of New Haven, and his willingness to take a stand on the issues. *(See Paul's article in the Neighborhood Section.)*

David & Ruthann Beckerman
Strongly committed to our community, Ruthann and David Beckerman, President of *Starter, Inc.*, a sportswear and sports accessories manufacturing company in New Haven.

Richard Bell
Dick Bell is a partner at Tyler, Cooper & Alcorn, and immediate past Chairman of the Community Foundation for Greater New Haven. He is a past Chairman of the Chamber of Commerce of Greater New Haven, and a well-known New Haven booster. Dick contributes his energy, warmth and enthusiasm

Harry Berkowitz
President of Yale Co-op, an unusual college emporium, and New Haven's largest department store. *(See page 264.)*

Bruno Bich
Chairman and CEO of The Bic Corporation, a Fortune 500 pen manufacturing company, and major employer in Milford.

Richard Bowerman
One of the most accomplished leaders in our region, Richard Bowerman, a senior corporate lawyer, became head of Southern Connecticut Gas Company in 1970s. He is the conscience of the business community, and a leading volunteer with the Chamber of Commerce and the Community Foundation.

Eleanor Boyd
A special education teacher and supervisor for the Board of Education since 1985, Eleanor Boyd works to improve our public schools. She also serves as President of "Q" House.

Richard H. Brodhead
The Dean of Yale College. *(See page 239.)*

Allan Bromley
Yale Dean of Engineering.

Theodore L. Brooks
Ted Brooks, a newly appointed Bishop, is long-time, respected pastor of Beulah Heights Pentecostal Church, where he focuses on "the wholeness of the family structure." He serves on the Vision Steering Committee, and on the Board of Yale New Haven Hospital, and sums up his beliefs in the African proverb: "It takes a whole village to raise one child."

Arvin Brown
For 28 years, Arvin Brown has been Artistic Director of the Long Wharf Theatre. Many of his productions go on to Broadway and London. His range, from Shakespeare to contemporary drama, attracts many fine actors who want to work with the company. *(See pages 72-73.)*

Bill Brown
Director and guiding spirit of the Eli Whitney Museum, Bill Brown has enriched the lives of kids of all ages. His intelligent programming offers rich opportunities for experiential learning, using many scientific media such as water, electricity, tool making, and trains, presented with flair and contagious enthusiasm for learning and discovery. *(See page 23.)*

Bill Brown
An innovative and exciting jazz performer, Bill Brown is also a composer of vitality and versatility. He informs his work with an intense personal style. He shares his musical gifts by teaching theory, jazz history, jazz and piano at Neighborhood Music School in New Haven.

Elizabeth Mills Brown
Author of *New Haven: A Guide to Architecture & Urban Design*, published by Yale University Press.

Gerard N. Burrow
Dean of the Yale School of Medicine. *(See page 242.)*

Mary Jane Burt
President and CEO of Burt Labs, a medical laboratory headquartered in Hamden, with branches throughout the area, Mary Jane Burt volunteers on many community boards.

David J. Butler
Editor of *The New Haven Register*.

Guido Calabresi & Anne Tyler Calabresi
This "dynamic duo" are great role models. Guido Calabresi, who immigrated from Italy to New Haven just prior to WWII, is former Dean of the Yale Law School. In 1995, he was appointed a Federal Judge to the 2nd Circuit Court of Appeals. His wife, Anne Tyler Calabresi, whose ancestors are among the original New Haven settlers, is the co-founder of Leadership, Education & Athletics in Partnership (LEAP), an inspired program of intervention to prevent school failure and social problems among inner city youth, which has received several awards.

Robert Cavanaugh
Managing partner of Wiggin & Dana, Robert Cavanaugh is a strong supporter of a wide variety of "happenings" in town, and an outstanding duck pin bowler.

Henry "Sam" Chauncey, Jr.
The former Secretary of Yale, Sam Chauncey is active in the arts and education. Sam is known everywhere in town. He was one of the people involved in founding Science Park, and served as its first President. He is past President of Gaylord Hospital in Wallingford.

Frances "Bitsie" Clark
Past President of the APT Foundation, Bitsie Clark is Executive Director of the Arts Council of Great New Haven, and serves on the boards of the United Way, Chamber of Commerce, and Vision for a Greater New Haven. A strong and effective advocate for the arts and other worthy community causes, Bitsie is hard working, focused, organized, and she knows everyone! *(See page 66.)*

Gerald S. Clark
Long-time force behind the Dixwell business community, Gerald Clark founded a successful insurance agency that still carries his name. In the 1960s, he helped develop the Dixwell Plaza concept for inner-city retailing, and also helped to found the Greater New Haven Business and Professional Assn. He was part of the team that began Science Park Development Corporation in the early 1980s, and is a past Director of the Chamber of Commerce.

Katrina Clark
Executive Director of the Fair Haven Clinic, Katrina Clark exemplifies caring and concern for our community.

Jared L. Cohon
Dean of the Yale School of Forestry & Environmental Studies. *(See page 247.)*

John Colleran
A long time New Havener and attorney, John Colleran is a Hillhouse High School graduate, and a Yale College and Law school graduate. He is a member of the New Haven Symphony Orchestra Board, and a past member of the Board of the Bank of New Haven. John is a Moderator of North Haven Town Meetings.

Leo Connors
The President of Founders Bank, and Board member of the Hospital of St. Raphael's, Leo Connors helps support a wide range of community activities.

Carmen Cozza
Coach of Yale's football team, the *Bulldogs*. *(See page 252.)*

John Crawford
President of the Regional Water Authority, John Crawford can be counted on to "come through" for our area. His exemplary management of United Way campaigns is a model of giving in action. John is active with the Hospital of St. Raphael and the Guilford Interfaith Housing Corp. He is a leading expert on regionalism, and one of its strongest advocates. He is the past chairman of the Regional Leadership Council and serves as its Director.

Joseph Crespo
President of Southern Connecticut Gas Company, he is also involved in the Regional Leadership Council.

Sumner & Sue Crosby
Sumner Crosby is a retired insurance executive and the Director of the Carolyn Foundation, a large family trust that consistently supports New Haven causes. His wife Sue is an avid gardener, active in the Garden Club of New Haven.

James J. Cullen
President & CEO of the Hospital of St. Raphael's. *(See page 283.)*

Elizabeth "Betty" Curren
A 1992 Distinguished Alumna of the University of New Haven, the first woman so honored, and a recipient of the YWCA "Women in Leadership" Award in 1987, Betty Curren can be found on most evenings all dressed up with someplace special to go. As the *New Haven Register's* Society Columnist, she captures in her column and with her camera, the flavor of the most exciting activities in town, from cultural events to fund-raising galas. If your party is "what's happening", it will be in Betty's column.

John Daniels
Former Mayor of New Haven. *(See page 130.)*

Virgil Dechant
Supreme Knight of the Knights of Columbus. *(See page 296.)*

Luisa DeLauro
Luisa DeLauro is known as "the Mayor of Wooster Square", which is her constituency, and her home for over 45 years. She was the first woman to serve on New Haven's Aldermanic Board, and is active in the Democratic party.

Rosa DeLauro
Like her mother, Luisa, Rosa DeLauro is a respected and popular politician, serving her second term as the Democratic Congresswoman from the 3rd District. Once a key aid for former Mayor Frank Logue, then the strategist who helped catapult Chris Dodd to his Senate seat in 1980, Rosa is married to President Clinton's chief pollster, Stanley Greenberg. Rosa knows New Haven, its people and its neighborhoods, and isn't afraid to speak on their behalf. She is a responsive representative with a long history of service to our area.

Fred DeLuca
As a local-boy-made-good, Fred DeLuca is founder and CEO of Subway, Inc., world's fastest growing franchise. Subway Inc. has 10,400 locations internationally, with new sites opening daily. In addition to the 500 people employed at the Milford Headquarters of the firm, Fred has helped to create jobs for 100,000 people worldwide, through his franchisees.

MORE PEOPLE...
Who help make us "Great"

Lawrence DeNardis
President of the University of New Haven. *(See page 231.)*

John DeStefano, Jr.
Mayor of New Haven. *(See page 4.)*

Biagio "Ben" DiLieto
Former Mayor of New Haven. *(See page 130.)*

David C. Driver
CEO and President of Science Park. *(See page 300.)*

Edwin Richardson Edmonds
The Reverend Edwin Edmonds was the pastor of the Dixwell Congregational Church for 35 years. His concerns for a better world has earned him many important honors, including awards from the NAACP, the Urban League of Greater New Haven, the Distinguished Community Service Award, Man of the Year from the United Negro College Fund and the Jefferson Award. He also received an Honorary Doctorate of Letters Degree from Quinnipiac College. Retired Emeritus from his Church in 1994, he is a role model for young people of all races.

Jonathan Einhorn
An attorney, former Alderman from Westville, and the leading Republican spokesman in town.

Louise Endel
A community activist for four decades, Louise Endel has used her vibrant energy to make a difference. Active in a wide range of endeavors, including Habitat for Humanity, Fellowship House, Hospital of St. Raphael's Foundation, Dixwell Community House, the YWCA, the Urban League, ISIS, Sage Services, Long Wharf Theatre, Artspace and Creative Arts Workshop, Louise was "the driving force" behind First Night, the Nine Squares Neighborhood Youth Leagues, City Spirit Artists, and Hello New Haven. Her current focus is LEAP.

James Farnam
A senior partner in Holt, Wexler, Farnam, Jim Farnam is a major grant-getter for the greater New Haven community, and a key consultant to a wide range of organizations.

Angel Fernandez-Chavero
One of the young talents in the region, Angel came to New Haven from Los Angeles to attend Yale and stayed on to become a leader in the redevelopment of the city. Executive Director of the Local Initiative Support Corporation, a national non-profit that helps community-based groups, Angel also worked for the City's office of Neighborhood and Housing, and the Hill Development Corporation.

Tom Ficklin 
CEO and editor/publisher of INNER CITY, Tom Ficklin's voice is heard loud and clear. A Brown University alum, he formed Pennfield Communications to reach new city audiences, with his newsy, down-to-earth reporting on local politics, cultural events and people.

Susan Fowler
General Secretary of Dwight Hall, umbrella organization for many of Yale's community service projects. *(See page 260.)*

Lewis Freifeld
President and General Manager of WTNH-TV Channel 8 in New Haven.

Edward Fusco & Lynn Fusco 
Ed Fusco owns the Fusco Corporation, a major construction company at Long Wharf's Maritime Center, built by the company. He is semi-retired. Lynn Fusco, Ed's daughter and the Marketing Director of the company, serves on many boards, such as the New Haven Development Commission, the Regional Leadership Council, and the Shubert. The innovative "adopt a school" program they started has meant a long-term commitment of the Fusco Corporation to Hillhouse High School, and the participation of eight other area companies who also adopted schools in New Haven.

Howard Fussiner 
Howard Fussiner, an artist and educator for 35 years, has exhibited in over 70 one-man art shows. He has won awards in major exhibitions. He taught at Southern Connecticut State University, retiring as Professor Emeritus in 1988. Howard joined an art mentoring program for inner-city youth through the Life Enrichment Activities Program in the late 1960s. His style has been called "an exuberance of light-soaked color" and examples of his work may be found in many local private collections, institutions and museums.

Murray & Suzanne Gallant
Murray and Suzanne Gallant are dedicated, community-minded people who actively and generously support many of greater New Haven's institutions and activities.

Barbara Geller and Thayer "Ted" Baldwin
Barbara Geller and her husband Ted Baldwin, an attorney, are politically savvy Wooster Square residents who have spent much of their lives in the public arena. Barbara is a community activist, and organizer who is also the Director of the anti-drug initiative, F*ighting Back*. *(See page 278.)*

Christopher Getman
Known as "Mr. Sports", Chris Getman is involved in everything from our hometown "AA" baseball club, the *Ravens*, to the summer Volvo tennis tournament. Chris is also the guardian of Handsome Dan, Yale's mascot bulldog.

Gary R. Ginsberg
A West Haven attorney with a long record of civic activity in greater New Haven, Gary Ginsberg is past President of the Jewish Home for the Aged, and currently Chairman of the Board of Trustees of the Hospital of Saint Raphael.

Melanie Ginter and John Lapides
Melanie Ginter is a practicing psychologist, and President of the New Haven Preservation Trust. She was also President of The Yale Club. Her husband, John Lapides, is the President of United Aluminum Corporation, a North Haven manufacturing company founded by his family.

Lindy Lee Gold

Vice President of Milford Travel Agency, Lindy Lee Gold has always found time to serve. She has been a member of many local boards, including Jewish Federation, the Jewish Community Center, and Fellowship House, for which she obtained a Community Development Block Grant. She also founded Cornerstone, a half-way house and served as its first president.

John F. Gontero

Senior New Haven partner of Coopers & Lybrand, John Gontero is immediate past Chairman of the Chamber of Commerce. He was also Chairman of the South Central Connecticut Chapter of the Red Cross, the Ben Hogan Connecticut Open, and Business Volunteers for the Arts.

William "Pete" Gray

Known as "Mr. Dixwell", Pete Gray has run the Dixwell Development and Neighborhood Corporations for as long as most people can remember. A strong fighter for the improved welfare and growth of the Dixwell neighborhood, Pete is active in local politics and as a leader of the community development corporation movement in the city.

Alan E. Green

The Executive Director of the Community Foundation for Greater New Haven, Alan Green brings to his work a long history of involvement in community building, and his experience as Associate Director of the Hartford Foundation for Public Giving. A graduate of the University of Hartford and the UCONN School of Law, he is also an adjunct professor at UCONN, where he teaches non-profit management.

Harold and Carole Greenbaum

Harold Greenbaum is the President of Wayside Furniture of Milford, Inc., which was founded by Carole's father, Yale Rubin, known for giving his "YALE" vanity license plate to Yale University. Carole and Harold are known throughout the area as loyal supporters of many of our most important cultural activities and institutions.

Alvin D. Greenberg

Alvin Greenberg is a neurosurgeon who trained at Yale and at London's National Hospital. He is the developer and President of Temple Medical Center, and also Chairman of Temple Surgical Center. Alvin is the President of the New Haven Medical Assn, and on the board of the New Haven Regional Advisory Board. He is the President of the Jewish Federation of Greater New Haven, and is on the board of the Shubert Performing Arts Center, and Quinnipiac College.

Stanley Greenberg

Stanley Greenberg is President Clinton's key political pollster, and is married to Democratic Congresswoman, Rosa DeLauro. Stan recently wrote *"Middle Class Dreams: The Politics and Power of the New American Majority"*, in 1995. Stan is a Miami University and Harvard alum, earning a Ph.D. there in Government in 1971. Stan was a Guggenheim Fellow, research associate at Yale, and co-ordinator of politics and human rights research for the Rockefeller Foundation. His firm specializes in surveys and polling to advance public issues.

Elinor Gregory

The Executive Director of the Greater New Haven Convention & Visitors Bureau, Elinor Gregory says that she has the best job in town! She loves welcoming visitors to New Haven and our region. Elinor serves on the board of the Chamber of Commerce, the VNA of South Central Connecticut, the Milford Fine Arts Council, and is past Chairwoman of Connecticut Tourism Association. *(See page 6.)*

Thomas Griggs

President of Creative Arts Workshop. *(See page 82.)*

Stuart and Velma Grodd

Philanthropists and community builders, Stuart and Velma Grodd have long given support to many important causes and institutions. Stuart was instrumental in launching the capital campaign for the new Jewish Community Center in Woodbridge. His multi-generational roofing company has an international clientele.

Richard Grossi

CEO of United Illuminating, Richard Grossi is Chairman of the Regional Leadership Council. He is a hard-working member of the community, always ready to participate in projects for the benefit of others.

Bonita Grubbs

Director of Christian Community Action.

Jean Handley

Long active in community affairs, Jean Handley was the first woman Vice President at SNET, and served on the Board of Long Wharf as Vice President of Long Range Planning. She is now involved in an exciting new project, the International Festival of Arts and Ideas, which is in the planning stages for the Summer 1996.

Dennis Hart

Director, Youth Fair Chance Grant, and former Director of Latino Youth.

Robert A. Haversat

President and CEO of ESSTAR Inc., a major architectural hardware manufacturing firm and parent company of Sargent. Robert Haversat is a graduate of Quinnipiac College and one of its major supporters.

More People... Who help make us "Great"

Richard Hegel
Richard Hegel and his favorite collaborator, Floyd Shumway, are the local "dons" of New Haven history. For details of their long-time collaboration, see write up and picture under Floyd Shumway in this section.

Betsy Henley-Cohn
President, CEO, and daughter of the late founder of Joseph Cohn & Sons Inc., an industrial painting contractor, Betsy Henley-Cohn is an active participant in the life of the city, and has served on many boards. She is engaged to Congressman Sam Gejdenson, from the 2nd Congressional District.

Linda Hershman
Vice President for External Affairs for SNET, Attorney Linda Hershman is an important figure in both the Volvo and SNET Women's Classic tennis tournaments.

Douglas Higgins
As the Executive Director of The United Way of Greater New Haven, Douglas Higgins helps many of our most important programs obtain the funding they need.

Leon Hirsch
President & CEO of U.S. Surgical Company, a major medical supply manufacturer, with a large plant in North Haven.

Jeanne J. and Ted Hogan
A former telephone company executive and senior mayoral aide, Ted Hogan is the President of "Q" House, and also a past Board member of the Community Foundation for Greater New Haven. His wife, Jeanne, served on the boards of the Connecticut Human Rights Commission, the New Haven Foundation, the New Haven Board of Education, and Yale-New Haven Hospital. She also served on the Board of Finance for the City of New Haven for 17 years, through three administrations. Jeanne is active with St Luke's Episcopal Church.

John Hogan, Jr.
A New Haven attorney active in community affairs, and the counsel for the Greater New Haven Chamber of Commerce.

Paul James
President of Pirelli Armstrong Tire Corporation until 1992, Paul James now devotes himself to non-profit work. Music is his special interest. He is active in the Great Connecticut Traditional Jazz Festival, and plays the tuba in a 10-piece Roaring '20s style hot jazz band.

Barbara Johnson
A Senior Vice President with People's Bank, Barbara Johnson was recently elected Chairwoman of the Board of the Greater New Haven Chamber of Commerce. She is the first woman to serve the organization in its top leadership position.

Birgitta Johnson
Birgitta Johnson, a senior executive with Bank of Boston, is the new President of the Quinnipiack Club. She is the first woman to head the "Q" Club in its long history.

Paul Johnson
President & CEO of Gaylord Hospital, Paul Johnson is the former Chairman of the Downtown Council, and former President of the old Connecticut Savings Bank. A key fund-raiser for many community capital campaigns, he is also past President of the Tennis Foundation of Connecticut.

Edward "Ted" Kennedy, Jr.
Ted Kennedy is on the Executive Committee of the 1995 Special Olympics World Summer Games, and works for Very Special Arts, an arts organization for people with disabilities. He was Executive Director of *Facing The Challenge*, a non-profit advocacy and public policy office on disability-related issues. He is a teaching fellow on disability policy at the JFK School of Government at Harvard. Ted is married to Katherine Kennedy, a Clinical Professor of Psychiatry at Yale Medical School.

Charles & Gretchen Kingsley
A senior partner with the law firm of Wiggin & Dana, Charles Kingsley is Chairman of the Executive Committee of the New Haven Symphony Orchestra. His wife Gretchen is President of the Investment Strategy Institute. Together they have a long history of involvement in community activities and worthy causes.

Fred Koetter
Dean of the Yale School of Architecture. *(See page 244.)*

Judith B. Krauss
Dean of the Yale School of Nursing. *(See page 246.)*

Anthony T. Kronman
Dean of the Yale Law School. *(See page 241.)*

Elizabeth "Betty" Kubler
Betty is an all around arts activist. She considers it a "great privilege" to have worked for the many organizations she has helped, including the New Haven Symphony, the Neighborhood Music School, the Arts Council, City Spirit Artists, the New Haven Chorale and Long Wharf Theatre, which she helped found in 1965.

Ezra Laderman
Dean of the Yale School of Music. *(See page 245.)*

John Lahey
President, Quinnipiac College. *(See page 228.)*

Ruth & Robert Lapides
Ruth and Bob Lapides are arts benefactors and patrons of New Haven's cultural life. Bob is the Chairman of United Aluminum Corporation in North Haven. Ruth is a painter and sculptor whose Tree of Life wall sculpture was recently installed at the Father McGivney Cancer Center.

Henry Lee
Henry Lee was born in China, speaks six languages and is a gourmet cook. He was a police Captain in Taiwan until he immigrated to the U.S. in 1965. He began the Forensic Department at the University of New Haven in 1975, after completing his Ph.D. in biochemistry at John Jay College in New York. In 1979, he took over the State's crime lab. He has made the news as part of O. J. Simpson's defense team, and for his generous contributions to the University of New Haven.

Richard C. Lee
Former Mayor of New Haven. *(See page 130.)*

Robert Leeney
Respected long-time editor of the *New Haven Register,* now Editor Emeritus, Robert Leeney is a loyal New Haven booster. Leeney Plaza on Audubon Street is named in his honor. He received the Seal of the City in 1994 from the New Haven Colony Historical Society.

Ann P. Lehman
Ann Lehman is a sculptor and arts advocate on the Yale faculty and the Creative Arts Workshop. She is head of the Sculpture Department of CAW, which she helped found in 1965. "Metal is the most versatile, malleable, strong, and permanent sculptural material." Her work was the subject of a major review in the Sunday New York Times: "Sculpture and Landscape in Graceful Tandem" (3/26/95). Ann is Huntmistress in Bethany and is involved in SOS – Save Open Spaces, a land preservation movement in Bethany.

Marvin Lender & Murray Lender
The "Bagel Brothers" sold their multi-generational bagel company (and name) to Kraft for millions. They are still into bagels, at Bagel Face, a bakery and restaurant in Orange. Marvin and Murray have been philanthropists on a grand scale for over two decades. They are strongly identified with the new Jewish Community Center, Quinnipiac College, and the local and national UJA.

Richard "Rick" Levin
President of Yale University. *(See page 235.)*

Susan Gray Lichtenstein
Sue Lichtenstein's New Haven-based *CT•Life,* founded in 1992, is a monthly lifestyle newspaper for 50+ adults with a readership of over 200,000. She was ad manager for *Connecticut* magazine before she began her own newspaper. Sue was the co-chair of the 1988 City Image Committee, and serves on the Boards of Edgerton Park, the Women's Health Initiative at Yale, and the South Central Agency on Aging.

Joseph I. Lieberman
A United States Senator, Joe Lieberman was appointed chairman of the Democratic Leadership Council in March, 1995. He began his political career as a State Senator in the 1970s, and later was Connecticut's Attorney General. He is on several important Senate committees: Armed Services; Environment; Public Works; Government Affairs; and Small Business. He lives in New Haven with his wife Hadassah.

Lawrence M. Liebman
Attorney Larry Liebman is past President of the New Haven County Bar Association, the Connecticut Bar Association and Woodbridge Country Club. A past Chairman of the Distribution Committee of the Community Foundation for Greater New Haven. He was one of the developers of Sound View Specialized Care Center, a rehabilitation facility in West Haven, built in the 1960s, which won awards for its unique architecture. Larry helped to found The Bank of New Haven. His wife, Susan, is Executive Director of the New Haven County Bar Association.

Linda Lindroth & Craig D. Newick
Linda Lindroth has been an artist for nearly two decades. In 1988, she served on the Mayor's Task Force for the Preservation of Public Art in New Haven. She is known for her luminous black and white photography of a wide range of subjects, often in collaboration with her husband, architect Craig Newick. In 1993, Yale commissioned her to photograph five past masters of Jonathan Edwards College. In 1994, her book *"Dear unknown friend," Children's Letters from Sarajevo,* produced for the Open Society Institute, received a Gold Award for Excellence in Communications. She is a past board member of Artspace and acts as an arts consultant to non-profit agencies.

Frank Logue
Former Mayor of New Haven. *(See page 130.)*

Ruth DuPont Lord
Ruth Lord, with friends C. Newton Schenck, Elizabeth Kubler, and Virginia Hepler, formed the original committee which opened Long Wharf Theatre on July 4, 1965. Ruth, whose childhood vacations and summers were spent at the DuPont's *Winterthur* estate in Delaware (now a national museum), worked as a volunteer and part-time staffer with Dr. Albert Solnit at the Yale Child Study Center. Ruth continues to support and enjoy the arts in our area.

Linda Koch Lorimer
Secretary of Yale University. *(See page 236.)*

Carlton Loucks
The owner of Connecticut Direct Mail, and President of the New Haven Colony Historical Society.

Robert Lyons, Jr.
President of Bilco Doors in West Haven, he has headed up a large number of capital campaigns for worthy institutions.

Frederick Mancheski
Long-time Chairman of the Echlin Corp., Frederick Mancheski is a major supporter of Connecticut Hospice, the alternative hospital for terminally ill patients located in Branford, Chairman of the Board of Quinnipiac College and active with many other civic organizations.

Ralph Marcarelli
An attorney in Wooster Square, and the Republican Town Chairman for New Haven.

Edward Marcus
New Haven attorney who is active in community affairs and the Democratic party, he is State Democratic Chairman.

Robert J. Mariano
President of the Branford Savings Bank.

Charles Mascola
This New Haven native began a nationally-recognized advertising agency. The unofficial public relations aide to New Haven Mayor John DeStefano, Chuck Mascola has chaired the past two major regional marketing efforts and is involved in many of the efforts to prepare the area for the Special Olympics. Son of famed Annex barber "Charlie", Chuck's office houses the oldest barber shop in town.

Edward Massey
Edward Massey is the Chairman of the Board of the *RAVENS* baseball team, New Haven's first "AA" team. *(See page 26.)*

F. Patrick "Pat" McFadden
President of the Bank of New Haven, Pat McFadden puts the "New Haven" in Yale-New Haven Hospital, due to his leadership and fund-raising skills. He has been extremely active on a wide variety of boards in our area, including the Regional Community Leadership Council.

Jo McKenzie
Formerly the owner of Robert Henry's, a 4-star French restaurant on Upper Chapel Street, now the Union League Café operated by her children. Jo McKenzie is a member of the Board of the Shubert Performing Arts Center, and is on the Republican Party's National Committee. She was Chairwoman of the Inaugural Ball held in January, 1995 for newly-elected Republican Governor John Rowland.

Julia McNamara
President of Albertus Magnus College. *(See page 227.)*

Leon and Phyllis Medvedow
Leon and Phyllis Medvedow are long-time dedicated workers for the New Haven Democratic Party, and generous community activists who support many worthwhile causes in our area. Phyllis is Director of Community and Government Relations for Yale-New Haven Hospital.

Roslyn "Roz" Milstein Meyer
Roz Meyer, a clinical psychologist with her B.A., M.S. and Ph.D. degrees from Yale, is known for her commitment to children, education and our community. Roz co-founded LEAP, which won the Children's Defense Fund Youth Development Award in 1995, helped develop Foote-Bridge, a new program of education and mentoring for disadvantaged youth, and is involved in the International Festival of Arts and Ideas scheduled for Summer 1996. She is a Trustee of Choate-Rosemary Hall in Wallingford, past President of the Foote School, and Vice President of Yale Hillel.

Jerome "Jerry" Meyer
Roz's husband, Jerry Meyer, is a psychiatrist and psychoanalyst in private practice, Assistant Clinical Professor of Psychiatry at Yale, and President of Western New England Institute for Psychoanalysis. He is serving as a French translator for the Special Olympic World Games. He is Chairman of the Education Committee of Long Wharf Theatre and a Trustee of the Jewish Federation. Jerry is a member of ISIS and a co-founder with his wife and Anne Calabresi of LEAP. He is also co-founder of BEEP, Bicycle Education and Enrichment Program.

Faith Middleton
Popular commentator and talk show host on CT Public Radio, she is the host of *Open Air New England*.

Daniel Miglio
Chairman and CEO of Southern New England Telephone Co., and Vice Chairman of the Regional Leadership Council.

Marta Moret
The Program Director of the Community Foundation for Greater New Haven and a community activist.

Douglas Morrill
On the Board of the Shirley Frank Foundation, an addiction treatment facility, Doug Morrill was also Chairman of Fund Raising for Opportunity House, a group home for autistic people. He is the President of Artspace and feels that "the arts are the very soul" of our area.

Richard "Rick" Nelson
A Senior Vice President at First Federal Bank, Rick Nelson is a very visible and active participant in our community. He is a past Chairman of the Chamber of Commerce, President of the New Haven Symphony, and President of the Tennis Foundation of Connecticut. Rick is also on the Board of the Community Foundation for Greater New Haven. He is on the Regional Leadership Council, a member of the Steering Committee for the Regional Economic Development Organization, and Director of Mercy Center Inc. in Madison.

Matthew Nemerson & Marian Chertow

Matt Nemerson is the President and Executive Officer of the Greater New Haven Chamber of Commerce and the Regional Leadership Council. He is active in efforts to involve the business community in activities including downtown development, regionalism, transportation issues, the arts, regional marketing and job attraction. He was a founder of Vision for a Greater New Haven. His wife, Marian Chertow, an expert on recycling and corporate environmental policy, is on the faculty of Yale School of Forestry & Environmental Science. She is a board member of the Shubert and WOWPAC, and involved in TECHCONN, an initiative to create high-tech companies in the state.

Vivienne Nemerson

A long-time arts activist, and Matt Nemerson's mom, Vivienne Nemerson is former Executive Director of Artspace. She is the Executive Director of RSVP, a program to encourage senior citizens to participate in meaningful volunteer efforts. She owned and operated a state-wide chain of gift stores, called Sweet Pea, and has been a retail consultant for many local developers, such as Joel Schiavone.

Herbert Newman

Herb Newman is a local architect with an international reputation. Among his many New Haven projects are Chapel Square Mall, Yale Law Library, the restoration of Union Station, the Whitney/Grove condominium and office complex, the City Hall renovation. He is committed to graceful, accessible urban architecture which "retains a sense of history."

William O'Brien

Bill O'Brien is a Vice President at Lafayette American Bank & Trust. He is best known for his role as Grand Marshall of the St. Patrick's Day Parade and is involved with Special Olympics. Bill is Chairman of Branford Sports Hall of Fame, on the Board of the Greater New Haven Chamber of Commerce, past President of the New Haven Labor Day Roadrace Board, and a co-chair of the 1994 United Way Campaign. Bill is past President of the Walter Camp Football Foundation which he still serves, and on the Advocacy Council of the Yale-New Haven Hospital. He has earned many honors, including the B'nai B'rith Youth Organization Tree of Life Award, the Jimmy Fund Award, and was recently elected the 1995 Irishman of the Year by the Branford Elks Club.

Thomas W. Ogletree

Dean of the Yale Divinity School. *(See page 240.)*

John Padilla

A well-known activist, John Padilla is on the Board of the Community Foundation, New Haven Enterprise Development, HOME Inc., Centro San José, and Long Wharf Theatre's New Audiences Committee. He also served on the Governor's Coalition for Literacy.

Michael Palmer

Music Director and Conductor of the New Haven Symphony Orchestra, Michael Palmer began his professional career at age 21 when he was invited by Robert Shaw to conduct the Atlanta Symphony Orchestra. While he was their Associate Conductor, he founded the Symphony Youth Orchestra. Michael is a gifted pianist. His major conducting teacher was Wolfgang Vacano, and he studied piano with Martin Marks and Alfonso Montecino. *(See page 79.)*

Philip Paolella

Former owner of Plasticrete Corporation of Hamden, Phil Paolella has a history of community activity and philanthropy. He was a key fundraiser for the Foundation to Restore the New Haven Green.

Robert Parker

Bob Parker is the Director of Educational Center for the Arts (ECA), a magnet arts program for gifted and talented South Central CT high school students. He feels that his job permits him to contribute very directly to the cultural life of the City, by encouraging and educating talented youth. *(See page 77.)*

Nicholas Pastore

New Haven Chief of Police. *(See page 163.)*

Robert Patterson

Robert Patterson is the Director of Special Programs for Southern New England Telephone, currently serving as a full time Public Relations Director for the 1995 Special Olympics World Games in New Haven.

Barbara L. Pearce

Barbara Pearce is President of H. Pearce Real Estate Company, started by her father in 1958. She is a Radcliffe graduate, with MBA and law degrees from Harvard. She serves on the Mayor's Business Advisory Group, and the Regional Leadership Council, and is Treasurer of Foote School. She is the President-elect of the Greater New Haven Real Estate Board, past Chairwoman of the Hospital of St. Raphael, a trustee of the Lippincott Foundation, President of Long Wharf Theatre, and a Conn. Real Estate Commissioner. Barbara is an Associate Fellow of Trumbull College at Yale.

Herbert Pearce

The founder and Chairman of the Board of the H. Pearce Co., currently managed by his daughter, Barbara, Herb Pearce worked for the A. C. Gilbert Company of New Haven, home of the American Flyer electric trains, and Erector Sets. At 29, he left his job and the 2,000 employees he supervised to begin his successful real estate venture. Herb was the developer of the Whitney-Grove Condominium and office project.

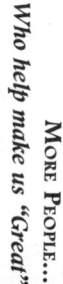

David Pease
Dean of the Yale School of Art. *(See page 244.)*

Cesar Pelli

Cesar Pelli is famous for designing commercial buildings "with...a spiritual presence." Cesar is quoted as saying: "The city is more important than the building; the building is more important than the architect." Born in Argentine, he moved to the U.S. in 1952 and served as Dean of the Yale School of Architecture from 1977 to 1984. His New Haven-based firm of Cesar Pelli & Associates, serves an international clientele. He is best known for the World Financial Center and Carnegie Hall Tower in New York, the United States Embassy in Tokyo, and Great Britain's tallest building, the 48-story Canary Wharf Tower in London. His New Haven projects include Boyer Center for Molecular Medicine at Yale, and One Century Tower. In January 1995, he won a Gold Medal for Lifetime Achievement from the AIA.

Mary L. Pepe

The current Chairwoman of the Community Foundation for Greater New Haven, Mary Pepe is director of human resources for TeleMedia of Western CT. She is immediate past President of the Valley United Way, a director of the Greater Valley Chamber of Commerce, and a trustee of Hewitt Hospital. Mary is also former President of the Valley Mental Health Center. Mary was honored by receiving the Good Neighbor Award from the Birmingham Group.

James Perillo

Jim Perillo, Executive Director of the New Haven Coliseum Authority since 1988, is responsible for the operation of the Veterans Memorial Coliseum, an arena with seating for 11,000. A former teacher, counselor and basketball coach in the West Haven schools, Jim was an alderman and ward chairman.

Charles Pignatelli

President of the Bank of Commerce in Woodbridge.

Charles "Charlie" Pillsbury

Charlie Pillsbury is a senior partner with Wiggin & Dana, and a community mediator. As a member of cartoonist Gary Trudeau's circle, he is widely rumored to be a character in the popular *Doonesbury* political strip. He has a long history of community involvement and caring.

Douglas Rae

Douglas Rae is a Yale professor of Political Science who served as an important advisor to Mayor John Daniels during his first term as mayor of New Haven. He is noted for his book on government entitled *Public Policy and Public Choice*.

Kevin Roche

The architect of the Veterans Memorial Coliseum, the Knights of Columbus World Headquarters in New Haven, and the Temple of Dendur Pavilion at the Metropolitan Museum in New York, Kevin Roche is an acclaimed expert on modern cities. He was born in Dublin in 1922, and, after earning a degree in architecture, he emigrated to the U.S., where he joined the Michigan firm of Eero Saarinen and Associates in 1950, as principal design associate, a position he held until Saarinen's death in 1961. Kevin, with his partner the late John Dinkeloo, completed such famous projects as the St. Louis Arch, the TWA Terminal at JFK airport, Dulles International Airport, and Union Carbide's World Headquarters in Danbury. In 1982, he won a Pritzker Prize for Architecture. His 1985 biography quotes: "I believe...one's ultimate responsibility is to use every opportunity to create a work of art."

Thomas "Tim" Rodd

Headmaster, The Hopkins School. *(See page 218.)*

Vincent Romei

Formerly the head of L. G. Defelice, Inc, a major international construction firm building roads, bridges, airports and tunnels, Vincent Romei is the general partner and manager of the Colony Inn Hotel and one of the original incorporators of the Bank of New Haven where he is still on the Executive Committee. Vincent helped begin the Greater New Haven Convention and Visitors Bureau and has served as its Chairman since its inception in 1993. *(See page 6.)*

Maritza Rosa

President of Latino Youth, and Chairwoman of the statewide Puerto Rican parade.

Peter A. Rosazza, D.D.

Bishop Peter Rosazza serves as Regional Bishop for the Archdiocese of Hartford. He lives in New Haven at his official residence on the grounds of the Hospital of St. Raphael. Born here in 1935, and ordained in 1961, he was elevated to this position in 1988. He is a member of the National Conference of Bishops for Latin America, and the Campaign for Human Development. Bishop Peter is also Chairman of the Steering Committee of Vision For A Greater New Haven, and helped to found the Naugatuck Valley Project, a coalition of churches and labor unions working to create jobs.

M. Edgar Rosenblum

The Director of Long Wharf Theatre, Edgar Rosenblum is convinced that "the arts are the best flagship for marketing our area." As he likes top point out, the non-profit arts world has always had patrons, going back to medieval times. "No civilization can survive without culture. It is our responsibility to better articulate the importance of art...to the corporate and business community." *(See page 68-69.)*

Harold Roth

Harold Roth, a Yale alumnus, worked extensively with Eero Saarinen and Roche-Dinkeloo of Hamden, before he began Roth and Moore, Architects in 1973. On the Board of *Perspecta* (Yale's Architectural Journal) and Long Wharf Theatre, he is a member of New Haven Preservation Trust, and Fellow of Pierson College. Past President of Connecticut Architecture Foundation, his special focus is on "producing distinctive and compelling buildings." Recent projects include: the Slifka Center for Jewish Life (Yale Hillel); the Computer Center, Observatory and Studio Arts Building (Vassar); Seeley Mudd Library and Watson Hall (Yale); the North Building at The Foote School, and Ingalls Rink Renovation (Yale). Among his many prizes is the 1993 Healthcare Facilities Award.

Willie H. Ruff, Jr.

A long time area resident and much loved musician who sold his nightclub and became an Adjunct Professor of Music at Yale, Willie Ruff was the Keynote Speaker at the 1994 Arts Awards Ceremony. His concern for the cultural life of our area is legendary, as is his joy in teaching.

William J. Rush

Publisher and CEO of the *New Haven Register*, William Rush plays a major role in the day to day life of Greater New Haven, with coverage of local events, politics and concerns. He is a past member of the United Way Board, and the Salvation Army Advisory Board and currently on the Boards of Long Wharf Theatre, Habitat for Humanity, the Regional Leadership Council, and the Gateway Community Technical College Foundation.

Humbert "Bert" V. Sacco, Jr.

The community's civil engineer, Bert Sacco is the man every mayor and developer turns to with the question, "will it work?" A Yale varsity baseball player, he is President of TPA Design, a national engineering and architecture firm, and an expert on roads, transportation, and mall development. Bert advocates increased job training, and a focus on manufacturing. Past Chairman of the Chamber of Commerce, he is on the Board of the Community Foundation and on the Executive Committee of the Private Industry Council.

Mustafa Abdul Salaam

The founder and first president of the Family Alliance, a group that brings together many human services in a co-ordinated manner, Mustafa Salaam has been working to improve the quality of life in the inner city, especially in the Dixwell and Newhallville neighborhoods, for over ten years.

Michael A. Schaeffer

Michael Schaeffer serves on the Development Commission for the City of New Haven, is co-Chair of the capital campaign for the Neighborhood Music School, and is active with the Corporation for Independent Living. In addition, Michael is an Adjunct Professor at the Hotel School of University of New Haven, and serves on its Advisory Board. He was the past co-Chair of the capital drive that raised money for the new Jewish Community Center building in Woodbridge, and is active on the Board of the Convention and Visitors Bureau. Michael is Director of Hotel Operations for a family-owned hotel management firm in New Haven.

Charles Newton "Newt" Schenck, III

Newt Schenck was born in New Jersey in 1923, and is a Yale University alumnus. He graduated from Columbia Law School in 1948. A Senior Partner of Wiggin & Dana, for 25 years he served as Founder and Chairman of Long Wharf Theatre, which renamed its center stage the Newton Schenck Stage. He was a Trustee and Founder of Goodspeed Opera House, President of the New Haven Housing Authority, the New Haven Board of Education, the United Way, and the New Haven Colony Historical Society. He is a Director and Secretary of the Regional Leadership Council, and Chairman of its Center City Committee; Chairman of the Committee of Proprietors for the New Haven Green; Vice-Chairman of the Board of Yale-New Haven Health Services Corp.; and on the Development Committee of the Community Foundation. He has received honorary degrees from Quinnipiac and Albertus Magnus Colleges, the *Service to the Arts* Award of the Arts Council, and the Community Service Award of the Chamber of Commerce. Newt is a committed New Havener who lives in the East Rock neighborhood, with his wife Ann.

Craig & Joel Schiavone

CEO & President of Schiavone Realty and Development, Joel Schiavone was the first real estate developer to see the potential of the theatre district in New Haven. He was the main force behind the rebirth of the Shubert, and the Palace and was instrumental in the revitalization of the entire Chapel and College Street area, now known as Shubert Alley. He developed the Taft Hotel/apartment complex, and ran New Haven Restaurant for a time on Chapel Street nearby. An avid amateur musician, Joel has his own group, *The Blue Mooners*. His wife, Craig, manages their real estate company.

Richard Schmalz

Richard Schmalz, a lawyer with Murtha, Cullina, Richter & Pinney, is active in community affairs, including the Community Loan Fund. He was also a New Haven Alderman.

Cornell Scott

Director of Hill Health Center. *(See page 272.)*

Gregory O. Scott
Vice President of the Beazley Company, a New Haven Real Estate firm with over 500 agents and associates in 26 branches throughout Connecticut, Gregory Scott is a Director of the New Haven Association of Realtors. Always ready to serve others, he is also Director of the Coordinating Council for Children in Crisis, the Community Soup Kitchen, and the toy drives for the pediatric departments at Yale-New Haven Hospital and the Hospital of St. Raphael.

Vincent Scully
Vincent Scully, a celebrated urban architect, and Professor at Yale School of Architecture, has said: "Urban glass boxes silence...(a) city's soul." Vince's lectures on the history of art and architecture are famous throughout the area, and beyond. He led successful local campaigns to save the Lincoln Theatre and the facade of the old City Hall Tower, which now fronts Government Center on Church Street. He is often seen sculling with his dog riding in the bow of his boat, in the waters off Branford.

Beau Segal & Ben Segal
Owners and operators of Oakdale Theatre in Wallingford, which Ben Segal founded in 1954 as part of a national movement to bring musicals and other productions to people living outside New York City, at prices they could afford. The term "summer stock" was born with Oakdale which pioneered the theatre-in-the round concept. Beau Segal grew up at Oakdale, where he worked every summer of his youth. A theatre major in college, Beau worked as a percussionist with folk singer Judy Collins, before returning to take over as CEO of Oakdale in 1984. Under his direction, Oakdale has become prominent as a year-round theatre, featuring plays, musicals and stars from television and Las Vegas.

Fenmore "Fen" R. Seton
Retired President of the Seton Name Plate Corp., Fen Seton attended Yale, M.A. 1956. From 1988-1992, he was President of Rehabilitation International, a worldwide group of 150 rehabilitation organizations from 89 countries. His work capped 58 years of service in behalf of disabled persons. Fen is past President of the New Haven Goodwill Center, the President's Committee on Employment of People with Disabilities, and the Community Foundation Development Committee. He is on the Board of University of New Haven, and an honorary Board member of the New Haven Symphony. His wife, Phyllis Zimmerman Seton, served for seven years on the Board of Education. She also worked with the Peabody Museum Associates, New Haven International Center, Save the Children Federation and the New Haven Colony Historical Society. She is Vice President of The Children's Center and involved with the Greater New Haven Rehabilitation Center and CT Easter Seals Society.

Lawrence Shanbrom
Larry Shanbrom's family-owned business is West Haven Lumber. He is former Vice President and Secretary of the Home Builders Association of Greater New Haven, and immediate past President of the JCC. He was involved in developing the new JCC facility in Woodbridge. He also served on the Executive Committee of the Federation. Larry is Chairman of the New Haven Committee of the Anti-Defamation League (ADL). He and his wife Sherry, a well-known interior designer, live in the Prospect Hill neighborhood.

Ronald G. Shaw
Ron is President and CEO of the Pilot Corporation of America, a leading pen manufacturing company and major employer in greater New Haven. In January 1995, the former stand-up comic was elected Chairman of the Board of the Shubert Performing Arts Center. Ron says: "A healthy arts community stimulates economic development." He actively promotes the arts to businesses in our area. He also is strongly committed to fighting against discrimination, and in 1993 led Pilot Pen's support of a public service campaign, "Prejudice Hurts." He is an active supporter of the Anti-Defamation League.

Mark Shiffrin
A Wooster Square resident and attorney, he is the new CT Commissioner of Consumer Affairs, appointed in 1995.

Timothy Shriver
President of the 1995 Special Olympics World Games, Tim Shriver is involved in New Haven, especially in education. He was in charge of the Young Men's Leadership Group at Hillhouse High School, the Extended Day Program in the New Haven Schools, and the Social Development Curriculum for grades K-12. He is directing many Special Olympics activities and events: the School Curriculum Guide; Art! Artists, Athletes; Neighborhood Clean-ups; Parade of Winners; 1,000 voice Choir; and Post Office Contests. Tim and his cousin Ted Kennedy, are continuing a long family tradition of compassionate involvement with disabled people.

Floyd Shumway (with Richard Hegel)
Retired Executive Director of the New Haven Colony Historical Society, Floyd Shumway and his colleague Richard Hegel co-edited *New Haven: An Illustrated History* (1981). Floyd is an Associate Fellow of Davenport College, and member of Yale's Sherlock Holmes Society. In 1989, he received the Elm Award and was Yale University Amistad Symposium co-chair. Floyd *(left, picture above)* recently wrote *The First Fifty Years of the Yale Club of New Haven*, which he co-authored with Richard Hegel *(right, picture above.)*

H. William Shure
A New Haven attorney who has been active in the Democratic party and who has served on many community boards and committees.

James Sinclair
Founder and Artistic Director of Orchestra New England (ONE) James Sinclair is an internationally known scholar of the Connecticut composer Charles Ives, and one of Ives' great champions. *(See page 78.)*

Mark and Judy Sklarz
An attorney in New Haven, Mark Sklarz is a past President of the JCC, and was co-chairman of the Building Committee, during the construction of the new facility in Woodbridge. He served as coach for the varsity basketball team at JCC for 18 years, and enjoys working with youngsters. Mark is on the Board of Trustees of Hopkins. He also served for 10 years as President of the New Haven Emons Bowen Babe Ruth League, an inner-city summer baseball program. Judy is on the Board of Clifford Beers Guidance Clinic, and the Greater NH Loan Fund, and is a grant writer serving the city of New Haven in the area of affordable housing.

DeForest "Frosty" W. Smith
Frosty Smith is a Yale alumnus and owner of George J. Smith & Son, Realtors in Milford. He is past President of the Greater New Haven Association of Realtors, and Realtor of the Year for 1985. He is adjunct professor of real estate at NYU, and a Senior Instructor for the Commercial Investment Real Estate Institute. Frosty is the author of *Only in Milford: An Illustrated History* and founder of Drug Free Milford, an award-winning anti-drug program. He is a Director of the Milford Bank and the US Basketball League. He is President-elect of the Yale Club of New Haven. In 1989, Frosty was honored as "Milford Citizen of the Year", and in 1990 received the "Businessman of the Year" award. In 1994, he received the Henry S. Harrison "Educator of the Year" Award from the Greater New Haven Association of Realtors.

Susan Smith
Susan Smith is Executive Director of Creative Arts Workshop, a fine arts and crafts education center on Audubon Street *(See p. 82)*. She is the past Membership and Development Officer for Yale's Peabody Museum. She is on the Board of the Peabody Museum Associates, and on the City's Transportation Task Force (Arena Block). Susan is involved with Yale Parents of New Haven School Children, the Vision Committee for New Haven (Arts Section), and the Review Panel of the Grants for Excellence program. Her husband, Steven B. Smith, is a Yale Professor of Political Science.

Christina Olson Spiesel & Sydney Z. Spiesel
Christina Spiesel is an artist whose work has often been shown locally and in New York. She teaches at Yale University and Bard College. Her local activities include nine years on New Haven's Cultural Affairs Commission, which she chaired for five years, and the leadership of two mayoral task forces. She is a prime mover in the founding of Artspace, and is a founding member of the Board of WOWPAC. Through the Sister Cities program, she has been involved in educational and cultural exchanges with our French Sister City, Avignon. Her husband, Sydney, is a pediatrician who also teaches at Yale. He is medical consultant for Opportunity House, for three group homes for autistic adults, and for several nursery schools and day care centers. Ex-president of Clinical Analytics Inc., Syd applies his interest in medical computer applications to an on-going immunization project for the Community Foundation, and has served on its commission on infant mortality.

Mike Spoerndle
As the owner and driving force behind Toad's Place, Mike Spoerndle is a "music impresario" with a major effect on the local and even the national music scene. Mike knows everyone in contemporary music, from rappers to bee-boppers, to heavy metal bands. As every kid over 10 in New Haven knows, Toad's Place features all ages shows as part of its audience outreach program.

Frederick Streets
Chaplain of Yale. *(See picture 259.)*

Charles Terrell
President, Treasurer and CEO of New Haven Savings Bank, Charlie Terrell is active with the Connecticut Bankers Association, Director and Vice Chairman of CT Public Broadcasting, and Chairman of the Finance Committee of the Chamber of Commerce. He is a Board member of the Hospital of St. Raphael's and the New Haven Symphony. He is a Director of the Regional Leadership Council, and on the Board of Governors of Southern CT State University.

Gail Thompson
Gail Thompson is the publisher of the *New Haven Advocate* and has been in New Haven for the past four years. She is active in the community and in addition to her role at the newspaper, her involvement includes the Board of Directors of the Greater New Haven Chamber of Commerce, the Steering Committee for Hearts for Life, and the Foundation Board for Gateway Community College. Gail was a YWCA "Women in Leadership" honoree.

Agnes W. Timpson

A mother of 6, Agnes Timpson is the Coordinator of Volunteers for Fellowship House, and a Trustee of the Hospital of St. Raphael and Quinnipiac College. She holds an honorary Doctorate from Quinnipiac College. She is serves with the Connecticut Commission on Aging, United Way, the YWCA/YMCA, the Community Foundation and First Constitution Bank. She received a community award from Women's Health Services, and a citation from the Connecticut General Assembly.

Henry & Deborah (Deb) Townsend

The Townsend family has lived in the same mansion on Townsend Avenue in the Annex for over 100 years. Both Henry and Deb Townsend have a long record of community service. Henry ran for Mayor in the 1960s, while Deb planted all the Japanese cherry trees in Wooster Square Park.

Charles Twyman

Vice Chairman-Elect of the Community Foundation, Charles Twyman received his Doctorate of Education from Columbia University. He served as District Director for Elementary Education and Supervisor for Curriculum Services for the New Haven School System. He is the former president of the Connecticut Children's Museum.

Cheever Tyler

A former senior partner at Wiggin & Dana, Cheever Tyler is known for his unselfish service to the community. He is President and Founder of Partnership for Connecticut Cities and Nonprofit Strategies Group, seeking private sector commitment to address urban problems. He is past President of the Shubert, United Way, the New Haven Public Education Fund, the Regional Housing Compact and the New Haven Bar Association. Cheever is past Chairman of the Community Foundation, the University of New Haven, and the Chamber of Commerce, and President-elect of the Arts Council. He has won many awards for distinguished service as a volunteer. *(See page 66.)*

Roger Vann

Roger Vann is an influential community leader and Director of the local NAACP.

Barry Vine

Barry Vine is the founder and CEO of Vine Products Co. in West Haven. He served on the boards of the American Diabetes Association, Recording for the Blind, Jewish Family Service and Federation. Barry ran Woodbridge Library's Capital Campaign, and did fund-raising for the new JCC.

Sister Anne Virginie

Sister Anne Virginie is the President of St. Raphael Healthcare System, and one of the most respected and visible people in New Haven. As Mary Margaret Grimes, she attended Post Elizabeth College, and took her vows as a Sister of Charity of St. Elizabeth. Sister Anne obtained a master's in hospital administration, at the request of the order. In 1973, she became the assistant to her predecessor, Sister Louis Anthony. Sister Anne has served on countless boards, and personifies a rare combination of total commitment, business acumen, and boundless human compassion. *(See page 268.)*

Laurel Vlock

Laurel Vlock describes herself as "a career volunteer" working in a professional capacity. For 26 years her weekly public service program *Dialogue with Laurel Vlock* ran on WTNH-TV, Channel 8, for the Anti-Defamation League, addressing "issues of tensions in a pluralistic culture." She is the Founder of the Fortunoff Video Archive of Holocaust Testimonies at Yale, and the Public Affairs Director of WHAI-TV, Ch. 43, started by Bridgeways Communications Corp., of which she is the founder and former President. She is the author of *Contraband of War*, and has received many awards for her work, including an Emmy.

Fred E. Walker

Fred Walker is Chairman of the Board of Long Wharf Theatre. He has been in radio and television for his entire career. He is the President and CEO of Broad Street TV, which operates KWQC-TV in Iowa. Active in the Radio Advertising Bureau and the National Association of Broadcasting, Fred served on the Board of CT Public Television for 12 years, and is an Associate Fellow of Berkeley College at Yale.

Horst Wallrabe

Horst Wallrabe is the CEO of Bayer, Inc., a pharmaceutical company and major employer, on Morgan Lane in West Haven. The company was formerly known as Miles Labs, until it changed its name to Bayer in April 1995.

Barbara Cooley Wareck

Barbara Wareck was born in New Haven. Her late husband, Steve, was President of the Board of Alderman, and active in Democratic politics and community affairs. She worked as Corporate Social Responsibility Specialist for United Illuminating, (1988-1994). In 1995, she received Habitat for Humanity's "Master Builder" award. She serves on many Boards: Habitat for Humanity; the Community Foundation; "Q" House; Jewish Family Service; the Hospital of St. Raphael; Sister Cities Program and the Neighborhood Music School. She was active with the Arts Council, School Volunteers for New Haven, Fortunoff Video Archives for Holocaust Testimonies, the Urban League, Jewish Federation of Greater New Haven, and the New Haven Public Education fund. Among her many awards are the Robert Eisner Memorial Award for Community Relations and the Women's Health Services Community Service Award in 1994.

Barbara Webster

Since January 1987, Barbara Webster has been the Executive Director of ARTSPACE, a center for the visual, literary and performing arts. Barbara is also an active member of the New Haven Rotary Club, and Chairwoman of Career Day for the past two years. *(See page 83.)*

Leon and Lillian "Lil" Weinberg
Leon Weinberg settled in New Haven after surviving the Holocaust in World War II in Europe. Leon's Bakery has grown into a large frozen baked goods provider located North Haven. Leon and his wife Lil are well-known in the area for their continued generosity. Leon has been instrumental in the Special Olympics program, and is an active member of the Holocaust Survivors group here in the city.

Martha Sue Weisbart
Martha Weisbart is the Director of Development for the Shubert Performing Arts Center. Her previous work in the non-profit sector culminated in her role as Capital Campaign Director for the new Woodbridge facility of the Jewish Community Center, where she was Associate Executive Director. Martha is a dedicated and effective volunteer, active with the American Heart Association as a CPR trainer since 1986. She has also served on the Board of the Jewish Federation.

Caroline Werth
President & CEO, Shubert Theatre. *(See page 69-71.)*

James E. Westhall
Jim Westhall is "Mr. Tennis Tournament," and the head of JEWEL productions. *(See page 27.)*

Courtland Wilson
The Executive Director of the Hill Development Corporation, Courtland Wilson has been an active and outspoken advocate for New Haven's neighborhoods for over thirty years. He is especially identified with the city's health care facilities. Courtland was the Director of Government Relation at Yale-New Haven Hospital and before that, was the Director of Personnel at The Yale Medical School.

F. Perry "Buck" Wilson
Buck Wilson is one of the business community's most resourceful activists. He is on the boards of the Chamber of Commerce and Vision for a Greater New Haven, and has served on many other boards and committees in the past.

Mary Lou Winnick
Woodbridge resident Mary Lou Winnick has served seven terms as Selectwoman in her town, focusing on elderly housing and human services. She served on the Jewish Federation Board for 12 years and is past President. She is the President of the Connecticut Jewish Federation Association, a member of the Board of Yale-New Haven Hospital since 1989, and past Chairwomen of the Advisory Council for INFOLINE. She received the *New Haven Register's* "Women Who Make A Difference" award, and was honored by Jewish Family Service and New Haven Business magazine as one of *Twenty Noteworthy Area Women* in 1994. She is married to New Haven attorney Edward Winnick.

Stan Wojewodski
Dean of Yale Drama School. *(See page 245.)*

Joseph Zaccagnino
President, Yale-New Haven Hospital. *(See page 266.)*

Rudolph and Jean Zallinger
Rudy Zallinger is famous for his Pulitzer Prize-winning panoramic mural of earth's history, covering roughly 300 million years. "*The Age of Reptiles*", which covers the entire east wall of Dinosaur Hall at the Peabody Museum is one of the world's largest scientifically accurate natural history murals. In 1989, on the 40th anniversary of his Pulitzer Prize, the Peabody Museum established the R.F. Zallinger Fellowship, a permanent endowment to support graduate level studies in natural history. His wife, Jean, is a Yale Art School graduate well-known for her illustrations of children's books.

Edward E. Zigler
The National Director of the Yale Bush Center in Child Development and Social Policy, and "Father of Head Start", which he piloted in New Haven under a Ford Foundation Grant in l965, Ed is currently involved in the School of the 21st Century program. He is also involved with a joint initiative called *CoZi*, in honor of Ed and Yale child psychiatrist and African-American activist, Dr. James P. Comer.

I suggest that the following person be added to the More People section for the next reprint of Harrison's Illustrated Guide: Greater New Haven.

Name _____

Accomplishments/Bio

_____

_____

_____

Contact phone # _____ Photo enclosed ( )yes ( ) no

Recommended by: _____ phone # _____

   To recommend people we should consider adding to the *More People* Section of this book for the next edition, make a photocopy of the form above and complete it as indicated. We are looking for men and women who make serious, long-term commitments to our communities, who work in the non-profit sector, and help make our day to day lives richer, more satisfying and easier. You may photocopy this form as many times as you wish. Thank you in advance for your input. Mail your suggestions to: The H² Company, 315 Whitney Avenue, New Haven, CT 06511 or FAX to 1(203) 624-5841.

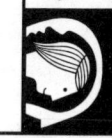

No need to tear your book -- just photocopy & complete the coupon below.

Harrison's Illustrated Guide: GREATER NEW HAVEN

Your purchase helps support the
**Community Service Student Loan
Reimbursement Scholarship Program**
of the Real Estate Educational Foundation, Inc.*

*Charitable Affiliate of the Greater New Haven Association of Realtors.

Name_____

Shipping Address_____

City_____ State_____ ZIP_____

I'd like to buy _____ copies of *Harrison's Illustrated Guide:* **Greater New Haven.**
I am enclosing $14.95 per book *(includes shipping, handling & sales tax.)*

_____ x $14.95 = $_____.

☐ My check is enclosed.   ☐ Please charge my credit card: M/C   Visa   Amex

Card #_____ Expiration_____

Signature_____

Order from: Henry S. Harrison, 315 Whitney Ave., New Haven, CT 06511

*For wholesale discounts on orders of 5 or more books
please call 1(203)562-5226 x222 or FAX 1(203)624-5841*

Harrison's Illustrated Guide
GREATER New Haven
A Great Place to Live, Work, Study & Visit

Item #300363   304 pages - Softcover

$14.95 per book
includes S & H & sales tax

Cover Art Posters
*High quality art posters for $ 9.95 each,
or buy both images for just $16.95!*

The lovely cover illustration artwork is also available for purchase as art posters. The front cover of this book depicts *New Haven*, a harmonious contemporary scene which brings to life the flavor and spirit of a great small city with its court house, library, offices, churches and people around the central Green. The back cover, *Yale*, is a view from an unusual aerial perspective, which offers a unique sense of Yale in its home environment.

Note: Art posters are illustrations only. No type.

FOR SALE BY THE ARTIST

Tony Falcone is a New England artist living in the rural township of Prospect. His Falcone Art Studio is located in a vintage dairy barn. There he has created murals, canvases & portraits for over 20 years.

DON'T TEAR YOUR BOOK -- JUST PHOTOCOPY & COMPLETE THIS COUPON!

Superb Art Prints

Olde New Haeven, 1982 $ 225.00   Print Size: 18" x 27"

Depicting the historic New Haven Green, this fine art print is painted in Falcone's "imaginistic" style, which combines realistic renderings with elements of the past and the present to produce images that are timeless. Available in 6-color limited edition print produced on 100% cotton rag paper, signed & numbered by the artist.

Fine Art from Tony Falcone

Please send me _____ posters of NEW HAVEN @ $9.95 =_____
Please send me _____ posters of YALE @ $ 9.95   =_____
Send me _____ sets of both posters for just $16.95 =_____

Please send me _____ signed and numbered
   fine art prints of *Olde New Haeven* for $225.00   =_____

Total purchases: $_____ + 6% CT tax _____ =$_____

Name_____
Shipping Address_____
City_____ State_____ ZIP_____

*Enclose checks or money orders and mail to:
Falcone Art Studio, 181 New Haven Road, Prospect, CT 06712*

DON'T TEAR YOUR BOOK -- JUST PHOTOCOPY & COMPLETE THIS COUPON!